OCR GCSE HISTORY

EXPLAINING THE MOD

D1765947

MODERN WORLD HISTORY

Period and Depth studies

BEN WALSH

HODDER
EDUCATION
AN HACHETTE UK COMPANY

This resource is endorsed by OCR for use with specification OCR GCSE (9–1) in History A (Explaining the Modern World) (J410). In order to gain OCR endorsement, this resource has undergone an independent quality check. Any references to assessment and/or assessment preparation are the publisher's interpretation of the specification requirements and are not endorsed by OCR. OCR recommends that a range of teaching and learning resources are used in preparing learners for assessment. OCR has not paid for the production of this resource, nor does OCR receive any royalties from its sale. For more information about the endorsement process, please visit the OCR website, www.ocr.org.uk.

Acknowledgements
The Publishers would like to thank the following for permission to reproduce copyright material. **p.31** North Chingford Branch of the League of Nations (1935); **p.40** Letter from Ronald and Margaret Hutton, two of Churchill's constituents, to Churchill in September 1938; **p.45** Reproduced with permission of Curtis Brown, London on behalf of The Estate of Winston S. Churchill. © The Estate of Winston S. Churchill; **p.48** Reproduced with permission of Curtis Brown, London on behalf of The Estate of Winston S. Churchill. © The Estate of Winston S. Churchill; **p.49** Things we forgot to remember by John Charmley (2011). © John Charmley; **p.58** Reproduced with permission of Curtis Brown, London on behalf of The Estate of Winston S. Churchill. © The Estate of Winston S. Churchill; **p.59** Reproduced with permission of Curtis Brown, London on behalf of The Estate of Winston S. Churchill. © The Estate of Winston S. Churchill; **p.284** Source 5 © 1955 Dr Martin Luther King Jr. © renewed 1983 Coretta Scott King; **p.288** Source 11 © 1957 Dr Martin Luther King Jr. © renewed 1983 Coretta Scott King; **p.291** Source 18 © 1963 Dr Martin Luther King Jr. © renewed 1983 Coretta Scott King; **p.291** Source 20 © 1963 Dr Martin Luther King Jr. © renewed 1983 Coretta Scott King; **p.322** 'I Feel Like I'm Fixin' To Die Rag'. © Country Joe and the Fish; **p.334** Source B © 1963 Dr Martin Luther King Jr. © renewed 1983 Coretta Scott King.

Every effort has been made to trace all copyright holders, but if any have been inadvertently overlooked, the Publishers will be pleased to make the necessary arrangements at the first opportunity.

Note: The wording and sentence structure of some written sources have been adapted and simplified to make them accessible to all pupils, while faithfully preserving the sense of the original.

Although every effort has been made to ensure that website addresses are correct at time of going to press, Hodder Education cannot be held responsible for the content of any website mentioned in this book. It is sometimes possible to find a relocated web page by typing in the address of the home page for a website in the URL window of your browser.

Hachette UK's policy is to use papers that are natural, renewable and recyclable products and made from wood grown in sustainable forests. The logging and manufacturing processes are expected to conform to the environmental regulations of the country of origin.

Orders: please contact Bookpoint Ltd, 130 Milton Park, Abingdon, Oxon OX14 4SE. Telephone: (44) 01235 827720. Fax: (44) 01235 400454. Email education@bookpoint.co.uk Lines are open from 9 a.m. to 5 p.m., Monday to Saturday, with a 24-hour message answering service. You can also order through our website: www.hoddereducation.co.uk

ISBN: 978 1 4718 6018 8

© Ben Walsh 2016

First published in 2016 by
Hodder Education,
An Hachette UK Company
Carmelite House
50 Victoria Embankment
London EC4Y 0DZ

www.hoddereducation.co.uk

Impression number   10 9 8 7 6 5 4 3 2 1

Year   2020 2019 2018 2017 2016

Cover photo © RIA Novosti/Topfoto

Illustrations by Julian Baker, Ron Dixon and Peter Lubach

Typeset by White-Thomson Publishing Ltd

Printed in Italy

A catalogue record for this title is available from the British Library.

Contents

Prologue: The historian's mind-set   4
   Features of this book   6

Part 1: Period study: International relations: the changing international order 1918–2001   7
   Explaining the modern world   8

1 The interwar years and the origins of the Second World War   10
   1.1 Hope for the future? The Treaty of Versailles and nationalism and internationalism in the 1920s   10
   1.2 'The hinge years': The impact of the Depression on international relations 1929–34   23
   1.3 'The dark valley': The failure of the League of Nations, Appeasement and the drift to war   29
   1.4 The big sell-out? Historical controversy 1: Changing interpretations of Appeasement   44

2 The Cold War   55
   2.1 A new world order: Causes of the Cold War 1945–50   55
   2.2 'Three minutes to midnight': Cold War crises and confrontations 1961–90   67
   2.3 The blame game: Historical controversy 2: Changing interpretations of the origins of the Cold War   97

3 The world after the Cold War   105
   3.1 End of an era: The end of the Cold War and the collapse of communism c1980–91   105
   3.2 New dangers: The post-Cold War world   116

Assessment focus   126

Part 2: Non-British depth studies: The people and the state   131

4 Germany 1925–55: Democracy to dictatorship to division   132
   4.1 Democracy to dictatorship: The rise and consolidation of the Nazi regime 1925–34   132
   4.2 A national community? Nazi Germany and its people 1933-39   148
   4.3 Destruction to democracy: The Second World War and its legacy in Germany 1939–55   171

Assessment focus   190

5 The USA 1919–48: Boom and bust, prejudice and progress   198
   5.1 The 'Roaring Twenties': The age of irresponsibility?   198
   5.2 The 1930s: Depression and New Deal   228
   5.3 The USA 1941–48: A land united?   246

Assessment focus   258

6 The USA 1945–75: Land of liberty?   266
   6.1 The Red Scare: Post-war challenges in the USA 1945–54   268
   6.2 Righting wrongs: African Americans and the struggle for civil rights in the USA 1945–75   278
   6.3 The times they are a-changing? Government and dissent c1964–75   310

Assessment focus   330

Glossary   338

Index   340

Acknowledgements   343

Prologue: The historian's mind-set

How historians work

If you think that history means reading a lot of information from a textbook and then memorising it, you are wrong. If you try to learn history in this way, you will probably end up feeling a bit like the picture above! Even historians get overwhelmed by the amount of historical information to be found in books, archives and other sources. They use a range of techniques to help them make sense of it all.

Focus

No historian can study every aspect of a period of history. To make the subject manageable, historians focus on particular areas. This book does the same – each of the studies focuses on selected parts of the story. The period study (Part 1) covers almost a century of history and focuses on political events and the relationships between countries. Each depth study in Part 2 focuses closely on a particular country at a particular time, investigating the lives of ordinary people.

Ask questions

Historians are investigators rather than just collectors of information. They search for new information about the past in order to tackle important questions.

Historians have different interests. They do not all investigate the same questions. So when studying the Vietnam War, for example, Historian A may be most interested in why the Americans could not win the war, while Historian B concentrates on the war's impact on the USA. Historian C, investigating Nazi Germany in the 1930s, might want to know why the Nazis faced so little opposition, while Historian D may be interested in what life was like for ordinary Germans at that time. A bit like two different builders, they use the same or similar materials but they ask different questions and tell different stories.

You will follow the same sort of process when preparing for your history exam. You need to learn the content of the specification, but you also need to practise *using this content* to answer important questions. The text in this book, as well as the Focus Tasks in each topic, are designed to help you think in this way.

Select

Another vital technique that historians use is selection. From all the material they study, historians must select just the parts that are relevant and useful to answer a question.

Selection is hard for a historian, but it may be even harder for you under the time pressure of an exam. You have learnt a lot of history facts and you want to show the examiner how much you know – but this is the wrong way of thinking. To begin with, you risk running out of time. Even more serious, you may end up not answering the question clearly because you have included things that are not relevant or helpful. Compare this process to a wardrobe full of clothes. You never wake up in the morning and put on every item of clothing you own! You choose what to wear depending on different factors:

- the weather
- what you will be doing that day (going to school, a wedding, a Saturday job, a sports match).

Organise

Once historians have selected the relevant information, they then have to choose what order to present it in to create a coherent argument. You must do the same. If you are responding to the question 'Why did the wartime allies fall out in the years 1945–48?', you need to do more than simply list all the reasons. You must build an argument that shows what you think is the most important reason. Listing all the events on either side of the Cold War does not necessarily explain why it happened. You need to link the events to the outcomes.

Fine tune

But don't stop there. Even the most skilled historians make mistakes when they write, and you might too. When you have finished writing, re-read your text and fine tune it to make it as clear and accurate as possible. When you are about to go out, what is the last thing you do before you leave the house? Check your hair? Check your make-up? That is fine tuning. It is a history skill too, and could make a real difference to how much an examiner enjoys reading what you write.

So remember:

- focus
- ask questions
- select
- organise
- fine tune.

Keep these points in mind as you work through your course. Good luck!

Features of this book

Sources

These help you understand the story more clearly because they reveal what events and ideas meant to people at the time – what they said, did, wrote, sang, celebrated or got upset about. You will not be asked source-based questions in the period-study assessment, but sources are still an important element when studying the history of a period. In the depth study, sources are a key part of the assessment.

Activity

Activities are designed to help you think through a particular question or issue. The thinking you do in these tasks is usually a building block towards your answer to a Focus Task.

Focus task

Focus Tasks are the main tasks for really making sure you understand what you are studying. They will never ask you to just write something out, take notes or show basic comprehension. These tasks challenge you to show that you know relevant historical information and can use that information to develop an argument.

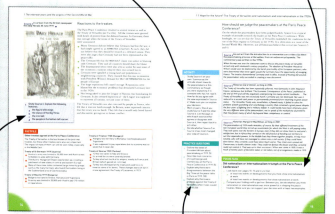

Topic summary

This appears at the end of every topic. It condenses the topic into a few points, which should help you get your bearings in even the most complicated content.

Margin questions

These useful little questions are designed to keep you on track. They usually focus in on a source or a section of text to make sure you have fully understood the important points in there.

Practice questions

These questions come at the end of major sections. They are designed to help you think about the kinds of questions you may come across in your exam. We do not know the exact questions you will be asked, but we know the *style* of question. Usually we have shown you the marks that might be available to give you a sense of how much time to spend on it. The question types are explained in the Assessment Focus sections.

Factfile

Factfiles are more or less what they say – files full of facts! These give you important background information to a story, without interrupting the narrative too much.

Assessment focus

This section takes you through the types of questions in the exam paper, how they are assessed and possible ways to answer them.

Profile

Profiles are essentially factfiles about people, summarising the key facts about a historical figure.

Glossary and Key Terms

Glossary terms are highlighted LIKE THIS and defined in the glossary on pages 338–39. Key Terms are listed at the end of each chapter.

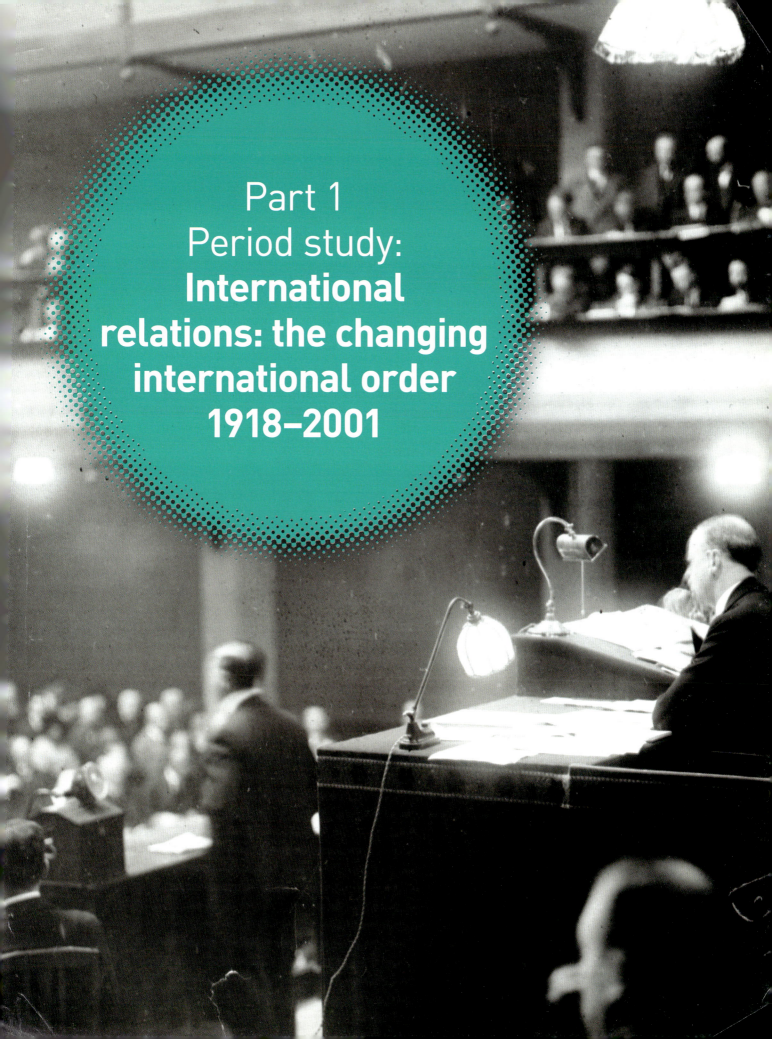

Part 1
Period study:
International relations: the changing international order 1918–2001

Explaining the modern world

The modern world is a big and complicated place, so explaining it is a pretty tall order! In this course we cannot really explain every aspect of everything that is happening around the globe today. However, right now the world is facing many problems, and almost all of these can be better explained and understood if we know where they came from – their history. The map below highlights some of the most significant issues at the present time and how the history in this book can help you understand them.

Nationalist feeling in Europe

There are concerns that groups of people in some countries have developed a negative view of immigrants and are supporting nationalist anti-immigrant organisations. This is particularly strong in Britain, France and Germany – countries in which large numbers of migrants from eastern Europe have settled in the hope of finding work. Tension has also arisen over the huge numbers of refugees fleeing to Europe from the war in Syria and Iraq. Many Europeans are concerned by the rise in nationalist feeling that these events are causing. Nationalism was a key cause of both world wars (see Topics 1.1 and 1.3).

Russia

Russia's oil and gas reserves have made it a wealthy and influential country. It is becoming increasingly powerful on the world stage. In recent years, Russia has intervened in the affairs of neighbouring Ukraine, taking control of the region of Crimea and supporting anti-government rebels in eastern Ukraine. Russia has also shown it will not be ordered around by the USA or any other country. We can trace the roots of this attitude back to Russia's rivalry with the USA in the Cold War (see Chapters 2 and 3).

The USA

The USA is the world's greatest power – the wealthiest and most influential nation on Earth. However, at the moment it is struggling to recover from an economic depression, and history shows that economic depression often causes political problems (see Topic 1.2). The USA has also become bogged down in conflicts in Iraq and Afghanistan, just as it did in Vietnam in the 1960s (see Topic 2.2).

Crisis in Syria and Iraq

In recent times Syria and neighbouring Iraq were both war zones, torn apart by different factions. There are many different armed groups but the largest and most powerful is Islamic State. This group has taken over from al-Qaeda as the main radical Islamist organisation. The roots of these problems can be found in two places. The first is the way that the Middle East was divided up after the First World War (see Topic 1.1). The second is the role of Afghanistan in the Cold War (see Topic 2.2) and in the years that followed. The crisis in Syria and Iraq has created millions of refugees, many of whom are fleeing to Europe.

China

China was referred to as a 'sleeping giant' in the first half of the twentieth century, but today it is a great global power. We can see the roots of China's rise in its relationship with the USA in the 1970s and 1980s in particular (see Topic 3.1). China now has the world's second-largest economy and it may soon overtake the USA to become number 1. How will the USA respond?

Historians in action

In this course we want you to *think like a historian* – answering important questions, making judgements and using your knowledge and the available evidence to back them up. The text and tasks in this book will help you to reach judgements on questions such as:

> How did Hitler's actions increase tensions in Europe in the period 1933–37?

> Why did Ronald Reagan have such a big impact on superpower relations?

> Why did al-Qaeda attack the USA in 2001?

However, one other really important step in thinking like a historian is to *study the work of other historians*. You will study two controversial historical issues:

> **Controversy 1: the policy of Appeasement**

> **Controversy 2: the origins of the Cold War**

Historians, politicians and ordinary people have disagreed (sometimes bitterly) about these issues. Interpretations have changed as new evidence has emerged and as new generations have challenged the views of the past. You will study *how* historians have interpreted these issues and also explain *why* historians have disagreed.

Why do interpretations differ?

Some people wonder why historians disagree and argue about the past. They say, 'The past is the past. Just tell me what happened!' In a way, they are right. There was a First World War, a League of Nations, an Adolf Hitler. There were wars in Vietnam in the 1960s and Afghanistan in the 1980s. We can discover a lot about these events from the many sources that survive. Historians agree on that. However, as soon as a historian starts trying to *explain* these things, they no longer simply record facts. They begin to put their own slant on events. They may choose to include some details while leaving out others. They will tell a version of the story that is influenced not only by the sources they have studied but also by their own views and experiences.

Once a historian has told their story, it is out there to be read by others – who might disagree, carry out further research and then write their own version of events. And so it goes, step by step, historian by historian. Our understanding of the past is gradually refined until we get close to what we are all seeking – the truth – while remaining aware that it is not the *whole* truth, only the closest we have come so far.

The problem of evidence

For some periods of history the problem is that we do not have much evidence. That is not a problem when studying the twentieth century, and particularly the subject of international relations. Quite the opposite, in fact! There are literally millions (maybe even billions) of sources that can help our understanding, and this is more than any person could study in a lifetime. This is why reinterpretation will carry on forever: there will always be something new to discover.

Welcome to the world of the historian!

1.1 Hope for the future? The Treaty of Versailles and nationalism and internationalism in the 1920s

FOCUS

The First World War was a traumatic event. It left 40 million people dead or injured. By the time the war ended in 1918, political leaders and ordinary people alike were determined that nothing like it should ever happen again. Many believed that the only way to achieve a lasting peace was to replace nationalism (states acting in their own interests) with internationalism (international co-operation). In this topic, you will investigate the attempts to achieve this in the post-war years:

- Was nationalism or internationalism the driving force behind the Treaty of Versailles in 1919?
- How successful was the League of Nations in encouraging international co-operation through the 1920s?

Preparing for peace

The First World War left a legacy of destruction and hatred, but despite this there were sincere hopes for peace and recovery. In the past, peace treaties had rewarded winners and punished losers (for example, the winners took land or money from the losers). This time it would be different.

The post-war treaties were to be agreed at the PARIS PEACE CONFERENCE in 1919. As DELEGATES prepared for their task one of the British officials at the conference, Sir Harold Nicolson, wrote in his diary: 'We were preparing not just for peace but Eternal Peace. There was about us the halo of divine mission.'

> **Source 1** US President Woodrow Wilson, speaking in 1918.
>
> *The day of conquest and self-interest is gone. ... What we demand is that the world be made fit and safe to live in; and particularly that it be made safe for every peace-loving nation which, like our own, wishes to live its own life, determine its own institutions, be assured of justice and fair dealing by the other peoples of the world as against force and selfish aggression. All the peoples of the world are in effect partners in this interest, and for our own part we see very clearly that unless justice be done to others it will not be done to us.*

PROFILE

Woodrow Wilson (1856–1924)

- Became a university professor.
- First entered politics in 1910. Became president of the USA in 1912 and was re-elected in 1916.
- An idealist and a reformer. People said that once he made his mind up on an issue he was almost impossible to shift.
- As president, he campaigned against corruption in politics and business. However, he had a poor record with regard to the rights of African Americans.
- From 1914 to 1917 he concentrated on keeping the USA out of the First World War.
- Once the USA joined the war in 1917, he drew up his Fourteen Points as the basis for ending the war fairly and to ensure that future wars could be avoided.

FACTFILE

Wilson's Fourteen Points
1   No secret treaties.
2   Free access for all to the seas in peacetime or wartime.
3   Free trade between countries.
4   All countries to work towards disarmament.
5   Colonies to have a say in their own future.
6   German troops to leave Russia.
7   Independence for Belgium.
8   France to regain Alsace-Lorraine.
9   Frontier between Austria and Italy to be adjusted.
10 Self-determination for the people of eastern Europe (they should rule themselves and not be ruled by empires).
11 Serbia to have access to the sea.
12 Self-determination for people in the Turkish Empire.
13 Poland to become an independent state with access to the sea.
14 League of Nations to be set up.

FACTFILE

The Paris Peace Conference 1919–20
● The Conference took place in the Palace of Versailles, a short distance from Paris.
● It lasted for 12 months.
● There were 27 separate delegations at the Conference. None of the defeated nations was invited.
● Five treaties were drawn up. The main one was the Treaty of Versailles, which dealt with Germany. The other treaties agreed how Germany's allies would be treated.
● All the important decisions on the fate of Germany were taken by the 'Big Three': George Clemenceau (prime minister of France), David Lloyd George (prime minister of Britain) and Woodrow Wilson (president of the USA).
● The Big Three were supported by hundreds of diplomats and expert advisers, but the leaders often ignored the advice they were given.

Woodrow Wilson and the Fourteen Points

President Wilson set out his vision for the post-war world in his FOURTEEN POINTS (see Factfile). His talk of DISARMAMENT, open dealings (and therefore no secret treaties) between countries, justice for small nations and international co-operation struck a chord with the people of Europe. His proposed LEAGUE OF NATIONS sounded like exactly what Europe needed: a place for countries to resolve their disputes without resorting to war. This was what people wanted to hear.

When Wilson arrived in Europe for the Paris Peace Conference, he was greeted as an almost saintly figure. Newspapers reported how some wounded soldiers in Italy tried to kiss the hem of Wilson's cloak and, in France, peasant families knelt to pray as his train passed by.

Behind the scenes, however, experienced politicians such as David Lloyd George of Britain and Georges Clemenceau of France had serious reservations about Wilson and his ideas. They doubted whether a peace treaty could live up to his RHETORIC. They felt that Wilson was being naive, not idealistic, and that he simply did not understand how complex the issues facing Europe were. They also worried about their own national interest. What if Wilson's Fourteen Points meant that France or Britain had to give up some of their own overseas empires? That would not go down well at home! Clemenceau and Lloyd George were not alone: plenty of people were asking whether INTERNATIONALISM could really work.

Source 2 A cartoon published in an Australian newspaper in 1919, commenting on the Paris Peace Conference. ▼

THE MELTING POT.

1   Look carefully at the features of the cartoon in Source 2. What is the cartoonist saying about disarmament?
2   Do you think the cartoonist favours nationalism or internationalism?
3   Would you say the cartoonist is optimistic or pessimistic about the prospects for peace? Make sure you can explain your answer with reference to details in the source.

Internationalism vs nationalism at the Paris Peace Conference

In Wilson's vision of the new world, all the delegates were supposed to discuss and agree major issues such as borders and REPARATIONS. In practice, this proved too complicated. Wilson quickly abandoned this principle and the BIG THREE ended up making the main decisions. However, even that proved difficult.

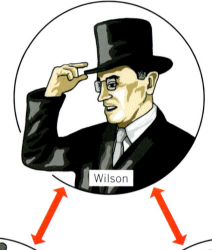

*Clemenceau clashed with Wilson over many issues but particularly on **how to treat Germany**. Wilson wanted Germany punished, but not too harshly. He hoped to see a democratic state emerge there. He feared that a harsh settlement would leave Germany wanting revenge. But France shared a border with Germany and Clemenceau wanted to make sure his own country would be secure from any future German threat. Even in defeat Germany had a larger, younger population than France, and a stronger economy. The French people were also demanding that Germany be harshly punished for their pain and suffering. In the end, Wilson gave way to Clemenceau on many issues relating to Germany.*

*Wilson and Lloyd George did not always agree either. Lloyd George was particularly unhappy with point 2 of the Fourteen Points, which allowed **all nations access to the seas**. Similarly, Wilson's views on **self-determination** seemed a potential threat if such ideas were to spread to the British Empire.*

*Clemenceau also clashed with Lloyd George on **how to treat Germany**. Like Wilson, Lloyd George wanted Germany to recover swiftly from the war, although he had different reasons. He wanted an economically strong Germany so it could pay Britain compensation for war damage. Germany could also be a valuable trading partner for Britain in peacetime. However, Lloyd George did not want Germany to keep its navy and its colonies, as these would be a threat to Britain and its empire. Clemenceau felt that the British were inconsistent: generous to Germany when it suited them; tough when it was against their national interests.*

Clemenceau and Lloyd George did give Wilson what he wanted in eastern Europe, despite their reservations about self-determination. The worry here was that there were so many people of different ethnic origins in different regions, it was almost impossible to create a state that would not have some minority groups in it. This issue affected the other four treaties much more than it did the TREATY OF VERSAILLES.

FACTFILE

The Treaty of Versailles

The Big Three co-operated enough to draw up the Treaty of Versailles, but none of them was completely happy with the terms of the treaty. After months of negotiation, each of them had to compromise on some of their aims.

1 War guilt

Germany had to accept the blame for starting the war. The Germans felt this was extremely unfair.

2 Reparations

Germany was forced to pay reparations to the Allies for war damage. The exact figure was debated for some time and announced in 1921. It was set at £6.6 billion. If the terms had not later been changed, Germany would not have finished paying until 1984.

3 Land

Germany's European borders were changed so it lost land to neighbouring countries (see map). The result was that Germany lost 10 per cent of its land and 12.5 per cent of its population. The treaty also forbade Germany to form a union (*Anschluss*) with its former ally Austria.

Germany also lost its overseas empire. This had been one cause of bad relations between Britain and Germany before the war. Former German colonies became mandates controlled by the League of Nations (which effectively meant that they came under the control of France or Britain).

4 Armed forces

The size and power of the German army was a major concern, especially for France. The treaty reduced German forces to well below their pre-war levels:

- The army was limited to 100,000 men and conscription was banned – soldiers had to be volunteers.
- Germany was not allowed armoured vehicles, submarines or aircraft.
- The navy could have only six battleships.
- The Rhineland (the border area between Germany and France) was demilitarised – no German troops were allowed there (see the pink area on the map).

5 League of Nations

Previous methods of keeping peace had failed and so the League of Nations was set up as an international 'police force'. Germany would not be allowed to join the League until it had proved its peaceful intentions.

A map showing the impact of the Treaty of Versailles on the borders of Europe. ▼

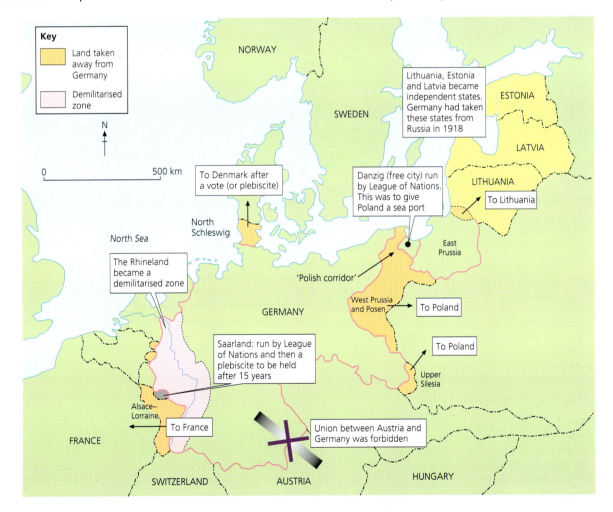

Source 3 A cartoon from the British newspaper the *Daily Herald*, 30 June 1919. ▼

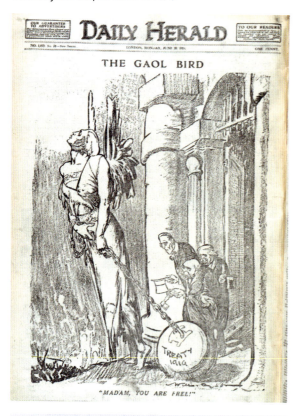

Reactions to the treaties

The Paris Peace Conference resulted in several treaties as well as the Treaty of Versailles (see Factfile). All the treaties were greeted with howls of protest from the defeated nations. In Germany, there was outrage when the terms of the Treaty of Versailles were announced:

- Many Germans did not believe that Germany had lost the war, it had simply agreed to an ARMISTICE (ceasefire). As such, they did not believe that they should be treated as a defeated nation. They were also angry that Germany had not been represented at the peace talks.
- The Germans felt that the WAR GUILT clause was unfair in blaming only Germany. They said that all countries should share the blame.
- The disarmament terms were also seen as unfair because none of the victorious countries reduced their own armed forces.
- Germans were appalled at losing land and population to neighbouring countries. They claimed that this was inconsistent with President Wilson's demand for SELF-DETERMINATION for the people of Europe.
- The huge reparations bill caused outrage. Reparations were blamed for the economic problems that devastated Germany later in the 1920s.
- Not being asked to join the League of Nations was humiliating for Germany. It also seemed hypocritical – the League was supposed to represent all nations, not just some of them.

The Treaty of Versailles was also criticised by people in France, who felt that it was not harsh enough. In Britain, some expressed concern that the treaty was *too* harsh. They felt that it would only breed hatred and discontent, giving rise to future conflict.

1   Study Source 3. Explain the following features:
   a   the figure with wings
   b   the stance of the Big Three
   c   the iron ball
   d   the people in the bottom left corner.

FACTFILE

Other treaties agreed at the Paris Peace Conference

The Treaty of Versailles is the best known of the post-war treaties, but these other treaties were also very important. The impact of many of them can still be seen today, especially in the Middle East.

Treaty of St Germain 1919 (Austria)
- Austria's army was limited to 30,000 men and Austria was forbidden to unite with Germany.
- The Austro-Hungarian Empire was broken up, creating a patchwork of new states in central and eastern Europe.
- Many of these new states contained large minority groups such as the many Germans who found themselves living in the Sudetenland area of Czechoslovakia.

Treaty of Neuilly 1919 (Bulgaria)
- Bulgaria lost land to Greece, Romania and Yugoslavia.
- Its army was limited to 20,000 and it had to pay £10 million in reparations.

Treaty of Trianon 1920 (Hungary)
- Hungary lost territory to Romania, Czechoslovakia and Yugoslavia.
- It was supposed to pay reparations but its economy was so weak that it never did.

Treaty of Sèvres 1920 (Turkey)
- Turkey lost lands to Italy and Greece.
- Its armed forces were severely limited.
- Turkey also lost much of its empire, mostly to France and Britain (which gained oil-rich Iraq).
- Turkey was dismayed at the treaty and used force to reverse some of its terms. These changes were set out in a new agreement, the Treaty of Lausanne, in 1923.

How should we judge the peacemakers at the Paris Peace Conference?

On the whole the peacemakers have been judged harshly. Source 4 is a typical example of attitudes towards the leaders at the Paris Peace Conference. With hindsight, we can see that the Treaty of Versailles established the conditions for the rise of the Nazi regime in Germany in the 1930s. As such, it is often seen as a cause of the Second World War. However, not all historians believe this is true (see Sources 5 and 6).

> **Source 4** A comment from an online article published in 2009. The title of the article was 'The Treaty of Versailles – the Peace to end all Peace'.
>
> *The Versailles Treaty was one of the most outrageous and predatory treaties in history. It was a blatant act of plunder perpetrated by a gang of robbers against a helpless, prostrate and bleeding Germany. Among its numerous provisions, it required Germany and its allies to accept full responsibility for causing the war and, under the terms of articles 231–248, to disarm, make substantial territorial concessions and pay reparations to the Entente powers.*

> **Source 5** Historian Zara Steiner, writing in 2004.
>
> *The Treaty of Versailles has been repeatedly pilloried, most famously in John Maynard Keynes' pernicious but brilliant 'The Economic Consequences of the Peace', published at the end of 1919 and still the argument underpinning too many current textbooks. ... The Treaty of Versailles was not excessively harsh. Germany was not destroyed. Nor was it reduced to a second rank power or permanently prevented from returning to great power status. ... The Versailles Treaty was, nonetheless, a flawed treaty. It failed to solve the problem of both punishing and conciliating a country that remained a great power despite the four years of fighting and a military defeat. It could hardly have been otherwise, given the very different aims of the peacemakers, not to speak of the multiplicity of problems that they faced, many of which lay beyond their competence or control.*

> **Source 6** Historian Margaret MacMillan, writing in 2001.
>
> *The peacemakers of 1919 made mistakes, of course. By their offhand treatment of the non-European world they stirred up resentments for which the West is still paying today. They took pains over the borders in Europe, even if they did not draw them to everyone's satisfaction, but in Africa they carried on the old practice of handing out territory to suit the imperialist powers. In the Middle East they threw together peoples, in Iraq most notably, who still have not managed to cohere into a civil society. If they could have done better, they certainly could have done much worse. They tried, even cynical old Clemenceau, to build a better order. They could not foresee the future and they certainly could not control it. That was up to their successors. When war came in 1939, it was a result of twenty years of decisions taken or not taken, not of arrangements made in 1919.*

ACTIVITY

1 Study Source 4 on your own. Summarise the attitude shown towards the peacemakers in this commentary as though you were explaining it to someone who has not read it.
2 How far do you agree with the view expressed in Source 4? Make sure you can explain your decision.
3 Work in pairs. One of you study Source 5 and the other Source 6. List the ways in which your source either agrees or disagrees with Source 4, then report back to each other.
4 Decide whether Source 5 or Source 6 has most changed your view of Source 4.

PRACTICE QUESTIONS

1 Outline the views of President Wilson about peacemaking in 1919. (5)
2 Describe the main concerns of Lloyd George and Clemenceau at the Paris Peace Conference in 1919. (5)
3 Explain why there were disagreements between the Big Three at the peace talks in Paris in 1919. (10)
4 Explain why there were protests against the Treaty of Versailles when it was issued in 1919. (10)

FOCUS TASK

Did nationalism or internationalism triumph at the Paris Peace Conference?

1 Look back over pages 10–15 and try to find:
   a at least two events or developments that you think show internationalism at work
   b at least two events or developments that show nationalism at work.
2 Compare your findings with a partner. Between you, decide whether you think nationalism or internationalism was more powerful in shaping the peace treaties. Make sure you can support your decision with at least two examples.

The League of Nations: internationalism in action in the 1920s

The most significant method of international co-operation in the post-war world was the League of Nations. The idea of an organisation like this had been around for some time, but it was President Wilson who really championed it. The single most important aim of the League was to solve international disputes without going to war. This was reflected in the COVENANT signed by all members (see Source 7).

1 Study Source 7. Explain why the covenant would have been popular and made people optimistic.
2 Imagine you are living in 1920. You are wondering how the League will perform. Using Source 7 and the Factfile, what would you say were its strengths and weaknesses?

Source 7 The introduction to the Covenant of the League of Nations.

THE HIGH CONTRACTING PARTIES, in order to promote international co-operation and to achieve international peace and security, agree to this Covenant of the League of Nations
- *by promising not to go to war*
- *by agreeing to open, just and honourable relations between nations*
- *by agreeing that governments should act according to international law*
- *by maintaining justice and respect for all treaty obligations.*

FACTFILE

How the League of Nations was organised.

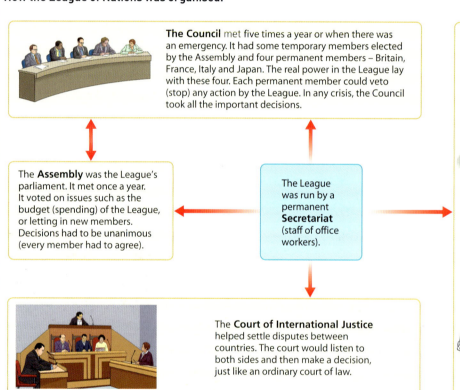

The Council met five times a year or when there was an emergency. It had some temporary members elected by the Assembly and four permanent members – Britain, France, Italy and Japan. The real power in the League lay with these four. Each permanent member could veto (stop) any action by the League. In any crisis, the Council took all the important decisions.

The **Assembly** was the League's parliament. It met once a year. It voted on issues such as the budget (spending) of the League, or letting in new members. Decisions had to be unanimous (every member had to agree).

The League was run by a permanent **Secretariat** (staff of office workers).

The League had a number of **commissions**, or committees, to tackle international problems such as helping refugees or improving health.

The **Court of International Justice** helped settle disputes between countries. The court would listen to both sides and then make a decision, just like an ordinary court of law.

The League began with 42 member nations. By 1939, there were over 50 members. But some powerful nations left the League and others, most notably the USA, never joined. The strongest influences were:

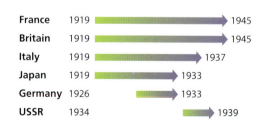

France	1919	1945
Britain	1919	1945
Italy	1919	1937
Japan	1919	1933
Germany	1926	1933
USSR	1934	1939

Wilson's vision

Once again Wilson raised expectations. He wanted the League of Nations to be like a world parliament, where representatives of all nations met regularly to solve problems. This was what people wanted to hear after the horrors of the war. All the major countries would join, binding themselves to the League's covenant. They would disarm. If they had a dispute with another country, they would take it to the League and accept its decisions.

League members would also promise to protect one another if attacked (this was called COLLECTIVE SECURITY). If any member broke the covenant and went to war illegally, other members would impose ECONOMIC SANCTIONS (i.e. they would stop trading with that country). Supporters of the League were particularly excited by this new weapon of economic sanctions. They believed it could be a powerful way of containing aggression without waging war. As a last resort, the League could take military action against an aggressor nation.

Doubts and reservations

Not all the leaders of the major powers were convinced by Wilson's vision for the League of Nations. Lloyd George wanted a simpler organisation that met only in emergencies. In fact, a body like this already existed, called the Conference of Ambassadors. Lloyd George was also determined that membership in the League would not commit Britain to take certain actions in emergencies – he wanted Britain to be free to act in its own interests. Clemenceau was also sceptical about the League. Like Lloyd George, he wanted his country to be free to act independently. The French leader also thought that the League needed its own army to achieve anything.

Although the League of Nations had been the US president's idea, the United States could not join it unless the US Congress agreed. In March 1920, after almost a year of debate, Congress refused. By that time, however, the League of Nations had officially opened for business, so it was left to Britain and France to take the lead in trying to make it work.

3 Match these visions for the League of Nations to each of the Big Three (Wilson, Lloyd George or Clemenceau):

 a a strong body with its own army

 b a world parliament with regular meetings

 c a simple group to meet when there was an emergency.

4 Study Source 8. How can you tell that the cartoonist had doubts about the League?

5 How do you know that the cartoonist who created Source 9 is hostile to the League of Nations?

Source 8 A cartoon from the magazine *Punch*, March 1919. ▼

PUNCH, OR THE LONDON CHARIVARI.—March 25, 1919.

OVERWEIGHTED.

PRESIDENT WILSON. "HERE'S YOUR OLIVE BRANCH. NOW GET BUSY."
DOVE OF PEACE. "OF COURSE I WANT TO PLEASE EVERYBODY; BUT ISN'T THIS A BIT THICK?"

Source 9 A Russian cartoon from 1919, commenting on the plans for the League of Nations. The caption reads: 'The League of Nations: Capitalists of all countries, unite!' ▼

КАПИТАЛИСТЫ ВСЕХ СТРАН СОЕДИНЯЙТЕСЬ!

The work of the League's commissions

The League's commissions worked hard to solve problems left over from the war. They were driven by a desire to make life better for ordinary people, but also by the belief that social problems and poverty were a cause of international tension. If these issues could be solved, future wars may be prevented.

The League did not employ its own experts. Instead, lawyers, trade unionists and financial experts from member countries came together and co-operated under the 'umbrella' of the League's organisation. This was internationalism in action to improve people's lives.

In the 1920s, the League's commissions made several important achievements:

- The **Refugee Committee** helped an estimated 400,000 people who had been displaced by the war or made prisoners of war return to their homes.
- The **International Labour Organisation** successfully campaigned for workers' rights – especially for women and children – in all countries.
- The League brought in the first **Declaration of the Rights of the Child**, which is still in force today.
- The **Health Committee** funded research into deadly diseases, developing vaccines against leprosy and malaria. The League also fought successful campaigns against DRUG TRAFFICKING and slavery. For example, it was responsible for freeing the 200,000 slaves in British-owned Sierra Leone.
- Another area of achievement was in finance. For example, in 1922-23 the ECONOMIES of Austria and Hungary collapsed. In response, the League's **Financial Committee** came up with an economic plan to raise loans and help these two economies recover.

A place to talk

The League also became a meeting place for experts in science, finance, law and health care, and for activists for women's and children's rights, working conditions and anti-slavery. Today, these groups might share information and ideas using the internet, but in the 1920s the League's commissions provided an important place for people to exchange ideas and introduce improvements.

Legacy

Even after the League was replaced by the United Nations in 1945, several of its commissions were kept on because they were so valuable. For example, the International Labour Organization still operates today. The League's Health Committee is now the United Nations' World Health Organization (WHO) and the financial planning done by the Financial Committee was the basis for the International Monetary Fund (IMF).

Source 10 The League Committee on Economic Questions, meeting in the 1920s. This was an official League of Nations' photograph. ▼

Source 11 The celebrations marking the opening of the League of Nations, January 1920. ▲

1 Study Source 11. This photograph was published in different newspapers in many countries. Do you think the different newspapers would have put the same caption on the picture? Explain your answer.

2 Compare Sources 10 and 11. If you were producing a booklet promoting the League of Nations, which of these two images would you choose for the cover? Explain your answer.

The League of Nations and international security

Despite the achievements of its commissions, the League was always going to be judged primarily on whether it could prevent war between member nations. Many countries faced severe financial problems due to the cost of the war. In addition, the peace treaties themselves created a whole new set of problems. For example, redrawing the borders of a country on a map was easy enough, but making this work in practical terms was much more difficult. The defeated nations despised the terms of the treaties, but it was the League's job to enforce these terms.

So how well did the League do? The Factfile shows just a few of the 66 disputes dealt with by the League in the 1920s and summarises what happened in some of the border disputes. Next, you will look at two disputes in more detail: Corfu and Bulgaria.

FACTFILE

A map showing the problems dealt with by the League of Nations in the 1920s.

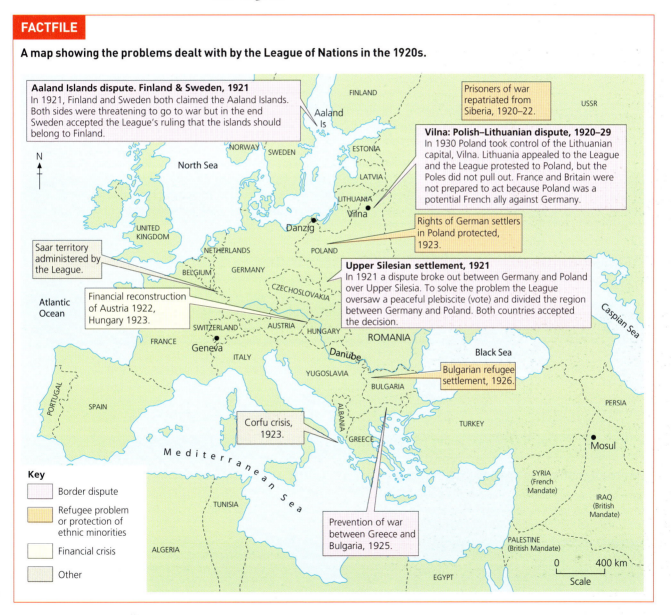

Aaland Islands dispute. Finland & Sweden, 1921
In 1921, Finland and Sweden both claimed the Aaland Islands. Both sides were threatening to go to war but in the end Sweden accepted the League's ruling that the islands should belong to Finland.

Prisoners of war repatriated from Siberia, 1920–22.

Vilna: Polish–Lithuanian dispute, 1920–29
In 1930 Poland took control of the Lithuanian capital, Vilna. Lithuania appealed to the League and the League protested to Poland, but the Poles did not pull out. France and Britain were not prepared to act because Poland was a potential French ally against Germany.

Rights of German settlers in Poland protected, 1923.

Saar territory administered by the League.

Upper Silesian settlement, 1921
In 1921 a dispute broke out between Germany and Poland over Upper Silesia. To solve the problem the League oversaw a peaceful plebiscite (vote) and divided the region between Germany and Poland. Both countries accepted the decision.

Financial reconstruction of Austria 1922, Hungary 1923.

Bulgarian refugee settlement, 1926.

Corfu crisis, 1923.

Prevention of war between Greece and Bulgaria, 1925.

Key
- Border dispute
- Refugee problem or protection of ethnic minorities
- Financial crisis
- Other

0   400 km
Scale

Corfu 1923

One of the borders that had to be decided after the war was between Greece and Albania. The Conference of Ambassadors was tasked with deciding where the border should be and it appointed an Italian general, Enrico Tellini, to supervise it. On 27 August 1923, while surveying the Greek side of the frontier area, Tellini and his team were ambushed and killed. The Italian leader Benito Mussolini was furious. He blamed the Greek government for the murders and demanded that Greece pay compensation to Italy and execute the murderers. When the Greek government refused to meet all of Italy's demands, Mussolini attacked and occupied the Greek island of Corfu. Fifteen people were killed. This attack violated the covenant, and Greece appealed to the League for help. The League condemned Mussolini's actions. However, it also suggested that Greece pay Italy the compensation.

Mussolini refused to let the matter rest. He claimed the Council of the League was not competent to deal with the issue and insisted that it should be decided by the Conference of Ambassadors. If Britain and France had stood together, Mussolini would probably have failed. However, the two leading League nations could not agree. Records from meetings of the British government show that they did not support Italy in the matter and were prepared to intervene to force Mussolini out of Corfu. The French backed Italy – probably because they were dealing with an issue in the RUHR region of Germany at the time, so they did not have the resources to support an armed intervention against Italy.

In the end Mussolini got his way. The Conference of Ambassadors ruled that the Greeks must apologise and pay compensation directly to Italy. On 27 September, Mussolini withdrew from Corfu, boasting of his triumph. There was much anger in the League over the Conference of Ambassadors' actions, but the ruling was never overturned.

1 'The main problem in the Corfu crisis was not the way the League worked, but the attitudes and actions of its own members.' Explain whether or not you agree with this statement.

Bulgaria 1925

In October 1925, some Greek soldiers were killed on the border with Bulgaria. Greek troops invaded and Bulgaria appealed to the League for help. The League demanded that both sides stand down and told Greek forces to withdraw from Bulgaria. Britain and France backed the League's judgement (it is worth remembering they were negotiating the LOCARNO TREATIES at the same time, see opposite). Greece obeyed, but pointed out that there seemed to be one rule for large states such as Italy and another for smaller ones such as themselves. The outcome of the incident was seen as a major success for the League, and optimism about its effectiveness soared. However, the main reason the League succeeded in this case was because the great powers were united in their decision.

FOCUS TASK

Internationalism vs nationalism in the 1920s

Look at the events and disputes on pages 18–20, then copy and complete the table below. You may decide that some disputes show examples of both internationalism (international co-operation) and nationalism (states putting their own interests first).

Dispute	Problem (who was involved and what they did)	Response (action taken by League, states or other organisations to solve problem)	Success for internationalism? (your judgement on whether nationalism or internationalism triumphed, with reasons)

Disarmament

All the peace treaties stated that nations should disarm and it was the League's role to make sure that they did. However, throughout the 1920s it largely failed in this aim. At the Washington Conference in 1921, the USA, Japan, Britain and France agreed to limit the size of their navies, but that was as far as disarmament ever got. This failure was particularly damaging to the League's reputation in Germany. Germany *had* disarmed – it had been forced to – but no one else did so to the same extent.

Source 12 A cartoon published in a British newspaper in December 1928. The caption reads: 'Peace (sadly): This looks very like the point we started from.' ▶

PEACE (SADLY): "THIS LOOKS VERY LIKE THE POINT WE STARTED FROM."

2   According to the cartoon (Source 12), how much progress has been made on disarmament? What details in the cartoon led you to this conclusion?

International agreements in the 1920s

Although disarmament failed, the major powers did work together to reach several agreements that seemed to make the world a safer and more secure place:

- **Rapallo Treaty (1922):** The USSR and Germany re-established diplomatic relations.
- **Dawes Plan (1924):** To avert an economic crisis in Germany, the USA lent it the money it needed to honour its reparations. These loans propped up the German economy and restored prosperity to the country in the mid-1920s.
- **Locarno Treaties (1925):** Germany accepted its western borders as set out in the Treaty of Versailles. This decision was greeted with great enthusiasm, especially in France, and it paved the way for Germany to join the League of Nations. However, nothing was said about Germany's eastern borders with Poland and Czechoslovakia. These states remained nervous about Germany.
- **Kellogg–Briand Pact (1928):** The official name for this was the 'General Treaty for Renunciation of War as an Instrument of National Policy' (also known as the 'Pact of Paris'). It was an agreement between 65 nations not to use force to settle disputes.
- **Young Plan (1929):** Reduced the total amount of German reparations.

So was the League of Nations irrelevant in the 1920s?

Each of these agreements was worked out by groups of countries working together rather than by the League of Nations, but this does not mean that the League was irrelevant. As long as such agreements were reached, it did not care whether or not it was involved. There is no doubt that during the 1920s the League was accepted as *one* of the ways in which international disputes were resolved, even if it was not the *only* way. Historian Zara Steiner has said that 'the League was very effective in handling the "small change" of international diplomacy'.

Source 13 Historian Niall Ferguson, writing in 2006.

Despite its poor historical reputation, the League of Nations should not be dismissed as a complete failure. Of sixty-six international disputes it had to deal with (four of which had led to open hostilities), it successfully resolved thirty-five and quite legitimately passed back twenty to the channels of traditional diplomacy. It failed to resolve eleven conflicts. Like its successor the United Nations, it was capable of being effective provided some combination of the great powers – including, it should be emphasized, those, like the United States and the Soviet Union, who were not among its members – had a common interest in its being effective.

Some historians believe that the League's biggest achievement was the way it helped to develop an 'internationalist mind-set' among leaders. In other words, it encouraged them to think of collaborating rather than competing. The significance of this should not be underestimated. Before the First World War, the idea of international co-operation was largely unknown and most states would have been suspicious of an organisation like the League. To some degree the League changed these views simply by existing. Countries both large and small felt that it was worth sending their ministers to League meetings throughout the 1920s and 1930s, so they could have a say when they might not have done so otherwise.

FOCUS TASK

Did nationalism or internationalism triumph in the 1920s?

1 Look back over pages 18–21 and try to find:
   a at least three events or developments that you think show internationalism being tried
   b at least three events or developments that show nationalism at work.
2 Compare your findings with a partner. Between you, decide whether you think that nationalism or internationalism was more powerful in the 1920s. Make sure you can support your decision with at least two examples.

TOPIC SUMMARY

Nationalism and internationalism in the 1920s

1 The Paris Peace Conference was dominated by Wilson, Clemenceau and Lloyd George (the Big Three), who disagreed on how to treat Germany, Wilson's Fourteen Points and the League of Nations.
2 Under the Treaty of Versailles Germany accepted blame for starting the war; had to pay reparations; lost land, industry, population and colonies; and was forced to disarm. People in Germany were appalled but they had no choice but to agree.
3 At the time, some thought the treaty was too soft on Germany, while others thought it was too harsh and could lead to another war. Most of the harshest criticisms came in the years just before and just after the Second World War, because critics blamed the peacemakers. Today, most historians think the criticisms are largely unfair. They believe the peacemakers had a near-impossible task and did a reasonable job in the circumstances.
4 The treaty set up a League of Nations to help prevent another war by encouraging international co-operation. The League's main methods of peacekeeping were diplomacy (talking), economic sanctions or, if necessary, using the armies of its members.
5 The League was the big idea of US president Woodrow Wilson, but his own country never joined. The leading members were Britain and France, but they had their own interests and bypassed the League when it suited them.
6 The League had some success in the 1920s, solving smaller international disputes and social, economic and humanitarian problems such as the refugee crisis.
7 The League also played a supporting role in helping the great powers sort out major international disputes, such as Corfu in 1923 (even though it failed to stand up to Italy).
8 The League was supposed to encourage disarmament, but failed to get any countries to disarm.

PRACTICE QUESTIONS

1 Outline the setting up of the League of Nations in 1919–20. (5)
2 Explain why the League of Nations had so much popular support when it was established. (10)
3 Outline the attempts by the League of Nations to maintain international peace in the 1920s. (5)
4 Explain why the humanitarian work of the League in the 1920s is generally seen as a success. (10)

1.2 'The hinge years': The impact of the Depression on international relations 1929–34

FOCUS

Throughout the 1920s, internationalism helped tackle many problems. By 1929, the world seemed a safer place than it had in 1919. However, from 1929 onwards the shadow of war returned. Historian Zara Steiner describes the period 1929–34 as 'the hinge years'. She sees this as the period when the balance of international relations changed for the worse. Steiner identifies four factors at work:

- the impact of a worldwide economic depression in 1929–34
- the emergence of powerful dictatorships in Europe
- the failure of the League of Nations over Manchuria in 1931
- the failure of disarmament in 1932–34.

In this topic, you will examine each of these factors to find out what went wrong and why.

Factor 1: Global economic depression and economic nationalism

World trade boomed in the late 1920s. The USA was the richest nation in the world and American business was the engine driving the global economy. Everyone traded with the USA and most countries borrowed money from US banks. As a result of this trade, many nations grew richer. This economic recovery helped to reduce international tension – for example, when the USA provided loans to stabilise the German economy after 1924.

Figure 1 A graph showing the rise and fall of industrial production in industrial countries 1928–34. ▶

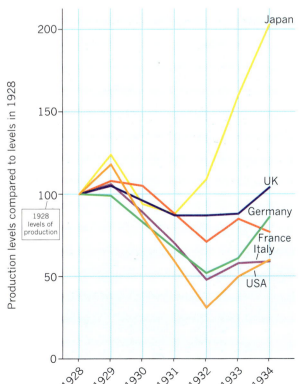

The Wall Street Crash

This period of prosperity came to a sudden end in October 1929. The US stock market (known as Wall Street) crashed, wiping out the savings of millions of Americans and causing the collapse of US banks and businesses. The Wall Street Crash marked the start of what became known as the Great Depression – a long period of economic decline – the effects of which quickly spread around the world (see Figure 1). The Depression had an impact on affairs *within* many countries as well as leading to important political changes *between* countries.

Economic nationalism

As the Depression hit, the internationalist spirit of the 1920s was replaced by a more selfish, nationalist approach:

- **Protectionism:** Some countries (including Britain, France and the USA) tried to protect their own industries by introducing TARIFFS to limit or stop imports. However, their trading partners did the same thing so trade simply worsened, leading to more businesses going bust and greater unemployment.
- **Rearmament:** Many countries (including Germany, Japan, Italy and Britain) began the process of REARMAMENT as a way of boosting industry and finding jobs for the unemployed. Afraid of being left weak while other states built up their armed forces, more and more countries did the same.

American loans called in

At the end of the First World War, Europe's economies were in ruins. Loans from US banks had helped Europe to recover in the 1920s. Most of the loans had gone to help rebuild the German economy, but the USA had also provided financial assistance to new states in central and eastern Europe, including Poland and Czechoslovakia. When the Depression hit in 1929, many US banks started to run out of money. As a result, they called in their loans, asking European banks to pay back the money they had borrowed.

Britain and France suffered great hardship, but the effects in Germany and other central European states were disastrous. Unemployment rocketed. When the USA, Britain and France also introduced tariffs from 1930 onwards and refused to lend money to Germany, the Germans felt bitter and betrayed.

1 According to Source 2, what is happening to the states of middle Europe?

2 What point is the cartoonist, David Low, trying to make about Britain, France and the USA?

3 How does Low show how serious the Depression was?

4 Do you think Figure 1 or Source 2 is more useful to a historian investigating the impact of the Depression? Explain your answer.

Source 2 A cartoon from a British newspaper, March 1932. The states of middle Europe include Germany, Austria, Poland, Czechoslovakia and Hungary. ▼

"PHEW! THAT'S A NASTY LEAK. THANK GOODNESS IT'S NOT AT OUR END OF THE BOAT."

5   What events are most worrying to the author of Source 3?

6   Is there any reason to doubt what he is saying about the state of international relations at this time?

7   The author of Source 3 was a committed supporter of the League of Nations. How can you tell this from the source?

Factor 2: The emergence of powerful dictatorships in Europe

Germany

After the First World War, Germany was rocked by economic and political crises. By the end of the 1920s it was much more stable and prosperous, thanks to a great extent to US loans (see page 133). When the USA called in the loans in 1929, the German economy collapsed. Unemployment rocketed. Many Germans felt that their government had let them down. People began to turn to extremist political parties. By 1933, the most extreme of all, the Nazis, were running Germany. There is little doubt that the Depression played a key role in destabilising Germany and bringing Nazi leader Adolf Hitler to power.

The Nazis believed in an aggressive political nationalism – putting Germany and the German people before anything else. Hitler offered radical solutions to Germany's economic problems, including:

- a massive rearmament programme
- extensive state control of industry and investment in projects such as road-building
- getting rid of the Treaty of Versailles and ending reparations payments.

Hitler wanted more than just economic recovery. His nationalist policies set him on a collision path with his European neighbours. He declared his intention to:

- reclaim land lost under the Treaty of Versailles
- carve out living space (LEBENSRAUM) for Germans in eastern Europe
- destroy communism in Germany and anywhere else it was found.

Italy

Italy had been under the control of the Fascist Party led by Benito Mussolini since 1922. FASCISM was a type of aggressive political NATIONALISM. Mussolini used the Depression to tighten his grip on the country by taking over its banks and industries. Mussolini's vision for Italy was a potential threat to international peace:

- Mussolini had long held ambitions to build an Italian empire, to bring back the glory days of the Roman Empire. He was hoping to gain territories in Africa.
- Mussolini also believed that established powers like Britain and France were in decline. He felt that Italy had more in common with Hitler's new regime in Germany, and he started to discuss an alliance.

The Soviet Union

The First World War had caused a revolution in Russia that eventually brought the communists to power there. COMMUNISM brought state control of industry and the economy, as well as a harsh dictatorship that clamped down on opposition. The communists also turned the Russian Empire into the Union of Soviet Socialist Republics (USSR). Through an organisation called COMINTERN (short for 'Communist International'), the USSR tried to spread communist ideas. The democracies, including Britain and the USA, were very suspicious of the USSR and feared it was trying to spread communism across the world.

By 1929, a new supreme leader had emerged in the USSR – Josef Stalin. Stalin was convinced that non-communist states would try to crush the communist USSR. The emergence of Germany and Italy, which were so strongly anti-communist, made Stalin feel even more threatened. He built up the USSR's industries to be ready for a future war. These actions and mutual suspicions all meant that the outlook for international relations was not good.

Factor 3: The failure of the League of Nations in Manchuria

Europe was not the only place where aggressive nationalist regimes emerged in the 'hinge years'. The Depression hit Japan hard. In rural areas there was widespread hardship and even famine. Worldwide economic problems, and particularly tariffs imposed by China and the USA, meant that Japan was unable to sell its products, especially silk and other textiles. The prices for Japanese goods fell by 50 per cent. As in Germany, the Japanese government began to take increasing control of the main industries, and of the economy as a whole. Here too, people began to blame the elected government and support more hard-line nationalist politicians. These men were in league with military commanders who believed that the solution to Japan's problems was to build up the military and take control of new territories that would give them access to raw materials and markets for their goods. Japan effectively became a MILITARY DICTATORSHIP (a country run by the army).

Source 4 A cartoon by David Low from a British newspaper, November 1931. The text in the middle reads : 'The concentrated disapproval of the whole world.'▼

Japan invades Manchuria 1931

In 1931, an incident in the Chinese region of Manchuria gave these nationalist leaders an ideal opportunity. The Japanese army controlled the South Manchurian Railway (see Figure 5). Claiming that Chinese troops had attacked the railway, they used this as an excuse to invade and set up their own government in Manchuria. Japan's civilian politicians protested, but the military was now in charge in Japan. China appealed to the League of Nations. This was a critical moment – would internationalism in the form of the League of Nations triumph over the aggressive nationalism of Japan?

Figure 5 A map showing Japan's invasion of Manchuria 1931–33. ▼

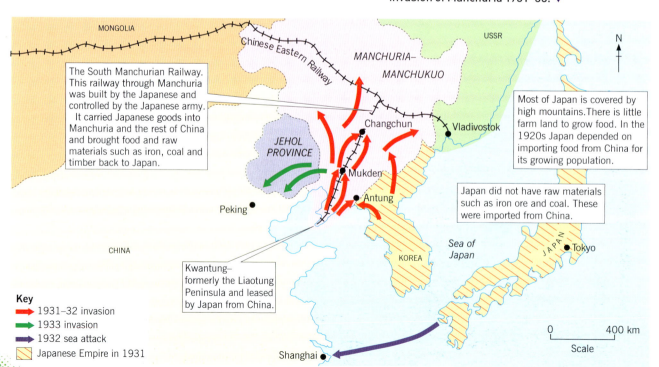

The South Manchurian Railway. This railway through Manchuria was built by the Japanese and controlled by the Japanese army. It carried Japanese goods into Manchuria and the rest of China and brought food and raw materials such as iron, coal and timber back to Japan.

Most of Japan is covered by high mountains. There is little farm land to grow food. In the 1920s Japan depended on importing food from China for its growing population.

Japan did not have raw materials such as iron ore and coal. These were imported from China.

Kwantung– formerly the Liaotung Peninsula and leased by Japan from China.

Key
- 1931–32 invasion
- 1933 invasion
- 1932 sea attack
- Japanese Empire in 1931

Source 6 A cartoon by David Low from a British newspaper, November 1932. ▲

1 Study Source 4. What is Low's attitude towards Japan in November 1931?

2 Do you get the impression from Source 4 that the cartoonist thinks Japan will get away with invading Manchuria?

3 Now study Source 6. Has Low's attitude towards Japan changed after one year?

4 Has Low's view of the League of Nations changed?

5 Study Source 7. What is the cartoonist's attitude towards Europe? What details make you think this?

The League's response

The League took a cautious approach. After all, Japan was one of its most powerful and important members. League officials, under the British Lord Lytton, were sent to investigate the issue in Manchuria. They took a full year to present their report, which was completed in September 1932. The report was detailed and balanced, and the judgement was clear: Japan had acted unlawfully and Manchuria should be returned to the Chinese.

However, instead of withdrawing from Manchuria, in February 1933 the Japanese announced that they intended to invade more of China. They claimed that China was politically unstable and that the invasion was necessary for Japan to protect itself. On 24 February 1933, the report from the League's officials was approved by 42 votes to 1 in the Assembly. Only Japan voted against it. A month later, Japan resigned from the League of Nations and invaded the Chinese province of Jehol.

The League discussed economic sanctions, but without the USA, Japan's main trading partner, sanctions would be meaningless. The League also discussed banning arms sales to Japan, but the member countries were worried that Japan would retaliate and the war would escalate. There was no prospect of Britain and France risking a war with Japan. Only the USA and the USSR would have had the resources to remove the Japanese from Manchuria by force, and they were not even members of the League.

Consequences

Several excuses were offered for the League's failure: Japan was so far away; it was a special case; the Japanese had a valid a point when they said that China was politically unstable. However, the significance of the Manchurian crisis was obvious: the League had proved powerless if a strong nation decided to pursue an aggressive policy. Japan had committed blatant aggression. Both Hitler and Mussolini looked on with interest. They would soon both follow Japan's example.

Factor 4: The failure of disarmament

You have already seen how the League of Nations and the great powers attempted – but largely failed – to reach agreements on disarmament in the 1920s. In the 1930s, there was increased pressure for the League to address disarmament.

The Disarmament Conference

In the wake of the Manchurian crisis, it became clear that something had to be done about disarmament. The US president, Herbert Hoover, encouraged states in Europe to come up with disarmament plans. In exchange, the USA offered to reduce or cancel their debts (see Source 7). In February 1932, the long-promised Disarmament Conference finally got under way. It came up with proposals to ban bombing of civilian populations and restrictions on some types of weapons. However, the various nations could not agree on how to *enforce* these restrictions.

◄ **Source 7** 'You can't have both!': a US cartoon from 1932, commenting on disarmament. It shows 'Europe' reading signs saying 'debt cancellation' and 'armament'. At this time most European countries were still in debt to the USA from their loans.

German disarmament

Under the Treaty of Versailles, Germany had been forced to disarm. Other countries were also supposed to, but they had not. By the time of the Disarmament Conference, most people accepted that Germany should be treated more equally. In December 1932 an agreement was finally reached, but this proved short-lived. In January 1933, Hitler took power in Germany and began rearming the country in secret. In October 1933, he pulled out of the conference altogether. By then most nations suspected that Hitler was rearming and accordingly they began to increase their own armed forces. The Disarmament Conference struggled on for another year, but few leaders paid much attention to it. Hitler publicly announced his rearmament programme in 1935.

PRACTICE QUESTIONS

1 Describe the problems caused by the worldwide economic depression. (5)
2 Describe the main events of the Manchurian crisis 1931–33. (5)
3 Explain why the Depression had such a bad effect on international relations. (10)
4 'The most serious challenge to international relations 1929–33 was the Manchurian crisis.' Explain how far you agree. (10)

FOCUS TASK

What went wrong in the 'hinge years' 1929–34?

The diagram below shows one way of summarising what went wrong in international relations in this period.

1 On your own copy of this diagram, add examples from this topic.
2 Use your diagram to answer this essay question:
   What went wrong in international relations in the years 1929–34?

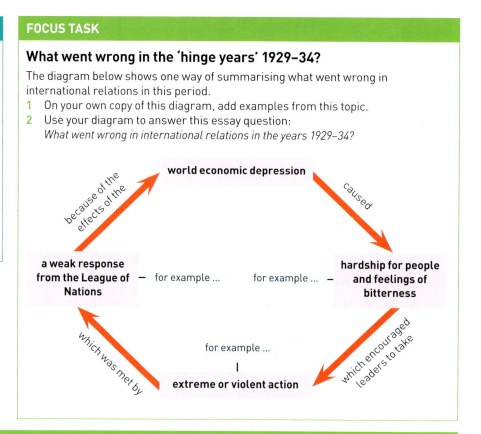

TOPIC SUMMARY

The impact of the Depression

1 The 1920s saw an economic boom in the USA. It lent money to many countries in Europe and Asia to help rebuild their economies.
2 In October 1929, the Wall Street Crash caused a worldwide economic depression. US banks asked for their loans to be repaid, which led to bankruptcies and unemployment in many countries.
3 Economic hardship led people to vote for extreme nationalist parties. The Nazis took power in Germany and the Fascist Party strengthened its grip in Italy. Both regimes planned aggressive expansion as a solution to their problems.
4 In Japan, the Depression caused major economic problems that led to political upheaval. The civilian government was effectively overthrown by the army and some politicians who supported it. Japan invaded Manchuria in China in 1931.
5 The League of Nations condemned Japan and ordered it to leave Manchuria. Japan refused and expanded further into China. The League was unable to stop Japan and the organisation's credibility was badly damaged.
6 The League of Nations tried to calm international tension by setting up talks on disarmament. However, many countries had used rearmament as a way to boost their economy. Few trusted their neighbours enough to disarm. Germany demanded that all states should disarm as they had been forced to. When this did not happen, Hitler left the talks in 1934 and openly announced German rearmament in 1935.

1.3 'The dark valley': The failure of the League of Nations, Appeasement and the drift to war

FOCUS

You have seen how international co-operation was replaced by nationalism in the period 1929–34, but there was worse to come. In this topic, you will examine:
- what went wrong in international relations between 1934 and 1939
- why these problems resulted in war.

'The dark valley'

The historian Piers Brendon referred to the 1930s as 'the dark valley'. This was a period when international relations became steadily worse and eventually resulted in war. The great powers turned away from internationalism and began to adopt more nationalist policies, forming secret military alliances against rivals and building up arms just as they had done before the First World War. The reasons for these actions were debated at the time and are still the subject of disagreement today. To understand what happened, we are going to look at four important developments in international relations:

1 the invasion of Abyssinia
2 the actions of Adolf Hitler
3 the policy of Appeasement
4 the Nazi-Soviet Pact.

ACTIVITY

As you work through this chapter, use a table like the one below to build your own timeline of the main events. Try to restrict yourself to a maximum of three events per year. Describe the event in column 2. Explain its importance in column 3. You might want to include more events in your first draft and then come back and cut some out when you reach the end of the topic.

	Event(s)	Why this event is important
1933		
1934		
1935		
1936		
1937		
1938		
1939		

Figure 1 A map showing the Italian invasion of Abyssinia. ▲

The invasion of Abyssinia: Why did this do so much harm to the League of Nations?

The Manchurian crisis had badly damaged the credibility of the League of Nations. In 1935, a new crisis developed when Italy invaded Abyssinia (now Ethiopia). This event really tested the League and its internationalist ambitions.

Britain, France and Italy all had colonies in northern and eastern Africa. Italy's leader, Mussolini, had his eye on the fertile lands and mineral wealth of Abyssinia, but above all he wanted to restore Italy to the glory of the days of the ancient Roman Empire. To do that, he needed military conquests.

In December 1934, Mussolini took advantage of a dispute over who owned the land around the Wal-Wal Oasis and prepared to invade Abyssinia. The Abyssinian emperor, Haile Selassie, appealed to the League for help. This was a clear case of aggression and Abyssinia lay close to British and French territories (see Figure 1), so they had an interest in events in this region in a way they had not had in events in Manchuria. Would the League be more successful in dealing with this crisis?

FOCUS TASK

What did the Abyssinian crisis reveal about international relations?
Copy the table below.

Abyssinian crisis	Headline	Evidence of internationalism (including the League) working	Evidence of nationalism winning over internationalism
Phase 1			
Phase 2			

1 As you study the events of the Abyssinian crisis, record evidence in columns 3 and 4.
2 When you have finished, decide on a good 'headline' title for each phase to sum up what was going on.

Phase 1: January to October 1935

In public, Britain and France were seen to be representing the League in trying to negotiate a settlement with Mussolini. However, it was a different story behind the scenes:

● In Italy, Mussolini began despatching forces to Africa and whipping up war fever among the Italian people.
● Britain and France were trying to protect their own interests. They wanted to stay on good terms with Mussolini because they believed he was a possible ally against Hitler. In April 1935, the British and French prime ministers met with Mussolini and agreed the Stresa Pact. This was a formal statement against German rearmament and a commitment to stand against Germany. They did not even discuss Abyssinia at their meeting. Some historians believe that Mussolini interpreted this as a promise that Britain and France would ignore his actions in Abyssinia.

There was strong support in Britain for action, possibly even military action against Italy. The British foreign secretary, Samuel Hoare, made a speech at the League Assembly, stressing Britain's commitment to collective security. A League committee was sent to investigate the Wal-Wal incident and reported back eight months later, in September 1935. The report concluded that neither side could be blamed and proposed giving Italy some Abyssinian territory.

Phase 2: October 1935 to May 1936

Mussolini rejected the League's proposals and invaded Abyssinia in October 1935. This was a clear case of a large, powerful state attacking a smaller one. The League had been established to deal with exactly this kind of dispute. After a frustrating delay that allowed Mussolini to build up his stocks of war materials, the League finally imposed sanctions. It banned arms sales and financial loans to Italy. It also banned the export to Italy of rubber, tin and metals, and prohibited imports from Italy.

However, the League delayed a decision for two months over whether to ban oil exports to Italy. It feared that the USA would not support such a sanction. Nationalist considerations also came into play. In Britain, the government learned that 30,000 British coal miners were about to lose their jobs because of the ban on coal exports to Italy. More importantly, the Suez Canal – which was owned by Britain and France – was not closed to Mussolini's supply ships. The canal was the Italians' main supply route to Abyssinia and closing it could have brought a swift end to Mussolini's Abyssinian campaign. Both Britain and France were afraid that closing the canal might result in war with Italy.

The Hoare-Laval Pact

There was worse to come. In December 1935, while sanctions discussions were still taking place, the British and French foreign ministers, Samuel Hoare and Pierre Laval, were hatching a plan. They aimed to give Mussolini two-thirds of Abyssinia in return for calling off his invasion. Laval even suggested that they approach Mussolini with this plan before they showed it to either the League of Nations or Haile Selassie. Laval told the British government that if it did not agree to the plan, the French would no longer support sanctions against Italy. However, details of the Hoare-Laval Pact were leaked to the French press. The people of France and Britain regarded the plan as an act of treachery against the League. Hoare and Laval were both sacked, but the real damage was to the reputation of the League, especially when the question about whether to ban oil sales was put aside.

1 In what ways was the Abyssinian crisis similar to the Manchurian crisis?
2 In what ways was it different?
3 Look at Source 2. In the cartoon, what has happened to the League of Nations?
4 Who has caused this?
5 What is the cartoonist trying to say about Samuel Hoare?

Source 2 A British cartoon from December 1935. The main figure is Samuel Hoare. He is holding a cosh – a small club often used by muggers. ▶

" YOU KNOW YOU CAN TRUST ME "

The situation worsens

The US Congress was appalled by the Hoare-Laval Pact and blocked a move by the USA to support the League's sanctions against Italy. In fact, US oil producers increased their exports to Italy. On 7 March 1936, German leader Adolf Hitler – timing his move to perfection – marched his troops into the Rhineland, in open defiance of the Treaty of Versailles. All hope of French support for sanctions against Italy was now dead. The French needed Italy as an ally against Germany and were prepared to sacrifice Abyssinia to this end. Italy continued to defy the League's orders and by May 1936 had taken control of the whole of Abyssinia.

Source 3 The front cover of the pro-Nazi magazine *Simplicissimus*, 1936. The warrior is delivering a message to the League of Nations (the 'Völkerbund'): 'I am sorry to disturb your sleep but I just wanted to tell you that you should no longer bother yourselves about this Abyssinian business. The matter has been settled elsewhere.' ▶

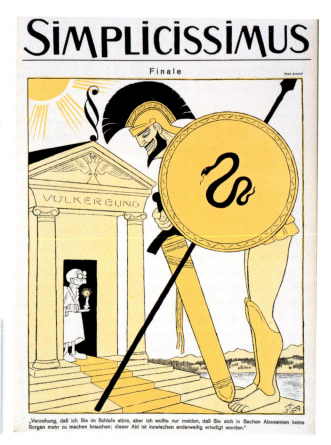

1 What does the large figure in Source 3 represent?
2 How is the League portrayed?
3 Do you get the impression that the cartoonist approves or disapproves of the situation?

The consequences of the Abyssinian crisis

The League of Nations had failed and collective security had been shown to be nothing but an empty promise. If the British and French had hoped that their handling of the Abyssinian crisis would strengthen their position against Hitler, they were soon proved wrong. In November 1936, Mussolini and Hitler signed an agreement of their own – the Rome–Berlin Axis.

Source 4 Historian Zara Steiner, writing in 2011.

The weakening of the League of Nations speeded up the retreat from internationalism to nationalism at every level. The Abyssinian crisis and Hitler's reoccupation of the Rhineland in 1936 affected the small states as well as the Great Powers. The small states turned their backs on Geneva and looked for other ways to protect themselves. The Great Powers returned to their pre-1914 practices: once again secret treaties, alliances, and arms races dominated the world scene.

FOCUS TASK

What were the consequences of the Abyssinian crisis for internationalism and the League of Nations?

1 Study Source 4 and the text on pages 30–32. Try to summarise the consequences of the Abyssinian crisis for internationalism and the League of Nations in a paragraph of just 100 words.
2 **Extension:** Discuss the following question:
Was it the League that failed its members or the members who failed the League?

The actions of Adolf Hitler 1933–37: Why wasn't Hitler challenged?

Between 1918 and 1933, Adolf Hitler rose from being an obscure and demoralised member of the defeated German army to become the all-powerful FÜHRER, dictator of Germany, with almost unlimited power. His is an astonishing story that you can read about in detail in Chapter 4. Hitler's emergence on to the international stage from 1933 marked another shift in international relations.

Hitler's beliefs

Hitler was strongly nationalist. He wanted to promote Germany's interests above all others. You have already seen how he hated the Treaty of Versailles and demanded that Germany's lost territories be returned. However, Hitler brought another, particularly dangerous dimension to international relations: his Nazi IDEOLOGY. He set out the main elements of this in his autobiography *Mein Kampf* ('My Struggle') in 1923–24.

Source 5 Historian Jeremy Noakes, writing in 1998.

Hitler had of course publicly stated his foreign policy 'programme' in his book 'Mein Kampf'. It is doubtful, though, whether the officials in the German foreign ministry had even read, let alone taken seriously, what he had written. And the officials in the French and British foreign ministries had certainly not read it or taken it seriously. It was assumed that the Nazis would be 'tamed' by less radical elements inside Germany.

Destroying communism

Hitler believed that communism (usually referred to as Bolshevism by the Nazis) was a disease that had to be wiped out. He persecuted communists in Germany. Since the USSR was a communist state, it seemed likely that the two countries would clash at some point.

Racial theory and *Lebensraum*

Hitler claimed that Germans were Aryans – a master race. He believed that Jews, Slavs (most of the peoples of eastern Europe including Czechs, Poles and Russians) were inferior. It was Germany's destiny to create an empire that would rule over these peoples and give Germans the *Lebensraum* ('living space') they needed.

Militarism

Hitler regarded war as a measure of the health and strength of a nation. Historians are still debating whether or not Hitler always intended to go to war. However, there is no doubt that within a short time of the Nazis coming to power, Hitler was preparing Germany for conflict.

ACTIVITY

It is 1933. Write a briefing paper for the British government on Hitler's plans for Germany. Conclude with your own assessment of whether the government should be worried about Hitler and his plans. In your conclusion, remember these facts about the British government:

- Britain is a leading member of the League of Nations and is supposed to uphold the Treaty of Versailles – by force if necessary.
- The British government does not trust the communist USSR, and thinks that a strong Germany could help to contain the communist threat.

1 How many of Hitler's actions between 1933 and 1936 were legal?
2 How many were illegal?

Hitler's actions

Hitler lost no time in turning his words into actions. Between 1933 and 1936, he defied many of the key terms of the Treaty of Versailles.

Leaving the League 1933: Hitler withdrew Germany from the League of Nations, claiming that his country was not being treated equally. This undermined the League's authority.

Rearmament 1933–35: Hitler began to rearm Germany in 1933. This was specifically banned by the Treaty of Versailles. He drafted thousands of unemployed workers into the army to reduce unemployment. He also began to STOCKPILE weapons, in secret at first. In 1933, he walked out of the League of Nations Disarmament Conference (see page 28). By 1935, he no longer bothered to hide Germany's rearmament programme. He publicly paraded his forces in a 'Freedom to Rearm' rally in Berlin, again boosting his prestige and support in Germany, particularly from the army commanders.

The Saar 1935: In 1919, the Saar region was run by the League of Nations (see Factfile on page 13). Hitler claimed it should be part of Germany. The League forced Hitler to agree to a PLEBISCITE. Nearly 90 per cent of people in the region voted to join Hitler's Germany, boosting his prestige in his country.

Remilitarisation of the Rhineland 1936: The Treaty of Versailles banned German forces from entering the Rhineland, a region on the border with France. In 1925, Germany had accepted this restriction in the Locarno Treaties. In February 1936, France and the USSR agreed a Mutual Assistance Treaty to protect each other in the event of an attack by Germany. Hitler claimed he was being encircled and therefore had the right to protect his own borders, so in March 1936 he ordered troops into the Rhineland. It was a huge gamble. If the British and French had sent troops he would have been forced to withdraw, but they were too concerned with the Abyssinian crisis. The League condemned Hitler's actions but no further action was taken.

Figure 6 A graph showing Germany's armed forces in 1932 and 1939. Under the Treaty of Versailles Germany was only allowed an army of 100,000 men, six battleships and no military aircraft. ▶

	Warships	Aircraft	Soldiers
1932	(30)	(36)	(100,000)
1939	(95)	(8,250)	(950,000)

Le peuple basque assassiné
par les avions allemands
GUERNICA MARTYRE _26 Avril 1937

Source 7 A postcard published in France to mark the bombing of the Spanish town of Guernica in 1937. The text reads: 'The Basque people murdered by German planes. Guernica martyred. 26 April 1937.' ▲

3 Study Source 7. Images like this were widely published in newspapers across the world. What effect do you think they would have had on public opinion?

The Spanish Civil War 1936

In 1936, a civil war broke out between two rival groups in Spain: republicans and nationalists. The war quickly developed an international dimension. The USSR supported the republican side with weapons and aircraft. Britain and France refused to intervene. Germany and Italy also said they would not intervene but then did exactly that. The nationalist leader General Francisco Franco had a similar ideology to Hitler and Mussolini. They helped Franco by supplying troops (claiming they were 'volunteers'), aircraft and other equipment. German aircraft also bombed republican strongholds to devastating effect (see Source 7).

This intervention had important consequences for international relations. Because Britain and France did not get involved in the Spanish Civil War, Hitler assumed that they would take the same attitude to any war. At the same time, the terrible impact of modern weapons, particularly bombing, convinced the British prime minister Neville Chamberlain that war must be avoided at all costs. The Spanish Civil War therefore encouraged Hitler in his plan to reverse the Treaty of Versailles. At the same time, the USSR became increasingly suspicious of Britain and France because of their reluctance to oppose Hitler and Mussolini.

The Anti-Comintern Pact and the Axis alliance 1936–37

Hitler and Mussolini had shown that their armed forces were effective and that they were ready to use them. Meanwhile, in the east, Japan had come under the control of hard-line nationalist commanders such as General Tojo. Hitler and Mussolini saw that they had much in common with the military dictatorship in Japan. In 1936, Germany and Japan had signed the Anti-Comintern Pact to pledge their opposition to communism (see page 25 for information on Comintern). In 1937, Italy also signed the pact. The new grouping of countries became known as the Axis alliance.

ACTIVITY

Look back at the briefing paper you wrote for the activity on page 33. That was in 1933. It is now 1937. Do you think you need to revise your report? Explain how, or revise it if you prefer. You might want to refer to how the events of 1933–37 have:
- increased Hitler's prestige and confidence
- weakened the authority of Britain, France and the League
- given Hitler new allies
- improved his military capability.

Why was Hitler able to achieve so much between 1933 and 1937?

It is clear to us today that Hitler's actions contributed to the outbreak of the Second World War. As Source 8 shows, there were plenty of commentators criticising the actions of Hitler and those who failed to oppose him. So you might wonder why no countries at the time, including Britain and France, took any steps to stop him. To understand why they did not do so, we need to clear our vision of hindsight as best we can. The statesmen of the 1930s did not know where these events would lead. We have to try see things from their perspective. Can we look inside the mind of a British prime minister in the late 1930s?

Look at the diagram opposite. You can see evidence of these ideas in British actions. For example, their response to Hitler's rearmament in 1935 was to sign a naval agreement with him that allowed Germany to build its navy up to 35 per cent of the size of the British navy. This clearly broke the terms of the Treaty of Versailles, but it must have made sense to the statesmen of the time. However, the result of such behaviour was to encourage Hitler to believe that Britain did not mind what he was doing. Indeed, he began to think Britain might even join him in an alliance against France and the USSR (he was wrong about this).

It is also important to understand the French point of view at the time, and why they may not have entirely trusted Britain. France shared a border with Germany, so the French were more worried about Hitler than they were about Stalin and any potential communist threat. France had been invaded from Germany many times before. The French therefore sought a formal alliance with Britain against Germany. When Britain refused, the French made a pact with Stalin instead (in 1936). This gave Hitler an excuse to remilitarise the Rhineland. It is also clear that British politicians failed to fully understand what Hitler was thinking.

Source 8 A cartoon by David Low, published in the *London Evening Standard*, 1936. This was a popular newspaper with a large readership in Britain. ▼

ACTIVITY

Write a short letter from Chamberlain to the cartoonist David Low in response to Source 8 (called 'Spineless leaders of Democracy').

1 Look at Source 8. What is the cartoonist's view of Hitler?
2 What is the cartoonist's view of the other leaders?
3 Would you say the cartoonist is more critical of Hitler or the other leaders?

We tried to recruit Mussolini as an ally but he proved to be unreliable and has sided with Hitler.

I'm not in a strong position!

The USA won't help us. It has isolated itself from Europe's concerns.

I am not even sure about France. We don't agree about how to treat Germany. The French are so paranoid they might even end up provoking Germany into war.

To be honest I'm more worried about Stalin and communism than Hitler! And Hitler is standing up to communism.

He has a point about the Treaty of Versailles. Some of its terms were too harsh on Germany.

He's right about disarmament. No one else has disarmed.

And as for all that extremist nonsense he spouts – he can't be serious!

Is Hitler really that bad?

The view from Britain

FOCUS TASK

How did Hitler's actions increase tensions in Europe in the period 1933–37?

To answer this question you need to do more than just list what Hitler did. You also need to explain how his actions caused tensions. It is important to plan and practise answering questions like this. If your planning is good, the writing is easy. Make a copy of this table and use it to plan an answer to the question above.

Hitler's actions	Reasons	How and why Britain and France reacted	Impact on international relations

Rather than writing your answer down, try explaining it to a friend. This will help show you if you have explained things clearly.

Appeasement 1937–38: A triumph or a sell-out?

Neville Chamberlain officially became British prime minister in 1937. However, he had been acting prime minister for two years already as the prime minister Stanley Baldwin had been ill. In that time, Chamberlain had begun a rearmament programme in Britain to prepare for the possibility of war, suggesting that he was realistic about the international situation. By 1937, Chamberlain was in regular contact with the French leader Edouard Daladier and was beginning to share his concerns about Hitler. You may think that the two men should have been planning a 'get tough' approach towards Hitler. In reality the policy Britain and France adopted in 1937–38 is known as Appeasement, and it basically meant giving Hitler what he wanted.

The *Anschluss*: Germany unites with Austria 1938

The next crisis came over Austria in 1938. The people who lived in Austria were mainly German. Hitler himself was Austrian. He wanted to unite the Germans in Austria with those in Germany. The treaties of Versailles and St Germain specifically forbade this, but that did not trouble Hitler. Austria had a strong Nazi Party and Hitler ordered these Nazis to campaign for union, or *Anschluss*, causing unrest. He then threatened to move troops into Austria to 'restore order'. The Austrian chancellor, Kurt Schuschnigg, asked Britain and France to put pressure on Hitler to make him back down, but they did nothing.

Hitler marched troops into Austria in March 1938. A plebiscite was organised, in which 99.75 per cent of the population agreed to the *Anschluss*. It was another significant success for Hitler. He had increased the German population and added Austria's reserves of gold and iron ore to Germany's industry. Britain and France had done nothing to stop him. In fact there was some agreement in these countries that the post-First World War treaties were unfair and that Germany and Austria should be allowed to unite if it was what the people wanted. Hitler began to believe that Britain and France would not fight to preserve the Treaty of Versailles – they might not be prepared to fight at all.

Figure 9 A map showing central Europe after the *Anschluss*. ▼

1. Read Source 10. Are you surprised by what it says about the reaction of Britain and France to the *Anschluss*?
2. What impression do you get of Chamberlain from Source 10?
3. Where is the next crisis likely to occur?
4. How is this source useful as evidence about international relations at this time?

Source 10 A US radio broadcast made immediately after the *Anschluss*.

Last night groups of cheering Nazis tore down the border posts on the Austrian–German border to signify they were now one nation. Over in London officials are watching every move Hitler makes. Prime Minister Chamberlain is determined to match Hitler gun for gun before openly pledging Britain's support for Czechoslovakia against a German invasion. In parliament today Chamberlain condemned Germany's actions in Austria. The prime minister is trying to win support for his big defence programme which may even include five years' compulsory military service. Britain's programme, currently in its second year, is to cost over 7 billion dollars and may rise to 10 billion. At the same time France has asked for renewed pledges of British support. France has vowed to fight for Czechoslovakia. Meanwhile the government in Washington is watching the whole European situation with close concern.

Source 11 One of a set of 50 cigarette cards circulated in 1938, giving advice on how to cope with air raids. Cigarette cards were collectible sets of cards included in cigarette packets. People were encouraged to collect the full set. ▼

The Sudetenland and the Munich Agreement 1938

After the *Anschluss*, the map of Europe shows Czechoslovakia looking a bit like a small creature about to be swallowed up by a large predator. That is probably a fair summary of how the Czechs felt. Czech leader Edvard Beneš was appalled by Germany's union with Austria. He asked for promises from Britain and France that they would protect his country against a German invasion. This time they gave those promises.

Hitler was interested in Czechoslovakia because the Sudetenland region of the country was mostly populated by Germans. As in Austria, Hitler got Nazis in the Sudetenland to stir up trouble and demand to join with Germany. In May 1938, Hitler expressed his support for the Sudeten Germans and threatened to invade if Czechoslovakia did not hand over the region to German control.

Beneš was prepared to fight. Czechoslovakia had a modern army and the support of Britain and France. Tension rose through the summer as the world braced itself for a new European war. In Britain, local councils began digging air-raid shelters. Magazines carried advertisements for air-raid protection and gas masks. Neither Hitler nor Beneš backed down.

Source 12 A photograph of air-raid shelters being dug in London, September 1938. ▶

Source 13 A cartoon published in Canada in 1938. ▲

Crisis talks – agreement at Munich 1938

By mid-September the situation had reached crisis point. Chamberlain made one last effort to avoid war.

- **15 September:** Chamberlain flew to meet Hitler. The meeting appeared to go well. Hitler moderated his demands, saying he was only interested in parts of the Sudetenland – and then only if a plebiscite showed that the Sudeten Germans wanted to join Germany. Chamberlain thought this was reasonable and that if Hitler got what he wanted, he would at last be satisfied.

- **19 September:** France and Britain put to Czechoslovakia their plans to give Hitler the parts of the Sudetenland that he wanted.

- **22 September:** Hitler increased his demands. He said he wanted the whole of the Sudetenland. Chamberlain told Hitler that his demands were unreasonable. War seemed imminent.

- **29 September:** Mussolini agreed to join Hitler, Chamberlain and Daladier at a Four Power Summit in Munich. The other leaders decided to give Hitler the Sudetenland. This became known as the Munich Agreement. The Czechs were not consulted about the agreement (nor was the USSR). The following morning Chamberlain and Hitler published a joint declaration, which Chamberlain said would bring 'peace for our time'.

1 Look at Source 13. Which do you think is a better summary of its message?
   a It is critical of Chamberlain because he is clueless.
   b It is sympathetic towards Chamberlain because he is beset by many problems.

Triumph or sell-out?

Many newspapers and newsreels at the time hailed the Munich Agreement as a triumph. Chamberlain was greeted by cheering crowds on his return to Britain. However, there were also many voices criticising the decisions made at Munich. There is evidence that the British public was still concerned. Opinion polls in September 1938 show that a majority of the British people did not think Appeasement would stop Hitler. There was also deep unease in the USA and in parts of the British Empire, especially Canada and Australia. You will investigate reactions to Appeasement in more detail in Topic 1.4.

FOCUS TASK

How did the policy of Appeasement affect international relations 1937–38?

To answer this question you need to do more than just list what Britain and France did. You also need to make sure that you can explain how these actions helped to ease tensions or made them worse. Copy the table below and use it to plan an answer to the question.

Example of Appeasement	Causes (actions of Hitler)	Reasons (why Britain and France did what they did)	Impact on international relations

SOMEONE IS TAKING SOMEONE FOR A WALK

Source 14 A British cartoon from 1939. ▲

Source 15 A Soviet cartoon from early 1939. CCCP is Russian for USSR and the other signpost points to western Europe. The police officers represent Britain and France. ▼

The Nazi-Soviet Pact: Why did such bitter enemies do a deal?

The end of Appeasement

Hitler moved his forces into the Sudetenland in October 1938. He stated that this was the end of his expansionist ambitions, but this was a lie. On 15 March 1939, German troops invaded the rest of Czechoslovakia. For Chamberlain this was a step too far. Unlike the Sudeten Germans, the Czech people had not been separated from their homeland by the Treaty of Versailles so Hitler had no claim to this land. If he continued unchecked, his next target was likely to be Poland. Britain and France told Hitler that if he invaded Poland they would declare war. The policy of Appeasement was ended. However, Hitler still did not believe that Britain and France would risk war by resisting him.

Poland under threat

Hitler definitely did have his eyes on Poland. In the short term he wanted to reclaim the Polish Corridor (see Figure 9 on page 38) and the city of Danzig. To do this he would have to fight Poland. He was confident he could defeat the Polish forces. He was also confident that Britain and France would do nothing. However, he was deeply concerned that Stalin would oppose him, since Poland bordered the USSR.

Stalin's concerns

Stalin's concerns about Hitler had grown throughout the 1930s. The USSR had joined the League of Nations in 1934 and agreed the Mutual Assistance Pact with France in 1936. But the Soviet leader had watched Britain, France and the League do nothing to stop Hitler rearming Germany or seizing territory in Europe. The Munich Agreement made Stalin even more suspicious. He was not consulted about it and it seemed that Chamberlain and Daladier were happy to point Hitler eastwards, towards the USSR (see Source 15).

2 According to the cartoonist, what is the relationship between Hitler and Stalin?
3 Do you think the cartoonist is more critical of Hitler or Stalin, or equally critical of both? Explain your answer.
4 What point is the cartoonist trying to make in Source 15?
5 How does this cartoon help to explain the Nazi-Soviet Pact of August 1939?

The Nazi-Soviet Pact

Stalin held discussions with Chamberlain and Daladier in March 1939 to try to arrange an alliance against Hitler. Negotiations continued through the spring and summer. However, at the same time Stalin was meeting with the Nazi foreign minister, Joachim von Ribbentrop, about a different alliance. In August, Stalin made up his mind. He opted for an alliance with Nazi Germany – a decision that stunned the world when it was announced on 24 August. By the terms of the pact, Germany and the USSR agreed not to attack each other. Privately, they also agreed to divide Poland between them and Hitler allowed Stalin to take the Baltic states of Lithuania, Latvia and Estonia.

Neither Hitler nor Stalin had any real faith in the agreement. Stalin was playing for time to get his forces ready for when Hitler turned against him (which he did in 1941). The Soviet leader had decided that Britain and France were probably too weak to stand up to Hitler and that even if they *were* strong enough, they could not be trusted to do so. In making this agreement, Hitler won the guarantee he needed to invade Poland.

The Second World War

Hitler invaded Poland on 1 September 1939 and German forces swept through the country. But this time Hitler had miscalculated. Britain and France had pledged to come to Poland's aid in the event of an invasion, and this time they honoured that promise. They declared war on Germany on 2 September. The Second World War had begun.

Who was responsible?

There has been a great deal of debate on this question and the arguments have swung back and forth. However, the majority of historians today believe that Hitler was responsible for the war. It could be argued that other factors helped Hitler, such as the failure of the League of Nations or the Depression. It might also be argued that Chamberlain or Stalin could be criticised for doing deals *not stopping Hitler*, but that is not the same as being responsible. They would not have started a war, whereas *Hitler wanted war.*

FOCUS TASK

Why did international relations get so much worse in the period 1933–39?

Make a copy of this table.

Factors	Impact on international relations	Explanation and/or example(s)	Most significant in causing Second World War (1–4)
Abyssinian crisis 1935			
Hitler's actions 1933–37			
Appeasement 1937–38			
Nazi-Soviet Pact 1939			

1 Look at some of the consequences of the factors in the table shown on the cards below.
   Decide which one(s) belong in column 2. You may use a consequence more than once.
   Explain the impact in column 3.

> Damaged credibility of League and internationalism.

> Meant Britain and France were seen as untrustworthy allies.

> Suggested Britain and France would not stand up to Hitler.

> Worried the USSR.

> Challenged Versailles Treaty.

2 Which of the four issues in the table do you think caused the most damage to international relations in this period? Rank them in column 4, giving an explanation of your top choice.

1 There are different kinds of cause:
  - a structural cause (a deep-seated problem like weak foundations in a building)
  - a trigger (like the storm that causes the weak building to fall over).

Work in pairs and decide whether you think the Nazi-Soviet Pact was a structural cause or a trigger.

PRACTICE QUESTIONS

1 Outline the main events of the Abyssinian crisis. (5)
2 Outline the actions of Adolf Hitler in the period 1933–37. (5)
3 Describe the policy of Appeasement followed by Britain and France in the 1930s. (5)
4 Explain why international relations became worse in the period 1933–38. (10)
5 Explain why Appeasement is considered one of the main causes of the Second World War. (10)

TOPIC SUMMARY

The failure of the League of Nations, Appeasement and the drift to war

1 Between 1933 and 1939, many countries abandoned internationalism and put their own national interests first. This led to major tensions and eventually to the Second World War.
2 Germany and its Nazi leader Adolf Hitler are often blamed for this. Through the 1930s Hitler pursued an increasingly aggressive policy, starting with rearming Germany in 1933. However other factors played a part as well.
3 The Abyssinian crisis of 1936 was triggered by Italy (under its nationalist, fascist leader Benito Mussolini) invading Abyssinia. This caused major confusion for the League of Nations and other European powers. They wanted Italy as an ally against Hitler but also wanted to defend Abyssinia. So they delayed and in the end did very little. The League of Nations was shown to be powerless.
4 Hitler chose this moment to make a decisive move to revoke the terms of the Treaty of Versailles. While the attention of world leaders was focused on Abyssinia, he marched his troops into the demilitarised zone of the Rhineland. He followed this up by sending aircraft to support the nationalists in the Spanish Civil War and by forming the Anti-Comintern Pact and Axis alliance with Japan and Italy.
5 Britain and France were once again thrown into indecision. They were deeply worried by Hitler but they were not ready or willing to fight him. Some people also had sympathy for Germany and were glad that the country was strong enough to be an important ally against the threat of communism if the need arose.
6 They followed a policy of Appeasement towards Hitler in 1937–38. They did not challenge the unification of Germany and Austria (the *Anschluss*). In the Munich Agreement, they allowed him to take parts of Czechoslovakia (the Sudetenland).
7 Appeasement came to an end when Hitler invaded the rest of Czechoslovakia in March 1939. Britain warned that any further aggression would result in a declaration of war. Hitler did not think Britain was serious – or he did not care. He struck a deal with his enemy Stalin to divide Poland between them.
8 The Nazi-Soviet Pact was a cynical short-term measure – Stalin knew that Hitler would one day fight him, but the deal gave him time to prepare for this. In September 1939, as Nazi tanks rolled into Poland, Britain kept its word and declared war. The European part of the Second World War had started.

KEY TERMS

Make sure you know what these terms mean and are able to use them confidently in your writing.
- communism
- democracy
- disarmament
- fascism
- Fourteen Points
- ideology
- internationalism
- League of Nations
- nationalism
- Paris Peace Conference
- plebiscite
- rearmament
- reparations
- self-determination
- Treaty of Versailles

1.4 The big sell-out? Historical controversy 1: Changing interpretations of Appeasement

FOCUS

You have seen that Appeasement was a controversial policy. In this topic, you are going to look in more depth at how and why attitudes to Appeasement changed. This section of the book is different from the others. We are less interested in *what* happened than in *how people's views of what happened* have changed and *why*.

The story of the story of Appeasement

We think the easiest way to begin this is to tell you 'the story of the story'.

	In 1938, there was some opposition to Appeasement but the majority of the population approved of what Chamberlain did at Munich.
Interpretation 1 **Popular majority view (1937–38)**	**'Well done Chamberlain!'** *Chamberlain kept the spectre of war at bay for as long as he could. He gave peace a chance.*
	The outbreak of the Second World War caused a major change in attitudes.
Interpretation 2 **Popular and political view (1939–48)**	**The 'Guilty Men'** *Appeasement was a foolish, cowardly and immoral policy that strengthened the dictators and weakened Britain.*
	Once the Second World War was over, the events that led to it were reassessed. The most influential historian was the wartime prime minister himself, Winston Churchill.
Interpretation 3 **Churchill (orthodox) view (1948–60s)**	**The appeasers misjudged Hitler** *Appeasement was a terrible misjudgement and miscalculation, even if it was based on good motives.*
	In the 1960s, many orthodox ideas were challenged by a new group of historians.
Interpretation 4 **Academic revisionist view (1960s–90s)**	**Rehabilitating Chamberlain** *Chamberlain was in an impossible position and he did the best that could have been done under the circumstances.*
	And then, as usually happens, the pendulum swung back the other way.
Interpretation 5 **Academic counter-revisionist view (1990s–2000s)**	**Chamberlain back on trial** *Chamberlain himself was part of the problem. His own personality and assumptions meant he could not deal satisfactorily with the situation.*

FOCUS TASK

Summarise the interpretations

Use note cards or draw up a table to produce your own summary of each interpretation. For each one note down:
- title of the interpretation
- main feature(s) of the interpretation
- why the interpretation developed at this time
- examples of this interpretation.

Interpretation 1
Popular majority view
1937–38

'Well done Chamberlain!'

Chamberlain kept the spectre of war at bay for as long as he could. He gave peace a chance.

Source 1 A photograph of part of the crowd that met and cheered Chamberlain on his return to London, 30 September 1938.

Summary

In 1937–38, most people approved of Chamberlain's actions. He was treated as a hero when he returned to Britain after signing the Munich Agreement. As he was driven from Heston Airfield to London, thousands of people lined the road in the pouring rain to cheer him. He received an estimated 40,000 letters and telegrams of support. He was applauded by the majority of members of parliament.

Unfortunately, we do not have any record of the discussions between Chamberlain and his ministers that must have followed. However, only one minister resigned and some ministers, including Lord Halifax, became even stronger supporters of Appeasement than Chamberlain was. The US ambassador to Britain, Joseph Kennedy, was also a strong supporter of Chamberlain's policies.

Source 2 Winston Churchill, speaking in October 1938.

We have suffered a total defeat. ... I think you will find that in a period of time Czechoslovakia will be engulfed in the Nazi regime. We have passed an awful milestone in our history. This is only the beginning of the reckoning.

Context

British people were haunted by memories of the First World War. The country was not united behind the idea of going to war over Czechoslovakia.

Impact

This interpretation did not last long. The euphoria was short-lived. People soon began to feel guilty about what had taken place in Czechoslovakia and that Britain had not stood up to Hitler. Most people in Britain realised that the Munich Agreement brought only a *chance* of peace – not much more. Opinion polls at the time showed that the majority of the population did not naively trust Hitler. They understood that Chamberlain had not really created lasting peace.

Challenges

There were powerful critics of Appeasement at the time, including politicians such as Winston Churchill (Source 2) and political cartoonists such as David Low (Source 8 on page 36). Their numbers grew steadily.

1 Use the framework in the Focus Task on page 44 to summarise this interpretation.

Source 3 The *Yorkshire Post*, December 1938.

By repeatedly surrendering to force, Chamberlain has encouraged aggression ... our central contention, therefore, is that Mr Chamberlain's policy has throughout been based on a fatal misunderstanding of the psychology of dictatorship.

Interpretation 2
Popular and political view
1939–48

The 'Guilty Men'

Appeasement was a foolish, cowardly and immoral policy that strengthened the dictators and weakened Britain.

Summary

During the Second World War, a new view developed that Appeasement was a foolish, cowardly and immoral policy. This was widely accepted among historians, politicians and the general public.

The key to this shift in attitude is likely to be a short book published in 1940 called *Guilty Men*, written by three journalists calling themselves Cato (see Factfile). Their basic argument was that since 1931 British leaders had made concessions to Japan, then Italy, then Germany, and that this had strengthened the dictators and weakened Britain. At the same time, these leaders had ignored the dictators' plans, failed to prepare Britain for war, and left it weak and defenceless. The appeasers were portrayed as being almost in league with the dictators.

> **Interpretation 2** An extract from *Guilty Men* by Cato, published in 1940.
>
> *Nazi Germany crossed the frontier of Poland and the world went to war in September 1939. How many warnings had previously been issued to the rulers of Britain? Hitler himself had written it in 'Mein Kampf'; the million speeches delivered by the Nazi leaders on the hustings of Germany; the denunciation of Versailles; the institution of Conscription in Germany; the Rhineland; Spain; Austria; Czechoslovakia; Munich; Prague – these and countless more. How many further proofs were needed?*
>
> *The Polish army was utterly obliterated. All the facts of Germany's prodigious capacity for war were known. Mr. Churchill had reiterated them to the House of Commons over the previous years. No room was left for doubt. The Nazis had been spending prodigiously. In the year before the war they spent £1,650,000,000 on armaments alone. Our rulers turned themselves to the task in a more leisurely manner. The British Government did not exert itself to any great extent in the arming of our country, even after we had clashed into war with the most tremendous military power of all times.*

Source 4 Chamberlain's Cabinet in 1940.

FACTFILE

Guilty Men

● *Guilty Men* was written by 'Cato' and published in July 1940. Cato was the name of a writer in ancient Rome who tried to improve life in the city.

● Cato was in fact three journalists (Michael Foot, Frank Owen and Peter Howard) who worked for Lord Beaverbrook.

● Although *Guilty Men* named 15 individuals, it was generally seen as a personal attack on Chamberlain and his policies.

● Beaverbrook had initially supported Appeasement but then turned against it completely once war broke out in 1939.

● When Churchill became prime minister in 1940, he asked Beaverbrook to join the government and made him minister of aircraft production.

Context

Many people felt ashamed of what had happened at Munich. When Hitler invaded Czechoslovakia, attitudes began to turn against Appeasement. These attitudes hardened after war broke out in 1939. Many wanted Chamberlain to be replaced as prime minister. These calls strengthened as the war went badly in the first few months. By May 1940, British forces had been defeated in Norway. Combined British and French forces were also defeated in France and the British army had to be evacuated. People were shocked and afraid that the Germans might invade.

They looked for a scapegoat and Chamberlain was an obvious choice. He resigned and Winston Churchill became the new prime minister. A bitter struggle followed between Churchill and the foreign secretary Lord Halifax (another of the appeasers). Halifax believed that Britain should make peace with Hitler, whereas Churchill wanted to keep fighting. For a time it looked as though Halifax had more support in the Cabinet and Churchill might be forced to resign. The powerful and influential newspaper publisher Lord Beaverbrook was a close friend of Churchill and strongly opposed Halifax. He published and promoted *Guilty Men* to help Churchill.

Impact

In the short term, *Guilty Men* had enormous impact. It helped Churchill defeat Halifax, who left the government soon after. Churchill became the undisputed leader of Britain's war policy. In 1945, however, it also helped unseat Churchill himself. In the general election that year, the Labour Party exploited the fact that it was a Conservative government that had been responsible for Appeasement, even though the war hero Churchill was their leader (see Source 7). They used Churchill's own condemnation of Appeasement to condemn his party. This helped them win the election and further damaged Chamberlain's historical reputation.

In the longer term, this interpretation shaped the way people thought about Chamberlain and Appeasement for years to come. It turned Appeasement into a dirty word – something no political leader would ever want to be accused of, even in countries beyond Europe (see Source 5).

> **Source 5** US historians Frederik Lovegall and Kenneth Osgood, writing in 2010.
>
> *Americans have fixated on it for seven decades. "Munich" and "appeasement" have been among the dirtiest words in American politics. American presidents from Harry Truman on have projected an air of uncompromising toughness lest they be branded as appeasers by their political opponents. As Truman put it in 1948: "Appeasement leads only to further aggression and ultimately to war."*

> **Source 6** British historian Derek Dutton, speaking in 2011.
>
> *Overall, 'Guilty Men' is less significant as an accurate assessment of Britain's political leadership in the 1930s than as a lasting influence on how people saw Appeasement. The book itself has few claims to historical scholarship. Even Michael Foot later admitted it was crude. Its black and white depiction of complex issues showed no understanding of the terrible dilemmas which confronted the policy makers of the 1930s, dilemmas to which there were no right answers.*

1 Use the framework in the Focus Task on page 44 to summarise this interpretation.

> **Source 7** Part of a Labour Party poster from the 1945 general election. Chamberlain is shown with Mussolini on the left and then Hitler on the right. Labour was careful not to criticise Churchill in the election campaign, just the rest of the Conservative Party.
>
>

Challenges

At the time there was virtually no challenge to this interpretation. However, later historians have been very critical of *Guilty Men* as a piece of historical writing.

Interpretation 3

Churchill's view, which became the 'orthodox' view

1948–60s

The appeasers misjudged Hitler

Appeasement was a terrible misjudgement and miscalculation, even if it was based on good motives.

Summary

The Second World War ended in 1945. Churchill lost the general election that year and devoted a lot of time to writing his history of the Second World War. The first volume, *The Gathering Storm*, was published in 1948. It was a bestseller and is still in print today.

Churchill took a slightly softer line on Chamberlain and Appeasement than *Guilty Men* had done. He was critical of Appeasement, but he did not say that Chamberlain had been weak or immoral. He argued that Chamberlain had been motivated by good intentions but that he had miscalculated and had misjudged Hitler.

Churchill also told the story in such a way that he appeared to be almost the only person to have opposed Appeasement in the 1930s. He claimed that Chamberlain should have tried to put together a 'grand alliance' of Britain, France, the USA and the USSR to stop Germany, Japan and Italy.

> **Interpretation 3** An extract from *The Gathering Storm* by Winston Churchill, published in 1948.
>
> *There was widespread and sincere admiration for Mr. Chamberlain's efforts to maintain peace. However, in writing this account it is impossible for me not to refer to the long series of miscalculations and misjudgements which he made. The motives which inspired him have never been questioned. The course he followed required the highest degree of moral courage. To this I paid tribute two years later in my speech after his death.*

Context

There are two important contexts for this interpretation, which are closely linked:

- **The 'Churchill Factor':** Churchill was well known for his self-promotion. In 1943, he actually said 'history will be kind to me because I shall write the history'. He was also bitterly disappointed at losing the 1945 general election and wanted to make sure his historical reputation did not suffer.
- **The Cold War:** At the end of the Second World War, two superpowers emerged – the USA and the USSR. Churchill was concerned about the USSR and saw it as a threat to Europe and the world. He believed that the USA and its allies (including Britain) should always stand up to Soviet leader Josef Stalin and not repeat the mistakes of the past.

Impact

It was not really true that Churchill was a lone voice in the 1930s. However, he had so much prestige after leading Britain through the war that his account became the accepted view – the orthodox interpretation of Appeasement. Throughout the 1940s and 1950s no *academic* historians challenged his account.

The Gathering Storm was also made into a TV documentary series in the 1960s (see Source 8) and influenced other TV and *popular* interpretations of the period.

> **Source 8** A review of a US TV documentary from 1960 called *Winston Churchill – the Valiant Years*. The first episode was based on Churchill's book *The Gathering Storm*.
>
> *'Winston Churchill – The Valiant Years' holds promise of developing into a stimulating and engaging series. 'The Gathering Storm', first of 28 projected filmed episodes, was shown last night. After tracing Sir Winston's family roots in America and Britain, the program moved rapidly through war's prologue period, from 1931 to 1939, when Churchill, a statesman in discard, a lone voice whose vibrant words were ignored, was forecasting the holocaust which Adolph Hitler would unleash.*

Churchill's views influenced politicians as well. In fact, long after historians began to challenge Churchill's views, politicians continued to be influenced by his account. For example, in the late 1940s and early 1950s US president Harry Truman took a very aggressive stance against the USSR, called the Truman Doctrine. In 1962, US president John F. Kennedy took the world to the brink of nuclear war with the USSR over Cuba. As late as 2003, British prime minister Tony Blair argued that it was important not to repeat the mistakes of Appeasement (see Source 9).

> **Source 9** British prime minister Tony Blair, commenting on Chamberlain in a speech in 2003. The main point of his speech was to persuade people that Britain should join the USA in invading Iraq that year.
>
> *In 1938 Chamberlain was a hero when he brought back the Munich Agreement and he did it for the best of motives. He had seen members of his own precious family, people he loved, die in the carnage of World War I. He strove for peace, not because he was a bad man. He was a good man. But he was a good man who made a bad decision.*

Challenges

As with Interpretations 1 and 2, there were very few challenges to this interpretation at the time. But later historians have been critical of Churchill's version of events (see Source 10).

> **Source 10** British historian John Charmley, writing in 2011.
>
> *The central flaw in Churchill's version of events is that it amounts to no more than an exercise in self-promotion. The sheer unlikeliness that everyone was out of step but our Winston is obscured by his iconic status as the man who won the war and as 'the prophet of truth' before it. His whole reading of events leading up to World War Two was badly flawed, and looks good only with the advantage of hindsight. ... It is also worth noting that Chamberlain could hardly have been that bad a choice as prime minister, or Churchill would hardly have seconded his nomination – a fact he somehow omitted from his memoirs.*

1 Use the framework in the Focus Task on page 44 to summarise this interpretation.

Interpretation 4

Academic revisionist view

1960s–90s

Rehabilitating Chamberlain

Chamberlain was in an impossible position and he did the best that could have been done under the circumstances.

Interpretation 4A British historian Donald Cameron Watt, writing in 1965.

The Orthodox view of Appeasement is now definitely on trial. The disenchantment has not spread to politicians or the reading public in Britain and the United States. But within the academic world of professional historians it is no longer so widely or easily accepted. Historians are now concerned to understand the processes which German and British politicians went through and the different kinds of advice they were receiving and the pressures that were on them. This is a welcome change from the dismissal of all of those involved in Appeasement as stupid, weak and ill-informed.

Interpretation 4B An extract from *The Realities Behind Diplomacy* by British historian Paul Kennedy, writing in 1981.

Appeasement in 1938 was a natural policy for a small island state gradually losing its place in world affairs, shouldering military and economic burdens which were increasingly too great for it, and which as a democracy had to listen to the desire of its people for peace.

Summary

Churchill's orthodox interpretation remained influential from 1948 onwards, especially with the public and politicians. However, in the 1960s some historians began to question the orthodox view. Historians often do this when new evidence comes to light or simply when they have new ideas. This practice is known as REVISIONISM.

The first historian to question the orthodox view was A. J. P. Taylor in 1961. He argued that Hitler did not have a clear plan in the 1930s, he simply grasped opportunities as they came along. This meant that Chamberlain could not be entirely blamed for not knowing what Hitler planned – Hitler did not know himself. Most historians did not accept Taylor's view, but it did start a revisionist process.

In 1965, the historian Donald Cameron Watt argued that Chamberlain faced many different problems and Hitler was just one of them – he had very few options and very limited resources.

Later in the 1960s, historians carried out studies into many different aspects of the events of the time – the financial issues, the military concerns, relationships with the empire and many others. A revisionist interpretation emerged, which stated that there was little else Chamberlain could have done in 1937–38.

Some historians went further and argued that Appeasement was actually the right policy because it bought precious time for Britain to build up its armed forces, particularly its air defences and the Royal Air Force. The fact that Hitler so clearly proved himself to be untrustworthy and dangerous in 1939 also helped to unite the country. By 1939, most British people still did not want to go to war but they no longer believed in peace at any price. Some historians went as far as to praise Chamberlain for his handling of the situation.

Interpretation 4C An extract from an article called 'Appeasement Revisited' by British historian David Dilks, 1972.

Chamberlain should be defended as a master politician pursuing the best, perhaps the only, policy possible in the difficult circumstances of Britain's declining power. Not only was Chamberlain's policy sensible, popular and of long standing, it was also skilfully executed: at Munich Hitler was out-manoeuvred. Subsequently British policy was to 'hope for the best and prepare for the worst'. When Hitler proved in March 1939 that he could not be trusted, Chamberlain's policy sensibly became one of deterrence and resistance. His careful handling of affairs through his whole premiership ensured that war came at the best possible conjuncture with the nation united and prepared.

Context

There were three developments that help explain the emergence of the revisionist interpretation:

- **Radical thinking:** The 1960s was a time when many traditional views in society were being questioned. History was one of many areas where new ideas emerged.
- **The Vietnam War:** During the 1960s the USA's dislike of Appeasement had drawn them into a war in Vietnam, which was going badly. This seemed to suggest that Appeasement may not have been a bad policy because without it Britain may have ended up in the same position.
- **New British sources:** Through the 1940s and 1950s historians relied on a fairly limited range of source materials, such as newspaper articles, private letters or interviews with key figures. But in 1958 the government passed the Public Records Act. This meant that official government papers could be studied 30 years after they were created. Previously the limit had been 50 years. This meant that by the late 1960s huge numbers of government documents became available. Historians were able to study documents from the Treasury, the armed forces, the Foreign Office and many other departments. This allowed them to get a detailed picture of the concerns that Chamberlain and his ministers had to face (shown below) and how seriously these concerns worried them.

Economic problems
Britain was still struggling with debts from the First World War, the effects of the Depression and unemployment. Britain could not afford a war. The Treasury blocked many of Chamberlain's plans to increase Britain's armed forces because of the cost.

Public opinion
For a democracy to fight a war successfully it needs the complete backing of its people. Chamberlain and his ministers did not believe the British people would support going to war in 1938.

The empire
The dominions (Britain's key allies in the British Empire – Canada, Australia, South Africa and New Zealand) were unsure about war with Germany. At the same time, Britain was struggling to hold its empire together. It faced problems in Palestine, an independence movement in India and its possessions in the Far East were threatened by Japan.

The military
British military commanders indicated they were not confident that their armed forces, particularly on land and in the air, were a match for Germany in 1938.

The USA
Chamberlain and his ministers knew they could not count on the USA. The USA was still isolationist in its thinking and was definitely not prepared to involve itself in European problems.

Fear of the USSR
Chamberlain's papers show he was concerned that Stalin as well as Hitler was a threat to Britain.

Impact

At this time, the debate had become an academic one not a popular one. Revisionist views did not have a huge impact on politicians or on public interpretations of Appeasement. Indeed, the popular and political interpretation of Appeasement remained Churchill's (Interpretation 3). However, these approaches *did* have an enormous impact among professional historians. After a relatively quiet period in which the orthodox interpretation was accepted, the 1960s, 1970s and 1980s saw many new studies and a lot of lively debate.

1 Use the framework in the Focus Task on page 44 to summarise this interpretation.

Challenges

It is the nature of history that each interpretation is re-evaluated by later historians. You can see how historians challenged the revisionist view in the 1990s in Interpretation 5 over the page.

Interpretation 5

Academic counter-revisionist view

1990s–2000s

Chamberlain back on trial

Chamberlain himself was part of the problem. His own personality and assumptions meant he could not deal satisfactorily with the situation.

Interpretation 5 An extract from *Chamberlain and Appeasement: British Policy and the Coming of the Second World War* by British historian Robert Parker, 1993.

Chamberlain succumbed to the temptation to believe that actions which were specifically his own were triumphing. Hitler helped. He appealed to Chamberlain's vanity and encouraged Chamberlain to think he had a special influence over him. Sir Neville Henderson, the British Ambassador in Berlin, encouraged Chamberlain even though he lost the confidence of his own colleagues in the Foreign Office. Chamberlain's appeasement was not a feeble policy of surrender. He never pursued 'peace at any price'. But he made big mistakes, especially after Munich. He could have built a strong alliance with France. He could have tried to ally with the USSR but he refused to try in any serious way. Chamberlain refused to listen to alternative views and his powerful personality probably stifled serious chances of preventing the Second World War.

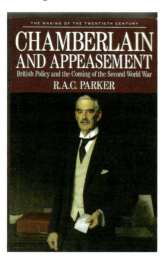

Summary

By the late 1980s and early 1990s, some historians began to question the idea that Chamberlain had virtually no choice in his actions in the 1930s. In 1993, Robert Parker developed the first of what came to be known as the counter-revisionist accounts of the 1930s.

Other historians agreed with Parker. They did not go back to the *Guilty Men* interpretation or even the orthodox interpretation, but they did not accept that Chamberlain was completely at the mercy of the problems he faced. In other words, they saw Chamberlain as at least partly responsible for Appeasement and its consequences. Their main arguments were as follows:

- Chamberlain overrated his own abilities and importance in thinking that he could talk Hitler into being reasonable.
- Chamberlain completely failed to understand Hitler because he was unable to change his own views about international relations.
- Chamberlain ignored the advice of many of his officials and colleagues.
- Whatever the reasons (including giving Britain time to rearm), Chamberlain did betray Czechoslovakia in 1938 and he should be held responsible for that.

Context

The two main drivers of the counter-revisionist interpretation were:

- **The historical debate:** It is an academic historian's job to disagree with earlier writers and challenge or refine their interpretations. A number of historians simply did not agree with the revisionist view because it let Chamberlain off the hook for Appeasement.
- **New Soviet sources:** In 1989, the Cold War ended and archives from the USSR began to be more available to historians. As well as Soviet documents, there were a lot of German documents that the Soviets had taken away when they captured Berlin at the end of the Second World War. These documents gave historians new insights into Appeasement, particularly the dealings between Hitler and Chamberlain.

Impact

The counter-revisionist view was not as dramatic as the orthodox or as controversial as the revisionist interpretation. As a result it did not have the same impact on politicians or the public. On the other hand, it continued to stir up debate among historians – and that debate still continues.

Some revisionist historians changed their view. For example, in 1991 revisionist historian Donald Cameron Watt argued that as well as the factors the revisionists emphasised, the behaviour and personality of Chamberlain also played a part. This is not unusual – historians often have to rethink their ideas as they research and find out more.

Source 11 British historian Paul Kennedy, writing in 1993.

The early writers about appeasement were severely critical because it was a failure of morality and willpower. By contrast, most of the later works have concentrated instead upon the compelling strategic, economic and political motives behind the British Government's policy during the 1930s. In seeking to explain appeasement, however, they have also tended to justify it. Yet the fact remains that some Cabinet ministers recognised that the dictators would have to be opposed. By 1939 at least, making concessions to Germany was neither as logical nor as 'natural' as might have been the case in 1936 or 1926. Instead, it was increasingly viewed as a policy which lacked both practical wisdom and moral idealism, but it was still being pursued in Downing Street. Individual conviction – in this case, Chamberlain's – obviously plays a critical role here.

Challenges

The revisionists have not simply let the counter-revisionists walk all over them! One of the most powerful arguments they have used is to ask what alternatives were open to Chamberlain. Several historians have used counter-factual history to think about this. Counter-factual history involves trying to understand what *did* happen by considering what else *might* have happened. For example, British historian Niall Ferguson used a complex computer-based historical simulation called *The Calm and the Storm* to test what might have happened if an alliance had been formed with France and the USSR and war declared in 1938. Source 12 is his conclusion.

Source 12 British historian Niall Ferguson writing in an article for the *New York Magazine*, 16 October 2006.

So how did my pre-emptive strategy stand up to a computer stress test? Not as well as I had hoped, I have to confess. The Calm & the Storm made it clear that lining up an anti-German coalition in 1938 might have been harder than I'd assumed. To my horror, the French turned down the alliance I proposed to them. It also turned out that, when I did go to war with Germany, my own position was pretty weak. The nadir [low point] was a successful German invasion of England, a scenario which my book [had ruled out] as militarily too risky!

Source 13 An extract from *Alternatives to Appeasement* by British historian Andrew Stedman, 2011.

It was easy to criticise Chamberlain from the side-lines. It was more difficult to suggest a constructive, coherent alternative. Critics were often confused and divided amongst themselves. One of Chamberlain's critics, Leo Amery, can be found in writing supporting at least four different approaches to dealing with Hitler.

So what were the other options open to Chamberlain?

1. *Isolation and absolute pacifism*
2. *Economic and Colonial Appeasement*
3. *League of Nations*
4. *Alliances*
5. *Armaments and Defence*
6. *War*

All of these options were considered by Chamberlain. Some were rejected and some were actually tried. In his ultimate failure Chamberlain's achievements deserve to be recognised. It is difficult to believe that the Nazis could have been deterred. War was the regime's main aim. In failing to achieve peace Chamberlain did at least make clear where the blame lay. History should give him credit for this.

1 Use the framework in the Focus Task on page 44 to summarise this interpretation.

PRACTICE QUESTIONS

Assessment questions on the historical controversy will usually be either type A or type B:

Type A: How fair is ...	Type B: Explain why ...
For example:	For example:
1 How fair is Interpretation A on Chamberlain? (25)	1 Explain why not all historians would agree with Interpretation C. (20)
or	or
2 How far do you accept the view of Interpretation B on Appeasement? (25)	2 Do you think most historians and commentators would agree with Interpretation D? (20)

1 Choose one of these questions and prepare an answer based on that interpretation below.
2 What would be a good question to ask about Interpretation E?

Interpretation A British historian Louise Shaw, writing in 1987.

To the dismay of his British colleagues and his French allies Chamberlain alone, motivated by his anti-Bolshevik prejudice, deliberately sabotaged the chance of an Anglo-Soviet alliance in 1939. Such an alliance would have been a workable solution for discouraging, or if necessary defeating, Hitler.

Interpretation B Conservative politician and political writer Lord Hailsham, speaking in 2008. He was a Conservative MP in 1938.

The question in September 1938 was whether we wanted war or whether we would give peace a chance – and it was just a chance. I was constantly being told that these dictators are only bullies and if you stand up to them they will run away. Well, the one thing we do know is that that would not have happened. Hitler proved that. If we had gone to war in 1938 we would have fought with outdated biplanes instead of Hurricanes and Spitfires and I don't think the people were sufficiently united. For a democracy to fight a war you have to be united and the people were divided.

Interpretation C Historian Donald Cameron Watt, writing in 1991.

The personality of Chamberlain is central to the discussion of Appeasement. He had a rather inflated sense of his own judgement and abilities and was unwilling to listen to anyone but himself. It could be said that he saw himself acting in the name of God or history. This earned him the disapproval of his people and historians.

Interpretation D British historian Zara Steiner, writing in 2011.

The leaders of the democratic states assumed that all those playing the game shared and accepted certain essential principles. All should, and hence would, agree that peace was preferable to war and that negotiation was more productive than fighting. These views were hardly appropriate for dealing with the Nazis, the Fascists, or the militarist Japanese leadership. Men like Chamberlain and Daladier, as well as their foreign ministers, because of their personalities, upbringing, education, and beliefs, barely understood a leader like Hitler. They, like so many others of the old élites, belonged to a world where statesmen made sensible choices, where rules and conventions were observed, and where men avoided bluff and reckless behaviour. The cataclysm of 1914–1918 had left the French and British leaders with the visceral horror of another war. Hitler suffered no such concerns.

Interpretation E British historian John Charmley, speaking in 2011.

'The Gathering Storm' has been one of the most influential books of our time. It is no exaggeration to claim that it has strongly influenced the behaviour of Western politicians from Harry S. Truman to George W. Bush.

Its central theme – the futility of appeasement and the need to stand up to dictators – is one that has been taken for granted as a self-evident truth in Western society, both during the period of the Cold War and subsequently.

2.1 A new world order: Causes of the Cold War 1945–50

FOCUS TASK

By the end of the Second World War, the balance of power had shifted. Britain, France, Germany, Italy and Japan were no longer great powers. The world stage was now dominated by two superpowers: the USA and the USSR. Although these two countries had fought together as allies in the war, they now regarded each other with suspicion. This developed into a new conflict – the Cold War. In this topic, you will examine how and why this happened between 1945 and 1950.

Allies or enemies?

Source 1 A photograph of US and Soviet soldiers shaking hands in Germany in 1945. ▼

Source 1 was a PROPAGANDA photograph, intended to show the unity of the USA and the USSR in the final weeks of their struggle against Nazi Germany. However, this unity would not last long:

- Within a year, Soviet and US leaders were accusing each other of breaking the promises they had made during the war.
- Within two years, the US president was promising his help to anyone who would stand up to the USSR.
- Within four years, war between the two SUPERPOWERS looked likely.

How did this happen? The timeline shows the main events and developments that led to this dangerous situation. Through the rest of the chapter you will examine these events in more detail.

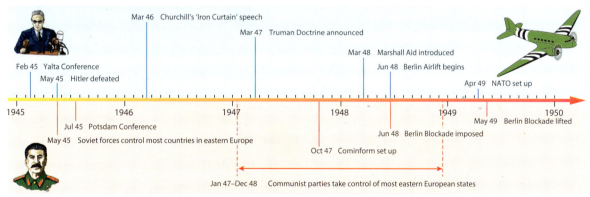

Origins of the Cold War 1945–50 ▲

Timeline:

- Feb 45 Yalta Conference
- May 45 Hitler defeated
- May 45 Soviet forces control most countries in eastern Europe
- Jul 45 Potsdam Conference
- Mar 46 Churchill's 'Iron Curtain' speech
- Mar 47 Truman Doctrine announced
- Jan 47–Dec 48 Communist parties take control of most eastern European states
- Oct 47 Cominform set up
- Mar 48 Marshall Aid introduced
- Jun 48 Berlin Airlift begins
- Jun 48 Berlin Blockade imposed
- Apr 49 NATO set up
- May 49 Berlin Blockade lifted

FOCUS TASK

Why did superpower relations worsen in 1945–50?

The timeline above lists the main events and developments of this period. As you work through this chapter, use a table like the one below to record how the events in the timeline affected relations between the USA and USSR.

Date	Event(s)	How this event made relations between the superpowers worse
February 1945		

Why did the alliance break down in 1945–46?

Conflicting ideologies

Historians have argued over this question since 1945, and they still disagree about the answer. There were many reasons why tensions rose between the superpowers. However, underpinning all the individual reasons was one fundamental factor: ideology. The USA and the USSR were founded on completely different sets of beliefs.

The USA	The USSR
The USA was capitalist. Businesses and property were privately owned.	The USSR was communist. All industry was owned and run by the state.
It was a democracy. Its government was chosen in free democratic elections.	It was a one-party dictatorship. Elections were held, but all candidates belonged to the Communist Party.
It was the world's wealthiest country. But as in most capitalist countries, there were extremes – there was some great wealth but also great poverty.	It was an economic superpower because its industry had grown rapidly in the 1920s and 1930s, but the general standard of living in the USSR was much lower than in the USA. Even so, unemployment was rare and extreme poverty was rarer than in the USA.
For Americans, being free of control by the government was more important than everyone being equal.	For communists, the rights of individuals were seen as less important than the good of society as a whole. So individuals' lives were tightly controlled.
Americans firmly believed that other countries should be run in the American way.	Soviet leaders believed that other countries should be run in the communist way.
People in the USA were alarmed by the theory of communism, which spoke of spreading revolution.	Communism taught that the role of a communist state was to encourage communist revolutions worldwide. In practice, the USSR's leaders tended to take practical decisions rather than be led by this ideology.
Americans generally saw their policies as 'doing the right thing' rather than as serving the interests of the USA.	Many in the USSR saw the USA's actions as selfishly building its economic empire and political influence.

> **Source 2** US historian John Lewis Gaddis, writing in 2011.
>
> *The war had been won by a coalition whose principal members were already at war—ideologically if not militarily—with one another. Whatever the Grand Alliance's triumphs in the spring of 1945, its success had always depended upon the pursuit of compatible aims [defeating Germany] by incompatible systems.*

It is not really surprising that the superpowers fell out after 1945. The USSR had been a communist country for more than 30 years. The majority of politicians and business leaders in the USA hated and feared communist ideas. In the past, the USA had helped enemies of communism. This made the USSR wary of the USA and its closest ally, Britain (especially after the policy of Appeasement in the 1930s). Britain and the USA were equally wary of the USSR.

The Yalta Conference February 1945

By February 1945, it was clear that Germany would be defeated. The 'Big Three' – Soviet leader Josef Stalin, US president Franklin D. Roosevelt and British prime minister Winston Churchill – met at Yalta in Ukraine. The aim of this conference was to decide what would happen after the war. The publicity photographs suggested the meeting was all smiles and friendly comradeship. However, while Roosevelt and Stalin got on reasonably well, Churchill was very wary of the Soviet leader.

> **ACTIVITY**
>
> Study Source 3 carefully. For each leader, write:
> - a speech bubble saying what he might have said publicly
> - a thought bubble indicating what he might have been thinking privately
>
> Make sure you can justify the contents of your bubbles by referring to the sources or other information on these pages.

◀ **Source 3** A publicity photograph from the Yalta Conference, showing Stalin, Roosevelt and Churchill. Although the USA and USSR were now far more powerful than Britain, Churchill was there because Britain's contribution to the war effort could not be ignored and because he was so well-respected.

1   What was the purpose of Source 3?
2   In what ways does Source 4 contradict Source 3?
3   On a scale of 1 to 10 (where 10 is very accurate) how far do you think Source 3 is an accurate representation of superpower relations at the Yalta Conference?

✓ The Big Three agreed on some important points	✗ But there were also worrying disagreements, particularly over Poland
• Stalin agreed to join the war against Japan. • Countries liberated from German occupation would be allowed to choose their government in free elections. • Nazi war criminals would be tracked down and made to pay for their crimes. • Germany would be divided into four occupied zones – US, Soviet, British and French. • To help Stalin ensure the USSR would not be invaded again, eastern Europe would become a Soviet 'sphere of influence'.	• Stalin wanted the border of the USSR to move westwards into Poland. Stalin argued that Poland, in turn, could move its border westwards into German territory. • Churchill and Roosevelt both disapproved of this plan but they agreed because in return Stalin agreed not to interfere in Greece, where the British were attempting to prevent the communists taking over.

Source 4 An extract from a top secret document called Operation Unthinkable. It was presented by army chiefs to Winston Churchill in May 1945. The research and planning for the operation had been taking place during the Yalta Conference.

OPERATION UNTHINKABLE

REPORT BY THE JOINT PLANNING STAFF

We have examined Operation Unthinkable. As instructed, we have assumed that Great Britain and the United States would have full assistance from the Polish armed forces and can count upon the use of German manpower and what remains of German industrial capacity. …

Owing to the special need for secrecy, the normal staff in Service Ministries have not been consulted.

AIM

The overall political aim is to impose upon Russia the will of the United States and British Empire. The only way we can achieve our object with certainty and lasting results is by victory in a total war.

The Potsdam Conference July–August 1945

The Big Three met again in Potsdam, near Berlin, after Germany's defeat. Although the press and the newsreels talked of harmony and co-operation, relations at Potsdam were more tense than they had been at Yalta:

- The war was almost over, so there was less pressure to show a united front.
- Soviet forces now controlled most of eastern Europe, after driving the Germans back to Berlin. Stalin set up a communist government in Poland, against the wishes of the Poles.
- The USA had a new president. Roosevelt had died in April 1945 and was succeeded by his vice-president, Harry Truman. Truman was much more anti-communist than Roosevelt and he was very suspicious of Stalin. He and his advisers believed that Soviet actions in eastern Europe were preparations for a Soviet takeover of the rest of Europe.
- The USA had tested an atomic bomb. Truman took Stalin to one side at the conference to tell him about it personally.

The Potsdam Conference led to more disagreements than agreements.

Disagreements at Potsdam		
Germany	**Reparations**	**Eastern Europe**
Stalin wanted to cripple Germany completely, to protect the USSR against future threats. Truman did not want to repeat the mistake of the Treaty of Versailles.	Twenty million Russians had died in the war and the Soviet Union had been devastated. Stalin wanted compensation from Germany. Initially Truman agreed, but he soon changed his mind. Stalin was confused and alarmed about why Truman would want to protect Germany.	At Yalta, Stalin had won agreement from the Allies that he could set up pro-Soviet governments in eastern Europe. He insisted that his control of the region was a defensive measure against possible future attacks (see Source 8). Truman became concerned about Soviet intentions and adopted a 'get tough' attitude.

FOCUS TASK

Why did the US–Soviet alliance begin to break down in 1945?

Look through pages 56–58 and find examples of how each of these factors caused the Allies to fall out in 1945:
- personalities
- actions by the USA
- actions by the USSR
- misunderstandings.

Place the factors in what you think is their order of importance and compare your view with those of others in the class.

Source 5 An extract from a British newsreel on the Potsdam Conference.

The three great leaders are now meeting in Potsdam, near Berlin. Marshal Stalin is the only one of the original Big Three from the Yalta Conference still in power, but the understanding forged in the war and strengthened at Yalta will continue to last. In continued harmony the British Commonwealth, the USA and the Soviet Union ensure the lasting peace of the world.

1 Read Source 5. How can you tell that this newsreel was approved by the British government before it was broadcast?
2 Find an image of the Potsdam Conference similar to Source 3 (which shows the Yalta Conference). Repeat the speech bubble activity from page 56.

Churchill's 'Iron Curtain' speech 1946

Despite their differences the superpowers continued to work together. The USSR had suffered huge loss and damage during the war. Some influential US officials argued that the Soviet Union should be given a loan of $10 billion to help its recovery. This was partly a political move, designed to improve relations between the two countries. It was also an economic move. The USA was worried that there might be another worldwide depression after the war, and US businesses would have no market for their goods if Europe was too poor to buy them. The USA offered the loan to Stalin in return for guaranteed freedom for US businesses to trade in eastern Europe. Stalin refused to accept the loan on these terms, fearing that it would give the USA power over his own 'sphere of influence'.

Over the next nine months, Stalin achieved the domination of eastern Europe. By 1946, Poland, Hungary, Romania, Bulgaria and Albania all had communist governments that were loyal to the Soviet leader.

During this period, Churchill lost his position as prime minister of Britain. However, he remained an extremely well-respected and influential figure, especially in the USA. He went on a world lecture tour, during which he expressed his belief that Stalin and the USSR posed a great danger to Europe and the world. In March 1946, he made a famous speech that some historians (especially Soviet historians) believe marked the start of the Cold War. It became known as the 'Iron Curtain' speech (see Source 8).

Source 6 A Soviet cartoon from 1947. Churchill is shown with two flags, the first proclaiming that 'Anglo-Saxons must rule the world' and the other threatening an 'iron curtain'. Notice who is formed by his shadow! ▼

Source 7 Churchill, speaking in the USA (in the presence of President Truman), March 1946.

A shadow has fallen upon the scenes so lately lighted by the Allied victory. From Stettin on the Baltic to Trieste on the Adriatic, an iron curtain has descended. Behind that line lie all the states of central and eastern Europe. The communist parties have been raised to power far beyond their numbers and are seeking everywhere to obtain totalitarian control. This is certainly not the liberated Europe we fought to build. Nor is it one which allows permanent peace.

Source 8 Stalin, replying to Churchill's 'Iron Curtain' speech.

The following circumstances should not be forgotten. The Germans made their invasion of the USSR through Finland, Poland and Romania. The Germans were able to make their invasion through these countries because, at the time, governments hostile to the Soviet Union existed in these countries. What can there be surprising about the fact that the Soviet Union, anxious for its future safety, is trying to see to it that governments loyal in their attitude to the Soviet Union should exist in these countries?

3   Some historians say that Churchill is as much to blame for the post-war distrust between the Soviet Union and the West as Roosevelt, Truman or Stalin. What evidence is there on pages 56–59 to support or challenge this view?

Stalin tightens his grip

The disagreements at Potsdam – and even Churchill's 'Iron Curtain' speech – did not discourage Stalin. He was determined to control the governments of eastern Europe to protect the USSR from future attacks. He made sure that communist governments took power right across eastern Europe. As the Factfile shows, it was an effective and sometimes brutal takeover.

In October 1947, Stalin also set up an organisation called the Communist Information Bureau (COMINFORM) to control these communist governments. Cominform regularly brought the leaders of each Communist Party to Moscow to be briefed by Stalin and his ministers. This allowed Stalin to keep a close eye on them. He spotted independent-minded leaders and replaced them with people who were completely loyal to him.

FACTFILE

How communists took control in eastern Europe 1945–48.

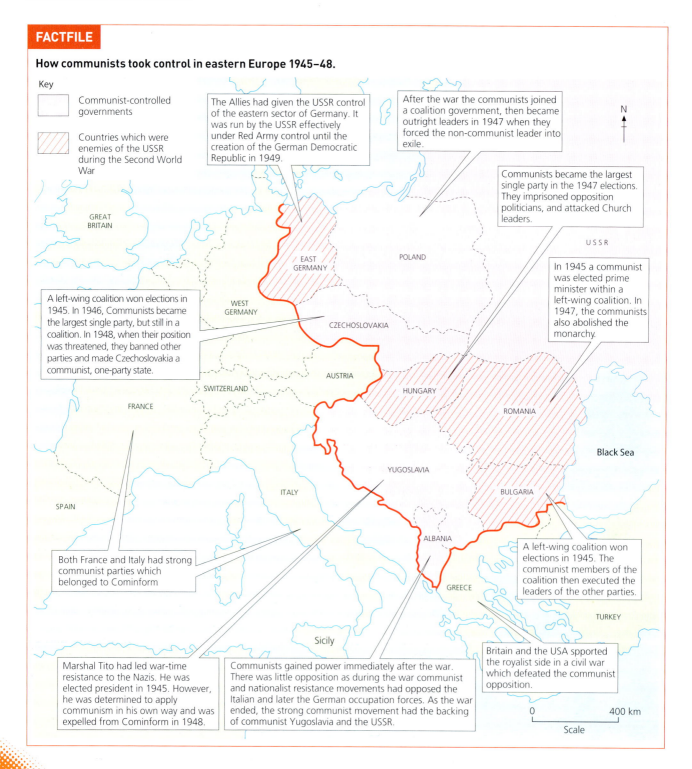

Key

■ Communist-controlled governments

▨ Countries which were enemies of the USSR during the Second World War

The Allies had given the USSR control of the eastern sector of Germany. It was run by the USSR effectively under Red Army control until the creation of the German Democratic Republic in 1949.

After the war the communists joined a coalition government, then became outright leaders in 1947 when they forced the non-communist leader into exile.

Communists became the largest single party in the 1947 elections. They imprisoned opposition politicians, and attacked Church leaders.

In 1945 a communist was elected prime minister within a left-wing coalition. In 1947, the communists also abolished the monarchy.

A left-wing coalition won elections in 1945. In 1946, Communists became the largest single party, but still in a coalition. In 1948, when their position was threatened, they banned other parties and made Czechoslovakia a communist, one-party state.

Both France and Italy had strong communist parties which belonged to Cominform

A left-wing coalition won elections in 1945. The communist members of the coalition then executed the leaders of the other parties.

Britain and the USA sported the royalist side in a civil war which defeated the communist opposition.

Marshal Tito had led war-time resistance to the Nazis. He was elected president in 1945. However, he was determined to apply communism in his own way and was expelled from Cominform in 1948.

Communists gained power immediately after the war. There was little opposition as during the war communist and nationalist resistance movements had opposed the Italian and later the German occupation forces. As the war ended, the strong communist movement had the backing of communist Yugoslavia and the USSR.

0 ___ 400 km

Scale

GREAT BRITAIN · EAST GERMANY · WEST GERMANY · POLAND · USSR · CZECHOSLOVAKIA · AUSTRIA · SWITZERLAND · FRANCE · HUNGARY · ROMANIA · YUGOSLAVIA · ITALY · BULGARIA · Black Sea · SPAIN · ALBANIA · GREECE · TURKEY · Sicily

FOCUS TASK

How did the USSR gain control of eastern Europe?

1 Study the information in the Factfile. Find examples of the communists doing the following to achieve power:
   a banning other parties
   b killing or imprisoning opponents
   c winning democratic elections.
2 Find examples of how the following factors helped the USSR take control:
   a the Red Army
   b communist involvement in resistance movements
   c agreements at Yalta.
3 'The only important factor in the communist takeover of eastern Europe was armed force.' How far do you agree with this statement? Explain your answer carefully.

Source 9 An extract from a report by the British foreign secretary to the Cabinet, March 1948. The title of the report was 'The Threat to Civilisation'.

The Soviet government is not prepared to co-operate with any non-communist government in eastern Europe, but it is actively preparing to extend its hold over the remaining part of continental Europe and, subsequently, over the Middle East and no doubt the Far East as well. In other words, physical control of Europe and Asia and eventual control of the whole world is what Stalin is aiming at – no less a thing than that.

Source 10 A US cartoon, commenting on Stalin's takeover of eastern Europe. ▼

1 How similar are Sources 9 and 10?
2 Do Sources 9 and 10 reveal more about Soviet policy or about British and US fears? Explain your answer.
3 According to Source 12, what are the aims of the Marshall Plan?

The US response 1947–48

Stalin claimed that his actions in eastern Europe were to protect his country from attack, but democracies in the West viewed them differently. To Truman and his supporters in both the USA and Britain, Stalin's actions looked more like empire-building (see Sources 9 and 10).

The Truman Doctrine

Despite his concerns, Truman was reluctant to get too involved in European affairs because it was not a popular policy in the USA. However, he was not prepared to stand by and let Stalin do whatever he liked, either. In March 1947, Truman made an announcement (known as the Truman Doctrine) that the USA would provide money, equipment and advice to any country he considered to be threatened by communism. This was the beginning of a policy that became known as CONTAINMENT – trying to stop the spread of communism.

Source 11 President Truman announcing the Truman Doctrine, March 1947.

I believe that it must be the policy of the United States to support free peoples who are resisting attempted subjugation by armed minorities or by outside pressures. ... The free peoples of the world look to us for support in maintaining those freedoms. If we falter in our leadership, we may endanger the peace of the world.

Marshall Aid

Truman believed that communism gained a foothold where there was poverty and hardship – and in 1947 people all across western Europe were suffering from the effects of the war. Truman sent an army general, George Marshall, to assess how bad the situation was. Marshall concluded that an aid programme of $17 billion was needed to rebuild Europe. At first the US Congress was reluctant to agree, but when communists banned all other political parties and took power in Czechoslovakia, US congressmen changed their minds and approved the plan in April 1948. There is no doubt that Marshall Aid was an extremely generous act by the USA, but there was also an element of self-interest. The USA wanted to create new markets for US goods to prevent another worldwide depression in the wake of the war.

Source 12 General George Marshall, setting out the aims of the Marshall Plan in 1947.

Our policy is directed not against any country or doctrine. Any government that is willing to assist in the task of recovery will get full co-operation from the United States Government. Any government which tries to block the recovery of other countries cannot expect help from us. Furthermore, governments or political parties which seek to exploit human misery for their own ends will face the opposition of the United States.

Source 13 Georgy Malenkov, a senior Soviet politician, speaking at a meeting of Cominform, September 1947.

The American imperialists have taken the path of outright expansion, of enslaving the weakened capitalist states of Europe and their colonies. It has chosen to hatch new war plans against the Soviet Union and the new democracies. The clearest evidence of this is provided by the Truman-Marshall plans, imitating Hitler. The new aggressors are using blackmail and extortion.

Source 14 A Soviet cartoon, commenting on Marshall Aid. The rope spells out the words 'Marshall Plan' and the lifebelt magnet is labelled 'Aid to Europe'. ▼

Source 15 Senior US official Dean Acheson, speaking in 1947.

We are willing to help people who think the same way we do, to continue to live the way they want to live.

1 How do Sources 13–15 present a different view of the Marshall Plan from the one in Source 12?

Just as Britain and the USA reacted with suspicion to Stalin's actions in eastern Europe, the Soviet leader reacted with concern to the Truman Doctrine and Marshall Aid. He believed that these policies would weaken his hold on eastern Europe. He also felt that the USA was trying to dominate as many states as possible by making them dependent on US money (see Source 14). Stalin forbade the eastern European states to apply for Marshall Aid.

FOCUS TASK

Why did superpower relations break down so badly in 1945–48?

You have been recording the events of 1945–48 and noting how they affected the relationship between the superpowers. Now it is time to reach some conclusions. Do these events prove that one side or other was responsible for the breakdown in superpower relations? Or were there other factors at work?

The table below will help you plan three paragraphs to explain the breakdown in relations between the superpowers in this period. Choose three paragraph starters (or come up with three of your own).

Paragraph starter	Use or reject?	Events I will use to argue that this was an important reason	How I will use these events to explain my point(s)
It was inevitable that relations between the USA and USSR would break down.			
National self-interest was the main reason why relations between the superpowers broke down between 1945 and 1948.			
Superpower relations broke down in this period because of the actions of the USSR.			
Superpower relations broke down in this period because of the actions of the USA.			
Superpower relations broke down in this period because of the way the USA interpreted the actions of the USSR.			
Superpower relations broke down in this period because of the way the USSR interpreted the actions of the USA.			
The main reason why relations between the superpowers broke down was ideology.			
There were other important factors which led to the breakdown of relations between the superpowers.			

The Berlin Blockade 1948–49

Historians are still debating exactly when the Cold War started, but most agree that it was underway by 1948. Stalin and Truman were locked into a pattern of action and reaction. Whatever one leader did, the other leader condemned. If one leader took any kind of action the other leader had to take an action to show his opponent, and his own people, that he would not be pushed around.

By 1948, the distrust between the USA and the USSR was so great that leaders were talking in public about the threat of war. Both sides increased their stock of weapons. Each side took every opportunity to denounce the policies or the plans of the other. A propaganda war developed. But despite all the threatening talk, the two sides still did not fire on each other. In this context the Berlin crisis of 1948–49 caused great anxiety.

Source 16 A Soviet cartoon from 1947. It shows (from left to right) the USA, Britain and France. The three sticks tied together are labelled 'American zone', 'British zone' and 'French zone'. The building is labelled 'Yalta and Potsdam Agreements'. ▼

Source 17 An extract from a report sent to Soviet minister Vyacheslav Molotov, March 1948.

The Western powers are transforming Germany into their strongpoint. They are making Germany part of a military and political bloc aimed at threatening the Soviet Union.

2   Look at Source 16. Explain what the cartoonist is saying about the USA and its allies.

3   How far do Sources 16 and 17 agree with each other?

4   Are you surprised that they agree at all?

Source 18 US General Lucius Clay, speaking in June 1948.

If we mean that we are to hold Europe against communism, we must not budge. I believe the future of democracy requires us to stay here in Berlin unless we are forced out.

FACTFILE

A map showing the zones of occupation in Germany after the Second World War.

The problem of Germany

After the war, Germany was divided into four zones (see Factfile). At first the US plan, known as the Morgenthau Plan, was to remove all German industry and make it an agricultural country so it could never again wage a modern war. However, as Truman grew more concerned about the USSR, he decided that a strong Germany might be a useful ally. It was also clear that if German industries were not allowed to recover then millions of Germans would simply starve. In 1946, Britain, France and the USA combined their zones. This region became known as West Germany in 1949.

Stalin blockades Berlin

Stalin felt he had to show western leaders that he would fight back if they encroached on the Soviet 'sphere of influence'. Although Berlin was also divided into four zones, the city itself lay deep in the Soviet zone and was linked to the western areas by roads, railways and canals. In June 1948, Stalin blocked these supply lines, stopping the western powers reaching their zones of Berlin. If the USA tried to ram the roadblocks or railway blocks, it could be seen as an act of war. Stalin expected Truman to announce a humiliating withdrawal from Berlin, which would give the Soviets control of Berlin and a propaganda victory.

The Berlin airlift

However, the Americans believed that the situation in West Berlin was an important test case. If they gave in to Stalin on this issue, the western zones of Germany might be next to fall to the communist USSR. Truman ordered that aircraft should fly supplies into Berlin. This was known as the Berlin airlift.

As the first planes took off from their bases in West Germany, everyone feared that the Soviets might shoot them down – an undeniable act of war. People waited anxiously as the planes flew over Soviet territory, but no shots were fired. For the next ten months, West Berlin received all the supplies it needed in this way – everything from food and clothing to building materials and oil. Stalin eventually lifted the blockade in May 1949. With US aid, West Germany began to recover.

What next for the Cold War?

What next for Berlin?

The end of the Berlin blockade did not signal the end of Cold War tensions. In fact, Berlin became a powerful symbol of Cold War rivalry: from the US point of view, it was an oasis of democratic freedom in the middle of communist repression; from the Soviet point of view, it was a cancer growing in the workers' paradise of East Germany. Berlin was also a Cold War flashpoint. It was one of the few places where US and Soviet troops faced each other directly (and on a daily basis), and it would be vulnerable if the Soviets chose to act. Later in the Cold War, Berlin would become even more significant.

Military alliances: NATO and the Warsaw Pact

During the blockade, war between the USSR and the USA seemed a real possibility. At the height of the crisis, the western powers met in Washington DC and signed an agreement to work together. The new organisation, formed in April 1949, was known as NATO (North Atlantic Treaty Organization). Source 19 shows the main terms of the NATO charter. Although the USSR was critical of NATO, Stalin took no further action until 1955, when the NATO powers allowed West Germany to join the organisation. In response, the USSR and the main communist states in eastern Europe formed an alliance known as the Warsaw Pact. Its members promised to defend each other if any one of them was attacked.

Source 19 Extracts from the NATO charter.

Article 3: To achieve the aims of this Treaty, the Parties will keep up their individual and collective capacity to resist armed attack.

Article 5: The Parties agree that an armed attack against one or more of them in Europe or North America shall be considered an attack against them all.

FACTFILE

A map showing the NATO and Warsaw Pact countries, centred on the North Pole.

Key

Warsaw Pact

NATO

More shocks for the USA

As if tensions over Berlin were not enough, the USA was in for more bad news in 1949:

- In August 1949, a shocked Truman heard the news that the USSR had successfully tested an atomic bomb. The Americans had thought the Soviets were years away from developing their own bomb and immediately began building up their own stock of nuclear weapons.
- In October 1949, the Chinese communist leader Mao Zedong finally triumphed over his nationalist rival Chiang Kai-shek, who had been supported by the USA. The country with the largest population in the world was now communist.

ACTIVITY

The Cold War often seems confusing because the two main sides involved never fought. Write a short paragraph in the style of the summary sections on Wikipedia, which defines the Cold War. You might want to mention:
- who was involved
- some reasons why it started
- how the war was fought (without fighting).

A pattern for Cold War conflict

Despite the mistrust shown by the superpowers, the crisis in Berlin suggested that there would not be a direct war between them. Instead, Cold War conflict was characterised by other features, which are outlined below.

Distrust and propaganda

- Each side would never trust the other and would never accept that the other had a valid case or was acting responsibly or morally.
- Each side would bombard the other with negative propaganda.
- They would also bombard their own people with propaganda about the greatness of their cause and the evil nature of their enemy.

Alliances

- They would form alliances for their own security while arguing that any alliances formed by the other side were aggressive and threatening.
- They would help any state, group or individual opposed to the other side, no matter what that state, group or individual was like.

Nuclear 'peace' and proxy wars

- In 1949, the USSR developed its own atomic bomb. It was clear that a nuclear war between the two superpowers would destroy the planet. With the stakes so high, the two sides went out of their way to avoid armed conflict (although there were many tense moments when open war seemed likely). In this way, nuclear weapons ensured peace, or at least prevented war between the superpowers.
- However, both sides became involved in 'proxy wars', supporting their allies in local conflicts while never directly fighting each other. The Factfile on this page shows just a few of these conflicts. You will look at some of them in more detail later in the book.

Source 20 A Soviet cartoon from 1948, showing President Truman. The title is 'Hysterical War Drummer'. ▼

1 Study Source 20. Do you think it was aimed at a foreign audience or at the Soviet population? Explain your answer.

FACTFILE

A map showing some key Cold War conflicts.

1979–90s: War in Afghanistan: the Afghan government supported by Soviet forces in fight against US-backed guerrilla fighters.

Korean War 1950–53: Communist North Korea invaded South Korea in 1950 with help from communist China. US and other forces intervened, leading to a stalemate in 1953. Korea is still divided into North and South to the present day.

Cuban Missile Crisis 1962 (see pages 74–79).

USSR

North Korea
South Korea

USA

Israel Afghanistan

Cuba

Vietnam War 1965–73 (see pages 80–89).

Vietnam

Angola

1960s–80s: In Central and South America the USA supported anti-communist regimes (e.g. General Pinochet in Chile). The USSR supported communist rebels.

Chile

1970s: Communist rebels in Angola helped by USSR and Cuba.

1967–80s: Israel supported by the US government in Middle East conflict with Arabs. The USSR supported the Palestinians and Arab states.

PRACTICE QUESTIONS

1 Outline Soviet actions in eastern Europe 1945–48. (5)
2 Outline the relations between the superpowers in the years 1945–49. (5)
3 Outline the actions of the USA in Europe in the period 1947–49. (5)
4 Explain why superpower relations got so much worse in the years 1945–48. (10)
5 Explain why the superpowers disagreed so violently over Europe in the years 1945–49. (10)
6 How far was the Cold War caused by ideology? (10)
7 How far was the Cold War the fault of the USA? (10)

TOPIC SUMMARY

Causes of the Cold War

1 After the Second World War, the world was dominated by two superpowers – the USA and the USSR. They had been allies against Hitler, but with their common enemy gone old ideological disagreements re-emerged, fuelled by new tensions over who would control post-war Europe.
2 The USA and the USSR were founded on completely different sets of beliefs. The USA was a capitalist democracy, which believed in individual rights. The USSR was a communist dictatorship, which believed in state control. Both sincerely felt their way of government was right.
3 US and Soviet leaders met twice in 1945. At Yalta in Ukraine in February 1945 they agreed on how to end the war, how Germany would be run after the war and that liberated countries should hold free elections. They also agreed that eastern Europe should be a Soviet 'sphere of influence' to protect the USSR against future attack.
4 In July 1945, they met again at Potsdam in Germany. Since Yalta, the USA had a new strongly anti-communist president and had developed a nuclear bomb. The Soviet army was still occupying most countries of eastern Europe. This conference saw major disagreements about how to treat Germany, about reparations and about eastern Europe.
5 Over the next three years, all countries in eastern Europe elected communist governments, although western leaders said these had been imposed and that elections had not been free. Churchill called the division between the communist east and the capitalist west an 'Iron Curtain', and the name stuck.
6 The USA poured Marshall Aid into Europe: money ($17 billion), equipment and advice was sent to any country that was threatened by communism, to help it rebuild. The USA was also deliberately trying to avoid the chaos that afflicted Europe after the First World War and to create a strong market for US goods.
7 Berlin was a divided city. The western (capitalist) part was rebuilt rapidly with US funds. Stalin blockaded Berlin to prevent any access between West Germany and West Berlin. In response, the Allies supplied West Berlin entirely by air for almost a year (the Berlin airlift). In May 1949, Stalin lifted the blockade.
8 During the Berlin blockade, war between the USSR and the USA seemed a real possibility. At the height of the crisis, the western powers set up an alliance called NATO. In response, the Soviet Union formed the Warsaw Pact. The members of each alliance promised to defend each other if any one of its members was attacked. This was a chilling reminder of how earlier conflicts had escalated.

Where next?

You now have a choice:

- Topic 2.2 continues the story of the Cold War through the next three decades.
- Topic 2.3 re-examines this story of the origins of the Cold War, but focuses on how interpretations have changed over time.

You can study these topics in either order.

2.2 'Three minutes to midnight': Cold War crises and confrontations 1961–90

By the mid-1950s, the world was divided into rival alliances. In this situation it was easy for local incidents to escalate into major crises that put the superpowers in conflict with each other. A similar thing had happened in 1914 and in the 1930s. It occurred many times during the Cold War (see Factfile on page 65). In this topic, you are going to examine four of the most serious crises and conflicts:

● Cold War crises: Berlin in 1961 and Cuba in 1962
● Cold War conflicts: the Vietnam War in 1954–75 and the Afghanistan War in 1979–89.

Make a copy of the table below and complete it after you have read about each crisis or confrontation. The first row has been done as an example.

Crisis/ confrontation	Local dimension	How/why the USA became involved	How/why the USSR became involved	What the outcome was for the USA/ USSR and why	Impact/ significance for the Cold War
Korean War	Communist North Korea invaded non-communist South Korea.	South Korea was an ally of the USA. The USA was worried about a 'domino effect' – if South Korea fell to communism then other Asian countries would follow.	North Korea was backed by communist China and the USSR. They were keen to see more of Asia become communist.	The USA became involved in a costly war, which resulted in a stalemate.	Maintained the balance of power in Asia. Also showed that the USA and China/the USSR would commit forces to conflict zones but not fight each other directly.

Source 1 Civilian and military casualties in the Korean War. ▼

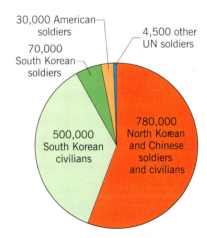

- 30,000 American soldiers
- 70,000 South Korean soldiers
- 4,500 other UN soldiers
- 780,000 North Korean and Chinese soldiers and civilians
- 500,000 South Korean civilians

Total killed: 1.4 million

Background: the Cold War in the 1950s

War in Korea

In 1950, communist North Korea, supported by communist China and the USSR, invaded South Korea – a DEMOCRACY and an ally of the USA. The USA and its allies immediately came to South Korea's aid. Chinese troops, with weapons and other support from the USSR, were sent to help the North Koreans. The Chinese troops were said to be 'volunteers', which meant that officially China and the USA were not fighting each other.

A bloody three-year war followed in which 1.4 million people died. For a while there seemed to be a real danger of this conflict escalating into nuclear war, after the US commander General Douglas MacArthur called for nuclear weapons to be used against China. President Truman sacked him, but many people in the USA felt that MacArthur was right.

Peaceful co-existence?

It was not all conflict in the 1950s, however. There were also some times when relations between the superpowers improved. When Stalin died in 1953, Cold War tensions eased a little, particularly when the new Soviet leader, Nikita Khrushchev, criticised many of Stalin's past actions and talked of PEACEFUL CO-EXISTENCE with the West. Nevertheless, many people remained suspicious of the USSR. These suspicions seemed well-founded when Khrushchev ruthlessly crushed the protests that broke out against communist rule in East Germany in 1953 and in Poland and Hungary in 1956.

The nuclear threat and the nuclear arms race

Throughout the 1950s, the threat of nuclear war was always present. After the USSR developed a nuclear bomb in 1949, both sides built up huge stocks of nuclear weapons and developed new bombers and missiles to deliver them. Each side accused the other of being aggressive, reckless and unreasonable. Soviet propaganda often showed the USA and its allies as loving or even worshipping nuclear weapons (see Source 2).

The poster on the left reads 'Glory to the policy of force!'

The poster on the right says 'St Madonna of the Hydrogen! We won't stop the tests!'

Source 2 A Soviet cartoon from 1957 called 'The Church of NATO'. It depicts war as the religion of the West. ▶

The box on the left is marked 'confessional'.

The poster on the confessional puns on a Russian word that means both 'forgive' and 'sell'. It says: 'We forgive/sell: 1) sins, 2) atomic weapons.'

The man with the gun is collecting 'for armaments'.

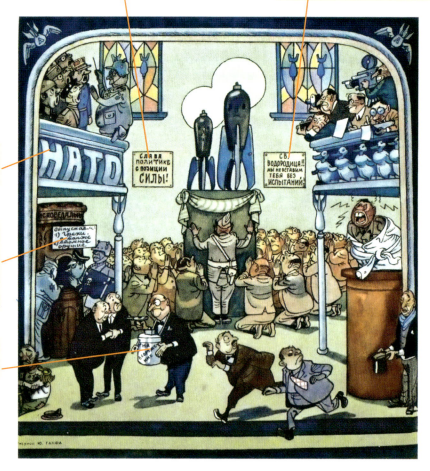

Against this strained background it was not surprising that local tensions developed into significant crises or confrontations. Sometimes the superpowers were dragged unwillingly into a local problem; at other times they tried to exploit a local problem to their own advantage. The rest of this chapter examines some of the most serious crises and confrontations.

Cold War crisis 1: The Berlin Wall 1961

What happened? An overview

At 2 a.m. on Sunday 13 August 1961, East German soldiers erected a barbed-wire barrier along the entire frontier between East and West Berlin, ending all free movement between the two sides. The fence was soon replaced by a concrete wall. Families found themselves living on different sides of the wall. Border guards kept a constant look-out for anyone trying to cross the barrier. They had orders to shoot people trying to defect. Hundreds were killed over the next three decades.

Source 3 An interview with an East German who opposed the regime and was eventually imprisoned.

When the GDR was established in 1949 many of us, especially young people, hoped it would mean a better, fairer life. But soon I turned against it because the ideology and reality did not match up. My grandfather owned some flats and rented them out. He was branded a capitalist, because he owned property. He wasn't then allowed to choose his tenants. They were nice flats so most of them got taken by government officials or their friends. And most of them just refused to pay him any rent and threatened him if he complained. Then it got worse in 1961 when they built the 'Anti-Fascist Protection Rampart' (the name given to the Berlin Wall). It wasn't protecting us at all, it was a prison.

1 Use the text and sources on this page to make a list of the reasons why people were leaving East Germany in the 1950s.
2 Organise the reasons into what you think is their order of importance. See if others in your class agree.

The local background: division, dissatisfaction and defection

The western zones of Germany were joined in 1949. The Soviets then created East Germany (the German Democratic Republic or GDR). Berlin was also divided into East and West. At first there was support for the communist regime in East Germany, but as time went on people became disillusioned. They resented the lack of freedom. They lived in fear of the Stasi (the secret police). Another complaint was corruption. Many government officials demanded bribes or made sure their friends and families got the best jobs and houses.

The greatest cause of dissatisfaction was the low standard of living, which contrasted with the prosperity of West Germany. The contrast between East and West Germany was particularly great in Berlin. In West Berlin, East Germans could see shops full of goods. They saw the freedom enjoyed by West Berliners. In the 1950s, East Germans could still travel into West Berlin. From there they could travel on into West Germany. Thousands did, but instead of coming back they DEFECTED (never came back). The flood of East Germans leaving Berlin was a propaganda gift to the USA. It would have to be stopped.

Figure 4 A bar graph showing the numbers of people crossing from East to West Germany 1950–64. ▼

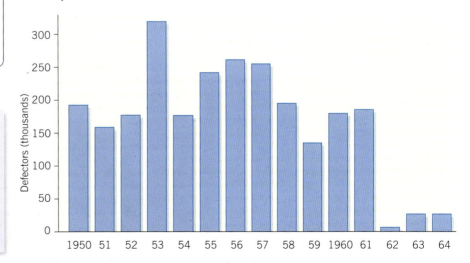

1 If you were in charge of propaganda for the USA, which of Source 3, Figure 4 and Source 6 would you find most useful? Explain your answer.

Source 6 Two photographs showing stages in the building of the Berlin Wall, August 1961 and October 1961. ▼

Why did it become a Cold War crisis?

By its very existence, Berlin was a Cold War flashpoint: West Berlin was a capitalist city in the middle of a communist state. You have seen how Stalin had tried and failed to force the USA out in 1948 (see page 63). However, specific circumstances led to the building of the Berlin Wall. The problem of defection was not new; in fact it reached a peak in the mid-1950s (see Figure 4). So what caused this crisis to erupt in 1961?

A new president

In January 1961, a new young president, John F. Kennedy, was elected in the USA. Kennedy recognised the significance of Berlin to the USA.

However, Kennedy's presidency did not get off to a great start. In April 1961, he backed a disastrous attempt to invade Cuba and remove its communist president, Fidel Castro (see page 75).

Khrushchev's demands

Khrushchev chose Kennedy's moment of failure in Cuba to call on him to remove US troops from Berlin. Khrushchev might have thought that the young, inexperienced president would give in, or he might have simply been playing to his audience back home who wanted him to act tough. But Kennedy stood firm.

The two leaders met in Vienna in July 1961, where Khrushchev repeated his demands. Not only did Kennedy refuse once again, he also ordered 150,000 US reservist troops to be called up for action in Germany and he increased funding to the US armed forces.

Accusations

Khrushchev accused Kennedy of provoking conflict. He claimed that the USA and its allies were using Berlin as a base for spies and for agents who were stirring up trouble in the GDR. There was probably some truth to that, although of course the Soviets were also using Berlin as a base for their own agents!

The Berlin Wall

Despite this tension, the creation of the Berlin Wall took many people by surprise. Through the night and day of 13 August, East German soldiers and workmen erected a barbed-wire fence all along the border between East and West Berlin. All crossing points from East to West were sealed, except for one. This became known as Checkpoint Charlie.

A

B

In official announcements, Khrushchev claimed that the wall was being built to protect East Berlin and East Germany from US spies and agents (see Source 7). However, this was a way of diverting attention from his main reason for ordering the wall to be built – stemming the flow of people out of East Germany.

> **Source 7** The official Soviet statement about the building of the Berlin Wall, 1961.
>
> *The western powers in Berlin use it as a centre of subversive activity against the GDR. In no other part of the world are so many espionage centres to be found. These centres smuggle their agents into the GDR for all kinds of subversion: recruiting spies; sabotage; provoking disturbances. The government presents all working people of the GDR with a proposal that will securely block subversive activity so that reliable safeguards and effective control will be established around West Berlin, including its border with democratic Berlin.*

Source 8 A Soviet cartoon from the 1960s. The sign reads: 'The border of the GDR is closed to all enemies.' Notice the shape of the dog's tail, which has been chopped off. ▶

2   According to Source 8, why is the Berlin Wall a good thing?
3   What is the significance of the dog's tail?
4   Look at the other cartoons in this chapter and see if you can find examples of the same claim being made. Why might the Soviets and East Germans want to emphasise this point?

Source 9 Colonel Jim Atwood, who was part of the US military mission in Berlin in 1961.

Instructions were given to our tank commander that he was to roll up and confront the Soviet tank, which was at the identical distance across from Checkpoint Charlie. The tension escalated very rapidly for the one reason that this was Americans confronting Russians. It wasn't East Germans. There was live ammunition in both tanks of the Russians and the Americans. It was an unexpected, sudden confrontation that in my opinion was the closest that the Russians and the Allies came to going to war in the entire Cold War period.

Source 10 Soviet tanks as seen from a US tank at Checkpoint Charlie, 27 October 1961. ▶

ACTIVITY

1 Look at Source 10. Write a caption that might have appeared alongside this photograph in a US newspaper at the time.
2 Now write a caption that might have appeared alongside the same photograph in a Soviet newspaper.

What happened next?

The building of the Berlin Wall was an extremely worrying development in the course of the Cold War. With hindsight, we know that events in Berlin did not trigger a war, but at the time no one could be sure what might happen as a result of this Soviet action. West Berliners genuinely feared this was the prelude to a Soviet invasion. They also feared a US withdrawal. The people of West Berlin staged a massive demonstration on 17 August 1961, calling for Kennedy not to withdraw US troops. In fact he sent 1,500 more.

Over the following weeks the Soviets and East Germans continued to strengthen and extend the wall. According to the agreements made at the end of the Second World War, US forces had the right to travel freely through East Berlin. Through September and October, US diplomats and troops crossed regularly into East Berlin to find out how the Soviets would react.

The most worrying day of the crisis came on 27 October. Soviet tanks pulled up to Checkpoint Charlie and refused to allow any further access to the East. All day, US and Soviet tanks, fully armed, faced each other in a tense stand-off. Then, after 18 hours, one by one, slowly the tanks pulled back.

What was the impact of the Berlin Wall crisis?

Taking the long view, we can see that the Cold War pattern held – another crisis, another retreat. The international reaction to the tanks pulling back was relief. Khrushchev ordered East German leader Walter Ulbricht to avoid any actions that would increase tension. Kennedy said: 'It's not a very nice solution, but a wall is a hell of a lot better than a war.' So the wall stayed, and over the following years it became the symbol of division – the division of Germany, the division of Europe, the division of communist East and democratic West.

Both sides presented their behaviour in this crisis as positively as they could. Kennedy had stood up to Khrushchev and he made good propaganda use of the wall. Khrushchev had shown he was tough by demonstrating that Kennedy could not stop him building the wall and by forcing the USA to accept that its troops and diplomats could no longer travel through East Berlin. The communists presented the wall as a protective shell around East Berlin. The western powers presented it as a prison wall. The superpowers had not gone to war, but there seemed little inclination for compromise beyond that.

Source 11 Extracts from a speech by President Kennedy in June 1963, soon after visiting Berlin.

Today, in the world of freedom, the proudest boast is 'Ich bin ein Berliner'. There are many people in the world who really don't understand, or say they don't, what is the great issue between the free world and the communist world. Let them come to Berlin. There are some who say that communism is the wave of the future. Let them come to Berlin. And there are some who say in Europe and elsewhere we can work with the communists. Let them come to Berlin. And there are even a few who say that it is true that communism is an evil system, but it permits us to make economic progress. Let them come to Berlin. Freedom has many difficulties and democracy is not perfect, but we have never had to put a wall up to keep our people in, to prevent them from leaving us.

Source 12 A cartoon by the German artist Ernst Lang, August 1961. Kennedy is saying 'This much and no further.' ▶

1 Source 12 was drawn by a German cartoonist. Do you think he was East German or West German?
2 Does the cartoon suggest that either Kennedy or Khrushchev triumphed in 1961? Explain your answer.
3 Is the cartoon critical or supportive of one or other figure?
4 Go back to the table you drew up for the Focus Task on page 67 and complete it for the Berlin Crisis of 1961.

»Bis hierher und nicht weiter ...«

FOCUS TASK

What kind of crisis was Berlin 1961?

1 Which of these descriptions best fits the Berlin crisis?
   a The superpowers were dragged in to a localised problem against their wishes.
   b The superpowers were keen to exploit a localised problem.
2 In groups, choose one of the following and explain how it contributed to the Berlin crisis:
   a nationalism or self-interest
   b ideology
   c personalities
   d economic problems
   e fear or misunderstanding.
3 Pool your ideas and decide which played the biggest role. You could turn it into a pie chart like the one shown here. Which section should be the biggest?

(pie chart sections: ideology, personalities, nationalism or self-interest, economic problems, fear or misunderstanding)

Cold War crisis 2: **The Cuban Missile Crisis 1962**

What happened? An overview

In October 1962, President Kennedy discovered that the USSR had been sending equipment and expert advisers to Cuba and that they were preparing to station nuclear missiles on the island. These missiles would be able to reach most US cities in 10–20 minutes. Kennedy sent US warships to intercept the Soviet ships carrying the missiles to Cuba. An incredibly tense period followed and war seemed a real possibility again. But on 28 October, both sides stepped back and agreed a compromise.

FACTFILE

A map showing the range of the nuclear missiles that the USSR wanted to place in Cuba in 1962.

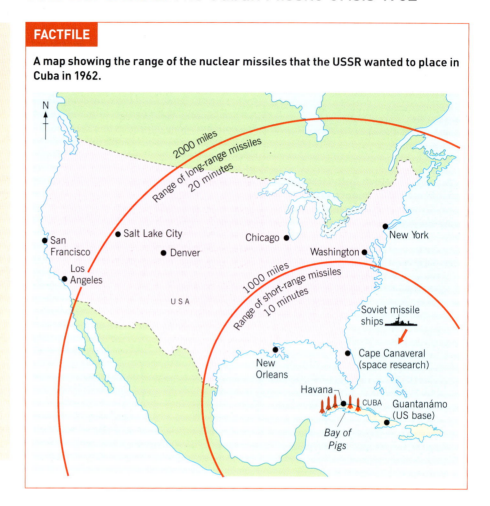

The local background: the Cuban Revolution 1959

Cuba is close to the coast of the USA. In the 1950s it was considered to be in the USA's 'backyard' and until 1959 it was practically a US colony. Cuba was ruled by General Fulgencio Batista. Batista was corrupt and deeply unpopular, but the USA supported him because he was fiercely anti-communist. In 1959, Batista was overthrown in a revolution led by the communist Fidel Castro. Castro killed or imprisoned many of Batista's followers. Thousands more fled into exile in the USA. These exiled Cubans pressured the USA to help oust Castro. The US president at the time, Dwight D. Eisenhower, ordered the Central Intelligence Agency (CIA) to investigate ways to overthrow Castro. The USA refused to trade with Cuba and began a propaganda campaign against the Cuban leader and his regime.

Why did it become a Cold War crisis?

Khrushchev supports Castro

Castro feared a US invasion of Cuba. He turned to the USSR for help. Khrushchev and Castro agreed a $100 million package of economic aid. Khrushchev also started sending military equipment and technical advisers to Cuba.

The Bay of Pigs invasion

In April 1961, the new US president, John F. Kennedy, decided to act. He authorised a CIA-backed plan to help 1,400 Cuban exiles – opponents of Castro – to land in the Bay of Pigs in Cuba and overthrow him. The plan was a disaster and a humiliating defeat for Kennedy. It also strengthened Castro's hold on Cuba. Worse still, it seemed to justify Khrushchev's actions because it seemed Cuba did need protection from a possible US invasion.

Khrushchev arms Castro

In May 1962, the Soviet Union announced publicly for the first time that it was supplying Cuba with arms. By September Cuba had thousands of Soviet missiles, plus patrol boats, tanks, radar equipment, aircraft and 5,000 Soviet technicians to help maintain the weapons. The Americans watched all this with concern, but the big question was whether the Soviet Union would put nuclear missiles on Cuba. On 11 September, Kennedy warned the USSR that he would take serious action if this happened. Khrushchev assured Kennedy that he had no intention of doing so.

Source 13 President Kennedy, speaking in 1963.

I believe there is no country in the world ... whose economic colonisation, humiliation and exploitation were worse than in Cuba, partly as a consequence of US policy during the Batista regime. I believe that, without being aware of it, we conceived and created the Castro movement.

1 Sources 13 and 14 are both US views. Why are they so different? (You may want to wait until you finish this section before you answer this question.)
2 How do you think the commentary for a Soviet or Cuban TV programme might have been different from the views expressed in Source 14?
3 The programme in Source 14 was actually funded by the US Air Force. Does this surprise you? Why, or why not?

Source 14 An extract from the commentary of a US TV programme made in 1962.

By October 1962 the historic friendship between Cuba and the USA was gone. Behind this change was the story of the betrayal of the Cuban people. It began with Fidel Castro triumphantly entering Havana in 1959. Castro promised democracy and freedom and for a time it appeared to most Cubans that they were liberated. But it soon became apparent that Castro had sold out to Premier Khrushchev of the communists.

The October crisis

Kennedy remained suspicious. On Sunday 14 October 1962, a US U2 spy plane flew over Cuba. It took amazingly detailed photographs that showed some worrying developments. It was clear to the CIA and US military experts that the images showed nuclear missile sites. US spy planes also reported that 20 Soviet ships were on their way to Cuba carrying missiles.

Why did Khrushchev place nuclear missiles in Cuba?

This was the first time that any Soviet leader had placed nuclear weapons outside Soviet territory. Why did Khrushchev take such an unusual step? He must have known that it would cause a crisis. This was not a covert operation – the missiles were carried openly on the ships. Historians have suggested various possible explanations, which are outlined below.

To bargain with the USA		To test the USA
If Khrushchev had missiles in Cuba, he could agree to remove them in return for some US concessions. The USA had missiles in Turkey and Iran, so Khrushchev may have been planning to do a deal on these. Or he may have wanted to make a deal over Berlin.		In the strained atmosphere of Cold War politics, the missiles were designed to see how strong the USA really was – whether it would step up or back down. Kennedy and Khrushchev had clashed the previous year in Berlin. Perhaps Khrushchev thought Kennedy would back down.
To close the missile gap	**To defend Cuba**	**To strengthen his own position in the USSR**
The USA had far more nuclear weapons than the USSR. Khrushchev was so concerned about the missile gap between the USSR and the USA that he would seize any opportunity he could to close it. With missiles on Cuba it was less likely that the USA would ever launch a 'first strike' against the USSR.	Cuba was the only communist state in the Americas, and it had become communist willingly rather than as a result of invasion by the USSR. In addition, Cuba was in the USA's backyard. Just by existing, Castro's Cuba was excellent propaganda for the USSR. It was also a potentially useful military base.	Khrushchev was not an all-powerful figure like Stalin had been. He had many critics within the Soviet Communist Party. A major success against the USA would strengthen his position and his authority.

What happened next? The '13 Days'

Events unfolded in an incredibly tense period of 13 days in October 1962.

Tuesday 16 October	Kennedy formed a panel of expert military and political advisers called Ex Comm. Some were 'Hawks', eager for a trial of strength with the USSR, even if that meant war. They proposed bombing the missile sites and possibly invading Cuba. Other advisers ('Doves') urged Kennedy to solve the problem through diplomacy.
Saturday 20 October– Sunday 21 October	Kennedy decided to blockade Cuba. US navy ships would stop Soviet ships 800 km from the Cuban coast. The US army also began assembling troops in Florida ready for a possible invasion of Cuba.
Monday 22 October	Kennedy announced the blockade on US TV and called on the Soviet Union to withdraw its missiles. Khrushchev told his troops in Cuba to expect – and to resist – a US invasion.
Tuesday 23 October	Kennedy received a letter from Khrushchev saying that Soviet ships would not observe the blockade. Khrushchev did not admit that there were nuclear missiles on Cuba.
Wednesday 24 October	The blockade began. The first missile-carrying ships, accompanied by a Soviet submarine, approached the blockade zone. Then suddenly, at 10.32 a.m., the 20 Soviet ships closest to the zone stopped or turned around.
Friday 26 October	Kennedy received a long personal letter from Khrushchev. The letter claimed that the missiles on Cuba were purely defensive. This was the first time Khrushchev had admitted the presence of the missiles. He indicated they might be withdrawn if Kennedy promised not to invade Cuba. By this point more than 120,000 US troops were assembled in Florida.
Saturday 27 October	Khrushchev sent a second letter revising his proposals. He now said he would remove the missiles from Cuba if the USA promised not to invade *and* withdrew its missiles from Turkey. Tension rose as a US U2 plane was shot down over Cuba. 'Hawks' demanded an attack on Cuba but Kennedy decided to delay. He also decided to ignore the second letter from Khrushchev, but instead accepted the terms suggested in the first letter, dated 26 October. He said that if the Soviet Union did not withdraw the missiles, an attack would follow.
Sunday 28 October	Khrushchev replied to Kennedy and agreed to remove the missiles 'in order to eliminate as rapidly as possible the conflict which endangers the cause of peace'.

Source 15 A cartoon by Vicky (Victor Weisz), published in the *London Evening Standard*, 24 October 1962. ▶

1 Source 15 is a British cartoon. Pretend you did not know this. Explain why it is unlikely to be a US or Soviet cartoon.

2 What is the cartoonist's attitude to the two sides in the crisis?

3 The cartoon was published on 24 October 1962. Do you think it would have been more relevant to the crisis on any other date? Explain your answer.

"INTOLERABLE HAVING YOUR ROCKETS ON MY DOORSTEP!"

How serious was the Cuban Missile Crisis?

Many people considered the Cuban Missile Crisis to be very serious indeed, as Sources 16 and 18 show. Even Source 17 hints at this (it was unusual for a British newspaper to criticise the USA in a Cold War crisis). It may reflect just how concerned people were about the possibility of war breaking out.

Source 16 The memories of poet Liz Lochead, who was a Scottish school student in October 1962.

It was the time of the Cuba crisis and everybody was scared, even the grown-ups. No one on the bus to school talked much, but those who did talked about nothing else and everyone's face was grim. On a placard outside the newsagents, black block capitals spelled WAR INEVITABLE. Even the newsreaders on television looked scared when they talked about 'the grave international situation'. We really expected that death. And the bombs might come falling.

Source 17 From an article in the *Manchester Guardian*, 25 October 1962.

THE YOUNG ONES IN REVOLT

– school strikes in protest at actions of superpowers

The two Ks – Kennedy and Khrushchev – will get a cable [telegram] from Britain's young ones in revolt today. The sender: Robin Mariner, 18-year-old head boy at Midhurst, Sussex, grammar school, and leader of a strike by 40 of the school's sixth formers yesterday. The strikers told their headmaster, Mr Norman Lucas, after morning assembly that they would not attend classes for two days.

Source 18 US defence secretary Robert McNamara talking about the evening of 27 October 1962.

It was a beautiful autumn evening, the height of the crisis, and I went up to the open air to smell it, because I thought it was the last Saturday I would ever see.

ACTIVITY

Read through these statements carefully:

A   Nuclear war was very close in October 1962.
B   The media thought nuclear war was very close in October 1962.
C   Ordinary people thought that nuclear war was very close in October 1962.
D   People 'in the know' thought nuclear war was very close in October 1962.

Each statement is making a slightly different point. They are similar, but not identical. For each statement explain:
● which sources support the statement
● why you feel the statement is supported by these sources.

Think carefully about each statement and be precise in your answers. You will find the '13 Days' timeline opposite helpful.

What was the impact of the Cuban Missile Crisis?

Both sides could claim something from the crisis, although they also had to accept compromises.

Khrushchev managed to keep Cuba communist and win a promise from the USA that Cuba would not be invaded. This was very important to the USSR. Khrushchev also managed to cause tensions between the USA and its allies, particularly Britain. On the other hand, Khrushchev had been forced to back down about the missiles and the missile gap between the USA and USSR never narrowed.

Castro was very upset by the deal Khrushchev made with the USA, but he had little choice. Cuba stayed communist and highly armed. The nuclear missiles were removed but Cuba remained an important base for communist supporters in South America. Castro also kept control of the American companies and other economic resources he nationalised during his revolution.

Kennedy came out of the crisis well. He made Khrushchev back down and he also stood up to the 'Hawks' in his own government. On the other hand, he had not managed to oust Castro and he removed US missiles from Turkey (although this part of the deal between him and Khrushchev was kept secret).

ACTIVITY

If the Cuban Crisis was an Olympic even which of Kennedy, Khrushchev or Castro would get gold, silver or bronze? Explain your answer.

1 Go back to the table you drew up for the Focus Task on page 67 and complete it for the Cuban Missile Crisis of 1962.

In terms of the Cold War, the crisis actually ended up improving relations slightly between the superpowers. The terrible possibility of nuclear war had never been so close. A permanent 'hotline' telephone link was set up between the White House (the office of the US president) and the Kremlin (the office of the Soviet president). In 1963, they signed a Nuclear Test Ban Treaty. It did not stop the development of weapons, but it limited tests and was an important step forward. Although it was clear that the USSR could not match US nuclear technology or number of weapons, it was also clear that this was not necessary. The Soviet nuclear arsenal was enough of a threat to make the USA respect the USSR.

This was the last 'head-on' confrontation between the superpowers in the Cold War. From this point on, the propaganda and the political arguments continued but for the rest of the Cold War the superpowers avoided direct confrontation – although, as you will see, they became deeply involved in other wars around the globe.

ACTIVITY

In 1945, an organisation called the Bulletin of Atomic Scientists was set up. Its aim was to bring together scientists, politicians and anyone else concerned by the threat of nuclear weapons. It had a Doomsday Clock Committee, which assessed how likely war seemed to be at particular times and expressed this by how close the world was to midnight (which marked the end of everything).

- When the USSR tested its atomic bomb in 1949 they set the clock at 11.57.
- During the Korean War, they set the clock at 11.57.

The committee was unable to meet in 1961 and 1962. If they had been able to, where do you think they would have set the clock for the following crises:

- the Berlin crisis in 1961
- the Cuban Missile Crisis in 1962?

FOCUS TASK

What kind of crisis was Cuba 1962?

You have used this task to analyse the Berlin crisis. Use the same steps to analyse the Cuban crisis.

1   Which of these descriptions best fits the Cuban crisis?
　　a   The superpowers were dragged in to a localised problem against their wishes.
　　b   The superpowers were keen to exploit a localised problem.

2   In groups, choose one of the following and explain how it contributed to the Cuban crisis:
　　a   nationalism or self-interest
　　b   ideology
　　c   personalities
　　d   economic problems
　　e   fear or misunderstanding.

3   Pool your ideas and decide which played the biggest role. You could turn it into a pie chart like the one below. Which section should be the biggest?

PRACTICE QUESTIONS

1   Outline the Berlin crisis of 1961. (5)
2   Describe the main events of the Cuban crisis of 1962. (5)
3   Which was a more serious threat to world peace: the Berlin crisis of 1961 or the Cuban Missile Crisis of 1962? (10)

FACTFILE

A map showing Vietnam in the mid-1960s.

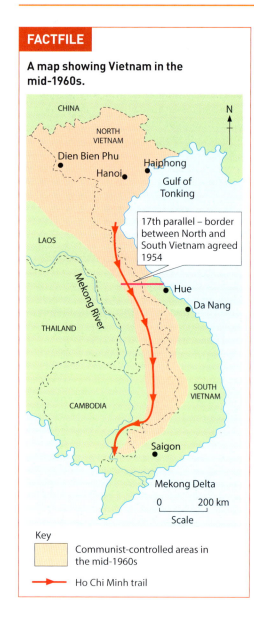

Key

Communist-controlled areas in the mid-1960s

Ho Chi Minh trail

Source 19 US historian John Lewis Gaddis, writing in 2011.

By 1963 Diem's government had become an embarrassment to the Americans ... so brutal—but at the same time so ineffective—that the Kennedy administration convinced itself that he had to be removed. Accordingly, it cooperated with a group of South Vietnamese colonels who overthrew the South Vietnamese president. But it was no solution. They were left with a deteriorating situation in South Vietnam while their own rhetoric had elevated the importance of Vietnam to an issue of global significance—but which they had no strategy for resolving.

Cold War confrontation 3: The Vietnam War 1954–75

What happened? An overview

The Vietnam War was one of the most significant Cold War confrontations. Like Korea, Vietnam was divided into communist North Vietnam and non-communist South Vietnam. The USA supported the South even though it was ruled by a corrupt and unpopular regime. North Vietnam used a mix of conventional and GUERRILLA WARFARE against the South. The USA poured in more and more support and eventually sent its own troops as well. They became bogged down in a long and costly war that they were never able to win. The USA effectively withdrew its forces in 1972 and South Vietnam fell in 1975. The war had a dramatic effect on the USA and its people, and a huge impact on the Cold War.

The local background: the liberation of Vietnam

Before the Second World War, Vietnam (or Indochina as it was called then) was ruled by France. During the war the Japanese took over and ruled the country very harshly. As a result, a strong anti-Japanese resistance movement (the Viet Minh) emerged under the leadership of Ho Chi Minh. Ho was just as much a nationalist as he was a communist. Above all else he wanted freedom and independence for Vietnam. He inspired the Vietnamese people to fight the Japanese. When the Second World War ended, the Viet Minh declared Vietnam independent. But the French had other ideas and they returned, wanting to rule Vietnam again. Nine years of war followed between the Viet Minh, who controlled the north of the country, and the French, who controlled much of the south.

Why did it become a Cold War confrontation?

From 1949, Ho was supported by money, weapons and equipment from communist China. President Eisenhower, following the US policy of Containment to restrict the spread of communism, poured $500 million a year into the French war effort. Despite this the French were unable to hold on to the country and pulled out of Vietnam in 1954. A peace conference was held and the country was divided into North and South Vietnam until elections could be held to decide its future.

Ironically for a country so keen on democracy, the USA prevented these elections because the government feared that Ho's Communist Party would win. Instead they helped his rival, Ngo Dinh Diem, to set up the Republic of South Vietnam. Diem was strongly anti-communist, but he was also deeply unpopular. He was a Christian and came from the landlord class. He showed contempt for the peasant population of his country and for their Buddhist religion. His government was also corrupt. He gave important jobs to his friends and family, and refused to hold elections even for local councils.

Diem was overthrown by his own army commanders in 1963 (with President Kennedy's knowledge), but the governments that followed were just as unpopular and corrupt. Despite this, the USA propped up these regimes with $1.6 billion. Why did it do this?

Containment and Domino Theory

US governments were sure that China and the USSR were planning to spread communism to countries in Asia. They thought that if one country fell to communism, the others would fall like a row of dominos. They were so determined to resist communism that they would support any anti-communist government, even if it was a brutal and undemocratic dictatorship. The US foreign policy chief, John Foster Dulles, admitted that 'we knew of no one better'.

1 In what ways was the situation in Vietnam similar to the situation in eastern Europe after the Second World War?

2 In what ways was the situation different?

3 How far do Sources 19 and 20 agree or disagree?

4 Which of these explanations of US policy in Vietnam up to 1964 do you think is more believable?
   a There was no strategy.
   b There was a clear strategy.
   c The military-industrial complex was in charge.
   Explain your answer.

> **Source 20** US defence secretary Robert McNamara, explaining US policy in 1964.
>
> *Our strategy is clear – to protect South Vietnam. First is the simple fact that South Vietnam, a member of the free world family, is striving to preserve its independence from communist attack. Second, Southeast Asia has great significance in the defence of the USA. For Hanoi, the aim is conquest of the south and national unification. For China, however, Hanoi's victory would only be a first step towards eventual Chinese dominance of the two Vietnams and Southeast Asia.*

Military-industrial complex

Some historians hold a more controversial view: they believe that powerful groups within the USA wanted a war. In 1961, President Eisenhower himself warned that the USA had developed a powerful MILITARY-INDUSTRIAL COMPLEX. The government gave huge budgets to the military commanders. This money was spent on weapons made by some of the USA's biggest companies. Thus, both the armed forces and business actually gained from conflict. Some historians believe that this was a factor in US involvement in Vietnam, but it is hotly disputed by other historians.

The USA gets drawn in

By the early 1960s, the South Vietnamese government was losing control of the countryside to the National Front for the Liberation of South Vietnam, usually called the Viet Cong. The Viet Cong was a communist-led rebel movement fighting to overthrow the hated South Vietnam regime. It was supported by North Vietnam, China and the USSR.

The USA supported the efforts of the South Vietnam government but it remained inefficient and corrupt. Step by step the USA was reluctantly drawn in. Kennedy sent military 'advisers' to help the South Vietnam forces. Kennedy's successor Lyndon Johnson continued to increase US involvement. In February 1965, he launched Operation Rolling Thunder, a massive bombing campaign against North Vietnamese cities, factories, army bases and the HO CHI MINH TRAIL. In March 1965, he sent ground troops in. Over the next eight and a half years thousands would serve and die there (see Figure 21).

Figure 21 US troops and deaths in Vietnam 1960–74. US troops were not the only foreign soldiers in the war. About 46,000 Australian and New Zealand troops fought too. ▼

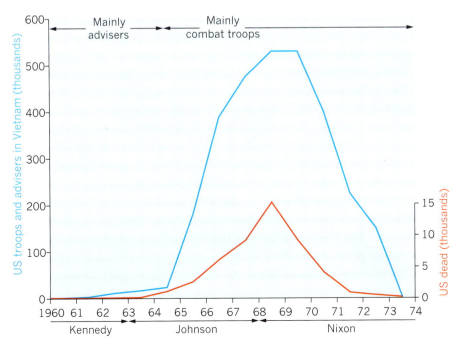

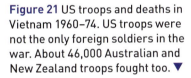

Source 22 John McNaughton, chief adviser to the US defence secretary (see Source 20), writing in 1965.

US priorities in Vietnam

70% – To avoid a humiliating US defeat which would damage our reputation as an ally and protector.

20% – To keep South Vietnam and neighbouring territory out of Chinese hands.

10% – To permit the people of South Vietnam to enjoy a better, freer way of life.

1 Study Source 22 carefully. Does it seem odd that the Viet Cong is not mentioned?

2 On a scale of 1 to 5 (where 1 is not at all), how well do you think these words describe Source 22: clear, ambitious, pessimistic, noble, sensible?

3 In pairs or small groups, come up with other adjectives to describe the source.

4 Write a caption for Source 23 to explain to visitors in a museum what it shows.

Source 23 A Viet Cong poster. ▼

What went wrong for the USA and its allies in Vietnam?

As US troops, aircraft, tanks, vehicles and naval forces rolled into Vietnam the outcome seemed certain. Surely the Viet Cong could not withstand this overwhelming firepower? But it did – and it turned Vietnam into a demoralising and humiliating disaster for the USA. So how and why did this happen?

The USA was propping up an unpopular regime

At the start the USA had been reluctant to get involved in Vietnam at all. President Johnson only committed troops when it was clear that the South Vietnamese regime was totally unable to deal with the Viet Cong. Johnson and other US politicians had become obsessed with the reputation and prestige of the USA in the Cold War. They could not be seen to lose out to communists anywhere. As such, they became the protectors of a brutal and corrupt South Vietnamese government, which was hated by many of its own people.

The Viet Cong was a formidable and committed enemy

Ho Chi Minh and his followers were used to fighting enemies with far greater resources. They had beaten the Japanese. They had beaten the French and the South Vietnamese despite US support. In early 1965, the Viet Cong had about 170,000 soldiers. It was heavily outnumbered and outgunned, and was no match for US and South Vietnamese forces in open warfare. However, Ho knew how to defeat a stronger enemy.

- **Guerrilla warfare:** Ho used guerrilla warfare tactics. Guerrilla literally means 'little war' and guerrillas did not fight large-scale battles. They wore no uniform, so they were hard to tell apart from the peasants in the villages. They had no known base camp or headquarters. They worked in small groups with limited weapons, attacking isolated units of soldiers or officials and buildings. They struck quickly then disappeared into the jungle, into the villages or into tunnels (see Source 24). US soldiers lived in constant fear of guerrilla AMBUSHES or booby traps (see Source 25).

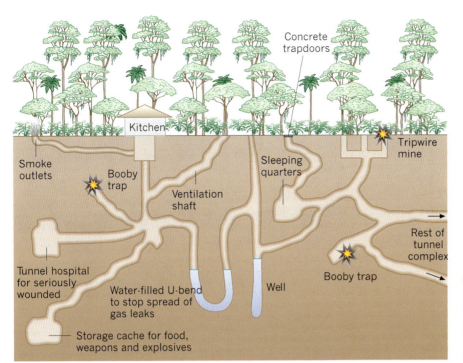

Source 24 A Viet Cong tunnel complex. To avoid the worst effects of US air power, the Viet Cong built a vast network of underground tunnels. ▲

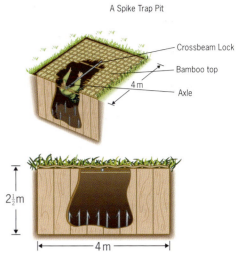

A Spike Trap Pit

Source 25 A diagram showing one type of booby trap. A trap pit was a large trap box with a bamboo top, with stakes made of bamboo inside. The top turned on an axle so it did not need to be reset to work again. ▲

Source 26 Le Duan, one of Ho Chi Minh's closest associates, writing in 1965.

We need to use the methods most suited for destroying the American troops – guerrilla forces encircling the American troops' bases. ... In the next few years, we should at least kill 40,000 to 50,000 Americans. We must not neglect the political war. Even though the US brings in more troops to Vietnam, they will fail to weaken our political power. The more troops the US brings in, the more military bases it builds, the larger area it occupies, the more sophisticated weapons it uses, the more B52 bombs it drops, the more chemical poisons it uses, the worse the conflict between our people and them becomes, the more our people hate them.

- **Civilian support:** Ho knew how important it was to keep the ordinary people on his side. The Viet Cong were expected to be courteous and respectful to the Vietnamese peasants. However, the Viet Cong could be ruthless – they were quite prepared to kill peasants who opposed them or who co-operated with their enemies. Between 1966 and 1971, the Viet Cong killed an estimated 27,000 civilians.
- **Supplies:** The Viet Cong depended on supplies from North Vietnam that came along the Ho Chi Minh trail (see the Factfile on page 80). US and South Vietnamese planes bombed this constantly, but 40,000 Vietnamese worked to keep it open at all costs.
- **Commitment:** The number of Viet Cong and North Vietnamese killed in the war has been estimated at 1 million – far higher than US losses. However, this was a price that Ho Chi Minh was prepared to pay. Whatever the casualties, there were replacement troops available. The greatest strength of the Viet Cong fighters was that they simply refused to give in.

5 On page 82 you chose adjectives to apply to Source 22. Do the same for Source 26. Which of these adjectives would apply: clear, ambitious, pessimistic, noble, sensible?

6 Is Source 23 or Source 27 more useful as evidence about the war in Vietnam? Explain your answer.

Source 27 Philip Caputo, a lieutenant in the US Marine Corps in Vietnam 1965–66, speaking in 1997.

I remember sitting at this wretched little outpost one day with a couple of my sergeants. We'd been manning this thing for three weeks and running patrols off it. We were grungy and sore with jungle rot and we'd suffered about nine or ten casualties on a recent patrol. This one sergeant of mine said, 'You know, Lieutenant, I don't see how we're ever going to win this.' And I said, 'Well, Sarge, I'm not supposed to say this to you as your officer – but I don't either.' So there was this sense that we just couldn't see what could be done to defeat these people.

Source 28 A ten-year-old Vietnamese girl, Phan Thi Kim, runs naked after tearing her burning clothes from her body following a napalm attack in 1972. This photograph won a Pulitzer Prize for journalism and became one of the most enduring images of the war. Kim later set up a foundation to help child victims of war. ▲

US tactics were ineffective and sometimes counterproductive

US and South Vietnamese forces had superior firepower, but it was often difficult to locate a target to use this against. The main tactics were:

- **Bombing:** US aircraft dropped more bombs on North Vietnam than had fallen on Germany in the Second World War. They bombed Viet Cong strongholds in South Vietnam as well as their supply routes. The bombing disrupted production of arms but it never closed down the Ho Chi Minh Trail, and because it killed many thousands of civilians it helped turn the Vietnamese people against the USA.
- **Search and destroy:** US patrols would surround a village and seek out Viet Cong forces. They had to report back with body counts of Viet Cong killed. Raids were often based on poor information and were chaotic. The raids did kill many Viet Cong but at a heavy cost: for every Viet Cong weapon captured, six Vietnamese were killed – most of them civilians.
- **Chemical weapons:** The USA used two main types of chemical weapons: AGENT ORANGE, a poisonous weed killer designed to DEFOLIATE the jungles where the Viet Cong hid, and NAPALM, which created a huge fireball that burned jungle, buildings and humans.

Many civilians were harmed by these weapons and the after-effects of Agent Orange can still be seen in Vietnam today.

The USA could not send its forces into North Vietnam or neighbouring Cambodia and Laos, which were sympathetic to the Viet Cong. This gave the North Vietnamese Army (NVA) and Viet Cong a huge advantage. They were able to retreat to these other countries, where they could reinforce their troops and replenish their equipment and ammunition.

The USA had increasingly inexperienced troops

In the early stages of the war, most US troops were professional soldiers. Morale was high and they performed well. However, as the war intensified the USA needed more soldiers, so it introduced the draft (CONSCRIPTION). The result was that, as the war went on, US troops were increasingly young (average age 19). They only served for a year. Many were not particularly committed to the war they were fighting, either. Inexperienced soldiers, poor information and the pressure and fear caused by Viet Cong tactics all took a terrible physical and psychological toll.

1 How far does Source 29 help to explain Source 28? Explain your answer.

> **Source 29** Fred Widmer, a US soldier, speaking in 1969.
>
> *In the end anybody who was still in that country was the enemy. The same village you'd gone in to give them medical treatment … you could go through that village later and get shot at by a sniper. Go back in and you would not find anybody. Nobody knew anything. We were trying to work with these people, they were basically doing a number on us. You didn't trust them anymore. You didn't trust anybody.*

Stalemate

From March 1965 to the end of 1967, the US troops and the South Vietnamese Army (SVA) fought a series of battles around the border between North and South Vietnam. In November 1965, in the La Dreng Valley, US forces killed 2,000 enemy soldiers, with a loss of 300 of their own troops. They also fought the Viet Cong in the countryside and killed large numbers of them, but they could not defeat them. However, nor could the Viet Cong and the NVA drive out the Americans. A stalemate was eventually reached, in which the Viet Cong controlled the countryside and the USA controlled major towns and cities and their own bases. The Americans could stay as long as they had the political will to do so, but this was about to be challenged.

FOCUS TASK

Why could the USA not defeat the Viet Cong?

Here are some key factors in successful warfare:
- clear aims
- effective tactics
- quality troops
- quality weapons and equipment
- effective supply lines
- support from the local population
- commitment.

Work in pairs or small groups. Give the USA and the Viet Cong a mark out of 10 each for their effectiveness in each of these areas.

Why did attitudes to the war change in the USA?

The Tet Offensive January 1968

Until the end of 1967, there was a general feeling in the USA that the war was going reasonably well. However, in January 1968, during the Tet new year holiday, Viet Cong fighters attacked over 100 cities and other military targets. US and SVA forces quickly retook the towns captured in the offensive and caused the Viet Cong heavy losses (around 10,000), but in the process they used enormous amounts of ARTILLERY and air power. In one of the fiercest battles, the ancient city of Hue was virtually destroyed and 116,000 civilians lost their homes. Back in the USA, people began asking questions. There were 500,000 US troops in Vietnam and it was costing $20 billion per year. How had the USA been taken by surprise in the Tet Offensive? How was the war in Vietnam going to be won?

The media

Until this point, media coverage of the war had been generally positive. During the Tet Offensive, however, the gloves came off. The respected CBS journalist Walter Cronkite asked: 'What the hell is going on? I thought we were winning this war.' Don Oberdorfer of the *Washington Post* wrote in 1971 that as a result of the Tet Offensive 'the American people and most of their leaders reached the conclusion that the Vietnam War would require greater effort over a far longer period of time than it was worth'.

The My Lai massacre

The reporting grew steadily more critical. One of the turning points was an article in *Life* magazine in December 1969, which reported an atrocity committed by US troops in the village of My Lai in March 1968. In this incident, US forces killed between 300 and 400 civilians. Some were gunned down in the fields, others were piled into a ditch and shot. What made the My Lai massacre worse in the eyes of the US public was that the troops and their commanding officer had initially been praised for their actions. It took the determination of one soldier, Ronald Ridenhour, and US army photographer Ron Haeberle to bring the incident to wider attention. One junior officer, Lieutenant William Calley, was eventually held responsible, but most soldiers – and most Americans – suspected that he had been made a scapegoat and that more senior commanders should also be blamed. It was another blow to support for the war. People in the USA wanted to know that their country was a force for good – fighting a just cause. The My Lai massacre challenged that view.

1 The Tet Offensive was technically a Viet Cong defeat. Explain why it was not seen that way in the USA.

2 Norman Cooling, a major in the US army, described the fight for Hue during the Tet Offensive as 'winning a battle but losing the war'. What do you think he meant?

Source 30 Ronald Ridenhour, a US soldier in Vietnam. Ridenhour was not at My Lai, but he interviewed many witnesses and started a campaign to pressure the US authorities to investigate the incident.

Most of the soldiers thought they were going to do something courageous on behalf of their country, something which they thought was in the American ideal. But it didn't mean slaughtering whole villages of women and children. One of my friends, when he told me about it, said: 'You know it was a Nazi kind of thing.' We didn't go there to be Nazis.

Source 31 A photograph taken by official US army photographer Ron Haeberle at My Lai, March 1968. ▶

3 What do you think was more damaging about My Lai:
a what US forces did
b the fact that Ridenhour and Haeberle had to struggle to bring it to light
c what My Lai made the US public think about themselves?

The peace movement in the USA

To continue a war on such a scale, the US government had to have the support of the people. With deaths and injuries to so many young Americans, public opinion had been turning against the war even before the Tet Offensive. After it, the trickle of anti-war feeling became a flood:

- **Cost:** The war was draining money that could be better used at home. The high-profile civil rights leader Martin Luther King pointed out that the US government was spending $500,000 to kill one enemy soldier while spending just $53 a year to help the poor in the USA.
- **Social inequality:** The draft exposed social and racial inequality in the USA. Young men could avoid the draft if they were going to study at college – these were mostly better-off middle-class Americans; 30 per cent of African Americans were drafted compared with 19 per cent of White Americans, and their casualty rates were higher. Moderate and radical civil rights campaigners criticised the war. Why should African Americans fight for a country that discriminated against them?

Most damaging of all, an increasing number of people felt deeply uncomfortable about what was going on in Vietnam. Television, radio and newspaper reports all showed worrying pictures of the fighting. Newspapers published photographs of children burned by US napalm bombs (see Source 28). Television showed prisoners being tortured or executed, or women and children watching with horror as their houses were set on fire. Such casual violence was deeply shocking to the average American. Was this why 900,000 of their young men had been drafted? Instead of Vietnam being seen as a justified crusade against communism, it had become a symbol of defeat, confusion and moral corruption.

Anti-war protests, led by students and civil rights campaigners, reached a peak during 1968–70. In the first half of 1968 alone, more than 100 demonstrations were held against the Vietnam War, involving 40,000 students. Frequently the protests would involve burning the US flag (a criminal offence). Students taunted President Johnson with the chant, 'Hey, hey LBJ; how many kids did you kill today?' As the protests escalated, the authorities were brought in to keep things under control. In one incident, at Kent State University, troops fired on student protesters, killing four and injuring several others. In November 1969, almost 700,000 anti-war protesters demonstrated in Washington DC. It was the largest political protest in US history.

Source 32 African American boxing champion Muhammad Ali, explaining why he would not go to fight in Vietnam, 1967.

Why should they ask me to put on a uniform and go 10,000 miles from home and drop bombs and bullets on Brown people in Vietnam while so-called Negro people in Louisville are treated like dogs and denied simple human rights.

ACTIVITY

A museum is putting together an exhibition to explain why support for the Vietnam War declined between 1968 and 1970. Choose three sources from this section that you think will help a visitor understand how and why support declined in this period, and how this affected the war effort. Write a caption of up to 100 words for each source.

4 Who or what is the cartoonist criticising in Source 33?

Source 33 A US cartoon from 1967. ▶

"There's Money Enough To Support Both Of You — Now, Doesn't That Make You Feel Better?"

—from The Herblock Gallery (Simon & Schuster, 1968)

◀ **Source 34** The front cover of *Life* magazine, reporting on events at Kent State University, 1970.

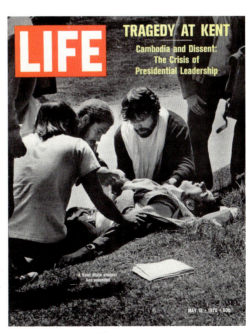

TRAGEDY AT KENT
Cambodia and Dissent: The Crisis of Presidential Leadership

MAY 15 · 1970 · 50¢

1 Draw a simple diagram
showing the relationship
between these four factors in
affecting US attitudes to the
Vietnam War:
- the Tet Offensive
- the role of the media
- the My Lai massacre
- the peace movement.

The end of the Vietnam War

After the Tet Offensive, President Johnson concluded that the war could not be won militarily. He began exploring the possibility of peace talks, and announced that he would not be standing for re-election as president. The main candidates in the presidential race all argued for an end to the war – a sign that the people of the USA were anxious to get out.

In November 1968, Richard Nixon was elected president. From 1969 to 1973, he and his national security adviser, Henry Kissinger, worked to end US involvement in Vietnam. They began a process of 'Vietnamisation' – handing responsibility for the war to South Vietnamese forces and withdrawing US troops. Between April 1969 and the end of 1971, almost 400,000 US troops left Vietnam. In Paris in January 1973, all parties signed a peace agreement. Nixon described it as 'peace with honour'. Others disagreed. By the end of March 1973, the last US forces had left Vietnam. Within two years, without the support of the USA, South Vietnam had fallen to the communists. After 30 years of constant conflict, the struggle for control of Vietnam had finally been settled – and the communists had won.

What was the impact of the Vietnam War?

The Vietnam War had devastating consequences for US society and the confidence of the international community in the USA:

- The USA had failed militarily. Even the USA's vast military strength had not been able to stop the spread of communism.
- The USA had failed politically. Not only did it fail to stop South Vietnam falling to communism, but by 1975 both Laos and Cambodia had communist governments as well.
- The USA had failed ideologically. The USA had always presented its campaign against communism as a moral crusade. However, atrocities committed by US soldiers, and the use of chemical weapons, damaged the USA's reputation. In terms of a crusade for democracy, the USA was seen to be propping up a government that did not have the support of its own people.

The US Congress had traditionally supported its presidents in foreign policy decisions. After the Vietnam War, this changed. Congress refused to allow US military aid to Cambodia in 1970, and in 1973 it introduced the War Powers Act, which limited the ability of the president to go to war.

These failures greatly affected the USA's future policies towards communist states. After the war, the USA tried to improve its relations with China. It ended its block on China's membership of the United Nations. The president made visits to China. The USA also entered into a period of greater understanding with the Soviet Union, known as DÉTENTE. In 1972, the two countries agreed the Strategic Arms Limitation Treaty (SALT) to reduce nuclear weapons. Leaders met at Helsinki, Finland, in 1975 to discuss borders and human rights. The USA was helped by the fact that China and the USSR had a series of clashes and, during the 1970s, both the Soviet Union and China enjoyed better relations with the USA than they did with each other. Americans also became suspicious of involving troops in any conflict that they felt could not be won quickly and convincingly. This was an attitude that would continue to affect US foreign policy into the twenty-first century.

2 Go back to the table you drew up for the Focus Task on page 67 and complete it for the Vietnam War.

Source 35 An extract from *The Tragedy and Lessons of Vietnam* by Robert McNamara, 1996. He had been defence secretary during the Vietnam War.

- *We misjudged the intentions of our adversaries ... and we exaggerated the dangers to the United States of their actions.*
- *We underestimated the power of nationalism to motivate a people to fight and die for their beliefs and values.*
- *We failed to recognize the limitations of modern, high-technology military equipment.*
- *We failed to adapt our military tactics to the task of winning the hearts and minds of people from a totally different culture.*
- *We failed to debate the pros and cons of a large-scale military involvement ... before we initiated the action.*
- *After the action got under way we did not fully explain what was happening, and why we were doing what we did.*
- *We did not hold to the principle that U.S. military action ... should be carried out only in conjunction with multinational forces supported fully (and not merely cosmetically) by the international community.*

ACTIVITY

Study Source 35 carefully. Do you think McNamara has provided a clear, accurate and complete explanation for the US failure in Vietnam? Give him a mark out of 100 and write a 50-word commentary on his explanation. Compare your marks with the marks given by other students.

FOCUS TASK

What kind of conflict was the Vietnam War?

You have used this task to analyse the Berlin and Cuban crises. Use the same steps to analyse the Vietnam War.

1 Which of these descriptions best fits the Vietnam War confrontation?
  a The USA was dragged in to a localised problem against its wishes.
  b The USA was keen to exploit a localised problem.
2 In groups, choose one of the following each and explain how it contributed to the USA's involvement in the Vietnam War:
  a nationalism or self-interest
  b ideology
  c personalities
  d economic problems
  e fear or misunderstanding.
3 Pool your ideas and decide which played the biggest role.
  You could turn it into a pie chart like the one below.
  Which section should be the biggest?

What happened? An overview

The USSR was huge and it had borders with countries in Europe, the Middle East and Asia. Just as in eastern Europe, the Soviets tried to establish friendly governments or client states on their borders. One of these states was Afghanistan. But in 1979 the government allied to the USSR was struggling to control the country. The Soviet leader Leonid Brezhnev took the decision to send Soviet forces to prop up the Afghan government. The Afghan War has often been called the USSR's Vietnam. Soviet forces were bogged down for ten years fighting in extremely difficult terrain against a formidable enemy backed by the USA and the wealth of Saudi Arabia. After 10 years and around 70,000 Soviet casualties, the USSR withdrew.

Source 36 The Soviet foreign minister Vasily Safronchuk, interviewed for a TV documentary in 1998.

Our major concern was the security of the southern borders of the Soviet Union. We also feared the spread of Islamic fundamentalism into Afghanistan from Iran.

Cold War confrontation 4: The Soviet war in Afghanistan 1979–89

FACTFILE

A map showing the location and terrain of Afghanistan.

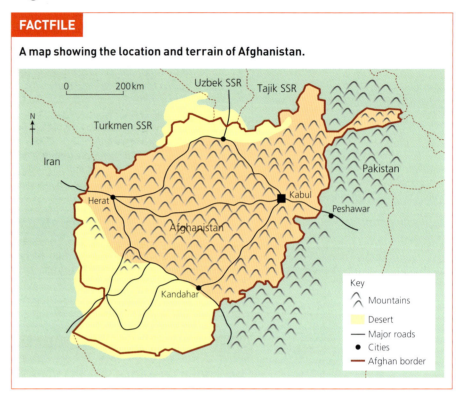

The local background: a communist coup in Afghanistan 1978

Afghanistan is an important country strategically. It sits on trade routes that are thousands of years old. For most of Afghanistan's history, great powers have tried to control it and the fierce tribes that inhabit the country have successfully resisted them. In the nineteenth century, Britain and Russia both tried to control Afghanistan. In the twentieth century, the USA and the USSR both tried to increase their influence in Afghanistan. In 1978, some pro-Soviet Afghan army officers, led by Nur Mohammad Taraki, overthrew the existing ruler and established a communist government there. The new government wanted to modernise Afghanistan. It brought in reforms to land ownership and also introduced social changes, such as education and other freedoms for women. These policies were generally accepted in the cities, but in the countryside traditional Islamic views were much stronger, and communism was an affront to this faith. Some of the powerful tribal warlords who ruled rural parts of Afghanistan opposed Taraki. He reacted harshly, executing an estimated 27,000 political prisoners.

The situation became more serious in 1979, when a revolution took place in neighbouring Iran. The shah (ruler) of Iran was overthrown by a militant Islamic group led by the Muslim cleric Ayatollah Khomeini. Soviet leaders had always been concerned about their Muslim republics, such as Kazakhstan and Uzbekistan. They did not want the radical Islamic views of Iran spreading to Afghanistan and then to the USSR itself. Ayatollah Khomeini gave support to the Afghan warlords, who became known as mujahidin, or 'soldiers of God'. They were tough fighters, who knew how to take advantage of the rough Afghan countryside to conduct a hit-and-run campaign against the government..

Why did Afghanistan become a Cold War confrontation?

Just as the USSR and China helped North Vietnam in the 1960s, so the USA helped the mujahidin against Taraki's government in Afghanistan. The USA secretly channelled funds and arms through Pakistan, even though the US president, Jimmy Carter, had publicly criticised Pakistan for human rights abuses and other actions (see Source 37).

> **Source 37** Charles Dunbar, a member of the US State Department, interviewed in 1998.
>
> *I think we had a double standard with respect to the Pakistanis. And we knew that there were big problems with drugs, and that there were big problems with nukes and we were prepared in various ways, in any way that we had to, to turn Nelson's eye [a blind eye] to those problems as long as the Afghan resistance was being supported via the government of Pakistan – and that's what we did.*

By March 1979, the communist government in Afghanistan was in trouble. It appealed to the USSR for help. The POLITBURO was divided about how to respond. In the end, they decided to send advisers and equipment to help the Afghan government, along with helicopter gunships and paratroopers disguised as technicians. This had little effect and by September 1979, the situation was critical. Soviet military commanders were opposed to sending troops into Afghanistan, fearing that it would be the equivalent of the USA's involvement in the Vietnam War. Taraki died the same month. The new Afghan leader, Hafizullah Amin, began to lose patience with the Soviets. KGB reports from the time show that the Soviets feared Amin would switch sides and ally Afghanistan with the USA, Pakistan and China in order to defeat his enemies.

> **Source 38** General Valentin Varennikov, commander of the Soviet forces in Afghanistan, interviewed for a TV documentary in 1998.
>
> *Andropov, the head of the KGB, became very concerned about Amin flirting with the Americans. Andropov felt that if we didn't introduce Soviet troops, Amin would claim that Moscow hadn't fulfilled its obligations. He would then turn to the Americans for help and they would put their own troops in.*

1 Read Source 37. Do you find it surprising? Explain your answer.
2 How does Source 38 help to explain why the USSR was so reluctant to intervene in Afghanistan? Refer to the Factfile on page 90 and the descriptions of Afghan terrain.

By December 1979, Politburo leaders were feeling the pressure. Intervention in Afghanistan was potentially risky and the military advised against it, but the danger of Afghanistan becoming either pro-USA or a militant Islamic state were also great. On 12 December, the Soviets decided to invade Afghanistan, depose Amin and set up their own pro-Soviet government. On 25 December, Soviet tanks rolled over the border into Afghanistan.

Source 39 Soviet forces moving into Kabul, January 1980. ▼

The US reaction

President Carter reacted quickly and furiously to the Soviet invasion:

- He called Brezhnev on the hotline and warned him that the invasion was a clear threat to world peace.
- He introduced trade sanctions, cancelling grain exports from the USA to the USSR.
- He began to channel economic aid and military supplies to the mujahidin through Pakistan.
- He completely abandoned any interest in the Strategic Arms Limitation Treaty (SALT II) and began a rapid increase in spending on weapons.
- The Olympic Games were due to take place in Moscow in August 1980. The Soviets wanted the Olympics to be a showcase for the greatness of the USSR and communism. Carter called for a BOYCOTT of the games. A few countries did boycott but the majority of nations, including Britain, took part.

Source 41 The opening ceremony of the Moscow Olympics in 1980. The majority of countries did not follow the US call for a boycott of the Games. ▼

Source 40 President Jimmy Carter, speaking on 23 January 1980.

The implications of the Soviet invasion of Afghanistan could pose a more serious threat to the peace since the Second World War. The vast majority of nations on Earth have condemned this latest Soviet attempt to extend its colonial domination of others. Any attempt by an outside force to gain control of the Persian Gulf region will be regarded as an assault on the vital interests of the United States, and such an assault will be repelled by any means necessary, including military force.

ACTIVITY

Some of the sources on pages 90–93 come from interviews for a TV documentary on the Cold War in 1998. By that time, Brezhnev and most of the other Politburo members who took the decision to invade Afghanistan were dead. Imagine what they might have said about it if they had still been alive at this time, 20 years after the event. Write some possible answers to these questions:

1 What was your motive for invading Afghanistan?

2 How do you feel about the decision now, 20 years later?

Source 42 A report from the British newspaper the *Independent*, February 1987.

At 11.55 a.m. local time yesterday General Boris Gromov walked out of Afghanistan. The final soldier had left and, after nine years and 50 days, Moscow's unwinnable Afghan war was over. 'As I left Afghanistan, I did not look back,' said the general, moved and close to tears. 'But I had many thoughts: above all for men who died in this war.' He leaves behind him not only 15,000 Soviet dead, but a raging civil war.

Why did the USSR fail in Afghanistan?

The Soviet commanders' reluctance to move troops into Afghanistan proved well-founded. Afghanistan was a country of mountains and deserts. There were few major roads, airports or rail links so it was difficult to move and supply a large army. The countryside also meant that Afghan society was very localised. The Afghan people knew the land very well and could turn this knowledge against an invading enemy. The conservative, strictly Muslim rural Afghan people disliked communism because it was an atheist ideology (it denied the existence of God). The Afghans disliked the communist government in Kabul for the modernising reforms it brought in, which challenged traditional views. They disliked the Soviets because they were seen as an invading army of foreigners. It was not difficult to find recruits for the mujahidin to resist them.

Soviet tanks were vulnerable to attack on narrow roads in high mountain passes. The Soviets had overwhelming air power but their targets were almost impossible to locate. They killed thousands of civilians and destroyed villages and homes in their attempts to hit mujahidin targets. They could not keep control of any territory they captured because the local people would not co-operate with them. Soviet fear and frustration often turned into atrocities against the Afghan people.

To make the situation even more difficult for the USSR, the mujahidin had support from Saudi Arabia (around $600 million a year in the course of the war) and the USA. In 1981, the new, fiercely anti-communist, president Ronald Reagan began sending money and supplies of weapons to the mujahidin via Pakistan. Pakistan itself received $3.2 billion in military and economic aid.

By the end of 1982, the Soviets had lost around 5,000 troops and airmen. They offered to withdraw if the USA and Saudi Arabia stopped supplying the mujahidin. However, Reagan and the other hardliners in the USA refused, hoping to weaken the Soviets. By the mid-1980s the strain of this conflict was beginning to tell on the USSR. Thousands of young men were being killed. The mujahidin were being supplied with US Stinger anti-aircraft missiles, which could destroy Soviet helicopters – the most important weapon the Soviets had against their enemies. This was a clear indication that the USA would do whatever it took to defeat the Soviets in Afghanistan.

FACTFILE

A map showing the extent of Soviet control in Afghanistan.

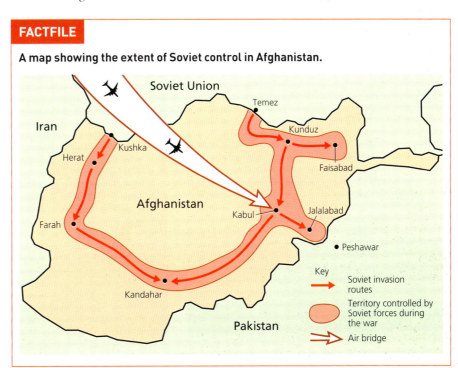

What was the impact of the war in Afghanistan?

By 1986 conditions were changing inside the USSR. A new leader had emerged, Mikhail Gorbachev. Gorbachev was a radical reformer and he was prepared to take actions that would have been unthinkable to old-style Soviet leaders such as Brezhnev or Andropov.

Gorbachev lightened the restrictions on the media, meaning more accurate reports on the war reached the Soviet people. The government began to receive letters from people demanding a withdrawal from Afghanistan. Early in 1987, the Soviet government withdrew its forces. It had been a long and futile war that had been carried out at a terrible cost:

- 15,000 Soviet soldiers dead and around 55,000 wounded
- an estimated cost of around $20 billion to the USSR
- over 1 million Afghans killed and around 5 million displaced as refugees, mostly to Iran or Pakistan.

The USSR's 'Vietnam'

Afghanistan was a humiliating defeat for the USSR. It had a similar effect on the USSR as the Vietnam War had on the USA, leaving the country traumatised and calling its foreign policy into question. It badly damaged confidence in the Soviet leaders. Furthermore (unlike the USA's experience) the Afghan war virtually bankrupted the Soviet Union.

The war demonstrated just how powerful the USA was, particularly under Reagan's leadership. The war also helped to bring Gorbachev to the forefront of Soviet politics. He made it very clear that the USSR was no longer prepared to use the military to prop up communist regimes around the world. He also started cutting down the USSR's armed forces and scrapping many of its nuclear weapons. Gorbachev's reforms were to have a startling effect on his country's relationship with the USA, bringing the Cold War to an abrupt and unexpected end in 1989.

FOCUS TASK

Was Afghanistan 'the USSR's Vietnam'?

Look back at Source 35 on page 89.
1 How many of these points do you think are also relevant to the Soviet war in Afghanistan?
2 Would you need to add any other points to fully explain the Soviet defeat?

Source 43 A Soviet convoy being ambushed by the mujahidin. ▼

Source 44 Mujahidin stand above a Soviet helicopter they have shot down. ▼

Source 45 Soviet troops returning home from Afghanistan in 1987. ▶

1 Go back to the table you drew up for the Focus Task on page 67 and complete it for the Afghanistan War.

ACTIVITY

Imagine you work for a picture library – a company that specialises in supplying pictures for the media. A publishing company has asked you to recommend an image to go on the front cover of a book about the war in Afghanistan. Write an email to the company explaining why Sources 43–45 might be appropriate. You need to explain:

- what each image shows
- how it tells at least part of the story of the war
- your personal recommendation.

If you are not happy with this selection you could use the websites of some picture libraries to search for more suitable images – or perhaps create a montage.

FOCUS TASK

What kind of conflict was the war in Afghanistan?

You have used this task to analyse the Berlin, Cuban and Vietnam case studies. Use the same steps to analyse the Afghanistan War.

1 Which of these descriptions best fits the Afghanistan War?
  a The USSR was dragged in to a localised problem against its wishes.
  b The USSR was keen to exploit a localised problem.
2 In groups, choose one of the following and explain how it contributed to the Soviet involvement in the Afghanistan War.
  a nationalism or self-interest
  b ideology
  c personalities
  d economic problems
  e fear or misunderstanding.
3 Pool your ideas and decide which played the biggest role. You could turn it into a pie chart like the one shown here. Which section should be the biggest?
4 We have called two of these case studies crises and two of them confrontations.
  a Why do you think we did this?
  b Is it a helpful distinction?

PRACTICE QUESTIONS

1 Outline the actions of the USA in Vietnam in the period 1954–72. (5)
2 Outline the main events of the Soviet war in Afghanistan 1979–89. (5)
3 Explain why the USA failed in Vietnam. (10)
4 In what ways were the Vietnam War and the war in Afghanistan similar? (10)

TOPIC SUMMARY

Cold War crises and confrontations

1 The first conflict of the Cold War was a real war – between North and South Korea and their allies. An international force (officially a United Nations army but dominated by the USA) fought for three years against a communist force backed by the USSR and China. It was a deadly conflict that left 1.4 million dead. The use of nuclear weapons was considered.

2 After the Korean War and the death of Stalin, the Cold War entered a different phase of propaganda and threats rather than outright warfare. There was also an 'arms race' to build more and better nuclear weapons. The ever-present threat of nuclear warfare was a source of great anxiety for politicians and ordinary people, but it also deterred aggression.

3 **The Berlin Wall:** Berlin, in the heart of Soviet-controlled East Germany, was a symbol of Cold War divisions and tension but also a regular Cold War flashpoint. In 1961, the USSR built a wall to divide the East and West. This was to prevent people leaving the GDR, but also to test Kennedy and get him to withdraw troops from West Berlin. Kennedy held firm, tanks faced each other over the wall for 16 tense hours, then withdrew. The wall remained a physical and symbolic barrier in the Cold War for 28 years.

4 **Cuba:** The USSR supported the communist regime in Cuba and placed its own nuclear missiles on the island. This significantly increased the nuclear anxiety in the USA because missiles from Cuba could reach the USA (although the USA had its own missiles in Turkey so could already do the same to the USSR). Kennedy's advisers wanted to invade Cuba, but he thought that was too risky and instead ordered a naval blockade. The world held its breath for a tense 13 days, then Khrushchev backed down. The impact on the Cold War was significant: secretly Kennedy agreed to remove US missiles from Turkey, and a hotline was established between the US and Soviet leaders so they could communicate better.

5 **The Vietnam War:** The USA was worried about communism spreading from country to country in Southeast Asia (the Domino Effect). To stop this happening they supported the anti-communist regime in South Vietnam and gradually got drawn into their war against communist guerrillas (the Viet Cong), who were funded and trained by communist China. Despite investing masses of money and soldiers, the USA could not win and withdrew its forces in 1971. South Vietnam fell to the communists, followed by neighbouring Laos and Cambodia, just as the USA had feared. The USA's failure in Vietnam, and the massive opposition to the war at home, humbled its political leaders, and for the rest of the Cold War they avoided direct military confrontation with communism.

6 **The Soviet war in Afghanistan:** This is sometimes referred to as 'the Soviet Union's Vietnam' and the similarities are significant. Just like the USA in Vietnam, the USSR was drawn into a costly and unwinnable war against fierce and committed guerrilla armies in Afghanistan, who were funded and trained by the USA and its allies. The Afghan War contributed to the end of the Cold War, as it bankrupted the USSR. The Afghan War also trained up a new group of fighters, such as Osama bin Laden, who would figure prominently in the terrorist movements of the post-Cold War world (see Topic 3.2).

KEY TERMS

Make sure you understand these terms and can use them confidently in your writing.
- Cominform
- détente
- guerrilla warfare
- ideology
- military-industrial complex
- peaceful co-existence
- propaganda
- superpowers

2.3 The blame game: Historical controversy 2: Changing interpretations of the origins of the Cold War

FOCUS

As you studied Topic 2.1 and 2.2, who did you blame most for the development of the Cold War? Historians have different views on this. In this topic, you are going to examine these different views – particularly the views held by US historians – and see how and why these interpretations have changed over time.

The story of the story

	Early US explanations of the Cold War were created by academics who had worked for the government and in an atmosphere of fierce anti-communism in the USA.
Interpretation 1 **US orthodox view (late 1940s–early 1960s)**	**The Soviet Union was to blame** *The Cold War was caused by aggressive expansion by Soviet leaders who wanted to spread communism to the whole world.*
	This view was not accepted by Soviet historians or politicians, but US academics would not worry about that; they might not even know. Other events would challenge the US orthodox view – notably the Vietnam War.
Interpretation 2 **US revisionist view (mid-1960s–mid-1970s**	**The USA was to blame** *The Cold War was caused by the aggressive actions of the USA, particularly its determination to ensure that it would dominate trade in Europe and Asia.*
	Hot on the heels of revisionism and the Cold War thawing, the post-revisionists tried to find common ground between the first two interpretations. They concluded …
Interpretation 3 **Post-revisionist view (1948–60s)**	**They just couldn't understand each other** *The Cold War was caused by the way the USA and the USSR each reacted to the actions of the other side, and those reactions were largely based on misunderstanding and mistrust.*
	With the ending of the Cold War, both Soviet and US historians had greater access to Soviet source material. However, the new sources brought no consensus.
Interpretation 4 **The new Cold War historians (1989 onwards)**	**We still can't be sure** *Access to Soviet archives still leaves historians divided. The sources just confirm what people already thought – that the USA/USSR (delete as appropriate) was most to blame.*

What do you think might happen next?

FOCUS TASK

Summarise the interpretations

Use note cards or draw up a table to produce your own summary of each interpretation. For each one note down:
- Title of the interpretation
- Main feature(s) of the interpretation
- Why the interpretation developed at this time
- Examples of this interpretation

Interpretation 1

US orthodox view

Late 1940s–early 1960s

The Soviet Union was to blame

The Cold War was caused by aggressive expansion by Soviet leaders who wanted to spread communism to the whole world.

Interpretation 1 US historian Thomas Bailey, writing in 1950. This was one of the earliest accounts of the Cold War, titled *America Faces Russia*.

The problem of negotiation with Russia was difficult enough under the Czars; now there has been erected the additional barrier of a fanatical Communist ideology. The pledges and agreements of the Russian Communists, like those of the Nazis, could not be trusted. Treaties have proved useful to the Kremlin as instruments for binding the hands of other countries, and freeing the Soviets to pursue their own world-conquering objectives. The American public, at least by 1947, concluded that a head-on clash between the American democratic system and the Soviet socialist system was inevitable, unless the Moscow directorate was prepared to deviate sharply and sincerely from the aim of world revolution.

Summary

There was no doubt in the mind of US historians and popular commentators in the 1940s who was to blame for the Cold War: it was Stalin and the Soviet Union. This was the orthodox view and it dominated US thinking for 15 years. Some of the main orthodox historians were Thomas Bailey, George Kennan and Herbert Feis.

- Bailey argued that the USSR wanted world revolution. The Soviets caused the Cold War by their actions in eastern Europe after the Second World War.
- Kennan argued that Stalin needed a threatening enemy (the USA) to convince the Soviet people that they needed his tough dictatorship to protect them. To achieve this, Stalin deliberately took actions to provoke the USA.
- Feis argued that the USSR was trying to spread communism across the world. He claimed that the USA had been forced to respond with the Truman Doctrine and Marshall Plan.

This was a popular view. Most Americans believed their own foreign policy was not driven by self-interest but by a desire to improve the world and be a force for good. They believed the USSR intended to export communism across the world by force if necessary. It was the USA's duty to stop it doing this.

Context

There were three important influences on the US orthodox view.

- **The 'Red Scare' in the USA:** Ever since the Russian Revolution in 1917 there had been worries in the USA about communist agents operating there. The first Red Scare was in the 1920s, when many communists were arrested. There was another Red Scare in the later 1940s. In the early 1950s, Senator Joseph McCarthy exploited this fear, claiming that the US government and other institutions were riddled with Soviet spies. Many intellectuals were accused of being communist sympathisers. We know that some historians in the USA and in Britain were monitored by the intelligence services. In this context, few US historians were keen to consider any explanations for the Cold War apart from the view that the USSR was responsible. There may not have been any official censorship of books or publications, but the climate of fear created by the Red Scare meant that academics censored themselves or each other. One historian who did not accept the orthodox view was William Appleman Williams (see Interpretation B on page 104). When he showed the draft of his book to a colleague at the University of Wisconsin in 1959, he was advised not to publish it because it would damage his career.
- **Personal experience:** Several of the historians who wrote orthodox accounts of the start of the Cold War had actually been involved in the events they were writing about. Kennan had been a senior US government official and was one of the key figures in the development of the US policy of Containment. Like Kennan, Feis had been an adviser in the US government at the start of the Cold War.

Source 1 The cover of a comic book published in the USA in 1947. ▼

IS THIS TOMORROW

AMERICA UNDER COMMUNISM!

Source 3 British historian Joseph Smith, summarising the Soviet view, 2001.

Soviet writers agreed on the importance of the Truman Doctrine in contributing to the conflict between East and West, but they regarded their country's response as defensive. In their opinion, American imperialism was the cause of the Cold War. This view reflected an official line which was consistently maintained throughout the Cold War. For example, only a day after the Truman Doctrine was enunciated, Soviet news agencies criticised it as part of a calculated strategy to expand the capitalist system throughout Europe. The Marshall Plan was similarly condemned as an American plot to encircle the Soviet Union with hostile capitalist states. In addition, the United States was accused of endangering Soviet security by creating NATO and proceeding to remilitarise West Germany.

1 Use the framework in the Focus Task on page 97 to summarise this interpretation.

- **Lack of sources:** In the early days following any event it is hard to access sources, but in this case the US sources were highly sensitive and secret. What was in the public domain was likely to be influenced by propaganda. And for the US historians, there was no hope at all of access to Soviet sources.

Source 2 An extract from the script of an educational film made in 1952. Called simply *Communism*, the film was widely shown in US schools.

Russia today is regarded as a grave threat to our nation, to our freedom, to the peace of the world. What makes it a threat? Looking close we see a clue: giant portraits of communist leaders on public display. These leaders have caused the world to stand guard. Here in Russia you see the reason why so many nations are building up their defences. Here in Russia you see the reason why we in the US are spending billions of dollars in defence production – why your family is paying the highest taxes in history. The leaders of Russia tell us their only concern is the defence of their own nation. Is this true, or are they really set on world conquest?

Impact

The orthodox view was widely accepted by historians and politicians for most of the Cold War. In addition, the orthodox view was widely accepted by the majority of the US public. This was partly because it was taken up in Hollywood movies (such as *The War of the Worlds* or *Invasion of the Body Snatchers*). It was also promoted by films that were funded and produced by the US government, such as *Make Mine Freedom*. Dramatic scenes of a possible communist invasion were also a common sight in public places and in books, comics and newspapers (see Source 1).

Challenges ... from the Soviet viewpoint

Not surprisingly, the main challenge to this interpretation came from Soviet historians and commentators. The Soviet view of the outbreak of the Cold War was more or less the opposite of the US orthodox view.

There are parallels between the factors influencing US and Soviet historians. The Soviet historians were influenced by:

- **Patriotism:** Many Soviet historians were just as patriotic as US historians, and wanted to defend the reputation of their country, especially in the years after the Second World War.
- **Censorship:** Soviet historians also had to work in a climate of censorship and suspicion. Historians who produced accounts of the Cold War that did not follow the official line might be passed over for promotion, lose their jobs altogether or even be arrested. However, many Soviet historians were loyal members of the Communist Party and genuinely believed that the US was the aggressor.
- **Lack of sources:** Soviet historians could not access Soviet or US sources.

Challenges ... from the US viewpoint

There were also US critics of the orthodox view at the time. William Appleman Williams argued that the Cold War was instigated by the USA and that Soviet actions were defensive. The British historian E. H. Carr was a great admirer of the USSR. In 1960 he published a history of the Soviet Union, in which he largely blamed the Cold War on the policies of the USA.

Interpretation 2

US revisionist view

Mid-1960s–mid-1970s

The USA was to blame

The Cold War was caused by the aggressive actions of the USA, particularly its determination to ensure that it would dominate trade in Europe and Asia.

Summary

In the 1960s there was a big change in interpretation. A large number of academic historians became highly critical of the US orthodox view. They claimed that:

- orthodox historians had overstated the Soviet threat
- orthodox historians were not really writing history; they were writing a justification for US policy in the years after the Second World War.

The revisionists also came up with new explanations for the origins of the Cold War:

- They argued that the USA provoked the Cold War by trying to achieve economic dominance in Europe and Asia, a policy known as 'Open Door', which would give the USA access to states it could then dominate economically and politically. They argued that the Marshall Plan was designed to prevent a post-war economic depression because that would harm US trade. This was why the USA only helped states that agreed to US-style democracy and capitalism and refused to help those with different ideologies.
- They also argued that Truman's get-tough attitude made the Soviets feel threatened and so it was hardly surprising that the USSR reacted aggressively.

> **Interpretation 2** US historians Joyce and Gabriel Kolko, writing in 1972 in *The Limits of Power.*
>
> *American foreign policy in the years 1945–54 was a drive to expand American capitalism through the world. Because Communism was the greatest enemy of this drive, American diplomacy had to oppose Communism everywhere in the world. The Cold War was not a conflict between Russia and the United States but an American campaign to dominate the world and reshape it in its own image. The Soviet threat to the West was a mirage conjured up by the Truman administration. NATO was created in order to regulate Western Europe to suit Washington's needs. American policy in Germany was designed to make Germany a fortress of capitalism in Europe. And the Marshall Plan was designed to shape Western Europe's economy to suit Washington. Instead of helping Europe, it strengthened Russian control over Eastern Europe.*

Context

Two developments fuelled the revisionist interpretation.

- **The Cuban revolution:** The first revisionist was William Appleman Williams, writing in 1959. He first began to question the orthodox view when he studied US actions in Cuba after Castro's communist takeover in 1958. Williams claimed that in this context, the USA behaved more like an aggressive, empire-building power than a force for good, trying to stop the Soviets developing their own empire. However, this was not a popular view and was not widely accepted in academic circles. Williams was not a lone voice, but he did not have many listeners!
- **The Vietnam War:** In the 1960s, a flood of young academics began making a similar argument. The USA had supported a corrupt regime in Vietnam, killed tens of thousands of civilians with bombing raids, used chemical weapons and neglected its poorest citizens at home. This had a profound impact on the trust the US public had in their government. It directly affected the way some US historians interpreted the actions of their country in the early years of the Cold War.

> **Source 4** US historian Thomas G. Paterson, describing how his views on the Cold War changed through this period, writing in 2007.
>
> *My undergraduate education at the University of New Hampshire, 1959–1963, featured, first, the work of George F. Kennan and, second, the "nationalist" school of Samuel Flagg Bemis, known for his grand narrative of American exceptionalism and benevolent imperialism. My superb professors showed me that an intellectual's responsibility was not only to build knowledge but also to be a sceptic of doctrine, a critic of fashionable thinking. From my graduate-school years of 1963–1967, I emerged a "revisionist." There is no mystery why. Influencing me were the horrific Vietnam War, the assaults and embargo against Cuba, and the invasion of the Dominican Republic—events that spawned anti-war teach-ins, protest songs such as Phil Ochs's "Cops of the World," the Fulbright Senate hearings, and essays by public intellectuals such as Henry Steele Commager on the abuse of American power. I took special notice of Senator Wayne Morse's vote against the Tonkin Gulf Resolution and his bold statement that "our hands are dripping with blood in Southeast Asia." The concurrent civil rights movement, antipoverty campaign, women's rights advocacy, and environmental movement also encouraged new ways of thinking, challenging prevailing assumptions and worldviews—especially at the University of California, Berkeley, in the days of the Free Speech Movement.*

Impact

Among **historians**, the revisionist view created a real stir. As one historian put it: 'They created some very rough seas for those sailing in the orthodox traditionalist boat.'

The **politicians** were less receptive to the revisionist view, not least because many had themselves been involved in the events.

Popular opinion was divided. Older people tended to feel uncomfortable with the revisionist view as they were usually more patriotic. However, there was a strong youth counterculture in the USA in this time and many young people strongly agreed with the revisionist view.

Challenges

Challenges largely came from traditionalists (see Source 5).

> **Source 5** Historian Thomas G. Paterson, describing how traditionalists reacted to his and others' revisionist works.
>
> ***After I submitted my first PhD chapters*** *about 1940s foreign policies, based on research into newly opened documents in the Truman Presidential Library and other archives, one of my advisers groaned, "You may be right, but this will ruin your career."*
>
> ***After ... I published an article in the American Historical Review*** *on "Red Fascism," which explored U.S. images of totalitarianism that moved policymakers toward an uncompromising, sometimes emotional, Cold War posture, contrary letters flowed to the journal, some impugning our scholarly integrity.*
>
> ***After my lecture at a military academy***, *one faculty member insisted that I had no business speaking on the Cold War because I had not lived through its early tortuous years. When I asked him what his own field of study was, he replied: "The Civil War."*
>
> ***At a professional meeting***, *one panellist uttered in essence "Go back to Russia where you belong," implying my critical approach somehow meant I was apologizing for the Soviets' brutal behavior in their empire or that I saw a moral equivalency between the United States and the Soviet Union. I did not, but that charge became familiar in the traditionalists' criticism.*
>
> *Herbert Feis, the State Department official turned diplomatic historian, belittled the writings of Revisionists as "just poor imitations of Communist official doctrine." A newspaper headline blared: "College Board Bans 5 Books from Curriculum." One of the five was the foreign-relations history textbook I wrote. During fierce debate, one board member declared that our text contained "a lot more funny pictures of Republicans and nicer pictures of Democrats."*

1 Use the framework in the Focus Task on page 97 to summarise this interpretation.

They just couldn't understand each other

The Cold War was caused by the way the USA and the USSR each reacted to the actions of the other side, and those reactions were largely based on misunderstanding and mistrust.

> **Interpretation 3** US historian John Lewis Gaddis, writing in 1972.
>
> *I have proceeded on the assumption that foreign policy is the product of external and internal influences, as perceived by officials responsible for its formulation. In seeking to understand their behavior, I have tried to view problems of the time as these men saw them, not solely as they appear in retrospect. I have not hesitated to express judgments critical of American policy-makers, but in doing so have tried to keep in mind the constraints, both external and internal, which limited their options. If there is a single theme which runs through this book, it is the narrow range of alternatives open to American leaders during this period as they sought to deal with problems of war and peace.*
>
> *In contrast to much recent work on the subject, this book will not treat the "Open Door" as the basis of United States foreign policy. Revisionist historians have performed a needed service by stressing the influence of economic considerations on American diplomacy, but their focus has been too narrow: many other forces – domestic politics, bureaucratic inertia, quirks of personality, perceptions, accurate or inaccurate, of Soviet intentions – also affected the actions of Washington officials.*

1 Use the framework in the Focus Task on page 97 to summarise this interpretation.

Summary

The leading post-revisionist historian was John Lewis Gaddis. He tried to take the most relevant and plausible elements of both orthodox and revisionist interpretations and put them together:

- He rejected the views of revisionists (especially Williams) that the Cold War was caused solely by US aggression and expansionism.
- He argued that a substantial proportion of the responsibility for the Cold War lay with the beliefs and actions of the USSR, and of Stalin in particular.
- On the other hand, he did accept that US policy was based on a misunderstanding and an exaggeration of Soviet strength and Soviet intentions, and that as a result the USA tended to overreact to Soviet actions, causing the USSR in turn to overreact.
- Gaddis did not believe that the Cold War was inevitable, but he saw it as the result of fear, confusion and misunderstanding on both sides.

Context

There are two main contexts for the post-revisionist approach:

- **Historical debate:** It was a time of intense debate. Historians were keen to find new ways of interpreting all history, including the Cold War. So even while the revisionists were challenging the orthodox view, Gaddis and other post-revisionists were challenging both orthodox and revisionist historians for being too simplistic in blaming one side or the other.
- **Thawing of the Cold War:** In the early 1970s, following the failure in Vietnam, Richard Nixon and his successors began a process of détente – trying to build better relations with communist China and the USSR. They agreed the Strategic Arms Limitation Treaty (SALT) in 1972 and even met to discuss human rights at Helsinki, Finland, in 1975. This influenced historians to think less in terms of blame and more in terms of misunderstanding.

Impact

Gaddis's work had a huge impact among historians. Many had recognised the weaknesses of the orthodox view but they had not felt comfortable with the revisionist view. The post-revisionist view provided a more complex and rounded approach, which they could accept.

Challenges

For a long time the post-revisionist interpretation dominated the thinking of historians about the Cold War. Some revisionist historians criticised it for being too close to the orthodox view. Carolyn Eisenberg said the post-revisionist view was really just the orthodox view with few archive references thrown in to back it up. However, on the whole it was widely accepted.

Interpretation 4

The new Cold War historians

1989 onwards

We still can't be sure

Access to Soviet archives still leaves historians divided. The sources just confirm what people already thought – that the USA/USSR was most to blame.

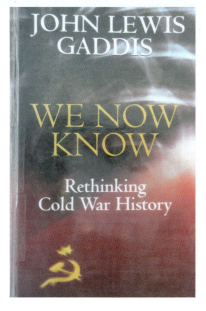

Summary

The Cold War ended with the fall of the Berlin Wall in 1989. Soon afterwards, the USSR collapsed. By the mid-1990s it was possible for western historians to access Soviet archives. However, rather than finally answering the question of the origins of the Cold War, these archives served to strengthen many existing divisions. The leading post-revisionist, John Lewis Gaddis, actually revised his views more towards the orthodox view (see Interpretation 4A).

> **Interpretation 4A** US historian Mervyn Leffler, reviewing Gaddis' book *We Now Know: Rethinking the Cold War* in 1999.
>
> *What is so distinctive about Gaddis's new book is the extent to which he abandons post-revisionism and returns to a more traditional interpretation of the Cold War. In unequivocal terms, he blames the Cold War on Stalin's personality, on authoritarian government, and on Communist ideology.*

In contrast, British historians Michael Cox and Caroline Kennedy-Pipe reached conclusions much closer to the revisionists, especially regarding the Marshall Plan (see Interpretation 4B).

Interpretation 4B British historians Michael Cox and Caroline Kennedy-Pipe, writing in 2005.

It was Stalin who eventually sealed the fate of Eastern Europe. However, the way that U.S. aid was originally conceived under the Marshall Plan ... propelled the Soviet Union into a more antagonistic and hostile stance, including the establishment of its own economic and political bloc. We do not assume Soviet ... innocence. ... Nevertheless, we would still insist ... that Soviet foreign policy was not just driven by ideology, but a series of responses and reactions that were just as likely to be shaped by the way others acted toward the Soviet Union as by Stalin's own outlook.

Context

Three connected developments provide the context for this reinterpretation:

- **The end of the Cold War:** This in turn led to…
- **New Soviet sources:** Throughout the Cold War, Soviet archives had been off-limits to US historians. They were even closed to most Soviet historians. Now there were millions of new sources to consider.
- **The Reagan factor:** With the Cold War over, you might expect historians to stop trying to allocate blame for the Cold War. However, in the USA the debate started to reflect the way politics inside the country had become polarised under Ronald Reagan. In the final years of the Cold War he had followed an aggressive policy towards the USSR, referring to it as the 'Evil Empire'. Many orthodox historians agreed with Reagan and found material in the Soviet archives to show that he had been right in his beliefs. However, not all Americans agreed with Reagan's policies. Some felt he had been reckless and taken unnecessary risks by being too aggressive towards the USSR. Many of these critics were revisionist historians. They found documents that supported their views!

Impact

It was expected that this new source of information would produce a final interpretation that all sides would accept. However, this has not been the case. Because he was so prominent, when Gaddis revised his ideas it created quite a big impression among historians. But not all historians were convinced by his change of mind, and wondered whether it had more to do with Gaddis' own political views than with his claim that the Soviet sources meant we finally knew what caused the Cold War.

1 Use the framework in the Focus Task on page 97 to summarise this interpretation.

PRACTICE QUESTIONS

Assessment questions on the historical controversy will usually be either type A or type B:

Type A: How fair is ...	Type B: Explain why ...
For example	For example
1 How fair is Interpretation A on the Soviet Union? (25)	1 Explain why not all historians would agree with Interpretation C. (20)
or	OR
2 How far do you accept the view of Interpretation B on the USA? (25)	2 Do you think most historians and commentators would agree with Interpretation D? (20)

1 Choose one of these questions and prepare an answer based on that interpretation below. You can find advice on how to do this on page 128.
2 What would be good questions to ask about Interpretations E and F?

Interpretation A An extract from a series of six lectures by US historian George Kennan, broadcast by the BBC in 1957.

From the time of their seizure of power in 1917 the Russian communists have always been characterised by their extraordinary ability to cultivate lies as a deliberate weapon of policy. Forty years of intellectual opportunism seem to have wrought a strange corruption of the Communist mind, rendering it incapable of distinguishing between fact and fiction in any field, but especially in its relations with the other powers. They have always lied to us and lied about us.

Interpretation F John Lewis Gaddis writing in his book *We Now Know: Rethinking the Cold War*, 1999.

As long as Stalin was running the Soviet Union a cold war was unavoidable. Stalin waged cold wars incessantly: within the international system, within his alliances, within his country, within his party, within his personal entourage, [and] even within his family.

Most important, Stalin was a revolutionary. He never gave up on the idea of an eventual world revolution, but he expected this to result ... from an expansion of influence emanating from the Soviet Union itself.

Interpretation B William Appleman Williams, writing in 1959. The 'Open Door' policy meant using US military, political and economic power to pressure other countries to adopt democracy and capitalism in the same way as the USA.

At the end of the 1940s a few Americans began to recognize and face the need to rethink the way the USA conducted its international affairs. But Truman and the other key decision makers in the US either discounted the need for such action or were carried along by the momentum of the long commitment to the expansion of US power and to reforming the world in the image of the United States. The US elite remained limited by the outlook that had crystallized during the 1890s: organize the world according to the principles of the Open Door policy and reap the benefits.

Interpretation C US historian John Lewis Gaddis, writing in 1997.

Here, then, was the difficulty after the war. The Western democracies wanted a form of security that would reject violence. Security was to be for everyone, it was not to be a benefit denied to some in order to provide it to others. Stalin saw things very differently: security came only by intimidating or eliminating potential challengers. The contrast, or so it would seem, made conflict unavoidable.

Interpretation D An extract from a review of Thomas Bailey's book *America Faces Russia*, written in 1951 by John Valery Tereshtenko and published in the *American Journal of Politics*. Tereshtenko was a researcher and academic based in the USA, but his family was originally Russian and he wrote books and articles about relations between Russia and America.

At present, there is no greater source of international concern than American-Soviet relations. Under these conditions the reader, deeply conscious of the frightening implications of the American-Soviet cold war, anxiously grasps the new books with the word "Russia" in their titles. But with this book the reader gets only more frustrated when he does not find anything new or of value. The study by Thomas A. Bailey, Professor of History at Stanford University is written in a lively and simple style. Yet there is something profoundly disturbing about it. The title of the book is misleading. The author expresses only the American perspective, and does not really address the relations between the countries or the reasons for the problems they face.

Interpretation E US historian Lynne Viola, writing in 2002.

The orthodox view of the Cold War greatly simplified the study of history for American audiences. There were enemies (them) and us and our friends. There were truth tellers (American historians) and there were liars (Soviet falsifiers). Best of all, there were no sources because no American historian could use a Soviet archive so it was very hard to challenge the view with evidence. As a consequence – and often because many American historians were either former politicians or wanted to become politicians – a great American success story unfolded as Americans and democracy were made to look very good indeed by their actions towards an unreasonable enemy.

3.1 End of an era: The end of the Cold War and the collapse of communism c1980–91

FOCUS

The Cold War dominated international relations from the 1940s to the 1980s. However, in the late 1980s the Cold War ended even more suddenly than it had started. In this topic you will consider how and why this happened. You will investigate:

- the roles of US president Ronald Reagan and Soviet leader Mikhail Gorbachev
- the importance of events in eastern Europe
- the importance of other factors.

The end of détente

In the 1970s, the USA and the USSR (and China) tried to improve relations. This was known as détente. By the early 1980s détente had broken down.

President Reagan
In 1981, a new president took power in the USA who believed in a much more aggressive foreign policy.

Nuclear weapons
The nuclear arms race restarted, with the USSR putting new SS-20 missiles in eastern Europe and the USA installing a deadly new weapon – the cruise missile.

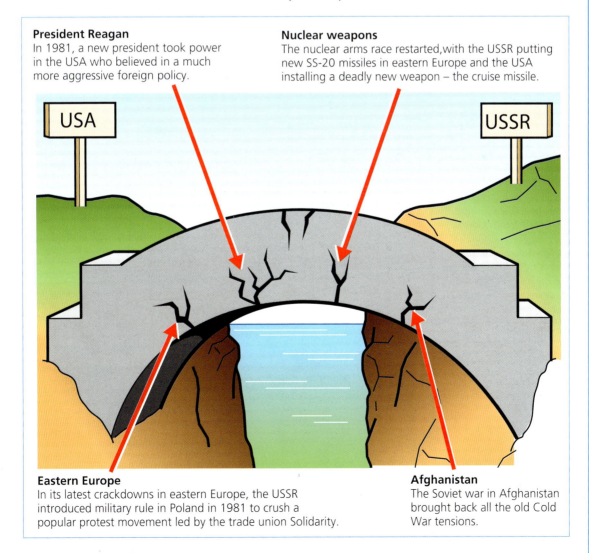

USA

USSR

Eastern Europe
In its latest crackdowns in eastern Europe, the USSR introduced military rule in Poland in 1981 to crush a popular protest movement led by the trade union Solidarity.

Afghanistan
The Soviet war in Afghanistan brought back all the old Cold War tensions.

How did Ronald Reagan change the Cold War climate?

Ronald Reagan took office as president of the USA in January 1981. Sources 1–5 give a picture of the personality and attitudes of this key figure in the history of the Cold War.

Source 1 Florence Galing, a Reagan supporter.

Ronald Reagan had the ability to convey whatever he was thinking of in terms that everybody understood. He just seemed to have a warmth about him that the people felt.

Source 2 Ronald Reagan, speaking on 8 March 1983.

I urge you to beware the temptation of blithely declaring yourselves above it all and label both sides equally at fault, to ignore the facts of history and the aggressive impulses of an Evil Empire, to simply call the arms race a giant misunderstanding and thereby remove yourself from the struggle between right and wrong and good and evil.

◄ **Source 3** Ronald Reagan with his Cabinet in 1981. Reagan is sitting on the desk on the left. On the right is the vice-president, George Bush Senior.

Reagan's policies

Reagan was a new type of leader. He had a simplistic but determined view of politics – essentially the Soviets were the bad guys and the Americans were the good guys. Reagan himself was not a great political thinker. The majority of his views were shaped by a THINK TANK of hard-line anti-communist advisers called the Committee on the Present Danger. This committee believed in increasing US defence spending and taking a tough line with the USSR wherever possible.

Reagan followed the think tank's advice closely. He supported anti-communist forces in Afghanistan and Nicaragua. More importantly, he increased the US defence budget dramatically (by $32.6 billion in his first two weeks in office). He also introduced new weapons systems, such as the B1 nuclear bomber.

In 1982, Reagan gave the go-ahead for the Strategic Defense Initiative (popularly known as Star Wars). This was a multi-billion dollar project to create a system using satellites and lasers that could destroy missiles before they hit their targets. Clearly, a weapon such as this could change the whole nature of nuclear war.

These plans were highly controversial. Reagan's supporters claimed that his main aim was to escalate the arms race in order to end it. He knew that the USSR simply could not compete with US spending on nuclear technology and would have to admit defeat. Reagan's critics suggested that his policies were about money rather than politics. They pointed out that defence companies had made huge donations to Reagan's election campaign. Was the president really challenging the USSR or was he paying back his friends in the defence industry?

Source 4 Ronald Reagan, speaking on 23 March 1983.

What if free people could live secure in the knowledge that their security did not rest upon the threat of instant U.S. retaliation to deter a Soviet attack? That we could intercept and destroy strategic ballistic missiles before they reached our own soil or that of our allies? I know this is a formidable technical task, one that may not be accomplished before the end of this century. I call upon the scientific community in our country, those who gave us nuclear weapons, to turn their great talents now to the cause of mankind and world peace – to give us the means of rendering these nuclear weapons impotent and obsolete.

Figure 5 An illustration of how SDI ('Star Wars') was supposed to work. ▶

Source 6 Reagan pictured holding up a car bumper sticker to news cameras at a meeting in the early 1980s. ▶

Reagan's impact

There is no doubt that Reagan had a huge impact on the course of the Cold War in the 1980s. His determination and charisma were vital assets. So was his willingness to invest in weapons development, which left the USA $4 trillion in debt. In addition, many of Europe's leaders at this time (including Britain's prime minister Margaret Thatcher and Germany's premier Helmut Kohl) supported his tough line against the USSR.

Perhaps the most significant factor in Reagan's success, however, was that the USSR itself was in crisis. The Politburo was made up of ageing politicians. Brezhnev died in 1982. He was succeeded by Andropov, but Andropov died in early 1984. These men had no real response to Reagan's policies other than to criticise him as a warmonger who was recklessly advancing the arms race. They could have attacked his links with the defence industry or pointed out that SDI was unlikely to work in practice, but they were no match for Reagan in getting across a message to the world. Politburo members were also aware that the USSR's economy was suffering due to the war in Afghanistan and Soviet support of its allies in Vietnam and Cuba.

Why did Gorbachev try to change the Soviet Union?

In the early 1980s the USSR was led by a series of elderly and unwell leaders. By 1985 it was clear this could not go on. A new leader with fresh ideas emerged – Mikhail Gorbachev. Gorbachev's ideas represented an unusual mix of realism, idealism and optimism:

- The **realist** in him could see that the USSR was in a terrible state. Its economy was very weak. It was spending far too much money on the arms race. It was locked in a costly and unwinnable war in Afghanistan. There had been almost no new thinking about how to run the Soviet economy since the days of Stalin.

- The **idealist** in Gorbachev believed that communist rule should make life better for the people of the USSR and other communist states. In the 1970s, he had travelled in western Europe and had seen that there were higher standards of living there than in the USSR. Gorbachev hated the fact that the USSR was the butt of jokes (Reagan in particular enjoyed anti-Soviet jokes, see Source 10).

- The **optimist** in him believed that communism could work. Gorbachev believed that a reformed communist system of government could give people pride and belief in their country. He did not intend to dismantle communism in the USSR and eastern Europe, but he did want to reform it radically.

Source 9 A US cartoon from 1981. The scene shown is based on the 1939 American film *The Wizard of Oz.* ▼

1 What was the US cartoonist of Source 9 trying to say about the USSR in 1981?

2 How might Gorbachev have reacted to seeing this cartoon?

Source 8 Mikhail Gorbachev, speaking in 1998.

The state of the Soviet Union and its society could be described very simply with a phrase used by people across the country, 'We can't go on living like this any longer!' That applied to everything. The economy was stagnating, there were shortages and the quality of goods was very poor.

3 Why do you think Reagan was so fond of jokes like the ones in Source 10?

4 Do you think it is strange that Gorbachev was upset by these jokes? Explain your answer.

Source 10 Anti-communist jokes told by Ronald Reagan to Mikhail Gorbachev at their summit meetings in the late 1980s.

A *The Soviet Union would remain a one-party state even if the communists allowed an opposition party to exist. Everyone would join the opposition party.*

B *When American college students are asked what they want to do after graduation, they reply: 'I don't know, I haven't decided'. Russian students answer the same question by saying: 'I don't know, they haven't told me'.*

Gorbachev had to be cautious because he faced opposition from hardliners in his own government, but gradually he declared his policies. The two key ideas were GLASNOST (openness) and PERESTROIKA (restructuring). *Perestroika* introduced economic reforms that allowed people in the USSR to trade for profit – a massive challenge to one of the basic beliefs of communism. *Glasnost* reduced state control of the media and, for the first time, the Soviet people began to get realistic reporting about issues such as the economy and the war in Afghanistan. Gorbachev launched a campaign against corruption in the USSR and began to attack the privileges that party and police officials had over ordinary citizens. He also made another momentous decision – he would talk to the US president Ronald Reagan.

5 What is the cartoonist who made Source 11 commenting on: Gorbachev's policies or the chances of his policies succeeding? Explain your answer.

Source 11 A US cartoon from 1987. ▼

PROFILE

Mikhail Gorbachev (b. 1931)

- One of his grandfathers was a *kulak* – a landowning peasant – who had been sent to a prison camp by Stalin because he resisted Stalin's policy of collectivisation. His other grandfather was a loyal Communist Party member.
- Studied law at Moscow University in the 1950s. Became a persuasive speaker.
- Worked as a local Communist Party official in his home area. He rose through the ranks and joined the Politburo in 1980.
- He was a close friend of Andropov, who became Soviet leader in 1983. He shared many of Andropov's ideas about reforming the USSR and was effectively Andropov's second in command.
- Became leader of the USSR in 1985.
- In October 1990 he was awarded the Nobel Peace Prize.

Source 12 Ronald Reagan and Mikhail Gorbachev at their first summit meeting in Geneva, November 1985. ▼

Source 13 Soviet foreign minister Eduard Shevardnadze.

I remember very clearly what Gorbachev said at that time. He said, 'There are two roads we can take. We can either tighten our belts, very, very tightly or reduce consumption – which the people will no longer tolerate – or we can try to defuse international tension and overcome the disagreement between East and West. And so free up the gigantic sums that are spent on armaments in the Soviet Union.'

The Gorbachev and Reagan summits

Economic policies

Gorbachev's job of reforming the Soviet Union would be a lot easier if he had more money available (see Source 13). The arms race was an enormous drain on the Soviet economy and Gorbachev recognised that his country could never hope to outspend the USA on nuclear weapons. He took the initiative and announced cuts in armament expenditure.

Relationship with the West

At the same time, Gorbachev brought a new attitude to the USSR's relations with the wider world. He withdrew Soviet troops from Afghanistan. He gave many speeches in which he talked about international trust and co-operation, rather than confrontation, as the way forward for the USSR. Gorbachev continued to suggest that he and Reagan meet face to face to discuss their differences.

Reagan was keen to discuss nuclear disarmament. He had been shocked to discover that the Soviets had almost launched a nuclear strike against the USA in 1983, because the Soviets had thought Reagan was planning to launch a first strike against them. The two leaders finally met at their first summit in Geneva on 19 November 1985, where they got on well. They held three more summits: in Reykjavik (October 1986), Washington (December 1987) and Moscow (June 1988). There were many tough negotiations but the real breakthrough came at the Washington summit in December 1987. Both sides reduced their missile stockpiles. Just as importantly, both sides agreed to co-operate fully with an inspection regime, which would ensure they kept to the terms of the treaty.

The final summit took place in Moscow in June 1988. It was mainly symbolic – it was the first time Reagan had been to the USSR and the first time he had met Soviet people. On the visit a British journalist, Jon Snow, asked Reagan whether he felt he was in an 'evil empire'. Reagan said he wanted to take back this earlier reference, not because he was wrong when he had coined the phrase, but because by 1988 the USSR was a very different country.

ACTIVITY

Study Source 14 carefully. On a copy of the source, add captions to each of the four images to describe how the relationship between Reagan and Gorbachev developed. You may be able to do this using presentation or other software. You could also search online for images to help tell the story.

Source 14 A cartoon from the British newspaper the *Daily Telegraph*, 10 December 1987. ▼

The Berlin Wall comes down

Gorbachev had shown that he was prepared to allow trading for profit in the USSR. He had shown that he was prepared to cut the funding of the Soviet military. He had shown that he was prepared to meet with Reagan. Next he was prepared to tell the hard-line communist leaders of eastern Europe that they had to change as well. The Factfile below shows how former Soviet leaders had dealt with dissent in eastern Europe. In March 1985, Gorbachev called the leaders of the Warsaw Pact countries together. He explained to them that he was now committed to a policy of non-intervention in the affairs of their countries.

Relationship with eastern Europe

Most of the Warsaw Pact leaders, including Erich Honecker of East Germany and Nicolae Ceausescu of Romania, were traditional, hard-line communists. They completely disagreed with Gorbachev's ideas and were sure that the USSR would not really abandon the communist countries of eastern Europe. Over the next few years these leaders came to realise they had made a serious error of judgement. As Gorbachev introduced his reforms in the USSR, demand rose for reforms in states across eastern European.

FACTFILE

Soviet treatment of dissent in eastern Europe 1953–81
- **East Germany 1953:** People's resentment at lack of freedom, poor living standards and availability of consumer goods turned into mass protests in many towns and cities across East Germany. The main protest in Berlin was crushed by East German police and Soviet troops.
- **Poland 1956:** There were mass protests demanding greater freedom and economic improvements. The premier, Wladyslaw Gomulka, promised reforms but when Khrushchev threatened Soviet military intervention, Gomulka abandoned reforms and clamped down on dissent.
- **Hungary 1956:** Protests against censorship, repression and Russian domination turned into a full-scale revolution, which was brutally crushed by Soviet tanks and soldiers. Many thousands were killed in the fighting. Hundreds of thousands of Hungarians fled the country.
- **Czechoslovakia 1968:** The Prague Spring – Czech leaders introduced reforms to end censorship and increase freedom – 'socialism with a human face'. They wanted to allow other political parties to exist. The USSR sent in tanks and troops to remove the leaders and crush the movement.
- **Poland 1980:** A trade union, Solidarity, which called for increased pay and greater freedom, turned into a nationwide movement with massive support. Soviet tanks and troops carried out 'training exercises' on the border to make clear that they would intervene if necessary, so the Polish army seized power, imposed martial law and imprisoned all Solidarity's leaders.

Gorbachev's policies gave the people of eastern Europe some hope for reform. In July 1988 he made a speech to the Warsaw Pact summit stating his intention to withdraw large numbers of Soviet troops, tanks and aircraft from other communist states. He reinforced these intentions in a speech to the Polish parliament soon afterwards. Hungary was particularly eager to see Soviet troops leave, and when the Hungarians pressed Gorbachev he seemed to confirm that troops would withdraw if Hungary wished. Gorbachev followed up this intention in March 1989. He again made clear to the Warsaw Pact leaders that they would no longer be propped up by the Soviet army and that they would have to listen to their people. In the months that followed, there was a sudden and dramatic collapse of communism across eastern Europe (see Factfile). Even the infamous Berlin Wall, symbol of the Cold War and of communist control of eastern Europe, could not withstand the pressure. In November 1989 guards on the Wall abandoned it and jubilant crowds began to dismantle it.

1 Can jokes such as those in Source 15 really be useful historical sources? Explain your answer.
2 If you think jokes are useful sources, do you think joke A or B is more useful? Explain your answer.

Source 15 Examples of anti-communist jokes collected by researchers in eastern Europe in the 1980s.

A Polish, Hungarian and Romanian dogs get to talking. 'What's life like in your country?' the Polish dog asks the Hungarian dog.

'Well, we have meat to eat but we can't bark. What are things like where you are from?' says the Hungarian dog to the Polish dog.

'With us, there's no meat, but at least we can bark,' says the Polish dog.

'What's meat? What's barking?' asks the Romanian dog.

B East German leader Erich Honecker is touring East German towns. He is shown a run-down kindergarten. The staff ask for funds to renovate the institution. Honecker refuses. Next he visits a hospital, where the doctors petition him for a grant to buy new surgical equipment. Honecker refuses. The third place on Honecker's itinerary is a prison. This is pretty dilapidated, and here too the governor asks for money to refurbish. This time Honecker immediately pulls out his cheque book and insists that not only should the cells be repainted but that they should be fitted with new mattresses, colour televisions and sofas. Afterwards an aide asks him why he said no to a school and a hospital, but yes to a prison. Honecker says, 'Where do you think we will be living in a few months' time?'

FOCUS TASK

Why did communist power in eastern Europe collapse?

Make a copy of the diagram below and use these pages to add links with labels, summarising how the factors worked together to destroy communist control. Add circles for other factors if you think anything has been missed out. Resize the factor circles if you think that one is more important than the others.

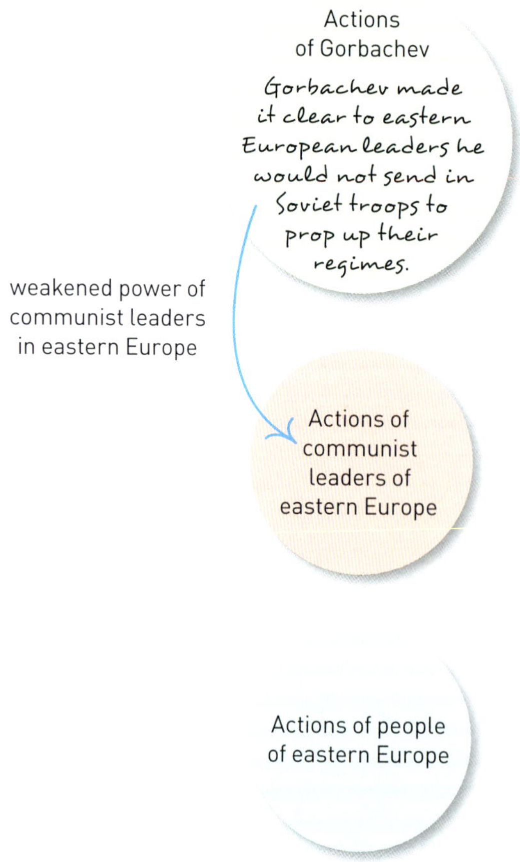

Actions of Gorbachev

Gorbachev made it clear to eastern European leaders he would not send in Soviet troops to prop up their regimes.

weakened power of communist leaders in eastern Europe

Actions of communist leaders of eastern Europe

Actions of people of eastern Europe

FACTFILE

The collapse of communism in eastern Europe.

1
May 1989
Hungarians begin dismantling the barbed-wire fence between Hungary and non-Communist Austria.

2 June
In Poland, free elections are held for the first time since the Second World War. Solidarity wins almost all the seats it contests. Eastern Europe gets its first non-Communist leader, President Lech Walesa.

3 September
Thousands of East Germans on holiday in Hungary and Czechoslovakia refuse to go home. They escape through Austria into West Germany.

4 October
There are enormous demonstrations in East German cities when Gorbachev visits the country. He tells the East German leader Erich Honecker to reform. Honecker orders troops to fire on demonstrators but they refuse.

Gorbachev makes it clear that Soviet tanks will not move in to 'restore order'.

5 November
East Germans march in their thousands to the checkpoints at the Berlin Wall. The guards throw down their weapons and join the crowds. The Berlin Wall is dismantled.

6 November
There are huge demonstrations in Czechoslovakia. The Czech government opens its borders with the West, and allows the formation of other parties.

7 December
In Romania there is a short but very bloody revolution that ends with the execution of the Communist dictator Nicolae Ceausescu.

8
The Communist Party in Hungary renames itself the Socialist Party and declares that free elections will be held in 1990.

9
In Bulgaria, there are huge demonstrations against the Communist government.

10 March 1990
Latvia leads the Baltic republics in declaring independence from the USSR.

N

FINLAND

NORWAY

SWEDEN

Estonia

Latvia **10**

Lithuania

U S S R

5
Berlin
4
EAST GERMANY

2
Warsaw

POLAND

WEST GERMANY

Prague **6**
CZECHOSLOVAKIA

FRANCE

SWITZERLAND

AUSTRIA

3

1 HUNGARY **8**
● Budapest

ROMANIA **7**

Bucharest ●

Black Sea

Belgrade ●

YUGOSLAVIA

BULGARIA **9**

ITALY

ALBANIA

TURKEY

Key

Territory taken over by USSR at end of Second World War

Soviet-dominated Communist governments

Other Communist governments

0   200 km
Scale

The collapse of the USSR and the end of the Cold War

The collapse of Soviet control in eastern Europe was astonishingly fast, but even more extreme events would follow. By October 1990, the Berlin Wall had been torn down and East and West Germany had been reunited. Gorbachev was reluctant to accept this at first, but he negotiated hard and eventually agreed. The new Germany was even allowed to become part of NATO. But there were still more changes to come. Throughout 1990–91, many of the republics that had made up the USSR began to demand independence as well. Gorbachev did not want to break up the USSR but in the end he had little choice.

In August 1991, a group of hard-line communists tried to overthrow Gorbachev, but this failed. Gorbachev survived the COUP, but it had not strengthened his position as Soviet leader. He had to admit that the USSR was finished – and he was too. In a televised speech on 25 December 1991, Gorbachev announced his resignation and the end of the Soviet Union (see Source 16).

1 Read Source 16 carefully. Three statements are in bold. Do you agree or disagree with each statement? For each statement, write a short paragraph to:
   a explain what it means
   b express your own view on it.

Source 16 Boris Yeltsin, writing about Mikhail Gorbachev in his autobiography in 1990.

What he has achieved will, of course, go down in the history of mankind. I do not like high-sounding phrases, yet everything that Gorbachev has initiated deserves such praise. He could have gone on just as Brezhnev and Chernenko did before him ... draped himself with orders and medals; the people would have hymned him in verse and song, which is always enjoyable. Yet Gorbachev chose to go another way. He started by climbing a mountain whose summit is not even visible. It is somewhere up in the clouds and no one knows how the ascent will end: Will we all be swept away by an avalanche or will this Everest be conquered?

Source 17 An extract from *History of Modern Russia* by historian Robert Service, 2003.

He had no grand plan and no predetermined policies; but if Gorbachev had not been Party General Secretary, the decisions of the late 1980s would have been different. The USSR's long-lasting order would have endured for many more years, and almost certainly the eventual collapse of the order would have been much bloodier than it was to be in 1991. The irony was that Gorbachev, in trying to prevent the descent of the system into general crisis, proved instrumental in bringing forward that crisis and destroying the USSR.

FOCUS TASK

How far was Gorbachev responsible for the end of the Cold War?

Imagine you are making a documentary film about the end of the Cold War. The film will be 60 minutes long.

1 Decide what proportion of this time should concentrate on:
   a Gorbachev's policies in the USSR
   b Gorbachev's policies towards eastern Europe
   c Gorbachev's relationship with Reagan
   d President Reagan
   e actions by individuals in eastern Europe
   f the war in Afghanistan
   g other factors.
2 Choose one of these aspects and summarise the important points, stories, pictures or sources that you would like to include in your film under that heading. You may be able to use presentation software to organise and present your ideas.

PRACTICE QUESTIONS

1 Describe the actions of Ronald Reagan towards the USSR in the 1980s. (5)
2 Describe the changes that Mikhail Gorbachev brought about in the 1980s. (5)
3 Explain why the USSR was so weak by the 1980s. (10)
4 Why did the USSR collapse in 1991? (10)
5 What caused the end of the Cold War? (10)

TOPIC SUMMARY

The end of the Cold War and the collapse of communism

1 Ronald Reagan was elected president of the USA in 1981 and he brought an uncompromising policy towards the Soviet Union. He called it an 'Evil Empire'. He could see the USSR was in crisis, struggling with the war in Afghanistan and running out of money.

2 He set up a new form of defence against nuclear weapons known as SDI (Star Wars), which never actually worked but upped the stakes and was a great propaganda tool for his policies. Historians disagree about whether SDI was his attempt to escalate the arms race in order to end it, or whether he was simply paying back his rich supporters by awarding them lucrative deals to make arms for the USA.

3 In 1985, the Soviet Union also got a new leader with fresh ideas: Mikhail Gorbachev. Gorbachev knew the USSR was in crisis and tried to remedy this with his new policies of *glasnost* (openness) and *perestroika* (restructuring). He allowed the development of capitalism (trading for profit). He withdrew Soviet troops from Afghanistan. He launched a campaign to remove corruption from the political system.

4 From 1985 to 1988, Gorbachev and Reagan held a series of summits where they agreed to reduce their nuclear weapons. The two leaders got on well and Reagan was prepared to change his view of the USSR, believing it had changed a great deal under Gorbachev's leadership.

5 Gorbachev's new approach also changed the situation in eastern Europe. He told the communist governments that the Soviet army would no longer be used to prop up their regimes and that they must reform or look after their own interests. Initially the communist leaders did not take him seriously, but people in eastern Europe did. In the summer of 1989 they began to test the limits by dismantling border crossings between communist east and capitalist west. When there was no reaction to this, the trickle became a flood and by mid-1990 all the communist regimes in eastern Europe had been overthrown.

6 Having unleashed such forces of reform, Gorbachev could not hold the Soviet Union together. It began to collapse, with the republics breaking free from Russian domination. The USSR was finished and Gorbachev resigned as leader on 25 December 1991. He was seen as a failure by the Russians, but treated as a hero in the West and was awarded the Nobel Peace Prize.

3.2 New dangers: The post-Cold War world

FOCUS

When the Berlin Wall came down and the Cold War ended in 1991 there was much celebration, especially in the USA and western Europe. However, as you have seen, wars tend to plant seeds that eventually grow into conflict again. The First World War sowed the seeds for the Second World War. That, in turn, sowed the seeds of the Cold War. In this topic, you will see how the legacy of the Cold War led to a new conflict in the 1990s and beyond. You will examine:
- how the Soviet war in Afghanistan affected militant fundamentalist Islamism
- the emergence of al-Qaeda.

The end of history?

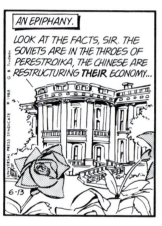   

Source 1 A US cartoon from 1988. ▲

Source 2 An extract from an article entitled 'The End of History?' by US political scientist Francis Fukuyama, 1989. The article was widely read at the time and is still being discussed today.

In watching the flow of events over the past decade or so, it is hard to avoid the feeling that something very fundamental has happened in world history.

The twentieth century saw the developed world descend into ideological violence, as liberal democracy contended first with absolutism, then Nazism, and finally faced Communism in a conflict that threatened to lead to the ultimate apocalypse of nuclear war. But the 20th century seems at its close to have given us a total victory of economic and political liberalism.

The triumph of the West, of the Western idea, is evident first of all in the total exhaustion of viable alternatives to Western liberal democracy. In the past decade, there have been unmistakable changes in the world's two largest communist countries, Russia and China. Both are adopting Western capitalist economic approaches and Russia is becoming increasingly democratic. The triumph of the West can be seen also in the spread of consumerist Western culture – color television sets now everywhere throughout China, the chain restaurants and clothing stores opening in Moscow, the Beethoven piped into Japanese department stores, and the rock music enjoyed alike in Prague, Rangoon, and Tehran.

What we may be witnessing is not just the end of the Cold War, or the passing of a particular period of post-war history, but the end of history. After a century of conflict between rival approaches we are seeing the universal adoption of Western liberal democracy as the final form of human government.

1 How similar are Sources 1 and 2 in terms of:
a the points they make
b the attitudes they display
c the general tone?

Source 1 sums up the feelings of many people in the USA at the end of the Cold War. The 'good guys' (the Americans) had triumphed over the 'Evil Empire' of the USSR. US businesses were selling their goods all over the world, exposing more and more people to the American way of life. Americans were confident that their way of life had triumphed because it was the best. They were eager to share it with the rest of the world and they genuinely believed that they were making the world a better place.

Source 2 took this viewpoint a stage further, with political writer Francis Fukuyama arguing that western liberal democracy had triumphed and that the world realised it. 'History' as people knew it – the story of competing nations, religions, ideologies – was now over. Everyone wanted US-style freedom and democracy, US goods and US culture, so there was no reason for conflict.

Was the end of the Cold War really the end of history?

Fukuyama's views were controversial at the time, and as the 1990s went on many critics claimed that he was being overly optimistic. Events across the world seemed to prove that the forces which caused conflict – nationalism, religion and ideology – were not things of the past.

Northern Ireland

A sectarian conflict between Catholic Nationalists and Protestant Unionists which had begun in 1969 was still going on in Northern Ireland.

The Balkans

After the collapse of communism, the former communist state of Yugoslavia split along religious and ethnic lines, resulting in a brutal and bloody series of civil wars.

Russia

Russia became a democracy and its economy became capitalist. However, many Russians resented US culture, which seemed to be swamping the Russian identity. The country was still a long way from US-style democracy, and capitalism only brought prosperity to a minority of Russians. At the same time, Russia faced a war in Chechnya as the Muslim Chechens wanted to break away from Russian control.

China

China embraced capitalism, but there was no relaxation of political control. The Communist Party remained firmly in charge.

Venezuela

During the Cold War, the USA had supported many corrupt dictatorships simply because they were anti-communist. This left resentment towards the USA once the Cold War ended. In Venezuela, people elected a SOCIALIST and deeply anti-US leader, Hugo Chavez.

Rwanda

In the mid-1990s, ethnic conflict broke out in Rwanda, resulting in GENOCIDE by the majority Hutu people against the minority Tutsis. This was just one of many ethnic and religious conflicts in Africa.

Philippines and Korea

US companies began to move production of their goods to factories in Asia. This reduced their costs and increased profits because wages were much lower in these places. However, working conditions were often poor. This generated resentment towards the USA. As in Russia, people in these countries also often felt that US culture was swamping their own culture.

117

The Middle East

Fukuyama's claims seemed particularly optimistic when it came to the Middle East.

Israel

The state of Israel had been founded in 1948. It was carved out of land that had been inhabited by Muslim Arabs for centuries. Most of the Muslim Arab states in the region (and Iran, which is not an Arab state) were hostile to Israel. Probably the only reason for Israel's survival was its close links with the USA. This in turn created resentment towards the USA among many Muslims.

Afghanistan

After the Soviet army withdrew from Afghanistan, civil war broke out between different factions. By the mid-1990s, the most powerful group was the radical Muslim organisation the Taliban. They believed in a strict form of Islam. They had support from Pakistan and were very suspicious of and hostile towards outside influence. In particular, the Taliban believed that US cultural influence was a threat to Islam. Many of the Taliban had been mujahidin (see page 90), so they had been armed and trained by the Americans – an unanticipated consequence of the USA's involvement in the Afghan war against the USSR.

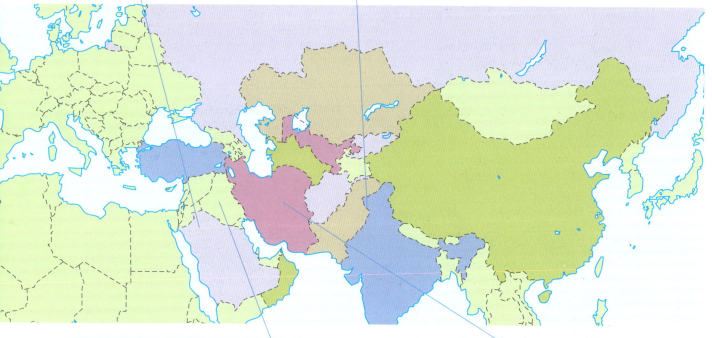

Iraq and the Gulf War

Iraq was ruled by Saddam Hussein from 1976. When he went to war with Iran in 1980, he initially had huge support (money and weapons) from the USA. However, in 1990 Saddam invaded neighbouring Kuwait – an ally of the USA. The USA led a coalition against Iraq and defeated Saddam in the first Gulf War of 1991. The USA stated that it was fighting to defend a country that had been illegally attacked. Most Muslims in the region believed that the USA was trying to control the region and its valuable oil supplies.

Iran

Iran had been hostile to the USA since an Islamic revolution overthrew the US-supported shah in 1979. The country had also long been a rival with Saudi Arabia as the most important country in the region. Iran was extremely hostile to Israel because Israel was in conflict with Muslim Palestinian Arabs. Both Israel and Saudi Arabia were important allies of the USA.

ACTIVITY

Use the information on pages 117–18 to write a 150-word article criticising Francis Fukuyama's views in Source 2 on page 116. You should mention nationalism, religion and ideology.

Source 3 A US cartoon published soon after 9/11. ▲

Source 4 A US cartoon published soon after 9/11. ▼

1 The cartoonist in Source 3 was making the point that 9/11 changed the way Americans saw themselves and the world. How does he get this point across?

2 Study Source 4. What explanation is the cartoonist giving for 9/11?

Source 5 US foreign affairs adviser Zbigniew Brzezinski, being interviewed in 2002.

Q: Do you regret having supported the Islamic fundamentalists, having given arms and advice to future terrorists?

A: What is most important to the history of the world? The Taliban or the collapse of the Soviet empire? Some stirred-up Muslims or the liberation of central Europe and the end of the Cold War?

The end of US optimism: 9/11

On the morning of 11 September 2001, two hijacked jet airliners were deliberately crashed into the Twin Towers of the World Trade Center in New York, killing around 3,000 people. The USA – and the world – looked on with shock. There was the obvious horror of the event itself but there was also a sense of disbelief that this should take place on US soil, in the heart of its biggest city. There was also great confusion – why anyone would want to do such a thing to them – the 'good guys'?

Sources 3 and 4 give a sense of how Americans struggled to understand what had happened and why. The only explanation most could come up with was that al-Qaeda, the group that carried out the attack, was just plain evil. But was there more to it than that?

The roots of al-Qaeda and 9/11

Al-Qaeda's roots lie in two countries: Saudi Arabia and Afghanistan. The story of al-Qaeda is also deeply influenced by the beliefs and experiences of its founder, Osama bin Laden.

The Afghan war 1979–86

As you have seen, the USSR invaded Afghanistan in 1979 to assist its communist government in dealing with a revolt by Muslim tribal leaders. Most Afghans in rural areas were very conservative and strictly Muslim. They deeply disliked and distrusted communism, an atheist system. These tribal leaders fought against the government because of its modernising reforms, which challenged traditional views. When the Soviets invaded, people flocked to join the mujahidin ('fighters of God') to stand against the invading enemy and the government.

The mujahidin were supported by neighbouring Muslim states, notably Pakistan. Their war against the Soviets was funded by the USA (for political reasons) and Muslim Saudi Arabia (for religious reasons), who saw this struggle as a JIHAD, or holy war. US president Ronald Reagan had no hesitation in supporting the mujahidin (see Source 6 on page 120). The USA and Saudi Arabia poured in money, food, medical supplies and the most up-to-date weapons. They also supplied trainers and advisers from their special forces units. These advisers provided the mujahidin with the equipment, training and skills to fight a larger, efficient modern army. This training would come back to haunt the USA in later years.

Source 6 US president Ronald Reagan, meeting with mujahidin leaders in 1983. ▼

Source 7 A Soviet cartoon, commenting on US involvement in the Afghan War. ▼

1 What is the cartoonist trying to say in Source 7 by the following features of the three figures?

 a facial expressions
 b hands
 c headgear.

Osama bin Laden and Abdullah Azzam

Osama bin Laden was one of many young Saudis who joined the Afghan war effort. At first he was involved in fundraising, but he eventually became a mujahidin fighter. While he was in Afghanistan, bin Laden and other Arab volunteers came under the influence of the radical Muslim preacher Abdullah Azzam. Azzam argued that Islam was under threat from enemies everywhere and that it was the responsibility of every Muslim to resist these attacks by taking part in jihad.

Azzam's ideas formed the basis of al-Qaeda's actions – that it should wage jihad in any form against:

- western democracies
- communism
- Jews and the state of Israel
- Muslim governments that were not strict enough or who co-operated in any way with al-Qaeda's enemies (the greatest enemy of all was the USA).

ACTIVITY

The official caption for Source 6 at the Reagan Archives is 'President Reagan meeting with Afghan Freedom Fighters to discuss Soviet atrocities in Afghanistan'. What other possible captions could be used with this source if it appeared in a textbook today?

PROFILE

Osama bin Laden (1957–2011)

- Father was a billionaire businessman in Saudi Arabia.
- Came from a very large extended family – Osama's father had many wives and around 50 children.
- Attended King Abdulaziz University in the late 1970s, studying civil engineering.
- While at university, he devoted much of his time to religious study.
- Left college in 1979 to fight in Afghanistan against Soviet forces.

Osama bin Laden is exiled

In 1990, bin Laden returned to Saudi Arabia. By this time, the country was divided between those who wished to modernise and accept US ideas and values, and those who rejected these values and demanded a strict observance of traditional Muslim practices. This division intensified in 1990 when Iraqi leader Saddam Hussein invaded Kuwait and threatened Saudi Arabia. Bin Laden offered the services of his fighters to King Fahd of Saudi Arabia, but the king refused. Instead he accepted the support of the USA and its allies. Bin Laden was appalled by the arrival of these foreign troops on the sacred soil of Saudi Arabia. He publicly criticised King Fahd. As a result he was forced into EXILE in Sudan and his family disowned him. He was stripped of his Saudi citizenship in 1994.

The development of al-Qaeda

Bin Laden was exiled from Saudi Arabia, but he still controlled much of his existing wealth. He also had allies in the Taliban in Afghanistan. He set about building up the strength of al-Qaeda and by the mid-1990s it was a force to be reckoned with.

- **Beliefs:** Al-Qaeda had a clear, simple and very powerful set of beliefs – originally laid out by the radical preacher Azzam and further developed by bin Laden.
- **Leaders:** It had a clever and charismatic leader in Osama bin Laden. He had proved himself as a fighter in Afghanistan and was widely respected as generous to his followers. His second in command, Ayman al-Zawahiri, was also extremely capable.
- **Well-trained fighters:** It had loyal, committed and effective operatives who were trained in all aspects of terrorist warfare in training camps in Afghanistan. These techniques had originally been taught to Afghan fighters by the Americans to help them fight the Soviets.
- **Secure bases:** Al-Qaeda was closely linked to the hard-line Muslim Taliban movement in Afghanistan, and could rely on security and secrecy.
- **Money:** Bin laden was from an immensely rich family and used his wealth to support the movement. The organisation also had generous funding from supporters in Pakistan and Saudi Arabia, along with the drugs trade in Afghanistan.
- **Technology:** It was aware of the potential of technologies such as the internet and mobile phones as tools for running a terrorist organisation.
- **Flexibility:** It was a very difficult movement to combat because it did not want anything material, such as land. It was also hard to combat because al-Qaeda was more like a franchise (see Source 8).

Its enemies, particularly the USA, were inadequately prepared to face this type of enemy.

> **Source 8** An extract from *Al Qaeda* by Jason Burke, published in 2006. The author is a journalist specialising in the Middle East and al-Qaeda.
>
> *Bin Laden did not kidnap young men and brainwash them. The young men who flocked to Afghanistan to seek military and terrorist training did so of their own free will. As is clear from the testimony of recruits in the training camps run by Al Qaeda in Afghanistan between 1996 and 2001, nobody was kept there against their will. Discipline was tight, but anyone who wanted to leave was allowed to go. Most of the volunteers were dedicated to the cause long before they reached the camps. Indeed, many overcame considerable obstacles to reach Afghanistan. Importantly, bin Laden's associates spent much of their time in the 1996–2001 period selecting which of the myriad requests for assistance they would grant. The requests – for money, expertise, advice and other logistical support – came from everywhere, from Morocco to Malaysia. These were not requests for help in building refugee camps or new mosques. They were requests for assistance with bomb attacks, assassinations and murder on a horrific scale. These requests, like the recruits who carried them, originated in the huge swathe of largely young men who were sufficiently motivated to want to devote substantial proportions of their lives and energies to the most extreme end of Islamic militancy.*

> **Source 9** Pakistani journalist Ahmed Rashid, speaking in 2014.
>
> *In the 1990s I used to regularly meet with American, British, European and United Nations officials. I was shocked by how little they knew or understood. I and others like me were telling them about the Taliban, al-Qaeda, bin Laden and the Arab fighters in Afghanistan and Pakistan. Nobody was interested.*

ACTIVITY

Study Source 9 carefully. Imagine that a visiting British or US official has shown an interest in what is happening. Use the information and sources to write a 150-word report explaining why the US and British governments should be concerned. Comment on aims, bases, funding and training. You could add examples of past events in the Cold War, where organisations with these strengths proved effective.

Al-Qaeda in action

Al-Qaeda was a terrorist group, but it was also more than that. In a sense there were three al-Qaeda movements.

- A hard-core militant terrorist organisation.
- A network sharing its views with other groups, and providing finance, training and support for them to carry out their own attacks.
- An idea or rallying point for modern militant Islam, providing inspiration, guidance, publicity and information (or propaganda) about the common aims of militant Islam across the world.

This made it very difficult to combat because many al-Qaeda attacks were not carried out by al-Qaeda operatives. For example, in 1993 a Pakistani militant called Ramzi Yousef attacked the World Trade Center in New York with a truck bomb. The bomb killed six people and caused $300 million in damage. Yousef claimed he was inspired by Osama bin Laden's teaching. He was not directly connected to al-Qaeda but he did share their views. He also attended a training camp in Afghanistan.

There was a similar attack in Saudi Arabia in November 1995 on the Saudi National Guard and US troops who were training them. The Saudi security services arrested four men, who claimed to have been inspired by bin Laden. They were later executed.

In 1998, bin Laden announced the formation of the World Islamic Front. He made very clear statements warning of attacks on the USA and hinting at the methods that might be used. Soon afterwards, al-Qaeda struck hard. On 7 August 1998, US embassies in Nairobi (Kenya) and Dar es Salaam (Tanzania) were hit by truck bombs. The Nairobi attack was particularly well-planned, with some of the al-Qaeda operatives settling in to the area for years before the attack took place, and even marrying local women. The Nairobi attack killed 213 and wounded around 4,600 people. In Dar es Salaam, 11 people died and 85 were wounded. In October 2000, suicide bombers drove a boat packed with explosives into the side of the US warship the USS *Cole*, killing 17 sailors.

Source 10 An extract from an interview by Osama bin Laden given to the US news network ABC early in 1998.

Any American who pays taxes to his government is our target because he is helping the American war machine against the Muslim nation. Terrorising oppressors and criminals and thieves and robbers is necessary for the safety of people and for the protection of their property.

Source 11 Scenes of devastation at the US embassy in Nairobi. The attack was carried out by a suicide bomber in a truck packed with explosives. ▼

1 According to Source 10, what kind of organisation was al-Qaeda? How would supporters of al-Qaeda have responded to this view?
2 Do Sources 11 and 12 provide convincing evidence that al-Qaeda was an effective organisation?

Source 12 Two comments on the bombings in Nairobi in August 1998.

A Daniel Benjamin, director of counterterrorism at the USA's National Security Council 1998–99.

I was shocked. I was astonished by the skill with which these attacks had been carried out. You only had to look at the first few pictures to realise that this was a different kind of terror, that this was terror which aimed at mass casualties in a way that previous attacks never had.

B Joe Billy, deputy director of counterterrorism for the FBI.

I was struck by the scale of the devastation in this bombing and that immediately told me of the capabilities of this organisation. We were not dealing with isolated, small groups of potential extremists. We were dealing with an organisational structure that had planned, thought it out, put all the mechanics in place and successfully carried it out.

9/11

The most significant attacks carried out by al-Qaeda were those of 11 September 2001. As well as the two planes that hit the World Trade Center, another targeted the Pentagon, the US military headquarters in Washington DC. A fourth was forced to crash land. The attacks resulted in the deaths of around 3,000 people, the majority of them civilians and many of them not Americans. It was the most destructive attack ever to take place on US soil.

Islamic militants celebrated what they saw as a great victory. Bin Laden again demonstrated his understanding of the power of modern communications by issuing a video praising the attackers. It was broadcast on the Arabic TV station al-Jazeera, although there were some doubts about whether it was genuine.

Source 13 A New York firefighter searches for survivors in the ruins of the World Trade Center. ▶

FOCUS TASK

Why did al-Qaeda attack the USA in 2001?

Look back at Source 4 on page 119. It suggests that al-Qaeda launched the 9/11 attacks because it was motivated by evil. Do you accept this view? Write a report explaining why you think the attacks happened. It is up to you how you explain it, but you may want to consider some of the following issues:

● the legacy of the war in Afghanistan
● US cultural influence around the world and its effects
● US economic influence around the world and its effects
● the impact of the Gulf War 1991
● the beliefs and nature of al-Qaeda.

The US response to al-Qaeda: the War on Terror

The US response to 9/11 was swift and devastating. On 20 September, the US president, George W. Bush, issued a demand to the Taliban leader Mullah Omar to turn Osama bin Laden over to the US authorities. The Taliban refused. The US quickly built a coalition of allies, with British prime minister Tony Blair playing a key role in this process. US-led forces then joined with Afghan opponents of the Taliban in a massive assault on the country in October 2001.

It began with a huge bombardment using long-range missiles and overwhelming airpower. The Taliban and their al-Qaeda allies had no weapons to equal this. Their bases and training camps were soon destroyed. The land campaign began in November 2001. The Taliban and al-Qaeda were no match for the British, US and NORTHERN ALLIANCE opponents. By the middle of November the Afghan capital, Kabul, had fallen. The Taliban's stronghold of Kandahar fell in December, and Mullah Omar fled to Pakistan. Other Taliban and al-Qaeda forces fell back to their mountain strongholds, including the Tora Bora complex. In hard fighting, this was taken on 17 December but there was no sign of Osama bin Laden, who had probably escaped through the mountains into Pakistan.

Al-Qaeda was defeated militarily and the USA and its allies then concentrated on new measures designed to fight al-Qaeda and its tactics in the future. However, this has been a long and difficult struggle with some unintended consequences.

Hearts and minds

It proved difficult to win the hearts and minds of the Afghan people. They were often caught in the crossfire between Allied forces and militants, and there were many civilian casualties as well as thousands of refugees from the fighting. Innocent Afghans were rounded up and interrogated as suspected militants. This made them reluctant to co-operate with the security forces or provide the intelligence so important when fighting an enemy like al-Qaeda.

Increased militancy

Although many governments in Asia and the Middle East allied with the USA, there was also much sympathy for Islamic militancy. The government of Pakistan, for example, struggled to control elements within its intelligence services and armed forces that were sympathetic towards the Taliban. Some US tactics, such as torture and detention, also undermined sympathy for the USA and increased support for militancy.

Consequences of the War on Terror

Control

Afghanistan proved very difficult to control. Taliban and al-Qaeda forces continued to mount hit-and-run attacks on western forces in an INSURGENCY.

Tensions

It has also caused tension between the media and the governments in Britain and the USA, who feel that the media has been too quick to criticise US forces and has ignored the actions of the terrorists. Reactions have been even more extreme on websites that support the War on Terror.

Heroin production

This had fallen under the Taliban, but it rose again and Afghanistan now supplies 90 per cent of the world's heroin.

Osama bin Laden was finally discovered and killed by US forces in 2011. However, militant Islamist fundamentalism did not die with him. Around the world large numbers of independent groups and individuals have continued the campaign. And in 2014 a large and significant jihadist group called Islamic State emerged and took control of significant areas of Syria and Iraq.

ACTIVITY

1 Look back at the article criticising Francis Fukuyama that you wrote on page 118. Add another 50–100 words, providing more evidence and examples.
2 Give Fukuyama's article a mark out of 10, bearing in mind that he was writing in 1989 and you are writing in 2016 or later.

REVIEW TASK

Key forces

In your study of international relations you have examined the importance and effects of key forces:
- nationalism (or national self-interest)
- internationalism
- religion
- political ideology
- economic forces.

1 Look back over your work in this section and put this list of factors in order of importance for the post-Cold War period (1990–2001).
2 Now do the same for the other two periods you have studied (1919–39 and 1945–89).
3 Finally, do the same again for the whole of the period 1918–2001.

You could follow this up with a whole class poll on this question.

PRACTICE QUESTIONS

1 Outline the development of al-Qaeda in the 1990s. (5)
2 Outline the main conflicts in the world after the end of the Cold War. (5)
3 Explain why al-Qaeda attacked the USA on 11 September 2001. (10)
4 The 9/11 attacks were the result of ideology and nothing else. Do you agree? (10)

TOPIC SUMMARY

The post-Cold War world

1 The rapid ending of the Cold War in 1989 was followed by a period of euphoria in democratic capitalist countries in the West. However, there were soon signs of new tensions emerging.
2 This optimism came under strain through the 1990s but it literally exploded with al-Qaeda's attacks on the World Trade Center in 2001 (known as 9/11).
3 Al-Qaeda was founded by Osama bin Laden, who supported the mujahidin in Afghanistan against Soviet occupation. During the Cold War, the USA had funded and trained the mujahidin. Ten years later, the USA and its allies invaded Afghanistan to remove al-Qaeda from its terrorist base in the mountains.
4 Al-Qaeda was a new kind of terrorist organisation with no fixed base or fighters. It was more a loose collection of militant groups who were opposed to the West and the USA in particular. Al-Qaeda inspired militant Muslims across the world, but did not directly manage them.
5 9/11 led directly to the USA's 'War on Terror', which was a new, more aggressive foreign policy. The USA secured the backing of many western allies for an invasion of Afghanistan, where Osama bin Laden was supposedly based. Despite this widespread support, there was much criticism of the policy by people and politicians in the West. Military victories were achieved but the battle for hearts and minds was not, and some of the actions of the War on Terror – such as the torture of prisoners – actually fed the forces it was trying to fight.

KEY TERMS

Make sure you understand these key terms and can use them confidently in your writing.
- coup
- exile
- *glasnost*
- insurgency
- jihad
- *perestroika*

ASSESSMENT FOCUS

How the international relations study will be assessed

The international relations study will be examined in Paper 1, along with your chosen depth study. The international relations section is worth 65 marks – 30 per cent of your total GCSE. The questions could be on any part of the content, so you need to revise it all.

Questions 1 and 2 will test the first two assessment objectives:
● AO1: knowledge and understanding
● AO2: explanation and analysis.

Questions 3 and 4 will test these objectives, too, but they will also test AO3: interpretations.

Above all, the questions are designed to assess your ability to think and work like a historian. In the introduction, you looked at how historians work (page 4). There we set out some steps that historians take:
1 focus
2 ask questions
3 select
4 organise
5 fine tune.

The exam questions have already chosen a focus (stage 1) and they have asked questions (stage 2). What the examiner wants from you is stages 3, 4 and 5.

Question 1

Question 1 will usually ask you to outline or describe events from one section of the course. It is a simple knowledge question, usually requiring a description of three or four events in sequence. For example:

> *Outline the actions of Adolf Hitler in Europe in the 1930s. (5 marks)*

Advice
Select: Hitler carried out a range of actions in the 1930s. You only need three or four for a good mark. But remember it is an outline – you do not need every detail.

Organise: The main point in a question such as this is the logical sequence. So, you might want to describe Hitler's actions in the Rhineland, Austria, Czechoslovakia and Poland.

Fine tune: Make sure that your spellings and dates are correct. Make sure that your answer is clear – in the pressure of an exam it is easy to accidentally say something you do not mean to say.

Example answer

> Hitler started the Second World War in 1939 when he invaded Poland. In 1936, Hitler moved German forces into the Rhineland area of Germany. This was banned under the Treaty of Versailles. The British and French failed to stop him even though they were supposed to do so under the terms of the treaty. They did not entirely agree about what to do about Hitler and had a number of arguments about it. In 1938, Germany joined Austria in the Anschluss.

Aim of the question
There are no tricks to this question. It is simply testing your knowledge. However, the examiner wants to see that you can *select* important events and *describe* them accurately. Selection is vital – this is not asking you to write down everything you know.

This answer has some good points. It would probably get two marks because it contains three relevant events.

However, it is not well organised. The answer is not in a logical sequence. The invasion of Poland is mentioned but not much more. The Rhineland is probably over-described and the *Anschluss* under-described.

To improve this answer, start with a clear framing statement, such as: 'In the 1930s Hitler pursued an aggressive foreign policy.' Then follow this with his actions that show this for example in the Rhineland, the *Anschluss*, Munich 1938 and Poland 1939 – in chronological order.

Question 2

Question 2 will usually demand more analysis and explanation than Question 1. It will ask you about the *importance* or *impact* of a factor, or *how successful* an organisation was. For example:

> ● *How important was the Depression in causing the Second World War? (10 marks)*

The Question 2 medal ceremony

 Bronze (up to 25% of marks): You describe the effects of the Depression but do not use these to answer the question, i.e. how they helped cause the war.

 Silver (up to 60% of marks): You describe how the Depression contributed to the war, but do not compare it with another factor.

 Gold (up to 100% of marks): You make it really clear how the Depression contributed to the war *and* compare it with another factor which caused the war *and* answer the question of how important the Depression was by comparing it with that other factor.

Even a Gold medal answer can be improved by ensuring you have:
● a clear conclusion that rounds off your argument
● supporting evidence: relevant knowledge to support each point you make
● a balanced answer that shows you understand that there might be more than one view about the question or explains how the different factors are connected.

Advice

Select: Focus on the effects of the Depression, not its causes, and obviously how these effects (e.g. unemployment) helped to cause war. Select one other cause to compare it with (e.g. Hitler's policies, the actions of Britain and France).

Organise: The important thing is to organise your knowledge in a relevant way to answer the question. In this question, a good way to organise your answer might be:

> The Depression was a very important cause of the Second World War but I do not believe it was the main cause. The Depression did contribute to war by … However, another factor was the policies of Adolf Hitler from 1936 to 1939. I believe this was a bigger factor because …

Fine tune: Do all the usual checking, but make sure you say which of your reasons you think is more important.

Example answer

> The Depression was a very important cause of the Second World War but I do not believe it was the main cause. The Depression did contribute to war by breaking down international trade between countries. To protect their own industries the USA and other countries brought in trade barriers called tariffs. This made imports from Europe and Japan more expensive. It was meant to protect US industries, but most other countries did the same thing and it caused resentment and mistrust. The Depression damaged internationalism and that helped to cause the Second World War, as Germany, Italy and Japan all tried to rebuild their economies and gain power.
>
> However, another factor was the policies of Adolf Hitler from 1936 to 1939. I believe this was a much bigger factor. It is quite likely that the Depression on its own would not have caused the Second World War. However, it is very likely that Hitler would have caused the war even without the Depression. He was determined to build Lebensraum for Germany and that would have made a war with the USSR inevitable at some point. Hitler also acted very aggressively in other parts of Europe. For example, he forced Czechoslovakia to hand over the Sudetenland in 1938 and then went on to invade the rest of Czechoslovakia in 1939.
>
> In conclusion, I believe that Hitler was a more important factor than the Depression because of the nature of his plans. However, we have to accept that without the Depression, Hitler might not have come to power in Germany in the first place, so there are important links between these two causes.

This is definitely a Gold medal answer and would probably get nine or ten marks.

It has a clear opening and it then sticks to the line that the opening suggests it will follow. There is a good analysis of the Depression, which is specified in the question. (You would be amazed how many answers miss out the issue specified in the question!)

Then there is a good analysis of another cause. Of course there are other causes that could have been included but do not be tempted to go into them all. This question only requires you to look at two. It could also have been answered by comparing the Depression with Appeasement or with the failures of the League of Nations.

There is not much need to improve this answer. It could possibly explain why Japan was hit so hard (e.g. silk exports collapsed), but otherwise this is very good.

Aim of the question

Examiners want you to show you understand the interpretation and that you can evaluate it by seeing how far events and developments of the time, and the work of other historians, support or challenge it.

Interpretation A US historian Herbert Feis, writing in 1957.

Soviet actions showed they were prepared to ignore the democratic votes of Eastern Europe's people. They also showed a ruthless will to make sure that all of Central and Eastern Europe was governed by its allies. This purpose clearly contradicted the vision of the United Nations Organization of a world in which all countries would join together to protect each other and to maintain peace. The Soviet Union wanted space, satellite peoples and armies, additional economic resources, and a favourable chance for Communism to spread its influence.

Question 3

Question 3 will usually ask you 'how fair' the view of a historian is or 'how far you agree' with a particular interpretation. You will be given an extract that sets out a particular interpretation and you will be asked to base your answer on that extract. For example:

> *Study Interpretation A.*
>
> *Do you think this interpretation is a fair comment on the policies of the USSR in the years following the Second World War? Use your knowledge and other interpretations of the events of the period to support your answer. (24 marks)*

The Question 3 'Evaluation toolkit'

Evaluation is probably the trickiest part of the assessment. Don't fall into the trap of simplistic comments like 'Historian X said this because he is Russian' or 'He might not have had all the sources'. This question demands more than that. Use as many of these evaluation 'tools' as you can:

Tool A The context of the historian: This is the context in which the historian is writing, not the events they are writing about. Think about how events, or the personal views or experiences of the historian, influenced the way they interpreted events.

Tool B The views of other historians: Use the views of other historians who have agreed with or criticised the original view or suggested alternative interpretations.

Tool C Relevant factual knowledge: Use your knowledge of specific events or developments to support or challenge any claim made by the historian.

The Question 3 medal ceremony

 Bronze (up to 25% of marks): You state why the interpretation is or is not fair, supported by knowledge of one or two events (e.g. 'It is fair. The Soviets did set up communist governments in eastern Europe.').

 Silver (up to 60% of marks): You summarise the main argument in the interpretation, followed by explanation of why it is fair or unfair, using one of tools A, B or C.

 Gold (up to 100% of marks): You write a clear summary of the main argument in the interpretation, followed by an explanation of why it is fair (using at least *two* of tools A, B or C) *and* why it is unfair (using at least *two* of tools A, B or C).

Even a Gold medal answer can be improved by ensuring you have:
- a valid conclusion that rounds off your argument
- a good range of different historians' views in your answer
- clearly explained why historians hold particular views.

Advice

Before you start: Be sure to read the interpretation carefully. It might be quite complex but you need to know exactly what it says to write a good answer.

Select: You need to select facts, events and developments that support or challenge the view in the interpretation. This interpretation focuses mainly on Soviet policy in eastern Europe, so it makes sense to select items from this part of your knowledge wardrobe.

Organise: A good way to start this question is to show you understand what the interpretation is saying. You will not get a lot of marks for this but it will give the examiner confidence that you know what you are doing. Then write a paragraph that explains how the interpretation might be seen as fair. Use *at least two* of the evaluation tools to do this. Then do the same thing to explain why the interpretation might not be seen as fair.

Fine tune: Do all the usual checking, but here it is worth making sure you have used at least two of the three evaluation methods. You will get more credit for using Tools A and B than Tool C.

Example answer

This answer is very good – a Gold medal again! It would probably get about 21–22 marks. The opening is a strong analysis of the interpretation. The candidate clearly understands what the historian is arguing. This then sets up the rest of the answer.

One paragraph explains why the evaluation might be seen as fair. This is sensible. It uses Tool B and Tool C well.

The next paragraph sets out the alternative view using Tools A and B. These do not need a great amount of detail. Some candidates may choose to name historians or groups (e.g. revisionists), but you do not have to.

Probably the only thing missing from this answer is a conclusion. It would be interesting to see which side of the argument the candidate found more convincing and why. For example, they might have argued that it is not convincing because it was just not possible for Feis to take an objective view and, since other US historians disagreed with him, that on balance the view was not fair.

In this extract Herbert Feis is basically saying that all of the tensions and problems in the late 1940s were the fault of the USSR. He says that it ruthlessly took control of eastern Europe and did not allow democratic elections and that the USSR simply wanted to control eastern Europe as a base to spread communism further.

In some ways this interpretation could be seen as fair. Feis claims that the USSR did not allow eastern Europe to hold democratic elections. This is basically true. Soviet leader Stalin installed a communist government in East Germany under Walter Ulbricht – a communist trained in Moscow. This view is supported by other US historians. For example, in the 1950s George Kennan accused the Soviets of being liars and deceivers and wanting to dominate the world. In the 1970s, Gaddis argued that the Cold War was the USSR's fault, although he believed that the USA should accept some responsibility.

On the other hand it could be argued that this interpretation is not fair. To begin with, we should look at Feis himself. At the time of the events he is writing about he was an adviser to the US government, so he cannot really be seen as an impartial observer. He was facing up to the Soviets in the late 1940s and helped to create US policy, so it seems likely that he would defend US policy at that time and criticise the Soviets and blame them for the tensions. Many US historians have criticised views like Interpretation A. For example, Thomas Paterson writing in the 1970s essentially argued that the USA was at least as much to blame for the Cold War. Paterson and other revisionist historians were writing at a time when the Vietnam War was coming to an end. That war changed the attitudes of many people in the USA and made them question whether the Americans really were 'the good guys'.

Question 4

Question 4 also focuses on interpretation. It provides you with an extract but this question is less focused on evaluation than was Question 3 and is more about showing your knowledge of the different interpretations and how they changed.

> **Interpretation B** British prime minister Tony Blair commenting on Chamberlain in a speech in 2003.
>
> *In 1938 Chamberlain was a hero when he brought back the Munich Agreement and he did it for the best of motives. He had seen members of his own precious family, people he loved, die in the carnage of World War I. He strove for peace, not because he was a bad man. He was a good man. But he was a good man who made a bad decision.*

Aim of the question

This question is asking you to show that you understand the interpretation and also to survey the differing views on the issue. It does not require the kind of evaluation demanded in Question 3. The question asks why not all historians and commentators would not agree, so you need to know about other interpretations and reasons for the differences. Here is a Question 4 checklist:

- Compare with other interpretations.
- Explain the reasons for similarities and differences (which will usually be because of the evidence they were using or the contexts in which historians were writing).
- Survey changing interpretations of this issue – i.e. tell the story of the story.
- Explain the reasons for those changes (again, this is usually new evidence or changing contexts in which historians were writing).

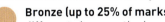

Explain why not all historians and commentators have agreed with this interpretation. Use other interpretations and your knowledge to support your answer.

The Question 4 medal ceremony

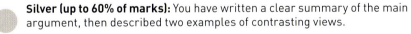

Bronze (up to 25% of marks): You have listed or described some similar or different views on the issue.

Silver (up to 60% of marks): You have written a clear summary of the main argument, then described two examples of contrasting views.

Gold (up to 100% of marks): You have written a clear summary of the main argument, followed by a description and explanation (i.e. how different *and* why different) of at least two examples of contrasting views.

Even a Gold medal answer can be improved by ensuring you have:
- a valid conclusion that rounds off your argument
- a good range of different historians' views in your answer
- clearly explained why historians hold particular views
- shown awareness of the degree of difference (interpretations might partially agree or partially disagree)
- offered some evaluation of the interpretation you have been given.

Advice

Before you start: Be sure to read the interpretation carefully. It might be quite complex but you need to know exactly what it says to write a good answer.

Select: Selection is extremely important in this question. There is so much that you could say. You need to select examples of interpretations from historians, politicians, journalists or popular interpretations that *disagree* with Blair. You do not need to explore which interpreters would agree.

Organise: A good way to start this question is to show you understand what the Interpretation is saying. You won't get a lot of marks for this but it will give the examiner confidence that you know what you are doing. After that you have a choice. You could either take a chronological approach and explain how particular historians at particular times would have disagreed with Blair. Alternatively, you could focus on the issues that Blair raises – Chamberlain being a good man and Appeasement being a bad policy – and explain how historians disagreed with them.

Fine tune: Do all the usual checking, but here it is worth making sure you have said what you think about the question. In questions like this, a conclusion usually means summarising the main reasons for disagreement *or* focusing on Blair's intentions.

Example answer

In this interpretation, Tony Blair is arguing that Neville Chamberlain was a good man and carried out the policy of Appeasement with the best of intentions. Blair also argues that even though he was treated as a hero at the time his policy was a terrible mistake and he should have gone to war with Hitler. Many historians and commentators would have agreed with Blair that Chamberlain was treated as a hero. However, there would be a lot of disagreement about what Blair says about Chamberlain as a man, and about his policies.

In the 1940s, historians like Cato disagreed that Chamberlain was a good man. Cato lists him as one of the 'Guilty Men' responsible for Britain doing badly in the war in 1940. However, Cato would have agreed with Blair that Appeasement was a bad policy.

In the 1960s, historians would not have completely agreed with Blair. Revisionist historians like Donald Cameron Watt began to question the view that Appeasement was a bad policy. They began to argue that Chamberlain made the best of a very bad situation because he faced a huge range of problems and had very few alternatives. The revisionists were influenced by events of the 1960s. The 1960s was a time when many traditional views in society were being questioned. History was one of many areas where new ideas emerged. Also, during the 1960s the US dislike of the Appeasement had drawn them into a war in Vietnam which was going badly. This seemed to suggest Appeasement may not have been a bad policy because Britain may have ended up in the same position. Through the 1940s and 1950s historians had to rely on a fairly limited range of source materials such as newspaper articles, private letters or interviews with key figures. But in 1958 the government passed the Public Records Act. This meant that official government papers could be studied 30 years after they were created. Previously the limit had been 50 years. So, by the late 1960s, huge numbers of government documents had become available. Historians were able to study documents from the Treasury, the armed forces, the Foreign Office and many other departments. This allowed them to get a detailed picture of the concerns that Chamberlain and his ministers faced and how serious they considered these to be.

In the 1990s, there were new views about Appeasement. Many counter-revisionist historians would have agreed with Blair about Appeasement being a bad policy but they would have disagreed about Chamberlain being a good man. Historians like Robert Parker argued that Chamberlain overrated his own abilities and importance in thinking that he could talk Hitler into being reasonable, and that Chamberlain ignored the advice of many of his officials and colleagues. Parker also argues that whatever the reasons (including giving Britain time to rearm), Chamberlain did betray Czechoslovakia in 1938 and that he should be held responsible for that.

This is a very full and thorough answer. It gives a good analysis of Blair's interpretation and then three really good examples of historians who would disagree. Two would probably have been enough. These are especially good because they show understanding of the partial agreement/disagreement. The only improvement might have been to pull paragraphs 2 and 4 together as they both cover the same theme.

KEYS TO SUCCESS

As long as you know the content and have learned how to think, this exam should not be too scary. The keys to success are:

1 Read the question carefully. This may sound obvious, but there is a skill to it. Sometimes students answer the question they *wish* had been asked rather than the one that has *actually* been asked. So identify the skill focus (what it is asking you to do). Does it want you to write a description, an explanation or a comparison? Identify the content focus (what it is about) and select from your knowledge accordingly.

2 Note the marks available. That helps you work out how much time to spend on answering each question. Time is precious – if you spend too long on low-mark questions you will run out of time for the high-mark ones.

3 Plan your answer before you start writing. For essays this is particularly important. The golden rule is: know what you are going to say; then say it clearly and logically.

4 Aim for quality not quantity: in the time limits of an exam you will not be able to write down everything you know and can think of – even if it is relevant. The marker would much rather read a short answer that really tackles the question than page after page of material that is not relevant.

5 Check your work. You will never have time in an exam to rewrite an answer but try to leave some time at the end to check for obvious spelling mistakes, missing words or other writing errors that might cost you marks.

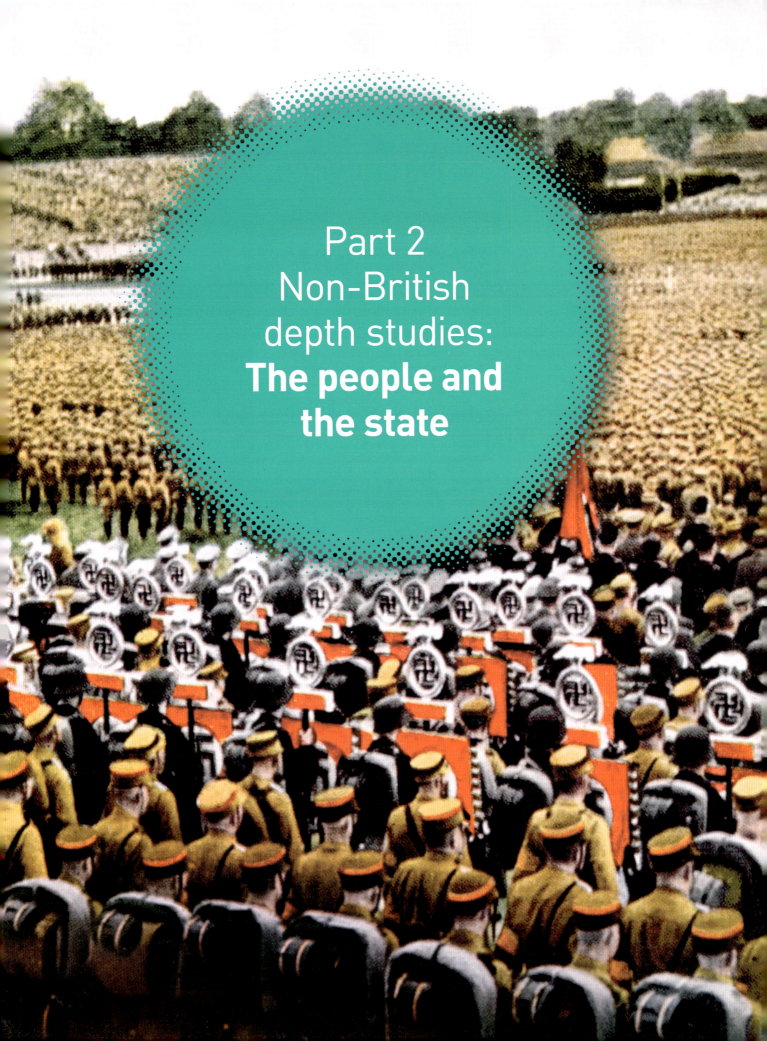

Part 2
Non-British
depth studies:
**The people and
the state**

4.1 Democracy to dictatorship: The rise and consolidation of the Nazi regime 1925–34

FOCUS

Although Germany emerged from the First World War in 1918 with many political, social and economic problems, by 1925 it appeared to be a stable democracy with its post-war problems behind it. Yet in less than ten years, the country transformed into an intolerant dictatorship under the Nazi leader Adolf Hitler. In this topic, you will look at how this change took place, the role the German people played in it and the effects these events had on the people. You will examine:

● how stable Germany was in the years 1925–29
● how the worldwide economic depression affected Germany
● how the Nazis took power and consolidated their hold.

1 Study Source 1. How is Berlin made to look attractive?

Source 1 A poster published by the London and North Eastern Railway Company (LNER) in 1925. It is advertising boat and rail services from Harwich (on the east coast of England) to Berlin. ▼

Germany in 1925 – the good news!

Source 1 is a travel poster from 1925, encouraging people in Britain to visit Berlin. They did so in their thousands – as did people from all over Europe and the USA. In 1925, Berlin (and Germany as a whole) was a major tourist destination. It had been through some dark times during the First World War (1914–18) and in the years that followed, but by the mid-1920s it had recovered well.

Political stability

Berlin was now an attractive tourist destination because it was safe. A few years earlier this had not been the case. From 1870 to 1918, Germany had been ruled by Kaiser Wilhelm I and then his son Wilhelm II. German people voted in elections and sent representatives to the REICHSTAG, but political parties had little real power. Power lay with the Kaiser himself, landowners and industrialists, and the army. However, by 1918 this old Germany had been crippled by four years of war. A new democratic government with a new constitution (see Factfile) had been set up, but it was not strong. The government was based in Weimar because Berlin was thought to be too dangerous. Extreme political groups on the Left (particularly the communists) and their opponents on the Right tried to overthrow it. The most recent attempt had been by Adolf Hitler's Nazi Party in 1923.

BERLIN
VIA HARWICH   TWICE A DAY

INFORMATION FROM CONTINENTAL TRAFFIC MANAGER L·N·E·R LIVERPOOL STREET STATION LONDON E.C.2;
OR HULL: 71 REGENT STREET WI   Wm.H.MULLER & Co (LONDON) LTD 66 HAYMARKET S.W.I   PRINCIPAL L·N·E·R STATIONS OFFICES & TOURIST AGENCIES

FACTFILE

The Weimar Constitution
Before the First World War, Germany was not a real democracy. The Weimar Constitution, introduced after the war, attempted to establish the most democratic system in the world – one in which no individual could gain too much power:

- All Germans over the age of 20 could vote.
- There was a system of proportional representation – for example, if a party gained 20 per cent of the votes, they gained 20 per cent of the seats in the German parliament (the Reichstag).
- The chancellor was responsible for day-to-day government, but he needed the support of at least half the Reichstag.
- The head of state was the president, but he stayed out of day-to-day government. However, Article 38 of the constitution gave the president emergency powers to rule the country directly, without having to consult the Reichstag, in extreme circumstances.

However, by 1925 most of these problems seemed to be over. In 1923, Gustav Stresemann had become chancellor of Germany and he served as chancellor and then as foreign minister until his death in 1929. Stresemann was a stabilising force, convincing Germany's more moderate parties to work together. He put together a COALITION of moderate left-wing Socialists (SPD) and moderate right-wing parties including the Catholic Centre Party, the German Democratic Party (DDP) and the German People's Party (DVP). Stresemann's coalition narrowly won the 1924 election, but the parties worked well together and in the 1928 election his coalition won 136 more seats in the Reichstag than the radical parties. The most extreme party of all, the Nazis, secured less than 3 per cent of the vote.

Economic prosperity

Another reason that people came to Berlin was that it was a good place to do business. The German economy was prospering after some difficult times. During the war, Germany had run up massive debts. It was struggling to pay war pensions to the wives and children of soldiers killed or injured in the war. Under the Treaty of Versailles (see page 13) Germany had to pay £6.6 billion in reparations to France and Belgium. When it refused to pay in 1923, French and Belgian troops invaded the Ruhr, Germany's main industrial region. In response, the German government ordered workers to go on strike, triggering an economic collapse. The German currency, the mark, became worthless. Millions of Germans faced ruin as their life savings became worthless.

Stresemann managed to tackle this crisis, too. He introduced a new currency called the Rentenmark. Under the Dawes Plan (see page 21), reparations payments were spread over a longer period, and 800 million marks in loans from the USA poured into German industry. Some of the money went into German businesses, replacing old equipment with the latest technology. Some of it went into public works such as the high-speed rail line from Berlin to Hamburg (see Source 2). These loans also paid for public swimming pools, sports stadia and apartment blocks.

As well as providing facilities, these projects created jobs. In 1928, Germany finally achieved the same levels of production as before the war and regained its status as the world's second greatest industrial power (behind the USA). Wages for industrial workers rose, and many Germans enjoyed a higher standard of living than they had for years. Reparations were being paid and exports were on the increase. The government was even able to increase welfare benefits and wages for state employees. Alongside this economic prosperity, there was a sense of German pride being restored.

Source 2 A train on the high-speed rail link from Berlin to Hamburg. These trains travelled at 230 km per hour. ▼

2 In what ways could Source 2 be seen as an advertisement for Germany at the time?

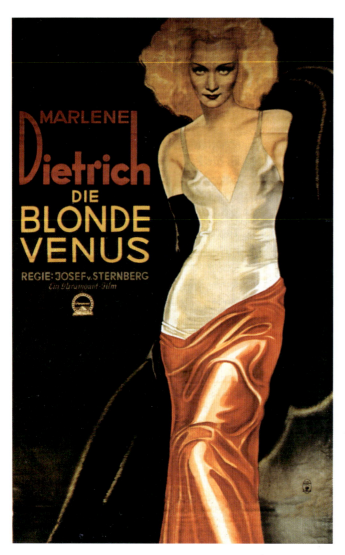

Source 3 A poster advertising one of Marlene Dietrich's films. ▲

Thriving culture

Perhaps the main reason why people wanted to visit Berlin was its cultural life. In the Kaiser's time there had been strict censorship, but the Weimar Constitution allowed free expression of ideas. Writers and poets flourished, especially in the capital. People flocked to see the work of artists like George Grosz and Otto Dix. The famous Bauhaus style of design and architecture developed. The first Bauhaus exhibition displayed designs for buildings from houses and shops to art galleries and factories, and attracted 15,000 visitors.

The 1920s were also a golden age for German cinema, producing one of its greatest international stars, Marlene Dietrich (see Source 3), and one of its most celebrated directors, Fritz Lang. Berlin became known for its daring and liberated night-life. People enjoyed going to clubs and in 1927 there were 900 dance bands in Berlin alone. Cabaret artists performed songs criticising political leaders that would have been banned in the Kaiser's days.

A peaceful Germany

Stresemann's greatest triumphs were in foreign policy. In 1925, he signed the Locarno Treaties, guaranteeing not to try to change Germany's western borders with France and Belgium. As a result, in 1926 Germany was accepted into the League of Nations. Here Stresemann began to work, quietly but steadily, on reversing some of the terms of the Treaty of Versailles, particularly those concerning reparations and Germany's eastern frontiers. By the time he died in 1929, Stresemann had negotiated the YOUNG PLAN, which further lightened the reparations burden on Germany.

1. What can we learn about Germany in the 1920s from Source 3?

Germany in 1925 – the bad news!

Weimar Germany in the 1920s may have been an exciting and attractive place for visitors, but what about ordinary Germans? Were they happy?

Political stability?

Despite the relative stability of the Weimar Republic in this period, there were worrying signs. Most Germans had come to accept and support democracy, but it was fragile. Only the influence of Stresemann and other party leaders held the coalitions together, and even during these stable years there were four different chancellors. Many Germans felt that politicians were more concerned with getting themselves the best job they could than with representing the people. There was much greater trust in other authority figures, such as army commanders and senior judges, many of whom disliked democracy.

Extreme political parties do not usually thrive during times of economic prosperity, yet in the elections held during this period, around 30 per cent of the vote regularly went to extremist parties that stood against the republic. Another event that would turn out to be significant was the election of Paul von Hindenburg as president in 1926. Hindenburg was opposed to democracy; he even wrote to the Kaiser in exile for approval before he took up the post of chancellor.

ACTIVITY

Imagine you work in the advertising department of LNER in the late 1920s. Write a 150-word advertisement to be printed on the back of a postcard version of Source 1. Your aim is to encourage people to come to Berlin and the rest of Germany. You will need to make Germany seem attractive and reassure people that the country is safe and peaceful.

Source 4 A photograph of a Wandervogel camp in the 1920s. ▼

2   How might a German farmer or middle-class lecturer, a shopkeeper or a local official have reacted to your advertising postcard in the Activity above?

Economic prosperity?

The economic boom in Weimar Germany was also precarious. The US loans could be called in at short notice, which would be devastating for Germany. The main economic winners were not the ordinary people but big businesses, such as the steel and chemicals industries, that controlled about half of Germany's industrial production. Other winners were landowners. Workers in the large industries gained as well, as most Weimar governments were sympathetic to the trade unions.

The main losers were peasant farmers and sections of the middle classes. After the war many peasants experienced a lack of demand for the food they produced. Many small business owners, particularly shopkeepers, saw their businesses threatened by large department stores (many of which were owned by Jews). In 1913, a university lecturer earned ten times as much as a coal miner. In the 1920s, he only earned twice as much. These people began to feel that the Weimar government was not meeting their needs.

Thriving cultural scene?

Weimar culture was colourful and exciting to many. Others, however, particularly those living in villages and country towns, felt that the culture of the cities represented a moral decline. The Bauhaus design college was situated in Dessau after being forced out of Weimar by hostile town officials. The Wandervogel movement was one reaction to Weimar's culture. The Wandervogel called for a return to simple country values and wanted to see more help for those in the countryside and less decadence in the towns. This was a powerful feeling, which the Nazis successfully took advantage of in later years.

A peaceful Germany?

There was also the question of international relations. German communists attacked the Locarno Treaties, claiming they were part of a plot against the communist government in the USSR. German nationalists attacked Stresemann for joining the League of Nations and for signing the Locarno Treaties because doing so suggested that Germany accepted the Treaty of Versailles. Most Germans still felt very bitter about the treaty, feeling it was a humiliating betrayal. They resented the fact that Germany was no longer a great power on the world stage. Germany was still a troubled place.

The Nazis in the wilderness 1924–29

One group of people who definitely thought the Weimar Republic was bad news was the Nazi Party. We will now examine how they fared in the 1920s. As you read this section, consider whether their story suggests that the Weimar Republic was strong or fragile in the 1920s.

The origins of the Nazi Party

The Nazis began as the German Workers' Party, led by Anton Drexler. In 1919, a young Adolf Hitler, fresh out of the army, joined the party. Drexler soon realised that Hitler had great talent and within months had put him in charge of propaganda and the party's political ideas. In 1920, the party announced its Twenty-Five Point Programme (see Factfile), and renamed itself the National Socialist German Workers' Party – 'Nazi' for short. In 1921, Hitler forced out Drexler and took his place as leader.

Hitler had a clear and simple appeal. He stirred nationalist passions in his audiences. His meetings were so successful that his opponents tried to disrupt them. To counter this, in 1921 Hitler set up the Sturmabteiling (SA), also known as 'storm troopers' or 'brownshirts'. These thugs protected Hitler's meetings but also disrupted those of other parties.

The Munich Putsch 1923

In 1923, the Nazis were still very much a minority party. However, Hitler had given them a high profile. On 8 November he put into action his plan to topple the Weimar government by sending his storm troopers to take over official buildings in Munich and announcing his planned revolution in a Munich beer hall. Government forces hit back and the rebellion broke up in chaos the following day.

In the short term, the Munich Putsch was a disaster for Hitler. People did not rise up to support him. He and other leading Nazis were arrested and charged with TREASON. At the trial, however, Hitler gained enormous publicity for himself and his ideas – every word he said was reported in the newspapers. In fact, Hitler so impressed the judges that he and his accomplices got off very lightly. Hitler was given only five years in prison, even though the legal guidelines stated that high treason should carry a life sentence. In the end, Hitler only served nine months of the sentence and did so in great comfort in Landsberg Castle.

This last point was very significant. It was clear that Hitler had won some sympathy and support from important figures in the legal system. During his time in prison, he wrote much of *Mein Kampf* – a book setting out his beliefs (see Factfile).

Source 5 Hitler, writing while in prison in 1923.

When I resume active work, it will be necessary to pursue a new policy. Instead of working to achieve power by armed conspiracy we shall have to take hold of our noses and enter the Reichstag against the Catholic and Marxist deputies. If out-voting them takes longer than out-shooting them, at least the results will be guaranteed by their own constitution. Any lawful process is slow. Sooner or later we shall have a majority and after that we shall have Germany.

ACTIVITY

After the end of the Second World War in 1945, the government banned the reprinting of *Mein Kampf* in Germany. It was able to do this because the government held the copyright to the book. In 2016, the copyright on *Mein Kampf* expired. There was much debate about whether to allow the book to be reprinted. What do you think? Search online to find out what actually happened.

FACTFILE

Hitler and *Mein Kampf*
Mein Kampf means 'My Struggle'. In this book and his later writings, Hitler set out the main Nazi beliefs:
- **National Socialism:** This stood for loyalty to Germany, racial purity, equality and state control of the economy.
- **Racism:** The Aryans (white Europeans) were the 'master race'. All other races – and especially the Jews – were inferior.
- **Armed force:** Hitler believed that war and struggle were an essential part of the development of a healthy Aryan race.
- **Living space (*Lebensraum*):** Germany needed to expand as its people were hemmed in. This expansion would come mainly at the expense of Russia and Poland.
- **The Führer:** Debate and democratic discussion produced weakness. Strength lay in total loyalty to the leader (the Führer).

Source 6 A Nazi election poster from 1928, saying: 'Work, freedom and bread! Vote for the National Socialists.' ▲

A change of tactics 1925

After leaving prison, Hitler reorganised the party. He realised that the Nazis would have to win power by democratic means (see Source 5). He saw the communists building up their strength with local branches and youth organisations, so he did the same by creating a network of local party branches and the Hitler Youth. He also enlarged the SA, drawing about 55 per cent of his storm troopers from the ranks of the unemployed. Many were ex-servicemen from the war. In addition, Hitler formed a new group called the Schutzstaffel (SS). The SS was similar to the SA, but its members were fanatically loyal to Hitler personally.

A change of focus 1927

Despite Hitler's efforts, the Nazi Party still failed to win wide popular support. In 1927, the Nazis were still trying to appeal to German workers (see Source 6), just as they always had. However, as you have seen, industry flourished in the period 1925–29 and life was good for workers. In the 1928 elections the Nazis gained only 12 Reichstag seats and only a quarter of the votes that the communists won. Although the Nazis' anti-Semitic policies gained them some support, they failed to win over the majority of workers. Most of them supported the Communist Party or the Social Democrats.

Source 7 A poster published by the Social Democratic party. It says: 'Women, for equal rights and treatment choose the Social Democrats'. ▶

1 Study Source 6. How is it trying to appeal to the working classes?

2 Compare Sources 6 and 7. In what ways are they similar or different?

3 Which would you say is better propaganda?

4 The Nazis failed to gain working-class support while the Social Democrats and Communists succeeded. Do you think propaganda had much to do with this, or was it more about what these parties stood for?

1 Compare Sources 8 and 9. Both are foreigners writing about Germany at this time. Why are they so different?

Support for the Nazis

However, the Nazis did gain support from groups who were benefiting less from Germany's success at this time. These included peasant farmers in northern Germany and middle-class shopkeepers and small business owners in country towns. Unlike Britain, Germany still had a large rural population – probably about 35 per cent of Germans lived and worked on the land. They were not sharing in Weimar Germany's economic prosperity. The Nazis highlighted the importance of the peasants in their plans for Germany, promising to help agriculture if they came to power. They praised the peasants as racially pure Germans. Nazi propaganda also contrasted the supposedly clean and simple life of the peasants with that in the allegedly corrupt and crime-ridden cities (for which they blamed the Jews). The fact that the Nazis despised Weimar culture also gained them support among some conservative people in the towns, who saw Weimar's flourishing art, literature and film achievements as immoral. The Nazis also began to collaborate closely with the right-wing Nationalist Party (DNVP) to make themselves appear more respectable.

More members, more activity …

With this change of focus, membership of the Nazi Party rose to over 100,000 by 1928. It was funded partly by members' subscriptions and partly by wealthy individuals or businesses.

Hitler appointed Joseph Goebbels to take charge of Nazi propaganda. Goebbels was highly efficient at spreading the Nazi message. He and Hitler believed that the best way to reach what they called 'the masses' was by appealing to their feelings rather than by rational argument. Goebbels produced posters, leaflets, films and radio broadcasts. He organised rallies and set up 'photo opportunities'.

… yet still on the fringes

Despite these shifting policies and priorities, there was still no electoral breakthrough for the Nazis. In 1928, they were still a minority party who had the support of less than 3 per cent of the population. They were the smallest party in the Reichstag, with fewer seats than the Communist Party. The prosperity of the Stresemann years and Stresemann's success in foreign policy meant that most Germans were not interested in extreme politics.

FOCUS TASK

How stable was Germany in the 1920s?

1 Look at the two images below. Which one do you think best represents the state of Germany in the 1920s?
 The rotten apple suggests that while things looked fine on the outside, inside were some nasty problems. The house of cards suggests that everyone knew the recovery was flimsy but were not expecting a gust of wind to blow it over.
2 Which image best reflects the issues highlighted on pages 132–38? Explain your answer, or come up with a better metaphor.

PRACTICE QUESTIONS

1 Describe one example of the main achievements of Weimar Germany in the period 1925–29. (2)
2 How stable was the Weimar Republic in the period 1925–29? Explain your answer. (10)

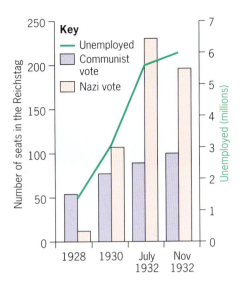

Figure 10 A graph showing unemployment in Germany and the changes in support for the Nazis and the communists in this period. ▲

The Depression and the rise of the Nazis

In 1929, the US stock market crashed, sending the country into a disastrous economic depression. In a very short time, countries around the world began to feel the effects of this. Germany was particularly badly affected. US bankers and businessmen lost huge amounts of money in the crash. To pay off their debts, they asked German banks to repay the money they had borrowed, causing economic collapse in Germany. Businesses went bankrupt, workers were laid off and unemployment rocketed.

The Depression was a worldwide problem – it was not just Germany that suffered. Nor was the Weimar government the only government struggling to solve the problem of unemployment. However, because Germany had been so dependent on US loans, and because it still had to pay reparations to the Allies, the problems were most acute there. In addition, it seemed that the Weimar politicians were either unwilling or unable to work together to find the policies needed to help the German people through this economic disaster. It seemed that democracy was failing them, so many Germans began to look to other solutions.

Source 11 An eyewitness describing unemployed vagrants in Germany in 1932.

No one knew how many there were of them. They completely filled the streets. They stood or lay about in the streets as if they had taken root there. They sat or lay on the pavements or in the roadway and gravely shared out scraps of newspaper among themselves.

Source 12 A photograph taken in Upper Silesia in 1932. Unemployed miners and their families moved into shacks in a shanty town because they had no money to pay their rent. ▼

Source 13 A Nazi election poster from July 1932. The Nazis proclaim 'We build!' and promise to provide work, freedom and bread. They accuse the opposing parties of planning to use terror, corruption, lies and other strategies as the basis for their government. ▼

Enter the Nazis

Hitler's ideas now had a special relevance:

- Is the Weimar government indecisive? Then Germany needs a strong leader!
- Are reparations adding to Germany's problems? Then kick out the Treaty of Versailles!
- Is unemployment a problem? Let the unemployed join the army, build Germany's armaments and be used for public works like road building!

The Nazis' Twenty-Five Points (see page 136) now seemed particularly attractive to those most vulnerable to the Depression: the unemployed, the elderly and the middle classes. Hitler gave these groups a focus for their blame for Germany's troubles: the Versailles Treaty, the 'November Criminals' (the socialist politicians who had signed the treaty), communists and Jews. These ideas had not won support for the Nazis in the Stresemann years, but now the democratic parties simply could not get Germany back to work. In the 1930 elections, the Nazis won 107 seats. Two years later this increased to nearly 200. They did not yet have an overall majority, but they were the biggest single party.

Why did the Nazis succeed in elections?

After the Nazis had fully established their power in the 1930s, their propaganda chief, Goebbels, created his own version of the events that brought Hitler to power in 1929–33. In this version, it was Hitler's destiny to become Germany's leader, and the German people finally came to recognise this. How valid was this view?

Nazi election campaigns

Nazi campaign methods were modern and effective. Posters and pamphlets such as Source 13 could be found everywhere. Nazi rallies impressed people with their energy, enthusiasm and sheer size.

Hitler's rise

Hitler ran for president in 1932 and although he was defeated, the campaign raised his profile hugely. As a powerful speaker, he was the Nazis' greatest campaigning asset. He was years ahead of his time as a communicator. Using films, radio and records, he brought his message to millions. He travelled by plane on a hectic tour of rallies all over Germany. He appeared as a dynamic man of the moment – the leader of a modern party with modern ideas. At the same time, he was seen to be a man of the people, someone who knew and understood ordinary Germans and their problems.

Policies and slogans

In their propaganda and at their rallies, the Nazis relied on generalised slogans rather than detailed policies – 'uniting the people of Germany behind one leader'; 'going back to traditional values'. This made it hard to criticise them. When they *were* criticised for a specific policy, they usually dropped it. For example, when industrialists expressed concern about Nazi plans to nationalise industry, they simply abandoned the policy.

The Nazis took every opportunity to state that Jews, communists, Weimar politicians and the Treaty of Versailles were the causes of Germany's problems. They expressed contempt for the democratic system and said that it was unable to solve Germany's economic problems.

1 Study Source 13 carefully and then complete this sentence:
This source is a very useful piece of evidence about Nazi campaigning in 1932 because ...

Nazi actions

The Nazis did not just impress people with their words, though. At a local level – where ordinary Germans would be most aware of them – the Nazis showed they were a political party that could get things done. For example, they organised soup kitchens and provided shelter in hostels for the unemployed. Out on the streets the uniformed SA and SS gave the impression of discipline and order. Many Germans felt the country needed the kind of order that Hitler's armed troops offered.

'Negative cohesion'

Not everyone was taken in by Hitler's magnetism, but even some sceptics supported the Nazis. The historian Gordon Craig believes that this was because of 'negative cohesion'. People supported the Nazis not because they shared Nazi views (that would be positive cohesion) but because they shared Nazi fears: if you hate what I hate, then I'll support you!

Disillusionment with democracy

Perhaps the biggest negative was dissatisfaction with democracy in Weimar Germany. Politicians seemed unable to tackle the problems of the Depression. The chancellor, Heinrich Brüning, actually cut government spending and welfare benefits during the worst of the Depression. He urged Germans to make sacrifices. Some historians think that he was deliberately making the situation worse in order to get the international community to cancel reparations payments. Other historians think that he was afraid of HYPERINFLATION, which had occurred previously, in 1923.

Brüning called new elections in 1930. This was a disastrous decision, as it gave the Nazis the opportunity to exploit the discontent in Germany. The elections resulted in yet another divided Reichstag. Many German people began to feel that democracy was not serving them well – unemployment was heading towards 6 million and the average person's income had fallen by 40 per cent since 1929. The Reichstag seemed irrelevant. It met for only five days in 1932. Brüning relied on President Hindenburg's emergency powers, bypassing the democratic process altogether.

Decadence

As for modern decadent Weimar culture, the Nazis could count on all those who felt traditional German values were under threat. They talked about restoring old-fashioned values. The Social Democratic Party made a grave mistake in thinking that German people would not fall for these vague promises and accusations. They underestimated the fear and anger that German people felt towards the Weimar Republic.

Source 14 Hitler speaking at an election rally, July 1932.

Our opponents accuse us National Socialists, and me in particular, of being intolerant and quarrelsome. They say that we don't want to work with other parties. They say the National Socialists are not German at all, because they refuse to work with other political parties. So is it typically German to have thirty political parties? I have to admit one thing – these gentlemen are quite right. We are intolerant. I have given myself this one goal – to sweep these thirty political parties out of Germany.

Source 15 The German interior minister, commenting on the rise of the Nazi and the Communist Parties, 1932.

The so-called race of poets and thinkers is hurrying with flags flying towards dictatorship ... the radicalism of the Right [Nazis] has unleashed a strong radicalism on the Left [Communists]. The communists have made gains almost everywhere. The situation is such that half the German people have declared themselves against the present state.

2   Study Sources 14 and 15. Explain how each source is useful for investigating:
    a   the actions of the Nazis and communists
    b   the concerns of the Weimar politicians
    c   the attitudes of the German people.

ACTIVITY

Make your own copy of the diagram below. Write in the blank boxes the sequence of problems, events and developments that led German people to support extremist parties (communists and the Nazi Party). Use a different type of diagram if you prefer.

Democracy → [ ] → [ ] → [ ] → Extremism

The Duties of German Communist Party Volunteers

Unselfishly they help the farmers to dry the harvest.

Particular detachments are responsible for improving transport.

They works nights and overtime getting together useful equipment.

They increase their fitness for the fatherland with target practice.

Source 16 An English translation of a 1931 Nazi election poster. ▲

1 Compare Source 16 with Source 13. Is it possible to say whether one is more useful to historians than the other?
2 Which of the posters do you think would have gained the Nazis more support? Explain your answer.

The communist threat

As the crisis deepened, support for the Communist Party rose too. At the same time gangs of communist activists fought street battles with the police. The Nazis turned this to their advantage. Fear of communism was another shared negative. The Nazis usually called the communists 'Bolsheviks', which was the name of the Russian Communist Party. This helped to frighten certain groups of people in Germany:

● **Business leaders** feared the communists because of their plans to introduce state control of businesses, just as the communists had in the USSR. They were also concerned about the growing strength of Germany's trade unions. They believed that the Nazis would combat these threats and some began to offer financial support to the Nazi Party.

● **Farmers** were also alarmed by the communists. In the USSR, the communist government had taken over all the land. Millions of peasants had been killed or imprisoned in the process. In contrast, the Nazis promised to help Germany's desperately struggling small farmers.

Source 17 Historian Simon Williams assessing the reason for Hitler's success, 1986.

The majority of Germans never voted for the Nazis. The Nazis made it clear they would destroy democracy and all who stood in their way. Why then didn't their enemies join together to stop Hitler? ... Had the Communists and Socialists joined forces they would probably have been strong enough both in the Reichstag and on the streets to have blocked the Nazis. The fact was that by 1932–3 there were simply not enough Germans who believed in democracy and individual freedom to save the Weimar Republic.

FOCUS TASK

Why did many Germans turn to the Nazis in the period 1929–32?

1 Did people rally to support Hitler for positive reasons as Goebbels claimed, or do you think Gordon Craig was right that it was for negative reasons – fear and disillusionment?
  To help you make up your mind look carefully at Sources 12–16. For each source, write two sentences explaining whether you think it is evidence that:
  a supports the view of Goebbels
  b supports the view of Craig
  c could be used to support either interpretation.
2 Now work through the text and other sources on these pages. Make a list of examples and evidence that seem to support either viewpoint.
3 Write a paragraph explaining which view you most agree with and why. Include one piece of 'killer evidence' if you can.

Joseph Goebbels

People voted for the Nazis because they shared Hitler's visions for Germany.

People voted for the Nazis because they were disillusioned with Weimar democracy and afraid of the communists.

Gordon Craig

How did Hitler become chancellor?

July 1932

July 1932: After the Reichstag elections of July 1932, the Nazis were the largest single party (with 230 seats) but not a majority party. Hitler demanded to be chancellor, but Hindenburg refused and kept the current chancellor, Franz von Papen. He then used his emergency powers to pass the measures that von Papen hoped would solve unemployment. However, von Papen was soon in trouble. He had virtually no support at all in the Reichstag and so called yet another election.

November 1932

November 1932: In November 1932, the Nazis again came out as the largest party, although their share of the vote fell. Hitler regarded the election as a disaster. He had lost more than 2 million votes, along with 38 seats in the Reichstag. The Nazis started to run out of funds. Hitler is said to have threatened suicide.

December 1932

December 1932: Hindenburg again refused to make Hitler chancellor. In December 1932 he chose Kurt von Schleicher, one of his own advisers, but he was forced to resign within a month. The Weimar system of proportional representation meant that no single political group could provide strong rule. This had left Hindenburg to more or less run the country using his emergency powers, supported by army leaders and rich industrialists. In one sense, Hindenburg had already overthrown the principles of democracy. If he was to rescue the democratic system, he needed a chancellor who had support in the Reichstag.

January 1933

January 1933: Throughout January 1933, Hindenburg and von Papen met secretly with industrialists, army leaders and politicians. On 30 January, to everyone's surprise, they offered Hitler the post of chancellor. With only a few Nazis in the Cabinet and von Papen as vice-chancellor, they were confident that they could limit Hitler's influence and resist his extremist demands. They intended that decisions would be made by the Cabinet, which was filled with conservatives. Hitler would get support in the Reichstag for those policies and control the communists. So in reality Hitler ended up as chancellor through a behind-the-scenes deal, not because he had won popular support. Both Hindenburg and von Papen were sure that they could control Hitler. They were wrong.

FOCUS TASK

How did Hitler become chancellor in 1933?

Here is a list of 14 factors that helped Hitler come to power.
1   Write each factor on a card with one example of how it helped Hitler. You may want to add other factors if you can think of them.
2   Give each factor a mark out of 10 for its importance in bringing Hitler to power.
3   Choose what you think are the five most important factors and write a short paragraph on each, to explain why you have chosen it.
4   If you took away any of those factors, would Hitler still have become chancellor?
5   Were any of those five factors also present in the 1920s? If so, explain why the Nazis had not been successful in the 1920s.

Nazi strengths

Hitler's speaking skills

Nazi policies

Propaganda campaigns

Support from big business

Criticism of the Weimar Republic

Violent treatment of opponents

Opponents' weaknesses

Failure to deal with the Depression

Failure to co-operate with one another

Attitudes of Germans to the democratic parties

Other factors

Weaknesses in the Weimar Constitution

Impact of the Depression on ordinary Germans

Scheming of Hindenburg and von Papen

Treaty of Versailles

Memories of the economic problems (hyperinflation) of 1923

How did Hitler consolidate his position?

When Hitler became chancellor in January 1933, he was in a precarious position (see Source 18). Few people thought he would hold on to power for very long. Even fewer thought that by the summer of 1934 he would be the supreme dictator of Germany. He achieved this through a clever combination of methods – some legal, others dubious. He also managed to defeat or reach agreements with those who could have stopped him.

1 How confident is the cartoonist in Source 18 that Hitler will hold on to power? Explain the cartoonist's view by referring to details in the picture and what happened to previous governments in the 1920s and early 1930s.

◄ **Source 18** A German cartoon from 1933. The people underneath the chair represent the powerful people in Germany such as army commanders, big business, lawyers and judges, and top public officials and civil servants. The caption says: 'Even if you are popular, the seat is often uncomfortable.'

Source 19 An extract from the diary of Victor Klemperer, a Jew who lived in Dresden and recorded his experiences, 17 March 1933.

The defeat in 1918 did not depress me as greatly as the present state of affairs. It is shocking how day after day naked acts of violence, breaches of the law, barbaric opinions appear quite undisguised as official decree. The Socialist papers are permanently banned. The 'Liberals' tremble. The 'Berliner Tageblatt' was recently banned for two days; that can't happen to the 'Dresdener Neueste Nachrichten', it is completely devoted to the government. … I can no longer get rid of the feeling of disgust and shame. And no one stirs; everyone trembles, keeps out of sight.

2 Read Source 19. How can you tell that Klemperer has been badly affected by the events of 1933?

3 Does the fact that he is a Jew make him an unreliable witness?

4 Who or what does he hold responsible?

The Reichstag fire

Once he was chancellor, Hitler took steps to complete a Nazi takeover of Germany. He called another election for March 1933 to try to get an overall Nazi majority in the Reichstag. Speeches, rallies, processions and street fighting all took place in cities across Germany. Hitler was using the same tactics as in previous elections, but now he had the power to control the media – for example, he could shut down opposition newspapers. He also had control of the streets (if communists attempted to disrupt Nazi rallies they were arrested by the police or beaten up by the SA with no police interference). Even so, success was not assured.

Then, on 27 February, there was a dramatic development: the Reichstag building was set on fire. Hitler blamed the communists and declared that the fire was the beginning of a communist uprising. He demanded emergency powers to deal with the situation and Hindenburg granted them. The Nazis used these powers to arrest communists, break up meetings and frighten voters. There have been several theories about what caused the fire, including that it was an accident, the work of a madman or a communist plot. Many Germans at the time – and many historians since – have suggested that the Nazis might have started the fire themselves.

The Enabling Act

In the election, the Nazis won their largest-ever share of the votes and, with the support of the smaller Nationalist Party, Hitler finally got an overall majority. He immediately banned the Communist Party. Using the SA and SS, he intimidated the Reichstag into passing the Enabling Act, which allowed him to make laws without consultation. Only the SPD voted against him. The Catholic Centre Party decided to co-operate with the Nazis rather than be treated like the Communist Party. The Enabling Act made Hitler a virtual dictator. If he wanted a new law, he could just pass it – there was nothing Hindenburg or anyone else could do.

Even now, however, Hitler was not secure. He had seen how the civil service, the judiciary, the army and other important groups had undermined the Weimar Republic. He was not yet strong enough to remove his opponents, so he set about a clever policy that mixed force, concessions and compromise (see Factfile).

FACTFILE

Nazi consolidation of power
1933

30 January	Hitler appointed chancellor; Goering minister of interior.
17 February	Goering ordered local police forces to co-operate with the SA and SS.
27 February	Reichstag fire. Arrest of 4,000 communists and other Nazi opponents on the same night.
28 February	Emergency Decree issued by Hindenburg: police to arrest suspects and hold them without trial, search houses, ban meetings, close newspapers and radio stations; Hitler took over regional governments.
5 March	Reichstag elections: government used control of radio and police to intimidate opponents. Nazi election slogan was 'The battle against Marxism'. Won 52 per cent of vote.
13 March	Goebbels appointed head of ministry for propaganda and took control of all media.
24 March	Enabling Act allowed Hitler to pass decrees without the president's involvement, making him a legal dictator.
7 April	Civil service administration, court and education purged of 'alien elements' – Jews and other opponents of the Nazis.
1 May	Workers granted May Day holiday.
2 May	Trade unions banned; all workers to belong to new German Labour Front (DAF).
9 June	Employment Law: major programme of public works (e.g. road building) to create jobs.
14 July	Law against the Formation of New Parties: Germany became a one-party state.
20 July	Concordat (agreement) with the Roman Catholic Church: government protected religious freedom; Church banned from political activity. In return the Church kept control of Catholic schools.
1934	
January	All state governments taken over.
30 June	Night of the Long Knives.
August	On death of Hindenburg, Hitler became Führer. German armed forces swore oath of loyalty to him.

The Night of the Long Knives

Within a year, any opponents (or potential opponents) of the Nazis had either left Germany or been taken to hastily created CONCENTRATION CAMPS run by the SS. Other political parties were banned. Hitler was *still* not entirely secure, however. The leading officers in the army were particularly suspicious of Hitler's SA and its leader Ernst Röhm. They thought that the SA was a disreputable force and were unsettled by Röhm's talk of making the SA into a second German army. Hitler himself was also suspicious of Röhm – his control over the 4 million SA men made him a potentially dangerous rival.

Hitler acted ruthlessly to eliminate this threat. On the weekend of 29–30 June, squads of SS men broke into the homes of Röhm and other leading figures in the SA and arrested them. Hitler accused Röhm of plotting to overthrow and murder him. Röhm and possibly as many as 400 others were executed that same weekend. These included the former chancellor, von Schleicher, who had fiercely criticised Hitler, and others who actually had no connection with Röhm. This purge came to be known as the 'Night of the Long Knives'.

Hindenburg thanked Hitler for his 'determined action which has nipped treason in the bud'. The army said it was satisfied with the events of the weekend.

The SA was not disbanded. It remained as a Nazi PARAMILITARY organisation, but was very much subordinate to the SS. Many of its members were absorbed by the army and the SS.

Source 20 A Swiss cartoon commenting on the Night of the Long Knives. Röhm was the head of the SA and Heines was his deputy. The caption for the cartoon was: 'And the Führer said: Only death can drive us apart.' ▼

The army oath

Soon after the Night of the Long Knives, Hindenburg died and Hitler took over as supreme leader (Führer) of Germany. On 2 August 1934, the entire army swore an oath of personal loyalty to him. The army agreed to stay out of politics and to serve Hitler. In return, Hitler spent vast sums on rearmament, brought back conscription and made plans to restore Germany as a great military power.

How did Hitler consolidate his power in 1933–34?

Work in groups of three or four. Take one of the following topics each. Report back your answers to the others in your group then try to summarise in just a headline how each of these factors helped Hitler consolidate power:
● the Reichstag fire
● the Enabling Act
● the Night of the Long Knives.

1 Look at Source 20. What is the cartoonist saying about Hitler? Explain your answer.
2 When researching this period, it was difficult to find German cartoons about the Reichstag fire or the Night of the Long Knives because of the censorship at that time. Would Hitler have allowed Source 20 to be published in Germany? Explain your answer.

Who killed German democracy?

In 1925, Germany was an apparently thriving democracy. By 1933, democracy had been rejected by the majority and the country was a dictatorship. Why did democracy fail? The table below gives some possible explanations. Work in pairs or small groups. Study each explanation, then on a copy of the table, find supporting or challenging evidence and then give it a final mark.

Suspects	The charge: they killed democracy because ...	Evidence	Rating (most guilty = 1)
the German people	... deep down they did not want democracy		
the politicians of Weimar Germany	... they failed to work together and so led Germans to lose faith in democracy		
the elite (e.g. Hindenburg, von Papen, Germany's military commanders and industrialists)	... they always hated democracy and looked for ways to re-establish their old power and control		
the communists	... they wanted to overthrow democracy and they inadvertently helped the Nazis		
the Nazis	... they wanted to overthrow democracy and when their chance came they took it		
the Depression	... all the other suspects had a motive but it was the Depression that gave them the opportunity		

PRACTICE QUESTIONS

Describe

1 Describe one example of the effects of the Depression on Germany 1929–33. (2)

2 Describe one example of the campaign methods used by the Nazis in elections 1929–33. (2)

3 Describe one example of Hitler's actions in 1933–34. (2)

Explain

4 Explain why the Nazis were able to gain so much support in the period 1929–33. (10)

5 Explain how the Nazis consolidated their hold on power in the period 1933–34. (10)

How far do you agree?

6 'The Weimar Republic fell because Germans never really supported it.' How far do you agree with this view? (18)

7 'The Nazis were only able to take power because they were led by Hitler.' How far do you agree with this view? (18)

TOPIC SUMMARY

Democracy to dictatorship 1925–34

1 In 1925, Germany had recovered well from the First World War and the post-war economic crisis, although many Germans had not forgotten it and had a lingering fear that things could all go wrong again.

2 Gustav Stresemann steered Germany through the late 1920s. He rebuilt Germany's international reputation and its economy and industry thanks to loans from the USA. By 1929, the majority of Germans were doing well.

3 The worldwide economic depression that followed the Wall Street Crash in 1929 hit German people particularly hard because Germany was so dependent on US money.

4 As businesses went bankrupt, millions of workers were laid off. The experience was devastating to many ordinary Germans. They wanted their government to help improve their lives, but the Weimar politicians did not seem able to do anything. This was partly because of a built-in problem in the Weimar Constitution. It was *so* democratic that no one had enough power to act decisively.

5 With the Weimar politicians looking weak, many more Germans started to vote for extremist parties – left wing (communist) and right wing (Nazi). They thought that extreme problems needed extreme solutions.

6 The Nazi Party did particularly well out of this. It had been labouring away for 10 years without achieving much, but now the economic problems helped it gain members, win more votes in elections and secure more influence. The Nazis convinced German voters that they could reduce unemployment and make Germany great again through their strong and charismatic leader Adolf Hitler.

7 They were particularly effective communicators and campaigners. No other party could match Hitler's speeches and Joseph Goebbels' propaganda. They kept their promises vague and used slogans rather than policies, which played on people's fears. But they said what many ordinary Germans wanted to hear. They particularly appealed to the farmers and the middle classes.

8 Their military organisation, the SA, also impressed some people (but alarmed others) by keeping order at Nazi rallies and fighting street battles with communists.

9 The Nazis became the biggest party in the Reichstag in 1932 and then, thanks to some back-door dealing by other Weimar politicians, Hitler became chancellor in March 1933.

10 Within months the Nazis started to dismantle Weimar democracy and transform German society. They banned other parties and trade unions, and imprisoned and executed political opponents. Eighteen months later Hitler became president as well as chancellor, the army swore an oath of personal loyalty to him as Führer. Germany was now a dictatorship.

4.2

A national community?
Nazi Germany and its people 1933–39

FOCUS

Hitler and the other leading Nazis were driven by their ideology. Their aim was to create a new Germany based on this ideology, as well as a German empire. Opposition would not be tolerated. At the same time, however, they wanted Germans (or the 'right kind' of Germans) to feel that they were part of a National Community. They must be loyal to the Führer and the state, but in return they would be cared for and protected. In this topic, you will examine:

- Hitler's vision for Germany
- how the Nazis controlled Germany and dealt with opposition
- the concept of the National Community
- how far different groups in Germany (workers, women, young people) accepted and became a National Community
- the treatment of Jews and other minority groups.

All non-Aryan people (such as Jews) would have no place in Germany. They would be sent away or killed.

Aryan people would get the best jobs and be encouraged to have lots of children.

All Germans would put the needs of the state (the National Community) above everything else – even the needs of their family and friends.

National Community

The armed forces would be built up.

War would make Germany strong. The German people would be mentally prepared for war.

The Nazis would destroy the USSR and all those who believed in communism.

Hitler's vision for Germany

Most Germans voted for the Nazis because they thought they would bring economic recovery and strong, stable government. They probably did not take too much notice of the Nazis' other plans for Germany. The diagram here summarises the Nazis' vision, but remember that we have the benefit of hindsight. The Nazis kept many of their harsher plans vague and many Germans assumed it was mostly tough talk. If they had known what was going to happen over the next 12 years, it is likely that very few would have supported Hitler. Most Germans felt that Nazi control was a necessary evil. Some saw the Nazis as a force for good with some bad elements, which they were prepared to tolerate to help Germany recover.

ACTIVITY

In pairs or small groups, look at Hitler's plans and aims. Take each one in turn. Decide whether you think each aim would gain Hitler the support of most Germans or whether it would put them off. Remember, most Germans wanted:

- national pride
- economic recovery
- strong, stable government.

Keep a record of your decisions. After you have worked through the rest of this topic, see if you were right.

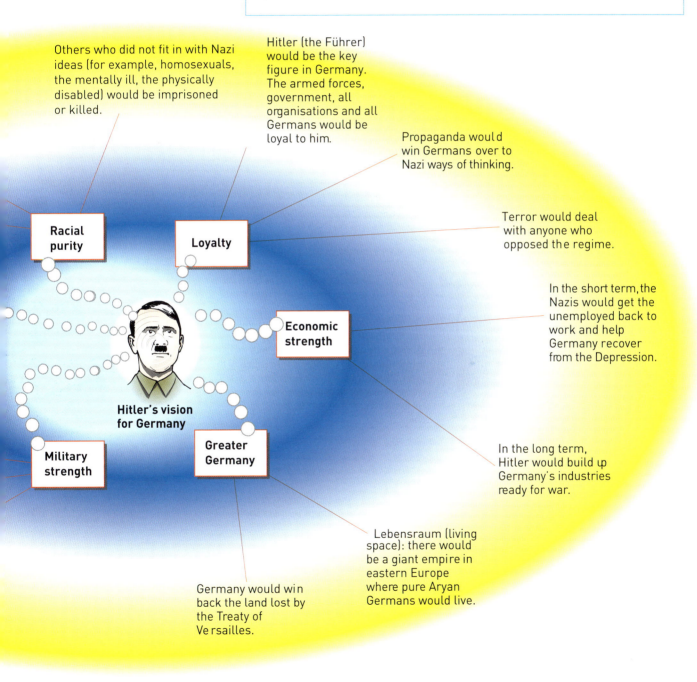

Others who did not fit in with Nazi ideas (for example, homosexuals, the mentally ill, the physically disabled) would be imprisoned or killed.

Hitler (the Führer) would be the key figure in Germany. The armed forces, government, all organisations and all Germans would be loyal to him.

Propaganda would win Germans over to Nazi ways of thinking.

Terror would deal with anyone who opposed the regime.

In the short term, the Nazis would get the unemployed back to work and help Germany recover from the Depression.

In the long term, Hitler would build up Germany's industries ready for war.

Lebensraum (living space): there would be a giant empire in eastern Europe where pure Aryan Germans would live.

Germany would win back the land lost by the Treaty of Versailles.

Racial purity

Loyalty

Economic strength

Greater Germany

Military strength

Hitler's vision for Germany

Crushing opposition: the Nazi police state

The Nazis wanted to create a TOTALITARIAN state. In a totalitarian state there can be no rival parties – no political debate. Ordinary citizens must divert all their energy into serving the state and doing what its leader wants. The Nazis had a range of powerful organisations and methods designed to control the German people.

These pages give the impression that Nazi Germany was run like a well-oiled machine – everyone there to do what the Führer demanded! Modern research suggests otherwise. It was chaotic and disorganised in many ways. Officials competed with each other to get Hitler's approval for particular policies. The result was often a jumble of different government departments competing with each other and getting in each other's way.

FACTFILE

A map showing the locations of SS bases and camps 1933–37.

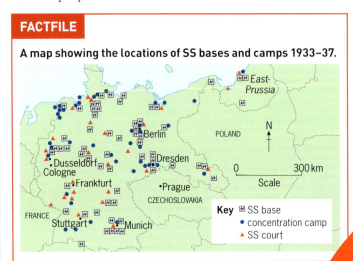

The SS

- The SS was formed in 1925 from fanatics loyal to Hitler.
- After virtually destroying the SA in 1934, the SS grew into a huge organisation with many different responsibilities (see Factfile). The SS was 240,000 strong by 1939 and 1 million by 1944. It was led by Heinrich Himmler.
- SS men were, of course, Aryans – very highly trained and totally loyal to Hitler. Under Himmler, the SS had primary responsibility for destroying opposition to Nazism and carrying out the Nazis' racial policies.

Source 1 SS guards after taking over the Berlin broadcasting station in 1933. ▲

- There were three particularly important sub-divisions. The SD was the SS's own internal security service. The Death's Head units were responsible for the concentration camps and the transportation and eventual murder of the Jews. The Waffen-SS were special SS armoured regiments that fought alongside the regular army.
- As its power grew, the SS set up its own courts and the SD carried out many activities similar to those of the Gestapo. Around 200,000 Germans were sent to concentration camps by these courts.

Source 2 The Gestapo, the German secret state police, in action. ▲

The Gestapo

- The Gestapo was the secret state police, under the command of Reinhard Heydrich.
- Gestapo agents had sweeping powers. They could arrest citizens and send them to concentration camps without trial or even explanation.
- They were reputed to have a network of 'informers' listening in on people's conversations.
- The Gestapo was perhaps the organisation that was most feared by ordinary citizens. However, recent research has shown that Germans believed the Gestapo was much more powerful than it actually was. As a result, many ordinary Germans informed on each other because they thought the Gestapo would find out anyway.

Source 5 Historian Frank McDonough, writing in 2015.

Nazi propaganda liked to give the impression that Gestapo officers were everywhere. Nothing could be further from the truth. In reality, the Gestapo was a very small organisation. In 1933, it had just 1,000 employees, rising to 6,500 in 1937 and 15,000 in 1939. A peak of 32,000 employees, including a team of administrators, was reached at the end of 1944. Gestapo offices in the localities were severely under-staffed. In Düsseldorf, with a population of 500,000, there were 126 Gestapo officers in 1937. Essen, with a population of 650,000, had 43. Duisburg, with 400,000 inhabitants, had 28. In 1942, Cologne with 750,000 inhabitants had a mere 69 officers. In small rural towns there was usually no Gestapo personnel at all. The number of active full-time Gestapo officers in Hitler's Germany never exceeded 16,000.

The police and the courts

- *Top jobs in local police forces were given to high-ranking Nazis reporting to Himmler. As a result, the police added political 'snooping' to their normal law-and-order role. They were, of course, under strict instructions to ignore crimes committed by Nazi agents.*

- *Similarly, the Nazis controlled magistrates, judges and the courts. They appointed all the judges and sacked those they disapproved of. This soon created a form of self-imposed control – magistrates knew what they were expected to do and did it. They knew they would not last long if they did not. This meant that opponents of Nazism rarely received a fair trial.*

Source 3 German judges swearing their loyalty to the Nazi regime at the criminal courts in Berlin. ▲

Concentration camps

- *Concentration camps were the Nazis' ultimate sanction against their own people. They were set up almost as soon as Hitler took power.*

- *The first concentration camps in 1933 were makeshift prisons in disused factories and warehouses. Soon, however, purpose-built camps were constructed, usually in isolated rural areas (see Factfile). These were run by SS Death's Head units. Prisoners were forced to do hard labour.*

- *Food was limited and prisoners suffered harsh discipline, beatings and random executions.*

Source 4 Political prisoners at the Oranienburg concentration camp near Berlin. ▲

- *Jews, socialists, communists, trade unionists, churchmen and anyone else brave enough to criticise the Nazis ended up in these camps. Historians estimate that around 1.3 million Germans spent at least some time in concentration camps between 1933 and 1939.*

- *By the late 1930s, deaths in the camps were increasingly common and very few people came out alive. However, these were not the same 'death camps' that the Nazis created during the Second World War. Concentration camps were generally smaller and their main aim was to 'correct' opponents of the regime or others who simply did not 'fit in'. Treatment there was harsh and violent, and there were many deaths, but they were not built with the purpose of killing people the way some of the later camps were.*

Source 6 Joseph Goebbels at his first press conference on becoming minister for propaganda, March 1933.

The Nazis gained 52 per cent of the vote in the March 1933 elections. This government will not be content with 52 per cent behind it and with terrorising the remaining 48 per cent, but will see its most immediate task as winning over that remaining 48 per cent. … It is not enough for people to be more or less reconciled to the regime.

1   Look at Source 8. How does the rally:
   a   make it clear who the leader is
   b   give people a sense of belonging
   c   provide colour and excitement
   d   show the power of the state
   e   show the Nazis' ability to create order out of chaos
   f   discourage opposition?

Propaganda, culture and mass media in Nazi Germany

No matter how powerful, a state could not control millions of people through fear alone. Hitler believed passionately in the importance of propaganda. Propaganda could impress or inspire. It could intimidate and discourage opposition from anyone it did not win over.

In Dr Joseph Goebbels, the minister for 'enlightenment and propaganda', the Nazis had a propaganda genius. Goebbels believed that Hitler was the saviour of Germany and his mission was to make others believe this too. Throughout the 12 years of Nazi rule, Goebbels kept his finger on the pulse of public opinion and decided what the Germans should and should not hear. He used every resource available to him to make people loyal to Hitler and the Nazis. Propaganda made it clear to people what the regime expected them to think. Even if they did not agree with this message, people were wary of contradicting it. They got into a habit of saying nothing rather than criticising.

Source 7 An extract from a secret report on attitudes in Nazi Germany, June 1937. It was written by socialists inside Germany and sent to socialist leaders who were in exile outside Germany.

The number of those who consciously criticise the regime is very small, quite apart from the fact that they have no way to express this criticism. The regime controls all of the press and radio stations. Propaganda is everywhere. It does not stop people feeling discontent but propaganda tells them that to complain is to threaten the Third Reich – a prospect which would leave them horrified. They have seen what happens to the Jews and do not wish to share their fate. It becomes increasingly evident that the majority of the people have two faces; one which they show to their family and friends and people they see as reliable. The other face is for the authorities. The private face shows the sharpest criticism of everything that is going on now; the official face beams with optimism and contentment.

The Nuremberg rallies

Goebbels organised huge rallies, marches, torch-lit processions and meetings. The most famous example is the Nuremberg rally, which took place every summer. There were bands, marches, flying displays and Hitler's brilliant speeches. The rallies brought some colour and excitement into people's lives and gave them a sense of belonging to a great movement. The rallies also showed the German people the power of the state and convinced them that others also fully supported the Nazis. Goebbels recognised that one of the Nazis' main attractions was that they were bringing order to Germany after a difficult and chaotic period, so the whole rally was organised to emphasise order.

Source 8 The annual rally at Nuremberg. The whole town was taken over and the rally dominated radio broadcasts and newsreels. ▼

A Hitler speaks to the assembled Germans.

B A parade through the streets.

C German youth marching with spades. These young men were ideal Aryans.

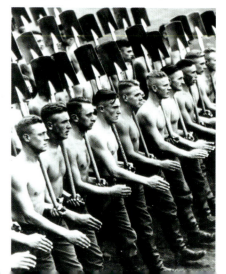

The media and culture

Less spectacular than the rallies but possibly more important was Goebbels' control of the media. In contrast with the free expression of Weimar Germany, the Nazis strictly controlled the media and all aspects of culture.

Throughout this period, the SS and the Gestapo supported Goebbels in his work. When he wanted to close down an anti-Nazi newspaper, silence an anti-Nazi writer or catch someone listening to a foreign radio station, he sent the SS and Gestapo.

Radio: *Goebbels loved new technology and quickly saw the potential of radio broadcasting for spreading the Nazi message. He made cheap radios available so all Germans could buy one and he controlled all the radio stations. Listening to broadcasts from the BBC was an offence punishable by death.*
For people without a radio, Goebbels placed loudspeakers in the streets and public bars. Hitler's speeches and those of other Nazi leaders were repeated on the radio over and over again until the ideas expressed in them – such as German expansion into eastern Europe and the inferiority of the Jews – came to be believed by the German people.

Films: *At this time, going to the cinema was one of the most popular leisure activities. People might go several times each week. Goebbels ordered that all films – factual or fictional, thrillers or comedies – had to carry a pro-Nazi message. The newsreels that preceded feature films were full of the greatness of Hitler and the achievements of Nazi Germany. There is evidence that Germans avoided these productions by arriving late! Goebbels censored all foreign films coming into Germany.*

Books: *No books could be published without Goebbels' permission (not surprisingly, the bestseller in Nazi Germany was Mein Kampf). In 1933, he organised a high-profile book-burning. Students came together publicly to burn any books that included ideas unacceptable to the Nazis.*

How did Goebbels control media and culture?

Posters: *If people missed the radio broadcasts, they would see the posters. Goebbels plastered Germany with posters proclaiming the successes of Hitler and the Nazis, and attacking their opponents.*

Newspapers: *Goebbels also controlled 'the news'. Newspapers were not allowed to print anti-Nazi ideas. Within months of the Nazi takeover, Jewish editors and journalists found themselves out of work and anti-Nazi newspapers were closed down. Newspapers became very dull reading and Germans bought fewer of them as a result – circulation fell by about 10 per cent.*

Art: *Artists suffered similar restrictions to writers. Only Nazi-approved painters could show their works. These were usually paintings or sculptures of heroic-looking Aryans, military figures or images of the ideal Aryan family.*

Music: *Goebbels banned jazz music, which had been popular in Germany and elsewhere around Europe at the time. He claimed that it was 'Black' music and Black people were considered an inferior race.*

Source 10 Albert Speer, a leading Nazi, speaking at the Nuremberg war trials after the Second World War. Speet always maintained he was a technical expert rather than a true Nazi.

Through technical devices like the radio and loud-speaker, eighty million people were deprived of independent thought. It was thereby possible to subject them to the will of one man. …

The nightmare of many a man that one day nations could be ruled by technical means was realised in Hitler's totalitarian system.

1 What does Source 10 tell you about the effectiveness of Nazi propaganda?
2 Is Source 9 or Source 10 more useful about Nazi propaganda? Explain your answer.
3 In what ways was the Berlin Olympics a propaganda success for Goebbels?
4 In what ways was it a failure?
5 Why do you think Nazi propaganda was more successful within Germany than outside it?

Case study: the 1936 Olympics

One of Goebbels' greatest challenges came with the 1936 Olympic Games in Berlin. Other Nazis were opposed to holding the Games in Berlin, but Goebbels convinced Hitler that this was a great propaganda opportunity, both within Germany and internationally.

Goebbels and Hitler also thought that the Olympics could be a showcase for their DOCTRINE that the Aryan race was superior to all others. However, there was international pressure for nations such as the USA to boycott the Games in protest at the Nazis' repressive regime and anti-Jewish policies. In response, the Nazis included one Jew in their team!

Goebbels built a brand-new stadium to hold 100,000 people. It was lit by modern electric lighting. He brought in television cameras for the first time. The most sophisticated German photo-electronic timing device was installed, as well as the largest stop clock ever built. With guests and competitors from 49 countries coming into the heart of Nazi Germany, it was going to take all Goebbels' talents to show that Germany was a modern, civilised and successful nation. No expense was spared. When the Games opened, visitors were amazed at the scale of the stadium, the wonderful facilities and the efficiency of the organisation. However, they were also struck – and in some cases appalled – by the almost fanatical devotion of the people to Hitler and by the clear presence of army and SS soldiers who were patrolling or standing guard everywhere.

Source 11 The Olympic Stadium built for the 1936 Olympics in Berlin. ▼

To the delight of Hitler and Goebbels, Germany came top of the medal table, way ahead of all other countries. However, to their great dismay, a Black athlete, Jesse Owens, became the star of the Games. He won four gold medals and broke two world records in the process. The ten black members of the American team won 13 medals between them. This defied everything the Nazis were teaching about Aryan superiority. To the majority of German people, who had grown used to the Nazi propaganda machine, the Games appeared to present all the qualities they valued in the Nazis – a grand vision, efficiency, power, strength and achievement. However, such blatant propaganda was clear to foreign visitors and it backfired on the Nazi regime.

Source 12 A Nazi poster from the 1930s. The text at the top says: 'The NSDAP [Nazis] takes care of the National Community'. The text at the bottom says: 'The people's needs can be taken care of by your local community group.' ▼

Nazi plans for the 'National Community'

One of the Nazis' key aims was the creation of a National Community (*Volksgemeinschaft*) of Aryan Germans, loyal to the Führer and the state. Under Nazi rule, workers, farmers and so on, would no longer see themselves primarily as workers or farmers but as Germans. Their loyalty would not be to their own social group but to Germany and the Führer. They would be so proud to belong to a great nation that was racially and culturally superior to all others that they would put the interests of Germany before their own.

Hitler's policies towards each group were designed to help win this kind of loyalty. Source 12 is a good example of the vision that was presented to German people. The ideal Aryan family is being protected under the sheltering wing of the Nazi eagle; Germans are being told that the Nazis take care of the National Community.

In this chapter so far you have read two extracts from the diaries of Victor Klemperer. Klemperer was a Jewish university lecturer. By 1937, he was clearly a frightened, disillusioned and very unhappy man. Source 13 suggests that Germans bought in to this idea and were willing members of the National Community, but can we accept what he says in Source 13 – that Hitler really did represent the 'soul of the German people'?

This is a complicated question with a lot of overlapping issues. For example, when we look at the relationship between the Nazis and women, we must remember that women were not just women – they were also workers, members of farming communities and young people as well. It is the same with Jews and other minorities. Even so, we are going to try to answer the question by dividing German society into groups and examining their relationship with the Nazis in the period 1933–39 (we will look at the effects of the war later, in Topic 4.3).

Source 13 An extract from the diary of Victor Klemperer, September 1937.

On the festival of Yom Kippur the Jews did not attend class. Kufahl, the mathematician, had said to the reduced class: 'Today it's just us.' In my memory these words took on a quite horrible significance: to me it confirms the claim of the Nazis to express the true opinion of the German people. And I believe ever more strongly that Hitler really does embody the soul of the German people, that he really stands for Germany and that he will consequently keep his position. I have not only lost my Fatherland. Even if the government should change one day, my sense of belonging to Germany has gone.

FOCUS TASK

Investigating propaganda

1   You have come across many examples of Nazi propaganda on these pages. Choose three (or more) examples that you think are most useful for explaining:
    a   the aims of propaganda
    b   the propaganda methods used
    c   the impact of Nazi propaganda.
    Write three paragraphs to explain your answer.

Which was more important – propaganda or terror?

2   In groups, discuss which of the following statements you most agree with.
    a   Goebbels' work was more important to Nazi success than that of Himmler (head of the SS).
    b   Himmler's work was more important to Nazi success than Goebbels'.
    c   The techniques of repression and propaganda go hand in hand – neither would work without the other.

The Nazis and young people

It was Hitler's aim to control every aspect of life in Germany, including children (see Sources 14 and 15).

Source 14 Dr Robert Ley, who was chief of the Labour Front, and in charge of making 'good citizens' out of the German people.

Our state is an educational state. … It does not let a man go free from the cradle to the grave. We begin with the child when he is three years old. As soon as he begins to think, he is made to carry a little flag. Then follows school, the Hitler Youth, the storm troopers and military training. We don't let him go; and when all that is done, comes the Labour Front, which takes possession of him again, and does not let him go till he dies, even if he does not like it.

◄ **Source 15** An illustration from a Nazi children's book. The children are being taught to distrust Jews.

At school

There is some evidence that the Nazis succeeded. If you had been a 16-year-old Aryan living in Nazi Germany you would probably have been a strong supporter of Adolf Hitler. The Nazis reorganised every aspect of the school curriculum to make children loyal to them. At school you would have learned about the history of Germany. You would have been outraged to find out how the German army was 'stabbed in the back' by the weak politicians who had made peace. You might well remember the hardships of the 1920s yourself, but at school you would have been told how these were caused by Jews squeezing profits out of honest Germans. By the time you were a senior pupil, your studies in history would have made you confident that loyalty to the Führer was right and good.

Your biology lessons would have informed you that you were special, as one of the Aryan race that was so superior in intelligence and strength to the *Untermenschen*, or sub-human Jews and Slavs of eastern Europe. In maths you might have been set questions like the one in Source 17.

Source 16 A German teacher, writing in 1938.

Children have been deliberately taken away from parents who refused to acknowledge their belief in National Socialism. … The refusal of parents to allow their young children to join the youth organisation is regarded as an adequate reason for taking the children away.

Source 17 A question from a Nazi maths textbook, 1933.

The Jews are aliens in Germany. In 1933 there were 66,060,000 inhabitants of the German Reich of whom 499,862 were Jews. What is the percentage of aliens in Germany?

Source 18 A German newspaper commenting on the school curriculum in 1939.

All subjects – German language, History, Geography, Chemistry and Mathematics – must concentrate on military subjects, the glorification of military service and of German heroes and leaders and the strength of a rebuilt Germany. Chemistry will develop a knowledge of chemical warfare, explosives, etc., while Mathematics will help the young to understand artillery, calculations, ballistics.

Source 19 Daily timetable for a girls' school in Nazi Germany.

8.00 German (*every day*)

8.50 Geography, History or Singing (*alternate days*)

9.40 Race Studies and Ideology (*every day*)

10.25 Recess, Sports and Special Announcements (*every day*)

11.00 Domestic Science or Maths (*alternate days*)

12.10 Eugenics or Health Biology (*alternate days*)

1.00–6.00 Sport

Evenings Sex Education, Ideology or Domestic Science (*one evening each*)

1 Read Source 14. Do you think that the speaker is proud of what he is saying?

2 What do you think is the purpose of Source 17? Do you think it is to improve mathematical skills or something else?

3 Read Source 19. Eugenics is the study of how to produce perfect offspring by choosing parents with ideal qualities. How would this help the Nazis?

Source 20 Henrik Metelmann, describing what it was like being a member of the Hitler Youth in the 1930s.

It was a great feeling. You felt you belonged to a great nation again. Germany was in safe hands and I was going to help to build a strong Germany. But my father of course felt differently about it. [He warned] 'Now Henrik, don't say to them what I am saying to you.' I always argued with my father as I was very much in favour of the Hitler regime which was against his background as a working man.

Source 21 A young German describing his feelings after a Hitler Youth rally.

Hitler looked over the stand, and I know he looked into my eyes, and he said: 'You my boys are the standard bearers, you will inherit what we have created.' From that moment there was not any doubt I was bound to Adolf Hitler until long after our defeat. Afterwards I told my friends how Hitler had looked into my eyes, but they all said: 'No! It was my eyes he was looking into.'

In the Hitler Youth

As a member of the Hitler Youth or the League of German Maidens, you would have marched in exciting parades with loud bands. You would probably be physically fit. Your leisure time would also be devoted to Hitler and the Nazis. You would be a strong cross-country runner and confident at reading maps. After years of summer camps, you would be comfortable camping out of doors and if you were a boy you would know how to clean a rifle and keep it in good condition.

Source 22 Members of the Hitler Youth in the 1930s. From a very early age children were encouraged to join the Nazi youth organisations. It was not compulsory, but most young people did join. ▲

4   Make a list of the main differences between your life and the life of a 16-year-old in Nazi Germany.
5   Totalitarian regimes through history have used children as a way of influencing parents. Why do you think they do this?
6   Study Sources 14–22. Choose one or two sources that you think provide useful evidence about:
   a   the aims of Nazi youth policies
   b   the methods used
   c   the impact of these methods.

At home

As a child in Nazi Germany, you might have felt slightly alienated from your parents because they were not as keen on the Nazis as you. They would expect your first loyalty to be to your family, whereas your Hitler Youth leader would have made it clear that your first loyalty was to Adolf Hitler. You might have found it hard to understand why your father grumbled about Nazi regulation of his working practices – you would have been taught that the Führer was only protecting him. Your parents would have found the idea of Nazi inspectors checking up on teachers strange. For you it was normal.

You can read what happened to young people in wartime on page 174.

Did all young people support the Nazis?

So far we have been describing these developments from the perspective of a loyal young Nazi. Henrik Metelmann (Source 20) was like this. He adored the Hitler Youth. But is this the whole picture? Probably not. It is possible that some of his friends joined the Hitler Youth just for the football and the holidays! There are many accounts from members of the Hitler Youth and BDM that suggest this is the case. These people talk about what fun they had. They also say that when the lectures about Nazi ideas began, they mentally switched off (see Source 23).

Remember that there were really no alternatives to the Hitler Youth. All other youth organisations had been absorbed or made illegal. Even so, only half of all German boys were members in 1933 and only 15 per cent of girls. It was not until 1939 that the Nazis made membership of the Hitler Youth compulsory.

Young people showed their resentment of Nazi control in different ways:

- **The Swing Movement:** Swing groups were anti-everything in a way. While some were also in the Hitler Youth, the Swing Movement resented the way the Nazis controlled people's lives. They showed their discontent through their interest in banned music, particularly American jazz and swing. They hung out in nightclubs and bars, and danced American dances. The Nazis acted against them by closing the bars they went to. Some Swing Movement members were arrested.
- **The Edelweiss Pirates:** This was a name given to many small groups of young people from many different parts of Germany. They wore the edelweiss flower (and other emblems) as a symbol of their resistance to the Nazis. The earliest groups appeared in 1934. By 1939, there were an estimated 2,000 Edelweiss Pirate groups. Some Pirate groups were like the Swing groups. They just opposed Nazi control of their lives. Others, like the group in Cologne, opposed Nazi political ideas. They made fun of Hitler Youth groups or even violently attacked them.

Source 23 A former member of the Hitler Youth, looking back after the war.

We didn't know much about Nazi ideals. Nevertheless, we were politically programmed: to obey orders, to cultivate the soldierly virtue of standing to attention and saying 'Yes, Sir' and to stop thinking when the word Fatherland was uttered and Germany's honour and greatness were mentioned.

FOCUS TASK

How did young people react to the Nazi regime?

Copy the table below and use the information and the sources on pages 156–58 to complete it.

Aims	Methods used to achieve these aims	Evidence that Nazi methods succeeded	Evidence that Nazi methods failed or were not completely successful

The Nazis and women

The Nazi Party was a male-dominated organisation and Hitler had a very traditional view of the role of the German woman (see Source 24). However, it is worth remembering that many women agreed with him. In rural areas and small towns, many women felt that their proper role was supporting their husband. Even in less traditional areas there was resentment towards working women in the early 1930s – it was felt they were keeping men out of jobs at a time of high unemployment. Hitler was also alarmed at the falling birth rate in Germany. All this created a lot of pressure on women to conform to what the Nazis called 'the traditional balance' between men and women. 'No true German woman wears trousers' said a Nazi newspaper headline when the film star Marlene Dietrich appeared in public wearing trousers.

Source 24 A painting showing the Nazis' view of an ideal German family. ▶

1 What does Source 24 tell historians about Nazi views on women and the family?

Persuasion

The Nazis could not terrorise women into being wives and mothers, but they could persuade them in different ways:

- Hitler offered financial incentives for married couples to have at least four children. They were awarded a 'Gold Cross' for having eight children and were given a privileged seat at Nazi meetings.
- Posters, radio broadcasts and newsreels all celebrated the ideals of motherhood and homebuilding.
- The German Maidens' League reinforced these ideas, focusing on a combination of good physical health and housekeeping skills. This was reinforced at school (see Source 19 on page 156).

With all these encouragements, the birth rate increased from 15 per 1,000 in 1933 to 20 per 1,000 in 1939. There was also an increase in pregnancies outside marriage. These women were looked after in state maternity hostels.

Source 25 A German woman and her Jewish boyfriend being publicly humiliated by the SA in 1933. The notices say: (woman) 'I'm the biggest pig in town and only get involved with Jews'; (man) 'As a Jewish boy I always take only German girls up to my room.' ▲

1 Why might the Nazis have allowed Source 25 to be published? Explain your answer.

FOCUS TASK

How successful were the Nazi policies for women? Look at these statements:
- Nazi policy for women was a failure.
- Nazi policy for women was confused.

Explain whether you agree or disagree with each statement. Use examples from the text and sources to support your explanation.

Limitations

There were some prominent women in Nazi Germany. Leni Riefenstahl was a high-profile film producer. Gertrude Scholz-Klink was head of the Nazi Women's Bureau, although she was excluded from any important discussions (such as the one to conscript female labour in 1942). Many working-class girls and women gained the chance to travel and meet new people through the Nazi women's organisation.

Overall, however, opportunities for women were limited. Married professional women were forced to give up their jobs and stay at home with their families. Discrimination against women applicants for jobs was encouraged. Many of them resented this restriction on their freedom.

U-turn

In the late 1930s, the Nazis seemed to change their minds about women, as they suddenly needed more female workers because there were no more unemployed men. This dilemma became even more marked once the war began. This sent a confusing message – did the Nazis want women to work or to be mothers?

Source 26 A US journalist, writing in 1937.

According to the statistics of the German Department of Labour, there were, in June 1936, 5,470,000 employed women, or 1,200,000 more than in January 1933. ... The vigorous campaign against the employment of women has not led to their increased domesticity and security. It has simply driven them into poorer jobs. Needless to say, this type of labour, with its miserable wages and long hours, is extremely dangerous to the health of women and degrades the family.

Source 27 British historian Tim Mason, writing in 1995.

It seems that the anti-feminist policies of the regime after 1933 were at least partially successful, in that they secured the approval, perhaps gratitude, of many German people, men and women alike. There is scarcely any evidence that the policies adopted on the family and on women's work were unpopular.

Source 28 German historian Ute Frevert, writing in 1988.

Even if most of the twelve million women in the numerous Nazi organisations of 1939 were not themselves ardent National Socialists, twelve years of being educated and bombarded with propaganda by the Volksgemeinschaft cannot have left individual consciousness and collective memory unmarked. In addition the impact of welfare measures reinforced popular loyalty. In a few areas, such as voting rights, access to the upper levels of the civil service, and family planning, the Nazis took women backwards. By contrast, in some areas the Nazis offered women novel opportunities for participation and recognition in public life. The evidence suggests that women who satisfied the political, racial and social requirements (the vast majority) did not perceive the Third Reich as a women's hell. Much of what it introduced was doubtless appealing, the rest one learned to accept.

The Nazis and workers, farmers and businesses

Hitler and the Nazis came to power because they promised to use radical methods to solve the country's two main problems – unemployment and a crisis in German farming. This was why the unemployed, farmers and businesses had voted for them. In return for work and other benefits, the majority of the German people gave up their political freedom. Was it worth it?

Economic recovery and rearmament

At first, many Germans felt it was, particularly the 5 million who were unemployed in 1933. Hitler was fortunate that by 1933 the worst of the Depression was over. Even so, there is no doubt that the Nazis acted with energy and commitment to solve some of the main problems. The brilliant economist **Dr Hjalmar Schacht** organised Germany's finances to fund a huge programme of work creation. The National Labour Service sent men on **public works projects** and conservation programmes, in particular to build a network of motorways, or **autobahnen**. Railways were extended or built from scratch. There were major house-building programmes and grand new public building projects such as the Reich Chancellery in Berlin.

Other measures brought increasing prosperity. One of Hitler's most cherished plans was **rearmament**. In 1935, he reintroduced **conscription** for the German army. In 1936, he announced a **Four-Year Plan**, under Goering's control, to get the German economy ready for war (this was one of the very few clear policy documents that Hitler ever wrote).

Conscription reduced unemployment. The need for weapons, equipment and uniforms created jobs in the coal mines, steel and textile mills. Engineers and designers gained new opportunities, particularly when Hitler decreed that Germany would have a world-class air force (the Luftwaffe). As well as bringing economic recovery, these measures boosted Hitler's popularity because they boosted **national pride**. Germans began to feel that their country was finally emerging from the humiliation of the First World War and the Treaty of Versailles, and putting itself on an equal footing with the other great powers.

Source 29 Previously unemployed men assemble for the building of the first autobahn, September 1933. ▼

ACTIVITY

As you read through pages 161–63, you will come across a number of individuals, organisations and terms in bold type in the text. Draw up a table containing definitions of the words, or explanations of their importance to the Nazis' economic policies. The completed table will help you with your revision. You could add more terms of your own.

Key word/ term/person	Definition/ explanation

Source 30 An extract from the memoirs of Henrik Metelmann, 1970. Metelmann came from a working-class family in Hamburg but was an enthusiastic member of the Hitler Youth and served in the German army in the Second World War.

Early one morning, a neighbour of ours, a trade-union secretary, was taken away in a car by the SS and police. His wife had great difficulty finding out what had happened to him. My mother was too scared to be seen talking to her and Father became very quiet and alarmed and begged me not to repeat what he had said within our four walls about the whole Nazi set-up. … I loved it when we went on our frequent marches, feeling important when the police had to stop the traffic to give us right of way and passing pedestrians had to raise their arm in the Nazi salute. Whenever we were led out on a march, it was always into the working-class quarters. We were told that this was to remind the workers, but I sometimes wondered what we wanted to remind them of, after all most of our fathers were workers.

The Nazis and the workers

Hitler promised (and delivered) lower unemployment, which ensured popularity among **industrial workers**. They were important to the Nazis: Hitler needed good workers to create the industries that would help make Germany great and establish a new German empire in eastern Europe. He won the loyalty of industrial workers through a variety of initiatives:

- Propaganda praised the workers and tried to associate them with Hitler.
- Schemes such as **Strength Through Joy (KDF)** gave them cheap theatre and cinema tickets, organised courses, trips and sports events, and even cut-price cruises on luxury liners. By 1939, over 2 million Germans had been on one of KDF's holidays.
- Many thousands of workers saved five marks a week in the state scheme to buy the **Volkswagen Beetle**, the 'people's car'. It was designed by Ferdinand Porsche and became a symbol of the prosperous new Germany, even though no workers ever received a car because all car production was halted by the war in 1939.
- Another important scheme was the **Beauty of Labour** movement. This improved working conditions in factories. It introduced features never seen in many workplaces before, such as washing facilities and low-cost canteens.

What was the price of these advances? Workers lost their main political party, the SDP. They lost their trade unions and for many workers this remained a source of bitter resentment. All workers had to join the **DAF (General Labour Front)** run by **Dr Robert Ley**. This organisation kept strict control of workers. They could not strike for better pay and conditions. In some areas, they were prevented from moving to better-paid jobs. Wages remained comparatively low, although prices were also strictly controlled. Even so, by the late 1930s, many workers were grumbling that their standard of living was still lower than it had been before the Depression (see Figure 31).

Figure 31 Annual food consumption in working-class families, 1927–37 (% change). ▼

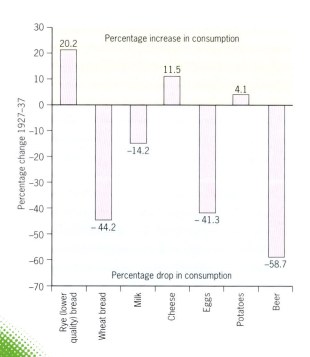

Figure 32 Unemployment and government expenditure in Germany, 1932–38. Economic recovery was almost entirely funded by the state rather than from Germans investing their own savings. Despite this, unemployment fell steadily and Germany was actually running short of workers by 1939. ▼

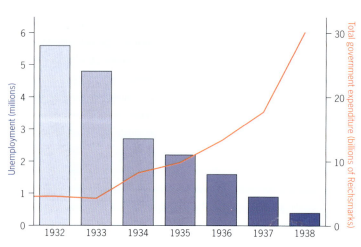

The Nazis and farming communities

The **farmers** had been an important factor in the Nazis' rise to power. Hitler did not forget this and introduced a series of measures to help them. In September 1933, he introduced the **Reich Food Estate** under **Richard Darre**. This set up central boards to buy produce from the farmers and distribute it across Germany. It gave the peasant farmers a guaranteed market for their goods at guaranteed prices. The second main measure was the **Reich Entailed Farm Law**. This gave peasants state protection for their farms: banks could not seize their land if people could not pay back their loans or mortgages.

The Reich Entailed Farm Law also had a racial aim. Part of the Nazi philosophy was '**Blood and Soil**' – the belief that the peasant farmers were the basis of Germany's master race. They would be the backbone of the new German empire in the east. As a result, their way of life had to be protected. As Source 33 shows, the measures were widely appreciated.

However, rather like the industrial workers, some peasants were not thrilled with the regime's measures. The Reich Food Estate meant that efficient farmers were held back by having to work through the same processes as less-efficient farmers. Because of the Reich Entailed Farm Law, banks were unwilling to lend money to farmers. It also meant that only the eldest child inherited the farm. As a result, many children of farmers left the land to work for better pay in Germany's industries. **Rural depopulation** was about 3 per cent per year in the 1930s – the exact opposite of the Nazis' aims.

> **Source 33** Lusse Essig's memories of the 1930s. Lusse was a farm worker who later worked for the Agriculture Ministry.
>
> *Thousands of people came from all over Germany to the Harvest Festival celebrations. ... We all felt the same happiness and joy. Harvest festival was the thank you for us farmers having a future again. I believe no statesman has ever been as well loved as Adolf Hitler was at that time.*

Big business and the middle classes

The record of the Nazis with the **middle classes** was also mixed. Certainly many middle-class business people were grateful to the Nazis for eliminating the communist threat to their businesses and properties. For the owners of small businesses it was a mixed picture. If you owned a small engineering firm, you were likely to do well from government orders, as rearmament spending grew in the 1930s. However, if you produced goods that might be considered luxuries (or non-essential), or you ran a small shop, you might struggle. Despite Hitler's promises, the large department stores that were taking business away from local shops were not closed.

It was **big business** that really benefited from Nazi rule. The big companies no longer had to worry about troublesome trade unions and strikes. Companies such as the chemicals giant IG Farben gained huge government contracts to make explosives, fertilisers and even artificial oil from coal. Other household names today, such as Mercedes and Volkswagen, prospered from Nazi policies. As these companies flourished, so did their managers. Their incomes rose much faster than those of their workers. There were very few recruits from the working class into management. Over 80 per cent of top management were university-educated middle-class men. As far as we know, most were perfectly content with the new regime.

> **Source 34** Average yearly wages in Germany in the 1930s.
>
> *Doctor: 12,500 marks*
> *Lawyer: 10,850 marks*
> *Office worker: 2,727 marks*
> *Industrial worker: 1,375 marks*

The Nazis and those who 'did not belong' in their National Community

The persecution of minorities

The Nazis believed in the superiority of the Aryan race. They persecuted members of other races and many minority groups, including Jehovah's Witnesses, Gypsies, homosexuals and mentally handicapped people. They persecuted any group that they thought challenged Nazi ideas. Homosexuals were a threat to family life; the intellectually disabled were a threat to Nazi ideas about Germans being a perfect master race; Gypsies were thought to be an inferior people. The persecution of such minorities varied. In families where there were hereditary illnesses, STERILISATION was enforced. Over 300,000 men and women were sterilised between 1934 and 1945. A so-called EUTHANASIA programme was begun in 1939. At least 5,000 severely intellectually disabled babies and children were killed between 1939 and 1945, either by injection or by starvation. Between 1939 and 1941, 72,000 mentally ill patients were gassed before a public outcry in Germany itself ended the extermination.

The extermination of the Gypsies, on the other hand, did not cause an outcry. Five out of six Gypsies living in Germany in 1939 were killed by the Nazis. Similarly, there was little or no complaint about the treatment of so-called 'asocials' – homosexuals, alcoholics, the homeless, prostitutes, habitual criminals and beggars – who were rounded up off the streets and sent to concentration camps. On these pages you are going to investigate this most disturbing aspect of Nazi Germany by tracing the story of Nazi treatment of the Jewish population. You will see how anti-Semitism turned to persecution in the 1930s and escalated into the slaughter of the Final Solution during the Second World War.

Hitler and the Jews

Anti-Semitism means hatred of Jews as a race. Throughout Europe, Jews had experienced discrimination for hundreds of years. They were often treated unjustly in courts or forced to live in GHETTOS. In the past, religion had usually been the reason for this persecution – Jews were blamed for the death of Jesus Christ. Another reason was jealousy. Jews tended to be well educated and therefore held well-paid jobs or ran successful shops and businesses.

Hitler hated Jews. In his years of poverty in Vienna, before he joined the army, he had become obsessed by the fact that Jews ran many of the most successful businesses, particularly the large department stores. This offended his idea of the superiority of Aryans. Hitler also blamed Jewish businessmen and bankers for Germany's defeat in the First World War. He thought they had forced the surrender of the German army. As soon as Hitler took power in 1933, he began to mobilise the full powers of the state against the Jews. They were immediately banned from the civil service and a variety of public services, such as broadcasting and teaching. At the same time SA and, later, SS troopers organised boycotts of Jewish shops and businesses. These premises were marked with a star of David.

◀ **Source 37** SA and SS officers enforcing the boycott of Jewish shops, April 1933.

Source 38 A cartoon from the Nazi newspaper *Der Stürmer*, 1935. Jews owned many shops and businesses. These were a constant target for Nazi attacks. ▲

1 Look at Source 37. How is this source useful in informing us about the actions of the Nazis in 1933?

2 Source 38 is very biased. Does that mean it is no use to historians? Why?

Nuremburg Laws

In 1935, the Nuremberg Laws took away German citizenship from Jews. Jews were also forbidden to marry or have sex with pure-blooded Germans. Goebbels' propaganda experts bombarded German children and families with anti-Jewish messages. Jews were often refused jobs, and shopkeepers refused to serve them. In schools, Jewish children were humiliated and then SEGREGATED.

Kristallnacht

In November 1938, a young Jew killed a German diplomat in Paris. The Nazis used this as an excuse to launch violent revenge on all Jews. Plain-clothes SS troopers were issued with pickaxes and hammers and the addresses of Jewish businesses. They ran riot, smashing up Jewish shops and workplaces. Ninety-one Jews were murdered. Hundreds of synagogues were burned. Twenty thousand Jews were taken to concentration camps. Thousands more left the country. This event became known as *Kristallnacht*, or 'the Night of Broken Glass'. Many Germans watched the events of *Kristallnacht* with alarm. The Nazi-controlled press presented it as the spontaneous reaction of ordinary Germans against the Jews. Most Germans did not believe this, but hardly anyone protested. The few who did were brutally murdered. Sources 39–42 on the next page give you a small sense of the shock that resulted.

Source 39 The Labour Corps leader, speaking in an interview in 1938, after *Kristallnacht*.

I hate the treatment of the Jews. I think it is a bad side of the movement and I will have nothing to do with it. I did not join the party to do that sort of thing. I joined the party because I thought and still think that Hitler did the greatest Christian work for twenty-five years. I saw seven million men rotting in the streets, often I was there too, and no one … seemed to care. … Then Hitler came and he took all those men off the streets and gave them health and security and work.

Source 40 An extract from an anonymous letter from a German civil servant to the British consul, 1938.

I feel the urge to present to you a true report of the recent riots, plundering and destruction of Jewish property. Despite what the official Nazi account says, the German people have nothing whatever to do with these riots and burnings. The police supplied SS men with axes, house-breaking tools and ladders. A list of the addresses of all Jewish shops and flats was provided and the mob worked under the leadership of the SS men. The police had strict orders to remain neutral.

1 Read Sources 39–42. How useful is each source to a historian looking at the German reaction to *Kristallnacht*?

2 Taken together, do these sources provide a clear picture of how Germans felt about *Kristallnacht*?

3 Could Germans have protested effectively about *Kristallnacht*? Explain your answer with reference to pages 164–66.

Source 41 Alfons Heck, a member of the Hitler Youth in 1938, interviewed for a television programme in 1989.

Until Kristallnacht, many Germans believed Hitler was not engaged in mass murder. [The treatment of the Jews] seemed to be a minor form of harassment of a disliked minority. But after Kristallnacht no German could any longer be under any illusion. I believe it was the day that we lost our innocence. But it would be fair to point out that I myself never met even the most fanatic Nazi who wanted the extermination of the Jews. Certainly we wanted the Jews out of Germany, but we did not want them to be killed.

Source 42 Henrik Metelmann, a member of the Hitler Youth, 1938.

[The day after Kristallnacht] the teachers told us: don't worry about what you see, even if you see some nasty things which you may not understand. Hitler wants a better Germany, a clean Germany. Don't worry, everything will work out fine in the end.

FOCUS TASK

Why did the Nazis persecute so many groups in Germany?

You have seen how the Nazis persecuted people who opposed them politically, such as the communists, socialists and trade unionists. But why did they persecute so many other groups? Make your own copy of the table below and complete it using the information on pages 164–66.

Groups persecuted by the Nazis	Reasons why they were persecuted	What happened to them

Why was there so little opposition to the Nazi regime?

You might wonder why nobody opposed the Nazis' persecution of all these different groups of people. To understand this we need to try and see Germany from the perspective of people at the time. There *was* opposition in the sense that people grumbled, complained, disobeyed. Some spoke out. But historians agree that considering how extreme Nazi policies were, there was remarkably little opposition.

Firstly, it is important to remember that many people in Germany approved of the Nazis. If you were a patriotic, able-bodied Aryan, with a job and a family or a farm or a business you might feel positive towards the Nazis and what they had achieved. You would not dream of opposing Hitler. Constant propaganda would help to keep you in this positive frame of mind. Goebbels and his team ensured that Germans were subject to an unrelenting diet of the glories of the Third Reich, of Hitler, of the duties of German citizens. Propaganda put the Nazi interpretation on any action that might alarm ordinary Germans, such as *Kristallnacht*.

However, this still leaves many people who had not voted for the Nazis, who opposed their policies and who were not taken in by the propaganda. The diagram opposite sums up the key reasons why there was so little opposition from these groups.

The speed and ruthlessness of the Nazi takeover 1933–34

One key factor – possibly the most important – is the speed with which the Nazis acted in 1933–34. You saw on pages 144–45 how they seized power and ruthlessly eliminated their enemies. Many of the most active, committed and capable opponents of the Nazis in the Communist and Socialist Parties were imprisoned or killed.

The result was that the Nazi takeover 'decapitated' the opposition movements. While there were still many communists and socialists in Germany, they lost their leaders. They were divided and could not work together.

Gleichschaltung (co-ordination)

The Nazis pursued a policy of *Gleichshaltung*, which means 'co-ordination' or 'bringing everything together'. They quickly and effectively took over existing organisations and put Nazis in charge. For example, the government took over the trade unions and the armed forces. This might not seem a surprising move at national level, but the Nazis argued that all organisations in Germany should be run by them. So, even at the local level, ambitious Nazi activists took control of sports clubs and youth groups – even town choirs.

This policy seeped into the workplace. If you worked in local government or the civil service you would be unlikely to get promotion if you did not join the party. If you were a business – perhaps a building contractor or a printer – you would not win government contracts unless you could show you supported the Nazi Party (usually with financial donations).

Even the churches joined in. The Catholic Church reached an agreement with the Nazis in 1933 and many of the Protestant denominations agreed to come together into the Reich Church. Many individual churchmen, including the Catholic Cardinal Galen and the Protestant ministers Dietrich Bonhoeffer and Martin Niemoller, criticised the Nazis publicly, but they were acting as individuals rather than representing their Churches.

The result was that people realised that they had to be a Nazi – or pretend to be one – to get anywhere; or they had to leave Germany. Around 300,000 potential opponents left the country between 1933 and 1939, probably as a result of pressures like these.

Fear

This overlaps with all the other points and operated at two levels:
- There was the obvious *personal fear* of the terror tactics of the SS, the Gestapo and their informers. In fact there were nothing like as many Gestapo agents as people believed, but because people *thought* agents were everywhere they conformed. The propaganda machine supported this. For example, the photographs on pages 150–51 were taken by the Nazis and distributed by them in order to feed people's fear and encourage their obedience.
- There was also a more *general fear* of economic or political instability (see Sources 43 and 44). Germany had been in chaos just a few years earlier. Many people who did not really like the Nazis thought the alternatives were worse.

The result was that people conformed and fitted in even if they did not support the Nazis.

The Hitler myth

The final factor was what historian Ian Kershaw has called 'the Hitler myth'. Kershaw found evidence that while many Germans disliked the Nazis, they respected Hitler personally and did not blame him for many of the unpleasant or unfair things that Nazi officials did. This belief remained strong and was only shaken towards the end of the Second World War.

The result was that people kept quiet and were prepared to overlook aspects of the Nazi regime that they disliked, because they admired Hitler and believed he had a good reason for doing what he was doing.

1 Sources 43 and 44 were written by people who opposed the Nazi regime. Does that affect the value of these sources as evidence? Explain your answer.

Source 43 A report by a socialist activist in Germany, February 1936.

The average worker is primarily interested in work and not in democracy. People who previously enthusiastically supported democracy showed no interest at all in politics. One must be clear about the fact that in the first instance men are fathers of families and have jobs, and that for them politics takes second place and even then only when they expect to get something out of it.

Source 44 Extracts from the diaries of Victor Klemperer.

November 1933: Millions of Germans are indeed won over by Hitler and the power and the glory are really his. I hear of some actions by the communists. ... But what good do such pinpricks do? Less than none, because all Germany prefers Hitler to the communists.

April 1935: Frau Wilbrandt told us that people complain in Munich when Hitler or Goebbels appear on film but even she (an economist close to the Social Democrats) says: 'Will there not be something even worse, if Hitler is overthrown, Bolshevism?' (That fear keeps Hitler where he is again and again.)

FOCUS TASK

Why was there so little opposition to the Nazi regime?

1 Throughout this topic, you have looked at the different reasons why the Nazi regime faced so little opposition in the 1930s. These can be summarised as terror and reward. Now it is time to reach a judgement: which was most important? Every individual was different but if you could assemble all the examples and all the evidence, which way do you think the balance would fall?

Write a paragraph to sum up your view.

2 **Extension:** There is a lot of debate among historians about exactly what is meant by 'opposition to the Nazi regime'. Ian Kershaw describes two main types of opposition in Nazi Germany:

a Fundamentalist opposition: people or groups who wanted to overthrow the regime.

b Societal opposition: people or groups who did not actively resist Nazi rule but kept their own identity and refused to accept and conform to Nazi ideals.

Would your answer to Question 1 be different for each type?

REVIEW TASKS

Did the Nazis succeed in creating a National Community?

The Nazi propaganda machine made many claims about Nazi achievements on their road towards establishing the National Community. For example:

We have restored traditional values for women and families.

Germany's young people are better off than ever before.

The Nazi state looks after its workers very well indeed.

Germans now have economic security.

There are no longer social classes in Germany, just loyal Germans.

The workers are loyal to the Nazi state.

The Nazis have ensured that Germany is racially pure.

The Nazis are on the side of the farmers and have rescued Germany's farmers from disaster.

You are now going to decide how truthful these claims actually are.

1. Look back over pages 148–68. Gather evidence that supports or opposes each claim. You could work in groups, taking one claim each.
2. For each claim, decide whether overall it is:
   a. totally untrue
   b. a little bit true
   c. mostly true
   d. totally true.
3. Discuss the following questions:
   a. Which of the groups you have studied in this topic do you think benefited most from Nazi rule?
   b. Who did *not* benefit from Nazi rule and why?
4. **Extension:** Do you think Victor Klemperer was right about Hitler representing the soul of the German people? What evidence can you find to support your point of view?

TOPIC SUMMARY

A national community? Nazi Germany and its people 1933–39

1 The Nazis wanted to win the hearts and minds of Germans – to mould the country and its people to their ideal. They wanted a 'National Community' of Germans who were prepared to work and fight for their country. They wanted to purify Germany of the weaknesses it had shown through the Weimar era.

2 They did not think everyone would do this willingly, so they ruthlessly repressed and persecuted anyone who opposed the regime through their network of Gestapo informers, SS officers and concentration camps. Ordinary Germans learned to keep quiet for fear of being arrested and sent to a concentration camp for doing or saying the wrong thing.

3 The Nazis also tried to win people's loyalty through relentless propaganda and censorship. Goebbels controlled what Germans could read, see at the cinema or listen to on the radio.

4 The Nazis used events like the Nuremburg rallies to show off their vision of military power and order and obedience. They tried to use the Olympic Games in a similar way to show off their ideas of a superior Aryan race, but this backfired as it turned out Aryans were not the best at everything!

5 Young people were central to the Nazi vision. The Nazis wanted children to grow up believing in and acting out Nazi ideals. They used the school curriculum and the Hitler Youth to indoctrinate young people. They trained boys to be soldiers and girls to be mothers. Young people were among the keenest supporters of the Nazis, although not all young people obeyed.

6 One of the most confusing parts of Nazi policy was its attitude towards women. The Nazis wanted German women to stop work and have lots of children to solve the problem of the falling birth rate. However, they found they also needed them as workers when many men were taken into the army.

7 Through the 1930s, the Nazis faced very little opposition because of terror (they had imprisoned or executed opposition leaders or frightened them into silence) but also because many Germans liked what the Nazis were achieving, particularly the version of it that was told in propaganda.

8 Many groups did do better under the Nazis – workers, farmers, business owners all benefited from Nazi investment in arms and in infrastructure such as road-building. However, many other groups did very badly, particularly those who did not fit the Nazi ideal such as the Jews or Gypsies.

9 Hitler was particularly anti-Semitic and started a systematic campaign to drive the Jewish population out of Germany by escalating persecution. He first limited their rights, then confiscated their property, then attacked their homes and businesses on *Kristallnacht*.

10 Historians do not agree about how far ordinary Germans accepted Nazi ideology. People learned to do what they were told and keep quiet because of terror, but did that mean they were converted? The big test of that would come in the war, when Germans were required to act out their required role in Hitler's aims.

PRACTICE QUESTIONS

1 Describe one example of how the Nazis terrorised the German people. (2)
2 Describe one benefit that German workers gained from the Nazis. (2)
3 Explain how the Nazis used propaganda to control the population of Germany. (10)
4 Explain why the Nazis devoted so much attention to youth policies. (10)
5 'The Nazis won the hearts and minds of the German people.' How far do you agree with this view? (18)

4.3 Destruction to democracy: The Second World War and its legacy in Germany 1939–55

FOCUS

Hitler had a vision of a 'thousand-year Third Reich': a great German empire. This new Reich would be forged in war and conquest. Hitler was convinced that the German people had not been completely ready for the First World War. Had he put that right by the time war began in 1939? In this topic, you will consider:

- the impact of the war on Germans
- the radicalisation of racial policy
- defeat and the division of Germany
- the experiences of Germans in East and West Germany.

The German people and the war effort

Hitler had been preparing Germany for war since he came to power in 1933. But how did the German people feel about it? As you have seen, it was difficult to express true opinions in Germany at the time if they contradicted Nazi doctrine. This makes it hard for historians to get a clear picture of how Germans felt. However, most experts agree that the German people were not enthusiastic about going to war. There were no celebratory parades or rallies. Many citizens still remembered the hardships of the First World War.

Control

During the war, the Nazis used all available methods to ensure the German people said and did the right things. For example, the Catholic minister Rupert Mayer had been in trouble with the Gestapo many times in the 1930s for openly criticising the Nazis. However, they had never managed to silence him. When war broke out in 1939, Mayer was taken away into 'protective custody' and sent to a concentration camp for the rest of the war.

The SD (a part of the SS) and the Gestapo monitored the mood of the people in more subtle ways, too, including placing agents in bars to listen to people's conversations. A typical example was Erich Weiss. In September 1939, Weiss was talking to a petrol station attendant, commenting on how millions of good Germans would be killed for nothing in the war. Records show that another customer overheard Weiss and reported him to the Gestapo. He spent six months in a camp.

The economy

Just as the government tightened control over the people, it also increased control over Germany's economy. War did not bring massive changes to the German economy at first. As German forces conquered territories, they seized raw materials and goods to supply the war effort. For example, Germany took around 20 per cent of Norway's entire production in 1940. From 1942, the German economy shifted further towards armaments to supply the army fighting against Russia. Huge corporations like IG Farben produced chemicals, explosives and the gas used to exterminate people in the death camps. German factories used forced labour from occupied countries. Estimates suggest that forced labourers made up around 25 per cent of the workforce. Production was hampered by Allied bombing and some factories were even moved underground. By 1944, there had been a vast increase in military production. Three times as many aircraft and tanks were built than in 1942.

Source 1 The cover of the Nazi magazine for women, *Frauen Warte*, 1 March 1940. It shows a house being built in conquered Polish territory. The caption says: 'Germany is building in the East'. ▲

1 Why was Source 1 published? How does it try to achieve its aim?

Successes and spoils

Limited food rationing was introduced soon after war began in September 1939. Clothes rationing followed in November 1939. Even so, from 1939 to 1941 it was easy to keep up civilian morale because the war went well for Germany. Hitler controlled much of western and eastern Europe, and supplies of luxury goods flowed into Germany from captured territories. There were other benefits too for German people. Pure Aryan Germans were encouraged to settle in the new territories that had been conquered (see Source 1). German industries prospered from war contracts, which meant there was a demand for workers.

The turning tide

The years 1939 and 1940 saw spectacular successes. However, in 1941 Hitler took a huge gamble and invaded the Soviet Union. For the next three years, German troops were engaged in an increasingly expensive and destructive war with Soviet forces, who 'tore the heart out of the German army', according to the British war leader Winston Churchill. By 1943, the tide was turning against Germany and its army was experiencing disastrous losses. Throughout the course of the war, around 18 million German men served in the armed forces. Of these, around 5 million were wounded and another 5 million were killed or went missing in action. Nine out of ten of German casualties occurred in the war against the Soviet Union on the Eastern Front. Very few German families were left untouched by these losses.

The impact of the war economy

With the war draining more and more German resources, Albert Speer began to direct Germany's war economy. All effort focused on the armament industries. Germans had to cut back on heating, work longer hours and recycle their rubbish. Goebbels increased censorship. He tried to maintain people's support for the war by asking them to make sacrifices to make them feel involved. They donated an estimated 1.5 million fur coats to help to clothe the German army in the USSR!

Postal services were suspended and postboxes were closed. All places of entertainment were shut down, except cinemas – Goebbels needed these to show propaganda films. Increasing numbers of women were drafted into the labour force. Country areas had to take evacuees from the cities and refugees from eastern Europe. With bombing and the arrival of slave labourers, accommodation and food were in short supply. The government rationed food much more tightly.

All these measures were increasingly carried out by the SS. In fact, the SS became virtually a state within the German state. This SS empire had its own armed forces, armaments industries and labour camps. It developed a business empire that was worth a fortune. New branches of the SS emerged to tackle particular issues: the Waffen SS (the military branch); the Race and Resettlement office (resettling Germans in occupied territories of eastern Europe); and the Office for Strengthening of Germanhood (in charge of racial policy in the occupied territories).

The impact of bombing

As things grew worse for the German army after 1942, civilians found their lives increasingly disrupted. One of the most direct ways in which the war affected ordinary people was the bombing campaign by the Royal Air Force and the US Air Force. In 1942, under Arthur 'Bomber' Harris, the British began an all-out assault on both industrial and residential areas of all major German cities. They intended to cripple German industry and to lower the morale of civilians and terrorise them into submission. These aerial attacks escalated over the next three years, culminating in the bombing of Dresden in February 1945, which killed between 35,000 and 150,000 people in two days.

> **Source 2** A translation of a leaflet dropped by the Allies on Berlin.
>
> *Goebbels does not always tell you the truth. When he tells you that England is powerless do you believe that? Have you forgotten that our bombers fly over Germany at will? The bombs that fell with these leaflets tell you. ... The war lasts as long as Hitler's regime.*

> **Source 3** Christabel Bielenberg, an English woman married to a German and living in Berlin in 1943.
>
> *I learned when I was living in Berlin that the impersonal killings, the barrage from the air which mutilated and destroyed, did not breed fear or a desire to give in. Instead it led to a fatalistic stubbornness, a dogged determination to survive and if possible, to help others, whatever their politics or religion.*

2 What was the purpose of Source 2?

3 Why do Sources 3 and 4 tell such different stories?

> **Source 4** A survivor describing the experience of bombing on Hamburg in 1943.
>
> *It is hard to describe the panic and chaos. Most people just put what they could on to bicycles or prams or just carried them on their backs and started, on foot, just to get away, to escape. People who were wearing Nazi party badges had them torn off their coats and there were screams of 'let's get that murderer!' The police did nothing.*

Source 5 A photograph showing the centre of Dresden after the air raids in February 1945. ▼

173

Women and the war effort

As more women entered the German workforce, many of them had to struggle with both family and work responsibilities. Even during the crisis years of 1942–45, when German industry could hardly cope with the demand for war supplies, Nazi policy on women remained torn between wanting German women to play the stereotypical role of mother and meeting the needs of the workplace. There was no opportunity for German women to serve in the armed forces, as there was in Allied countries.

Young people and the war effort

In 1939, membership of a Nazi youth movement was made compulsory. However, by this point such organisations were in crisis. Many of the experienced leaders had been drafted into the army. Others – particularly those who had been leaders in the days before the Nazis came to power – had been replaced by those who were more supportive of the regime. Youth movements were often now run by older teenagers who rigidly enforced Nazi rules. They even forbade other teenagers to meet informally with their friends. As the war progressed, the activities of the youth movements focused increasingly on the war effort and military drill. Their popularity decreased and an anti-Hitler Youth movement, including organisations such as the Edelweiss Pirates, even appeared.

The Nazis were obviously deeply concerned about this. In December 1942, the Gestapo broke up 28 groups of Edelweiss Pirates containing 739 adolescents. However, as long as the Nazis needed future industrial workers and soldiers, they could not simply exterminate these teenagers or put them in concentration camps. They therefore responded uncertainly – sometimes arresting the Pirates, sometimes ignoring them. In 1944 in Cologne, Pirate activities escalated. They sheltered army deserters and escaped prisoners. They stole armaments and took part in an attack on the Gestapo during which its chief was killed. In response, the Nazis rounded up the ringleaders and publicly hanged 12 of them.

Source 6 An extract from a report by the Nazi youth leadership, 1942.

The formation of cliques, i.e. groupings of young people outside the Hitler Youth, has been on the increase before and particularly during the war to such a degree that one must speak of a serious risk of political, moral and criminal subversion of our youth.

1 How does Source 6 help you to understand Source 7?
2 Why do you think the executions shown in Source 7 were carried out in public and photographed?

Source 7 The public hanging of 12 Edelweiss Pirates in Cologne, 1944. ▶

FOCUS TASK

Germany at war (2)

Look back at the Focus Task on page 172 and add any points you have learned about:
- the effectiveness of Germany's war economy
- the impact of the war on German people
- how far German people were committed to the war effort.

The effect of war on the persecution of Jews

You have already seen how the Nazis persecuted Jews and other minority groups in Germany in the 1930s. Once the war began, this persecution reached new depths of brutality. At the same time, it became more carefully organised.

Polish ghettos

After invading Poland in 1939, the Nazis set about 'Germanising' western Poland. This meant transporting Poles from their homes and replacing them with German settlers. Around one in five Poles died either in the fighting or as a result of racial policies in the period 1939–45. Polish Jews were rounded up and transported to the big cities. Here they were herded into sealed areas, called ghettos. Able-bodied Jews were used for slave labour but the young, the old and the sick were left to die of hunger and disease.

Mass murder

In 1941, Germany invaded the USSR. Within weeks the Nazis found themselves in control of 3 million Soviet Jews (in addition to the Jews in all the other countries they had conquered). German forces had orders to round up and shoot Communist Party activists and their Jewish supporters. The executions were carried out by special SS units called Einsatzgruppen. By the autumn of 1941, mass shootings were taking place all over occupied eastern Europe. In Germany, all Jews were ordered to wear the star of David on their clothing to mark them out.

The 'death camps'

In January 1942, a group of senior Nazis met at Wannsee, a suburb of Berlin, to discuss what they called the 'Final Solution' to the 'Jewish Question'. There, Himmler, head of the SS and Gestapo, was put in charge of the systematic killing of all Jews within Germany and German-occupied territory. Slave labour and death camps were built at Auschwitz, Treblinka and Chelmno in Poland, among other places. The old, the sick and young children were killed immediately. The rest were sent to work at the labour camps. Some were used for medical experiments. Six million Jews, 500,000 European Gypsies and countless political prisoners, Jehovah's Witnesses, homosexuals and Russian and Polish prisoners of war were sent to these camps, where they were worked to death, gassed or shot.

Was the 'Final Solution' planned from the start?

Historians have long debated whether or not Hitler had planned the 'Final Solution' for some years. Some historians (intentionalists) believe that the whole process had been carefully planned. Others (structuralists) argue that there was no clear plan and that the policy of mass murder evolved during the war years. Once again, lack of evidence makes it difficult to know for sure. Hitler made speeches in which he talked of the annihilation of the Jews, but there are no documents with his signature and no record of him ever giving any orders directly relating to the extermination of the Jews. The Nazis kept the programme as secret as they could, so there are relatively few documents.

> **Source 8** US historian Gordon Craig, writing in 1978.
>
> *The extermination of the Jews is the most dreadful chapter in German history, doubly so because the men who did it closed their senses to the reality of what they were doing by taking pride in the technical efficiency of their actions and, at moments when their conscience threatened to break in, telling themselves that they were doing their duty … others took refuge in the enormity of the operation, which lent it a convenient depersonalisation. When they ordered a hundred Jews to get on a train in Paris or Amsterdam, they considered their job accomplished and carefully closed their minds to the thought that eventually those passengers would arrive in front of the ovens of Treblinka.*

Source 9 A child's drawing of prisoners arriving at the Auschwitz death camp. ▲

1 The systematic killing of the Jews by the Nazis is generally known today as the Holocaust, which means 'sacrifice'. Many people prefer the Jewish term *Sho'ah*, which means 'destruction'. Why do you think this is?

2 There are many websites, TV programmes and books about the mass murders during the war. Some of these resources contain shocking images of dead bodies, gas chambers, cremation ovens and other horrors. We have chosen Sources 9 and 10. Why do you think we did this?

Although historians disagree about whether there was a plan, they do generally agree that Hitler was ultimately responsible. However, other individuals and organisations were also responsible. The genocide would not have been possible without:

- **the Civil Service bureaucracy:** this collected and stored information about Jews
- **police forces in Germany and the occupied territories:** many victims of the Nazis were actually taken by the police rather than the Gestapo or SS
- **the SS:** Adolf Eichmann devised a system of transporting Jews to collection points and then on to the death camps. He was also in charge of looting the possessions of the Jews; the SS Death's Head battalions and Einsatzgruppen also carried out many of the killings
- **the Wehrmacht (German armed forces):** army leaders were fully aware of what was going on
- **industry:** companies such as Volkswagen and Mercedes had their own slave labour camps; the chemical giant IG Farben competed with other companies for the contract to make the Cyclon B gas that was used in the gas chambers
- **the German people:** anti-Semitism was widespread, even if these feelings did not include support for mass murder; many Germans took part in some aspect of the HOLOCAUST, but ignored the full reality (see Source 9).

Resistance

Many Jews escaped from Germany before the killing started. Other Jews managed to live under cover in Germany and the occupied territories. Some joined resistance groups. Gad Beck, for example, led the Jewish resistance to the Nazis in Berlin. He was finally captured in April 1945. On the day he was due to be executed, he was rescued by troops from the Jewish regiment of the Soviet army. There were 28 known groups of Jewish fighters, and there may have been more. Many Jews fought in the resistance movements in the Nazi-occupied lands. In 1945, the Jews in the Warsaw ghetto in Poland rose up against the Nazis and held out against them for four weeks. There were armed uprisings in five concentration camps, and Greek Jews managed to blow up the gas ovens at Auschwitz.

We know that many Germans and other non-Jews helped Jews by hiding them and smuggling them out of German-held territory. The industrialist Oskar Schindler protected and saved many people by getting them on to his 'list' of workers. The Swedish diplomat Raoul Wallenberg worked with other resisters to provide Jews with Swedish and US passports to get them out of the reach of the Nazis in Hungary. He disappeared in mysterious circumstances in 1945. Of course, high-profile individuals such as these were rare. Most of the successful resisters were successful because they kept an extremely low profile and were discovered neither by the Nazis at the time, nor by historians since then.

◄ Source 10 Wedding rings taken from people killed at Buchenwald concentration camp.

Did the war increase opposition to the Nazi regime?

You have already read some examples of opposition to Nazi control during the war, such as the Edelweiss Pirates and Gad Beck leading Jewish resistance in Berlin. The diagram below shows some other examples of opposition.

RESISTANCE GROUPS

One of the best-known resistance groups was the White Rose, run by Hans and Sophie Scholl and some of their close friends. The White Rose published and distributed anti-Nazi leaflets. This was a small movement, although its members were certainly brave. The Scholls were executed in February 1943.

THE ARMY

The only group that really had much chance of overthrowing the Nazis was the army, but as the war progressed the army became increasingly integrated with the Nazi regime. Even so, there were attempts by senior army officers to assassinate Hitler. We know of five attempts between June 1940 and December 1943, but they all failed. The closest to success came in July 1944. By this stage, many army officers were sure that the war was lost and that Hitler was leading Germany into ruin. One of these was a colonel in the army, Count von Stauffenberg. On 20 July he left a bomb in Hitler's conference room. The plan was to kill Hitler, close down the radio stations, round up the other leading Nazis and take over Germany. It failed on all counts because the revolt was poorly planned and organised. Hitler survived and the Nazis took a terrible revenge, killing 5,000 people.

CHURCH LEADERS

Many clergymen – both Catholic and Protestant – opposed the Nazis.
- *The Catholic bishop Clemens Galen criticised the Nazis throughout the 1930s. In 1941, he led a popular protest against the Nazi policy of killing mentally ill and physically disabled people, forcing the Nazis to stop this programme temporarily. Galen had such strong support that the Nazis decided it was too risky to try to silence him – they did not want social unrest while Germany was at war.*
- *Protestant pastor Martin Niemöller was one of the most high-profile critics of the regime in the 1930s. Along with Dietrich Bonhoeffer, he formed an alternative Protestant Church to the official Reich Church. Niemöller spent the years 1938–45 in a concentration camp for resisting the Nazis.*
- *Dietrich Bonhoeffer preached against the Nazis until the Gestapo stopped him in 1937. He then became involved with members of the army's intelligence services who were secretly opposed to Hitler. He helped Jews to escape from Germany. Gradually he increased his activity. In 1942, he contacted Allied commanders and asked what peace terms they would offer Germany if Hitler was overthrown. He was arrested in October 1942 and hanged shortly before the end of the war, in April 1945.*

Wartime opposition

BUT …

We must be careful not to exaggerate resistance or opposition to the regime or the war effort. Support for the war remained strong for most of its duration.
- *The Nazis maintained strong control. There are many examples like that of Protestant minister Wilhelm Kenath, who was reported by several mourners after criticising the war at the funeral of a young soldier in Bruckshaven in May 1943.*
- *Many Germans still believed in Hitler. The 'Hitler myth' described by historian Ian Kershaw (page 167) remained intact. Even in 1944, with the war going badly for Germany, there is evidence that many people still believed Hitler would lead them to victory (although that faith does not seem to have extended to the rest of the Nazi leadership).*

LOW-LEVEL RESISTANCE

There were other types of lower-level resistance as well.
- *SS and Gestapo reports show that they were becoming increasingly concerned about the discontent caused by bombing raids, shortages and heavy casualties (see Sources 11 and 12).*
- *Anti-Nazi jokes were a common form of resistance, allowing people to express their discontent without much risk.*
- *Some civilians dared to go further by hiding food from the authorities or refusing to give the 'Heil Hitler' salute.*
- *Others went further still by hiding Jews or helping them to escape.*

Source 11 An extract from a Gestapo report, December 1942.

One of the strongest causes of unease among those attached to the Church and in the rural population generally is the news from Russia in which shooting and extermination of the Jews is mentioned. The news frequently leaves great anxiety. According to the population it is not at all certain we will win the war and if the Jews come again to Germany they will exact dreadful revenge upon us.

Why did Germans fight to the bitter end?

It was clear from 1944 that the Germans would lose the war, but the Nazi leadership would not admit defeat. One reason for this may have been because they felt they had nothing to lose. They knew that they would be tried and perhaps executed for war crimes. This may also have been true of other Germans, who were aware of the atrocities being carried out and felt they would receive no mercy at the end of the war.

The propaganda minister himself, Goebbels, remained totally committed until the bitter end. In July 1944, he was made 'Plenipotentiary (minister) for Total War'. In 1945, Hitler ordered the formation of the Volkssturm ('People's Storm'), a force similar to the British Home Guard, and put Goebbels in charge. He had to organise teenagers and old men to fight the invading Soviet, US and British forces. Most of these people were inexperienced and untrained. This was a desperate and hopeless measure that illustrates the stubborn persistence of the regime and its leaders.

Source 12 An extract from a German government report, spring 1943.

The rumour mongers are still with us, or rather they are busier than ever. An especially dangerous situation is that some people are openly risking criticism of the Führer himself, attacking him in the most hateful and vulgar manner. Unfortunately, too many of our countrymen blabber and repeat everything we are told and sadly our local party members have been very lax. They witness this subversive behaviour but they do nothing about it.

Source 13 Goebbels awarding the Iron Cross to a young member of the Volkssturm. ▲

In 1945, when Himmler dared to start negotiations with the British and Americans, Hitler ordered his arrest and he was forced to go into hiding. Even through spring 1945, when the Germans were losing ground on all sides, the army was ordered to keep fighting. They only surrendered when Soviet troops entered Berlin and Hitler committed suicide. The Nazi Reich was over. Germany was left to count the cost of Hitler's vision.

1 Study Sources 11 and 12. Which is more useful in explaining attitudes in Germany during the war?

FOCUS TASK

What was the most significant impact of the war on German people?

A TV company is making a one-hour documentary on the effects of the war on Germany. They are trying to decide how much time to give to each topic. At the moment they are planning to organise the film in four 15-minute sections as shown here.

Your job is to tell the TV company:
● what examples and details should be covered under each category
● whether they have covered everything they should
● whether they have things in the right order
● whether this is the right amount of time for each topic – does it reflect their relative importance?

You could write your report or do it as a presentation.

[Diagram: a circle divided into four quadrants labelled:]
- Bombing
- War economy
- Final Solution
- Control

FOCUS TASK

Germany at war (3)

Look back at the Focus Task on page 174 and add any more points you have learned about:
- the effectiveness of Germany's war economy
- the impact of the war on German people
- how far German people were committed to the war effort.

Defeat, division and denazification

Since 1943, the Allies had been discussing what to do with Germany after the war ended. They had many conflicting ideas, but they did agree that the country should be divided up into four zones, run by the USA, the USSR, Britain and France (see page 63). They also agreed that Germany would be demilitarised, denazified and democratised.

A new life?

Demilitarisation was not much of a problem. Germany was shattered – it was in no state to fight on and its people had no will to do so. Most were struggling simply to find food and shelter amid the ruins of war.

People got on with forgetting and rebuilding as soon as they could. Very soon women known as the Trümmerfrauen ('rubble women'), working individually or in groups, started clearing the remains of bombed buildings with their bare hands, brick by brick, laying them neatly in piles ready for the rebuilding to start. As time went on, the work became more organised and they were given equipment to use.

Meanwhile, Germany was facing an extreme refugee crisis as Germans in eastern Europe fled or were forced to leave their homes. The official Allied policy was that all German speakers in eastern Europe would move to Germany to avoid revenge attacks. However, such attacks still took place. The Germans of the Czech Sudetenland suffered particularly brutal treatment from the advancing Soviet army.

An estimated 12–14 million German speakers became refugees. There were no powered vehicles available, so refugees walked the hundreds of kilometres across eastern Europe towards Germany, pulling simple hand carts (see Source 15) containing as many of their possessions as would fit. For many of them, Germany had never been their home, nor were they welcome when they arrived – people felt they just added to the problems in the now-ruined country. Historian Neil McGregor comments on this post-war German refugee crisis that 'outside Germany little is known about this. Inside Germany, it is part of almost every family's history.'

Source 14 Trümmerfrauen working in Berlin, 1946. ▼

2 Look at Source 14. How is this picture useful in telling us about the impact of war on German towns and cities?

3 What impression does the source give of the mood of Germans in 1946? What other sources might you use to check whether or not this image is typical?

4 Imagine one of the carts from Source 15 is displayed in a museum. Write a 100-word caption to go with it to explain its significance.

Source 15 One of the many lines of refugees arriving in Berlin in summer 1945. ▶

Denazification in the Soviet sector

The Soviets had suffered terribly in the war. At least 20 million people had died, and possibly many more. Since one of the key principles of Nazism was a commitment to crushing communism, the communist USSR was determined to stamp out Nazism as effectively as possible. The first step was tearing down evidence of the Nazis in the streets and buildings (see Source 17). All Nazi symbols, flags, banners, etc. were destroyed and it became illegal to display them. Higher-ranking Nazis were imprisoned in Soviet-run camps. Thousands of government officials, military commanders and others were also sent to camps. The Soviets removed around one-third of German teachers – those believed to be Nazi sympathisers – and they scrapped the Nazis' school curriculum and textbooks. They also sacked large numbers of public servants.

Getting rid of Nazism in wider society proved more difficult. The Soviet military administration set up local commissions across the Soviet sector, which investigated the thousands of individuals who had been members of the Nazi Party. However, there were simply not enough Soviet officials to handle such a huge job so they appointed German officials to carry out this process. The Soviet administration pressured these commissions to deal quickly with known or suspected Nazis. In practice, however, the TRIBUNALS took a long time and were usually sympathetic to Germans who had been Nazi Party members, because they understood the pressures people had been under. Overall around 300,000 Germans were convicted of low-level involvement with the regime. Some were imprisoned, others banned from positions of authority.

By 1948, the USSR had reinstated elected government in its sector of Germany. This was run by the communist East German leader Walter Ulbricht. Ulbricht grew tired of the slow process of the commissions and abandoned the whole process, preferring to 'look forwards rather than backwards'.

Source 16 Historian Timothy Vogt, writing in 2000. Vogt carried out a detailed study of the work of the Soviet local commissions in the Soviet sector.

The process of denazification was far less politicized and much more fair-minded than the earlier histories written by western historians during the Cold War has led us to believe. People of different classes, age or gender were treated in the same way and the commissions were sympathetic towards the situation of "nominal" party members, people who by force of circumstance and pragmatism had joined the Nazis, the Hitler Youth, and related organizations.

Source 17 A photograph from 1945 showing Soviet troops beginning the process of removing and destroying Nazi symbols. ▼

Denazification in the Western zones

The western powers (the USA, Britain and France) also took the challenge of denazification seriously. US and British army intelligence units began gathering information on Nazis as early as October 1944, fearing that many Nazis would try to hide away after the war. Once Germany surrendered, the Allies put various measures in place to remove any remaining Nazi influence.

Leading Nazis were quickly arrested. All Germans over the age of 18 had to complete a questionnaire detailing their past political activities and beliefs, and the jobs they had held. Allied intelligence officers investigated all senior public officials (local councillors, lawyers and judges, police officers, etc.) and around 50,000 of them were dismissed. They also investigated teachers and members of the health and medical professions, then spread their net wider to look into leaders of businesses, industries and worker organisations as well.

1. Read Source 18. This commentary is aimed at US audiences. Do you think that the commentary would have been changed (apart from translation) for German audiences?
2. One of the purposes of this newsreel was to explain to people in the USA why not all US troops were returning from the war immediately. How can you tell?
3. Do you think US audiences would have been reassured by this newsreel?

Source 18 An extract from the commentary on a US newsreel, 1946.

After the First World War, the German Kaiser and his friends were allowed to seek safety in Holland. Today, proven war criminals must answer for their crimes. After the last war, German education was untouched. Today all Nazi doctrine is being destroyed. New textbooks have been prepared for German youth – under American direction, not German direction. We have come to Germany not as liberators but as conquerors. And this time we shall remain, for ten years, for twenty years, if necessary forever. The average German, let's call him Karl Schmidt, will determine when we go. Karl must realise that he himself is responsible not only for Germany's past but also its future. We have rid him of Hitler and Nazism, but we have not rid him of his history and traditions. That he must do for himself.

Just like the Soviets in their sector, the western powers soon discovered what a mammoth operation this was. In September 1945, they created German Review Boards, run by Germans appointed by the Allied military and answerable to it. By 1948, these boards had investigated around 3.5 million cases. There were about 5,000 trials with around 4,000 people found guilty. Just under 500 of these were executed. Around 200,000 individuals were held prisoner but were later released as there was not enough evidence to put them on trial.

Source 19 Historian Martin Kitchen, writing in 2011.

Soldiers who were guilty of the most appalling crimes were released on the grounds that they were simply obeying orders. The army was absolved of all crimes, until historians began to uncover the full extent of its complicity with a criminal regime. All the occupation powers made use of Nazis with desirable skills, whether as scientists, administrators, or publicists. Many opportunistic Nazis in the Soviet zone found the transition from one dictatorial regime to another easy to make. In the Western zones the difficulty of finding competent officials who were completely untainted was so great that a blind eye was all too often turned. This was particularly true of the legal profession, where a large number of singularly unsavoury characters remained in office. The French were the most lenient in dealing with their Nazis, the Americans the most stringent, although they quickly lowered their standards as tensions with the Soviet Union began to worsen. All in all the denazification program was an expensive and time-consuming failure. There were precious few devout Nazis left by1945, degrees of complicity were hard to establish, and the need to rebuild the country was such that even those with a heavy burden of guilt were forgiven after a few years.

In addition to tracking down Nazis, the western Allies introduced a programme of re-education. They wanted to expose Germans to the full horror of what the Nazis had done. German citizens were forced to view pamphlets, photographs and newsreels, although we cannot know what kind of impact these measures had. In 1948, the western powers wound down the denazification programme and began focusing on rebuilding Germany.

Source 20 An Allied publication showing Nazi atrocities, published in Germany in 1945. The headline reads: 'These Atrocities: Your Fault!' ▶

1 What is the purpose of Source 20 and how does the publication try to achieve it?
2 Do you think it is an effective technique to denazify the population?

ACTIVITY

Study Source 20 carefully. Imagine you are advising US, British and other Allied intelligence agencies about how to fight extremism in different parts of the world. What lessons do Source 20 and the other information in this section provide?

FOCUS TASK

How effective was denazification?

1 Look back at your work on pages 171–82. In pairs or small groups make a list of reasons why:
   a it was difficult to 'measure' the effects of Nazi propaganda
   b it was difficult to be sure whether propaganda or terror had more effect
   c there was little effective opposition.
2 Now look back over the denazification programmes of the Soviets and the western powers and answer the following questions:
   a Did they face the same problems?
   b In what ways did they take similar or different approaches?
   c Was one more effective than the other?

Two Germanies: democratisation and rebuilding

At the end of the war there was much discussion about whether Germany would be reunited. However, during this period relations between the USA and the USSR grew steadily worse, and Germany became the centre of a tense stand-off (see page 62). By 1949, it was clear that the country would remain divided.

Source 21 Konrad Adenauer photographed in his office. Note the crucifix in the background. Adenauer was a Catholic. ▼

Democratisation and rebuilding in the Western Zone

In 1949 the US, British and French zones were merged to become the Federal Republic of Germany (often called West Germany) with a new capital in Bonn. Today we think of Germany as a successful democracy, but it took several factors to allow this transition to happen. The FRG was founded on a constitution called the Basic Law (see Factfile). West Germany was still divided and governments still relied on coalitions similar to the Weimar period, but the new constitution and the watchful Allies made sure that a new Nazi or communist threat could not emerge.

Konrad Adenauer

The key figure in the new FRG was the chancellor, Konrad Adenauer. Adenauer had been the mayor of Cologne when the Nazis took power. He was no friend of the Nazis and had been arrested several times. He had no sympathy for communism, either. In 1945, he formed the Christian Democratic Union Party (CDU). The CDU attracted around 30 per cent of the vote in Germany and Adenauer was able to form coalitions with other parties. He was chancellor from 1949 until 1963.

Adenauer did not have an easy job. Germans were still divided over the direction the country should take, and there was still a lot of support for radical political organisations. Adenauer banned the right-wing Socialist Reich Party (SRP) in 1952 and the Communist Party (KPD) in 1956 because they were felt to be a threat to the country's constitution.

Whitewashing history: *Betriebsunfall*

Betriebsunfall means 'accident in the works'. Many Germans struggled to come to terms with what had happened in the war. One response to this was the theory that the Nazi period had been a 12-year aberration – an accident in the works. It was effectively written out of Germany's history. *Betriebsunfall* probably helped some people feel loyal to the new state. It allowed many German institutions and businesses to convince themselves there was no need to change. In some ways this was a positive factor – it brought stability. However, it also meant that the best opportunities in education and jobs still went to the wealthy middle and upper classes. Adenauer was concerned that this would lead some sections of society to feel that the new republic did not offer them much – and that was a major reason that the Weimar Republic had failed. In the election of 1949, 22 per cent of Germans did not bother to vote, which suggested that Adenauer was right.

FACTFILE

The Basic Law
In some respects, the Basic Law was similar to the constitution of the Weimar Republic (see Factfile on page 133). However, the Basic Law built in important safeguards to protect democracy. The position of president was much less powerful. No party could send any representatives to the new parliament unless it gained 5 per cent of the vote. This was to stop aggressive minority parties like the Nazis or the Communist Party causing problems.

The West German 'economic miracle'

What really won the German people's support for the FRG was an extraordinary 'economic miracle'. Between 1948 and 1954 the German economy grew by 8 per cent every year. It had started from a low position because of the effects of the war, but even so this increase was impressive. By the early 1950s, Germany was again exporting high-quality manufactured goods all over the world. Unemployment fell from 8 per cent to 4 per cent by 1955, despite the dramatic rise in population due to the arrival of hundreds of thousands of refugee Germans from eastern Europe.

Source 22 A CDU election poster from 1949. It says: 'We cannot work magic but we can provide work. Vote CDU in the elections.' ▼

Source 23 An election poster from an opposing party in 1950. The text reads: 'Rubbish on the path. To achieve unity Adenauer and Krupp must go.' ▶

Adenauer pursued a cautious policy, promising no radical changes. The German people felt this was sensible – they had seen enough upheaval. More importantly, West Germans began to associate democracy with economic success and prosperity. Adenauer's share of the vote rose steadily and in 1957 the CDU gained an outright majority – over 50 per cent.

Causes and consequences of the economic miracle

The West German economic miracle was helped by Marshall Aid from the USA (see page 61), but there were other important factors. Many East German immigrants had valuable technical skills and so boosted the economy. The government also introduced a compensation scheme for Germans who had lost property or savings in the war. Many of these people were middle-class business owners who used their compensation to set up new businesses, which helped the economy grow.

Source 24 A typical West German supermarket in the 1950s. ▲

Another key factor was government involvement in industrial relations. Under the Co-determination Law of May 1951, large businesses had to allow trade union officials to sit on the board of directors to represent their workers. In 1952, firms were obliged to set up Works Councils. These made it compulsory for companies to keep workers informed about management plans. Both the unions and the managers disliked being forced into this arrangement but on the whole it seemed to work. Unions became less suspicious of managers and far fewer strikes took place in West Germany than during the Weimar years. This undermined support for communism. At the same time, better industrial relations encouraged big industries to accept democracy.

Agreement with France

Of course life in West Germany was not perfect. The country was still divided. Wealth was not distributed equally. The big industries that had helped the Nazi regime seemed to be thriving again. Adenauer looked for ways to reassure his European neighbours that Germany was now a peaceful nation. In 1950, Germany and France formed the European Coal and Steel Community, essentially making coal and steel a joint industry between the two countries. This was the first step towards the European Union that exists today. It tied one of Germany's key war industries to France, making it harder to fight another war.

By 1954, West Germany was seen to be stable, democratic and trustworthy enough to be allowed its own armed forces again, and to join NATO (see page 64). From 1955 to 1989, West Germany remained a stronghold of democracy in Europe. It continued to be so after East and West Germany were reunited in 1990.

1 Write your own 10-word summary of Source 25.

Source 25 Historian Mary Fulbrook, writing in 2011.

The period is an exceedingly difficult one to evaluate. From one point of view it can be pointed out that:
- *many former Nazis received minimal, if any, punishment for their crimes or complicity in an evil regime. It can even be shown that entrepreneurs who built up vast personal fortunes on the basis of Nazi 'aryanization' policies (forcible expropriation of Jewish concerns) and exploitation of slave labour, working Poles and Jews to the bone before their death by exhaustion, starvation or gassing, were able to use the capital thus amassed to continue successful entrepreneurial careers in the Federal Republic – and to influence prominent politicians in their favour.*
- *there was a massive wastage of talent, as thousands of courageous people who had refused to compromise with the Third Reich found their paths to postwar careers in the Civil Service blocked, as positions were retained or refilled by Nazi time-servers.*

- *the chance of a fundamental restructuring of German society was missed, as neither structure nor personnel were radically changed in an era of conservative 'restoration'.*

Against all this it can be asserted that:
- *without the integration of former Nazis, and without the startling economic success, Bonn democracy might have had as little chance of survival as Weimar democracy. Radical anti-system opposition on the part of a few activists would have combined with mass discontent based on economic misery and uncertainty to provide powerful forces for political destabilization.*
- *the end, retrospectively, might have justified the means: actions which can be criticized on moral grounds might have had consequences which even the critics would applaud.*

Source 26 GDR leader Water Ulbricht inspecting East German police in the 1950s. ▲

Democratisation and rebuilding in the Eastern zone

The Soviets introduced elected assemblies in the eastern sector of Germany quite early on. They also allowed political parties to be formed. On the creation of the FRG, the Soviet zone became the German Democratic Republic (GDR), often called East Germany. In theory this was a multi–party democracy, which held free elections to an assembly and was headed by a president. In reality, the USSR ensured that the East German Communist Party, the SED, was the dominant force. The key figure in East Germany was the leader of the SED, Walter Ulbricht. Ulbricht was German, but he was a deeply committed communist. He had been trained in the USSR during the war and was installed by the Soviets when they took over East Germany.

FOCUS TASK

The FRG and Weimar Germany: similarities, differences and lessons learned

You learned about Weimar Germany on pages 132–33. Your task now is to compare what you found out about Weimar Germany with the description of the FRG on pages 183–85.

1 What similar or different problems did they face?
2 What similar or different solutions did they try?
3 Do you think the FRG tackled its problems successfully?
4 What would you say were the two *main* differences between Weimar Germany and the FRG?

ACTIVITY

Draw a 'life graph', showing the attitude of Victor Klemperer towards communism in East Germany. Mark on your graph some of the key events and developments from this topic. Add notes explaining their impact on him.

Source 27 Extracts from the diary of Victor Klemperer, 1945–59.

26 July 1945: I am unsure whether to join the Communist Party. I do not want to take a decision in accordance with my – vacillating – emotions, not out of pure idealism, but coolly and calculatingly in accordance with what is best for my situation, my freedom, the work I still have to do, and yet nevertheless serving my ideal task, back the right horse. Which is the right horse? Russia? USA? Democracy? Communism? Unpolitical? Politically committed? Question mark upon question mark.

23 November 1945: I shall today hand in my application to join the KPD. My application states: 'I have never belonged to a party, but in my opinions and as a voter have stood by the Liberals. I nevertheless request to be admitted to the Communist Party, then for the following reasons: I believe, that to remain unattached to a party today is a luxury. I believe that only a very resolute left-wing movement can get us out of the present calamity and prevent its return. As a university teacher I was forced to watch at close quarters, as reactionary ideas made ever greater inroads. We must seek to remove them effectively and from the bottom up. And only in the SED [the Communist Party] do I see the unambiguous will to do so.

24 May 1950: I have not been awarded the honour I was hoping for. Perhaps more bitter than this defeat is my great divergence from the SED on many important matters, especially free speech. But I cannot just move over to the West – it is even more repugnant to me. Over here it is the 150%ers, that I loathe, but over there it is everything.

8 July 1953: In the very final analysis I am a liberal not a communist. I believe in freedom.

19 January 1955: If 'the people' themselves really are the rulers, what is the SED Party, what is the Central Committee, what is the Politburo, what is Ulbricht?? And why the game with parties, when only one rules? I do not understand it.

2 August 1956: Met with my publisher. Door was left open so all could hear our conversation and we could not be accused of anything. The atmosphere was as if we were threatened by the Gestapo again. It became clear to me, that communism is equally suited to pulling primitive peoples out of the primeval mud and pushing civilised peoples back into the primeval mud. I have finally become an anti-communist. This cannot have been Marx's ideal condition.

---

1 Read Source 27. How would you describe the changing tone of Klemperer's views on communism?
2 What do you think he means by 'the 150%ers'?
3 Given what you know about Klemperer, how reliable do you think his account of life in East Germany is?

Life in East Germany

As the war ended, many Germans fled from the Soviet zone to the Western zone but far more stayed in the East. Just as in the West, the majority of people were concerned only with finding food and shelter in the immediate aftermath of the war. Some welcomed the Soviets and the emergence of communism. One of these was Victor Klemperer, whose diaries you came across earlier in this chapter. Klemperer was a Jewish university professor. He survived the war with a bitter hatred of Nazism, and he hoped that communism might transform Germany for the better. Source 27 shows how his views changed over time.

The communist approach to rebuilding Germany

Source 28 A youth festival march in the GDR, 1951. ▼

The experiences of those living in the Soviet sector of Germany were probably harsher than in the western sectors. In the years 1945–47, the Soviet leader Josef Stalin was determined that Germany should pay for its wartime actions in the USSR. Food, industrial equipment (including 1,400 entire factories) and countless other resources were gathered up and shipped out of East Germany to the USSR. Looting and rape were widespread.

By 1948, this phase had largely ended and a new communist government was established under Walter Ulbricht. He continued the communist policies that the Soviets had begun. Around 7,000 large landowners had their estates confiscated and the land was mostly redistributed to peasants. Ulbricht also abolished private schools and brought in free education for all. Policies like these encouraged people like Victor Klemperer to believe that communism might improve life in East Germany.

Ulbricht effectively scrapped East Germany's democratic constitution in 1950. He reorganised the SED along the same lines as in the USSR, creating a Central Committee and a Politburo, with himself as head of state. A PURGE of political opponents began. The state took control of the media and the education system. Teachers were watched closely to ensure they were teaching approved ideas. The newly formed Stasi (secret police force) kept a close eye on potential enemies of the new state.

In 1952, Ulbricht announced a new programme for East Germany – the Building of Socialism. People hoped that this might bring economic improvements, but they were disappointed. There was no 'economic miracle' in East Germany. Ulbricht took his orders from Stalin, and Stalin wanted East Germany to produce goods that would help the recovery of the USSR. This meant engineering equipment and similar industrial items rather than the consumer goods that drove West Germany's economic boom.

Ulbricht also brought in compulsory state control of agriculture. In doing so, he hoped to grow enough food to feed the population with a surplus that could be shipped to the USSR, but the programme did not have much success. In addition, he decided to build up the military in East Germany. This was an unpopular move: many Germans were forced into military service and the programme took up around 10 per cent of the country's wealth. For East Germans the result of Ulbricht's policies were shortages and repression. Basic foods like butter and sugar had to be rationed. Consumer goods were scarce and very expensive. Any attempts to protest or challenge Ulbricht were dealt with harshly by the Stasi.

Source 29 A table showing the percentage of East German households owning consumer goods in 1955.

Item	Percentage of households owning item
car	0.2
motorbike	11
radio	77
TV	1
fridge	0.4
washing machine	0.5

4   Is it possible to make a comparison between East and West Germany using Source 24 on page 185 and Source 29?

Protest

The result of the problems was violent protest. In June 1953, workers in East Berlin went on strike and began protesting in the streets. Within days, an estimated 1 million people in towns and cities across East Germany followed suit. Ulbricht responded quickly and ruthlessly. East German police, alongside Soviet tanks and troops, moved in and crushed the rebellion. Estimates put the death toll at around 500. Around 5,000 people were arrested and more than 1,200 of these served long prison sentences. There was outrage in the West at Ulbricht's actions, but little could be done. It was clear that two Germanies were following entirely different paths.

Source 30 Soviet tanks in East Germany, June 1953. ▼

1 Source 30 was published in West Germany. Does this mean it is not a useful source of information about events in 1953?

FOCUS TASK

Comparing the two Germanies

You have been asked to write an article for a British newspaper with the title: *Ten years on: Two Germanies 1945–55*. The article has a word limit of 250 words. You should aim to include:

● examples of two *similar* problems faced by the two Germanies
● examples of two *different* solutions tried
● two examples of the *experiences* of Germans in each area
● two sources.

You could use a table like the one below for your research – once for each problem.

	East Germany	West Germany
solution		
experience		
source		

REVIEW TASK

What had the biggest impact on the German people 1939–55?

The period 1939–55 was a time of immense and catastrophic change in Germany. Imagine it was possible to survey the population and ask them what changes had the biggest impact on their lives. Look back over this chapter and do some plausible reconstruction. Based on the events of the period 1939–55 what do you think the German population might have said about the following? Record your ideas in your own copy of the table

Key event/development	Was impact positive or negative?	Explanation	Rating from –5 (biggest negative) to +5 (biggest positive)
early successes in war			
bombing			
war economy			
racial policy			
defeat and occupation			
denazification			
division			
rebuilding economy			

PRACTICE QUESTIONS

1 Describe two examples of the effects of occupation in Germany. (2)
2 Explain how war affected Germans in the years 1939–45. (10)
3 Explain why denazification proved to be a difficult task in the years 1945–48 in Germany. (10)
4 'The biggest change that affected Germans in the period 1939–45 was war.' How far do you agree with this view? (18)

KEY TERMS

Make sure you understand these key terms and can use them confidently in your writing.
- coalition
- concentration camps
- Holocaust
- Reichstag

TOPIC SUMMARY

The Second World War and its legacy in Germany 1939–55

1 Germany had been preparing for war since the mid-1930s. When it started, war was not celebrated by ordinary people but most of them played their part as demanded by the Nazi regime.
2 The war went well at first, bringing wealth to Germany from occupied countries.
3 From 1941, the tide turned. A long campaign of Allied bombing of German cities became increasingly ferocious, culminating in a catastrophic few days in Dresden in which 50,000 people died.
4 The war with the USSR sapped more and more resources from Germany – the war economy took over and Germans found themselves short of everything. Women and young people now found new roles in the war industries.
5 Propaganda increased through wartime, giving good news and encouragement.
6 War increased terror. The worst escalation of this was in the treatment of Jews. Nazi persecution turned into the 'Final Solution' – a deliberate policy of mass murder. Jews were taken away to death camps, where they were worked to death or gassed on arrival.
7 Once it was clear that the Nazis were going to be defeated, Hitler faced increased opposition and disillusionment, including an assassination attempt by his own generals. However, the German people fought loyally to the end. Despite defeat in battle, the regime remained strong.
8 When the Nazis surrendered, the Allies divided Germany into four zones, run by the USA, the USSR, Britain and France. They began a programme to demilitarise, denazify and democratise Germany. However, due to Cold War tensions beyond Germany the policies changed: the US, British and French sectors were combined as the Federal Republic of Germany (West Germany).
9 West Germany flourished. Democracy was re-established and there was rapid economic growth. East Germany, under Soviet and communist control, was characterised by repression, shortages and lack of freedom.
10 For those Germans living with the memory of Nazi war crimes, the idea developed that the Nazi era had been an accident – *Betriebsunfall*. They put it behind them and devoted all their energy to building a new Germany.

ASSESSMENT FOCUS

How the non-British depth study on Germany 1925–55 will be assessed

This section is worth 40 marks – 20 per cent of your total GCSE. The questions could be on any part of the content, so you need to know it all.

Three questions will assess:
● AO1: knowledge and understanding (total 15 marks across all questions)
● AO2: explanation and analysis (15 marks across all questions).

One question will assess:
● AO3: analyse, evaluate and use sources (10 marks in one question).

Above all, the paper is trying to assess your ability to think and work like a historian. Before you read this guidance you might want to look back at the introduction on how historians think on page 4. There, we set out some steps that historians take:
1 focus
2 ask questions
3 select
4 organise
5 fine tune

The exam questions have already chosen a focus (stage 1) and they have asked questions (stage 2). What the examiner wants from you is stages 3, 4 and 5.

Question 1

Question 1 will usually ask for a short description of an event or feature from one section of the course. It is a simple knowledge question, usually requiring some accurate description. For example:

Aim of the question
This is designed to start the exam with a relatively simple, knowledge-based question. The examiner wants to see that you can select and describe important events accurately, without simply writing down everything you know.

> **Describe one example of Nazi policy in the 1920s. (2 marks)**

Advice
Select: Choose one action and either describe it in a couple of sentences or describe why the government took the action. You do not need every detail.

Organise: The main thing to remember here is not to write too much.

Fine tune: Make sure that your spellings and dates are correct. Make sure that your answer is clear – in the pressure of an exam it is easy to accidentally say something you do not mean to say.

This answer is correct and has adequate description. Examiners are not looking for a lot, this is just about right.

This answer needs no improvement – move on to Question 2!

> One example of a Nazi policy in the 1920s was the demand for the abolition of the Treaty of Versailles. It was seen as an unjust *diktat* and blamed for many of Germany's problems in the 1920s.

Question 2

Aim of the question
There will usually be at least two reasons or results to consider in a question like this, and examiners want to see you *explain* them rather than just describe events. You can argue that one reason or result was more important than another, or you may argue that they were equally important – or perhaps that they were connected.

Question 2 will demand more analysis and explanation than Question 1. It might ask you about the importance or impact of a factor, or how successful an organisation was. For example:

> **Explain how the Reichstag fire helped the Nazis to secure control of Germany in 1933. (10 marks)**

A useful way to improve your answers is to assess them yourself. Examiners use mark schemes but you do not really need anything that complicated. Think of it like an Olympic medal ceremony. Read some of your practice answers and ask yourself which of these medals your answer deserves.

The Question 2 medal ceremony

 Bronze (up to 25% of marks): You list some of the events but do not answer the question (e.g. 'After the fire, a communist called van der Lubbe was arrested').

 Silver (up to 60% of marks): You describe the events that followed the fire in greater detail (e.g. 'Hitler claimed it was a communist plot', 'Hitler persuaded Hindenburg to give him emergency powers') but you do not fully explain how these events helped the Nazis secure power.

 Gold (up to 100% of marks): You go beyond description of the events to explain how they helped the Nazis (e.g. you explain how it helped them get rid of their opponents).

Even a Gold answer can be improved by ensuring you have:
- a clear conclusion that rounds off your argument and makes it really clear what you think the answer to the question is
- a balanced answer that shows you understand that there might be more than one view about the question, or explains how the different elements are connected
- supporting evidence – using relevant knowledge and a good range of examples to support each point you make.

Advice

Select: Focus on how the Nazis capitalised on the fire and the actions they took after it.

Organise: The important thing is to use your knowledge in a relevant way.

Fine tune: Do all the usual checking but for an explain question check that you have really explained how the fire helped the Nazis and not just described what happened afterwards.

> This is a good answer – a Gold medal! It would probably get 9–10 marks.
>
> It has a clear opening and it then really does explain two factors. The first explains how the fire led to Hitler getting emergency powers. The second factor explains how those powers helped the Nazis do well in the election that followed.
>
> There is no need to improve this answer. It does the job!

> The fire gave Hitler a tremendous opportunity to consolidate his power. He used the fire to claim that it was the signal for an imminent communist uprising. This in turn allowed Hitler to convince Hindenburg to give him special emergency powers, which were passed on 28 February. These powers allowed the police to hold suspects without trial. The Nazis used this to round up their opponents. Around 4,000 communists and other Nazi opponents were arrested. Obviously this weakened the opposition to the Nazis.
>
> The fact that the opponents were so weak helped the Nazis do well in the elections in March 1933. The Nazis could campaign on slogans like 'The Battle against Marxism'. Hence they won the election, although with a smaller majority, which shows how much they needed to attack the communists.

Question 3

Question 3 requires an evaluation of sources. The question will always be worth 10 marks and it will always contain two sources. However, it can appear in two formats:

Format A: separate questions

This format asks a separate question on each source (worth 5 marks each).
For example:
- Why was the source published?
- How is this source useful to historians?
- What is the viewpoint of the artist/author?
- How reliable is this source?

Format B: comparison question

This format asks you to compare two sources (10 marks). For example:
- How similar are Sources A and B?
- How far do the sources agree?
- Why do they disagree?
- Is one source more reliable than the other?
- Is one source more useful than the other?

Aim of the question
These questions ask you to show your understanding of two sources from the period you are studying by producing a clear answer and supporting that answer from the sources. Some examples of questions are shown below, but we cannot cover all types. You will find it helpful to look at the Assessment Focus for the other depth studies as well (pages 258 and 330), which give examples of the different types of questions and advice on how to tackle them.

The Question 3 source evaluation guide

Here are some rules to help you evaluate sources.

Sources are not textbooks. Do not treat them as if they are.

Textbook authors use many sources and then generalise to give the overall picture. Textbooks tell you what happened. Sources tell you how individuals or groups *felt* about what happened. If a source says something different from your textbook, this does not mean it is wrong. It might be atypical and something the textbook author did not have space to cover.

Do not criticise a source because of what it does not say.

You could make this point about almost any source – a source on the USA in this period does not tell you about Germany in the 1800s. Neither does this morning's newspaper. It is not a helpful approach.

Back up your points with examples from the source.

It is amazing how often candidates fail to do this. They may write something like 'Source B is hostile to immigrants', but then fail to say what they found in Source B that led them to this conclusion.

In comparison questions, compare content first ...

... Then go on to compare purpose, attitude, context, etc.

Use comprehension to work out *what the source says* and then use inference to see *what it can tell you.*

Comprehension means understanding what the source actually says – such as an advertisement trying to sell vacuum cleaners or a newspaper article criticising immigrants. An inference builds on your comprehension – it is something not stated in the source but which can be worked out from it. For example, you might be able to look at an advertisement from the 1920s and decide that it is aimed at women. This is an inference, because the poster does not state this openly. Similarly, you might be able to infer that the writer of an article wants controls in immigration, even though they might not actually say that. Using inferences can also stop you making mistakes about bias (see right).

Use your evaluation to answer the question – not for its own sake.

Candidates often use useful tools like the five Ws (Who? Why? When? Where? What?). However, it is also common for candidates to forget to use those findings to answer the question! If you are going to use the five Ws or a similar technique, make sure the information it gives you helps support your answer, otherwise it is irrelevant.

Never dismiss a source because it is biased or unreliable. All sources are useful about something and reliable about something.

The *story in the source* might be biased or unreliable (e.g. an election poster). However, that means *the story of the source* is very useful – somebody went to the trouble of exaggerating, lying or distorting the facts in order to achieve a particular aim. We can use the source to learn about the people who created it, their aims and their attitude towards the people they are lying about. Sources will almost always reveal something about values, attitudes, fears, concerns, beliefs and reactions.

Only use contextual knowledge when it helps you answer the question.

If you have some relevant contextual knowledge that supports your answer, use it. If you just want to show the examiner you know stuff, don't!

Commenting on tone or language is not evaluation.

A comment on the tone or language of a source can be used to support a point you make about purpose, attitude or some other aspect of evaluation, but in itself is not evaluation.

Aim of the question

The focus of the question is on usefulness. The best way to show that something is useful is to use it! So this question is testing whether you can make use of the source – whether you understand the content and can make inferences and support them the way historians do.

Source A An extract from a secret report on attitudes in Nazi Germany in June 1937. It was written by socialists inside Germany and sent to socialist leaders in exile outside Germany.

The number of those who consciously criticise the regime is very small, quite apart from the fact that they have no way to express this criticism. The regime controls all of the press and radio stations.

Propaganda is everywhere. It does not stop people feeling discontent but propaganda tells them that to complain is to threaten the Third Reich – a prospect which would leave them horrified. They have seen what happens to the Jews and do not wish to share their fate.

It becomes increasingly evident that the majority of the people have two faces; one which they show to their family and friends and people they see as reliable. The other face is for the authorities. The private face shows the sharpest criticism of everything that is going on now; the official face beams with optimism and contentment.

This is a Gold medal answer – 5 marks.

The candidate makes two very good inferences (in bold).

There is supporting detail from the source, which is used to support the answer.

The only improvement would be to provide a little context from the candidate's own knowledge, either about the propaganda machine in Germany or the terror state. But this answer is so good it would get full marks without the context.

Example 3A: separate question format

One common question type asks you about the usefulness of a source.

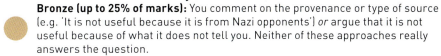

> **Study Source A. Explain how this source is useful to a historian studying Nazi Germany. (5 marks)**

The Question 3 medal ceremony (usefulness)

Bronze (up to 25% of marks): You comment on the provenance or type of source (e.g. 'It is not useful because it is from Nazi opponents') *or* argue that it is not useful because of what it does not tell you. Neither of these approaches really answers the question.

Silver (up to 60% of marks): You answer the question and support your answer with extracts or details from the sources.

Gold (up to 100% of marks): You answer the question using context, provenance, purpose, attitude or other inferences to support the answer.

Even a Gold answer can be improved by ensuring you have:
- a valid conclusion
- more than one type of evaluation.

Advice

Select: Candidates often criticise sources as not useful because they do not say what the candidate already knows. This is not a helpful approach, so in some ways the best advice we can give is to *not* select knowledge from your wardrobe! Instead you are using your knowledge and understanding of the period to make use of the source. Similarly, stay away from comments about bias unless you can show how the bias makes it useful.

Organise: The most important thing is to work out what you want to say before you start writing. A good structure for this question is:

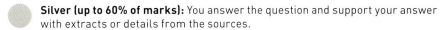

Source A is useful because it provides some interesting information. For example …

However, it can be even more useful to historians. When we look at it more carefully we can infer that … because …

In some ways the source is biased because … This is actually useful because …

Fine tune: Do all the usual checks, but here it is worth making sure you have answered the question using content and then evaluation.

Example answer

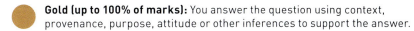

Source A is useful because it provides some interesting information. For example, the source tells us that the Nazis controlled the press and radio stations.

However, it can be even more useful to historians. When we look at it more carefully we can infer that **Nazi control over the population was very strong**. We can see this because the source says people are afraid to complain even though they do not really support the Nazis.

In some ways the source is biased because it was written by opponents of the Nazis. This is actually useful because it is the opposition telling us that the Nazis are powerful, not the Nazis themselves. The source is useful to the historian because **it gives really strong evidence about why opposition groups found it difficult** in Germany.

Source B A poster published in Germany in 1943. The caption means 'The enemy sees your lights! Blackout!'

Example 3B: separate question format
Another common question type is about purpose.

> *Study Source B. Explain why this source was published at this time.* **(5 marks)**

The Question 3 medal ceremony (purpose)

- **Bronze (up to 25% of marks):** You comment on the general context (e.g. 'Germany was at war').

- **Silver (up to 60% of marks):** You explain the message of the source – what it is trying to say (e.g. 'There were air raids').

- **Gold (up to 100% of marks):** You make an inference to explain the purpose of the poster (e.g. 'To get people to obey the blackout') and support your answer with extracts or details from the source.

Even a Gold medal answer can be improved by ensuring you have:
- explained the attitude of the creator, not just the message of the source
- included more than one type of evaluation.

Advice
Select: Many candidates need to be more selective when tackling this type of question. If you have some relevant contextual knowledge that supports your answer, use it. If you just want to show the examiner you know stuff, don't!

Organise: The most important thing is to work out what you want to say before you start writing. With purpose questions, a good way to organise your answer is:

> The purpose of this source was to ... [change laws/attitudes/behaviour].
>
> The poster tries to achieve this by ...

Fine tune: Do all the usual checks, but here it is worth making sure you have answered the question using content and then evaluation.

Example answer

> The poster was published **to make sure Germans obeyed the blackout regulations** in force. In 1943, Germany was being bombed by the Allies and the poster shows a British bomber bringing death to the Germans. The bomber can drop bombs much more accurately if it can see what is below at night, hence it was essential for Germans not to show any light but to ensure there was a blackout. Not only did bombs damage houses in the cities but they also put industrial complexes out of action, as in the Ruhr.

Source C An extract from a speech given by Robert Ley in 1933. Ley was in charge of the German Workers' Front, which replaced trade unions and controlled industrial workers.

We have power, but we do not yet have the whole nation. We do not have the 100 per cent support of you workers. We will not leave you alone until we get your support. Workers, without you there is no German nation. I swear to you we will not only preserve the rights you have, we shall extend them and we shall improve your pay and working conditions. You will be made worthy and respected members of the nation.

Aim of the question
The focus of the question is on the differences between the sources. You want to identify how they disagree and give reasons for that based on your evaluation of the sources and your background knowledge.

Example 3C: comparison format

Source D An extract from the diaries of Victor Klemperer, a Jewish university lecturer in Germany.

September 1937: On the festival of Yom Kippur the Jews did not attend class. Kufahl, the mathematician, had said to the reduced class: 'Today it's just us.' In my memory these words took on a quite horrible significance: to me it confirms the claim of the Nazis to express the true opinion of the German people. And I believe ever more strongly that Hitler really does embody the soul of the German people, that he really stands for Germany. There is no will or even desire to resist him. Consequently he will keep his position. I have not only lost my Fatherland. Even if the government should change one day, my sense of belonging to Germany has gone.

> *Study Sources C and D. Why do these two sources disagree? (10 marks)*

The Question 3 medal ceremony (disagreement of sources)

- **Bronze (up to 25% of marks):** You comment on the provenance or type of source (one is written by a Nazi, the other by a Jew) *or* summarise each source. Neither of these approaches really answers the question.

- **Silver (up to 60% of marks):** You answer the question by explaining how they are different and support your answer with extracts or details from the sources.

- **Gold (up to 100% of marks):** You answer the question as above, but use context, provenance, purpose, attitude or other inferences to support your answer.

Even a Gold medal answer can be improved by ensuring you have:
- a valid conclusion
- more than one type of evaluation.

Advice
Select: Only use your knowledge if it helps you make use of the sources. Do not select knowledge from your wardrobe for its own sake.

Organise: The most important thing is to work out what you want to say before you start writing. A good structure for this questions is:

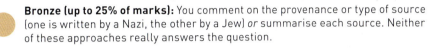

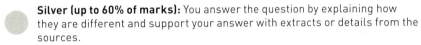

Fine tune: Do all the usual checks, but here it is worth making sure you have answered the question using content and then evaluation.

Example answer

This is a Gold medal answer, probably gaining 9 out of 10.

It picks out information from each source and explains clearly how they are different.

It then steps up a level and uses contextual knowledge and inferences to explain why they disagree. These sections are in bold.

The only way you could improve it would be to point out that Klemperer was talking about middle-class university professors and not German workers, so he would not have had a very clear idea of their views.

These two sources disagree because they say completely different things. For example, Source C shows the Nazi Workers' leader Robert Ley stating that at least some workers do not support the Nazis. In contrast, Source D claims that Hitler really does represent the soul of the German people and there will never be any resistance to him.

There are important reasons for these differences. **Firstly they come from different times. In 1933, German workers did not support the Nazis – most voted SPD. That is why Source C contradicts Source D. Also, Klemperer was writing in 1937. Although most German workers did not support the Nazis they did not resist them.** This was partly because they were afraid to lose their jobs but it probably seemed to Klemperer that they supported the Nazis.

Another reason was that by 1937 Victor Klemperer was very disillusioned. We can see in Source D that he thinks most of his fellow workers at the university support Hitler. As a Jew, he would have been suffering severe discrimination for many years. During the 1930s Jews were pushed out of jobs and encouraged to emigrate. This explains why Klemperer thought other Germans did support Hitler.

Question 4

Question 4 is a traditional essay-style question. For example:

> *'The Nazi regime in Germany in the 1930s faced relatively little opposition because most Germans were afraid of it.' How far do you agree with this statement? (18 marks)*

Aim of the question
Examiners want to see a balanced answer. You can state your view strongly and clearly, but make sure you have fully considered the alternative view.

The Question 4 medal ceremony

 Bronze (up to 25% of marks): You describe aspects of Nazi Germany without answering the question (e.g. 'There was a lot of propaganda').

 Silver (up to 60% of marks): You argue yes or no and support your argument by describing example(s) of the actions of the Nazi regime.

 Gold (up to 100% of marks): You write a balanced answer which explains that there is evidence to support both a 'yes' and a 'no' argument. The answer may support one side or the other but must acknowledge that there is an alternative view even if you think it is wrong.

Even a Gold answer can be improved by ensuring you have:
- a clear conclusion that rounds off your argument and makes it really clear what you think the answer to the question is
- a balanced answer that shows you understand that there might be more than one view about the question or explains how the different elements are connected
- used relevant knowledge and a good range of examples to provide supporting evidence for each point you make.

Advice
Select: Focus on the reasons. A common error is to describe the actions of the regime and forget to explain why these actions (or other factors) stopped opposition. It may seem obvious to you but examiners cannot read your mind. They will not credit something unless you spell it out in your answer.

Organise: Take one factor and explain it in a paragraph of its own. Then move to the next paragraph.

Fine tune: Make sure that your spellings and dates are correct. Make sure that your answer is clear – in the pressure of an exam it is easy to accidentally say something you do not mean to say. In this question examiners like you to say which side of the argument you support.

Example answer

> The statement is true to a great extent. Nazi Germany was a terror state. The state controlled the police forces and the judiciary, so if you were accused of a crime you had very little chance of a fair trial. Even more terrifying, the regime also had the secret police or Gestapo, which had informers everywhere and had a terrible reputation for torturing opponents of the regime. Finally there was also the SS. The SS ran the concentration camps and was responsible for persecuting Jews. This was not hidden as it terrorised the rest of the population.
>
> On the other hand, another reason why opposition to the Nazi regime in the 1930s was limited was that the opposition groups were weak and divided or they were too small-scale and lacked resources. Even before the Nazis came to power the communists and the socialists fought against each other rather than uniting against the threat of the Nazis. Communists and socialists and other groups like trade unions were weakened when most of the leading figures were arrested after the Reichstag fire in 1933. Another reason was that for many Germans life under the Nazis was acceptable in that they had work after the terrible unemployment of 1929–33.
>
> Another important factor was that the Nazis had improved life for many Germans. They had reduced unemployment from 6 million in 1933 to almost nothing. They also helped farmers and provided schemes for workers like Strength Through Joy....

This is an excellent answer – definitely a Gold – and would probably get 17 marks.

It has a clear opening and it then sticks to the line that the opening suggests it will follow.

There is a good analysis of two factors.

It is worth noting that this answer does not cover every aspect of Nazi Germany. It does not need to! The level of detail shown here is enough for a top mark.

The only way to improve this would be with a conclusion, perhaps along these lines: 'So overall, the statement is only partially true. Fear was probably the biggest factor because we know that Germans did grumble and complain in private but they did not do so in public, suggesting that even if they supported the opposition groups they would have been too scared to do anything about it.'

KEYS TO SUCCESS

As long as you know the content and have learned how to think, this exam should not be too scary. The keys to success are:

1   Read the question carefully. This may sound obvious, but there is a skill to it. Sometimes students answer the question they *wish* had been asked rather than the one that has *actually* been asked. So identify the skill focus (what the question is asking you to do). Does it want you to write a description, an explanation or a comparison? Identify the content focus (what it is about) and select from your knowledge accordingly.

2   Note the marks available. That helps you work out how much time to spend on answering each question. Time is precious – if you spend too long on low-mark questions you will run out of time for the high-mark ones.

3   Plan your answer before you start writing. For essays this is particularly important. The golden rule is: know what you are going to say; then say it clearly and logically.

4   Aim for quality not quantity: in the time limits of an exam you will not be able to write down everything you know and can think of – even if it is relevant. The marker would much rather read a short answer that really tackles the question than page after page of material that is not relevant.

5   Check your work. You will never have time in an exam to rewrite an answer but try to leave some time at the end to check for obvious spelling mistakes, missing words or other writing errors that might cost you marks.

5.1 The 'Roaring Twenties': The age of irresponsibility?

FOCUS

After the First World War ended in 1918, the USA immediately withdrew from the world stage. The new president, Warren Harding, promised to return the USA to 'normalcy' – how things were before the war. And these policies seemed to work ... for some. The US economy boomed in the 1920s and so did cultural life. Many groups in US society flourished. However not everyone shared in the prosperity. Some faced poverty, prejudice and intolerance. In this topic, you will find out about those contrasting experiences and the reasons for them. You will examine:

- what caused the economic boom
- how far the economic boom benefited all Americans
- how women's lives changed in this period
- the reasons for and impact of the prohibition of alcohol
- the experiences of immigrants, African Americans and minority groups in the 1920s.

Source 1 Newspaper headlines announcing Charles Lindbergh's successful first crossing of the Atlantic by air in 1927. ▶

Source 2 A photograph of the parade welcoming Lindbergh back to New York, June 1927. ▼

Source 3 A postage stamp issued in the USA, June 1927. ▲

Charles Lindbergh and the *Spirit of St. Louis*

Sources 1–3 tell part of the story of Charles Lindbergh. In many ways Lindbergh sums up the spirit of the Roaring Twenties in the USA. His story reads like a Hollywood movie. Lindbergh flew across the Atlantic – a major feat in the aircraft of the time – to win a $25,000 prize. He had to battle against the odds to achieve this: financial problems, technical problems, bad weather. He made it across the Atlantic in 33.5 hours. He got a hero's welcome in France, and on his return to the USA in June 1927 he was greeted by the president. Every newspaper, magazine and radio show wanted to interview him. The *Spirit of St. Louis* (funded by businessmen from St. Louis) even had a postage stamp made in its honour (see Source 3).

So what made a poster boy out of Charles Lindbergh? In the 1920s, many Americans loved celebrity and glamour just as they do today. They loved new technology and people who could use it. They admired and sought wealth. It was an exciting, even a reckless, time and a young, handsome risk-taker like Lindbergh appealed to the spirit of the Roaring Twenties.

The spirit of this era was not all media hype. The USA was undergoing some fundamental changes that shaped the character of the decade.

1. Study Sources 1–3. How can you tell that Charles Lindbergh was big news at this time?
2. Study Source 4. Is the artist positive or negative about the building boom taking place in US cities in the 1920s? How can you tell?

What was changing in the 1920s?

More people lived in towns and cities than ever before

In 1920, for the first time in US history, over 50 per cent of Americans lived in towns and cities rather than in the countryside. The percentage continued to grow as the decade progressed. The skylines of expanding cities, especially New York and Chicago, were powerful symbols representing a new age of prosperity, opportunity, freedom and excitement.

Source 4 A painting from 1920 called *The Builder*. The artist was Gerrit A. Benecker, who had worked for the US government producing posters in the First World War. ▼

The entertainment and leisure industries were booming

During the 1920s, average wages rose and working hours fell. Much of this spare time and money went on entertainment:

- **Radio:** Almost everyone listened to the radio. Even in the poorer urban areas there was a radio to every one or two households. In August 1921, there was one licensed radio station in the USA. By the end of 1922, there were 508. By 1929, the NBC network was making $150 million a year.
- **Music:** Radio brought new music to new audiences. Jazz swept the nation and the 1920s are often referred to as the 'Jazz Age'. It was associated with young people – both men and women – drinking and partying, dancing outrageous modern dances like the Charleston.
- **Cinema:** Cinema exploded in popularity in the 1920s. Based in a small suburb of Los Angeles called Hollywood, it became a multi-million dollar industry. Even the poorest could afford the 10 or 20 cents entrance fee. Stars such as Charlie Chaplin, Buster Keaton, Douglas Fairbanks and Mary Pickford became national celebrities in the era of silent films. When talking movies ('talkies') arrived in 1927, Hollywood became even more popular.

Source 5 An advertisement for *The Jazz Bride*, a movie released in 1928. ▲

Old attitudes were being challenged

Young women in particular gained new freedom in the 1920s. The emergence of the 'flapper' – a young woman who partied, drank and smoked just like her male friends – was widely commented upon. The flapper became one of the symbols of the 1920s.

Before the war, sex was a taboo subject in society – nobody spoke of it openly. In the 1920s, however, sex and morality were discussed freely in newspapers and magazines, and radio shows and movies exploited its appeal. There were female sex symbols like Clara Bow in *Get Your Man* (1926) and male sex symbols like Rudolph Valentino in *The Sheik* (1921). These films would not seem risqué to an audience today, but they were very daring at the time.

Car ownership was increasing, which increased people's freedom

The motor car made all the other freedoms of the 1920s easier. Over 7 million vehicles were registered in the USA in 1922, and manufacturers were turning out around 1.5 million more every year. Cars helped the cities to grow by offering access to the suburbs. They allowed boys and girls to travel beyond the moral gaze of their parents. Cars carried their owners to and from their entertainments and opened up a wider range of leisure pursuits: sporting events, beach holidays, shopping trips, picnics in the country, or simply visits to their family and friends.

1. Source 5 is an advertisement designed to persuade people to pay to see the film. How does it do this?
2. Is it reasonable to infer that that target audience of Source 5 was women? Explain your answer.
3. Which of these statements do you agree with more?
   a. Source 4 is more useful to historians than Source 5.
   b. Sources 4 and 5 are both very useful to historians, but about different aspects of the Roaring Twenties.
4. In his *History of the USA*, the historian Hugh Brogan titled the chapter on the 1920s 'Irresponsibility'. From the evidence on pages 198–200, can you understand why he did this? Do you agree?

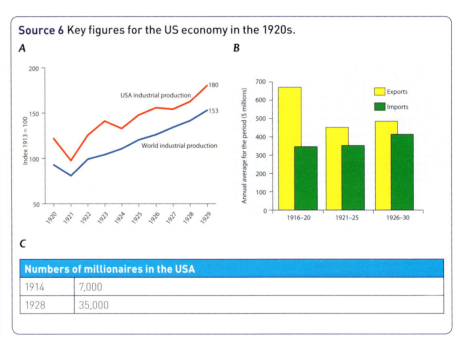

Source 6 Key figures for the US economy in the 1920s.

A — USA industrial production (180), World industrial production (153). Index 1913 = 100, years 1920–1929.

B — Exports / Imports. Annual average for the period ($ millions), periods 1916–20, 1921–25, 1926–30.

C

Numbers of millionaires in the USA	
1914	7,000
1928	35,000

FOCUS TASK

What were the Roaring Twenties all about?

You have been commissioned by a US company that wants to build a Roaring Twenties history attraction. Your job is to write a proposal (maximum 150 words) about what they should feature. The company has a limited budget so you need to:

- recommend exhibits (e.g. a reconstructed movie theatre)
- explain how these exhibits represent the Roaring Twenties
- Indicate which exhibits you think should take priority over others (in case they cannot afford all of the exhibits you propose).

The US system of government

- **The federal system:** Individual states look after their own internal affairs (such as education). Federal issues, such as questions that concern all states, are dealt with by Congress.
- **The Constitution:** The Constitution lays out how the government is supposed to operate and what it is allowed to do.
- **The president:** Presidents are elected every four years. They are powerful, but they have to work with Congress and the Supreme Court to govern effectively.
- **Congress:** Congress is made up of the Senate and the House of Representatives. Congress and the president run the country, often arguing but usually working out some kind of compromise.
- **The Supreme Court:** This is made up of judges, usually experienced lawyers. Their main task is to make sure that US governments do not misuse their power or pass unfair laws. They have the power to block laws they see as unconstitutional (against the Constitution).
- **Parties:** There are two main political parties: the Republicans and the Democrats. In the 1920s and 1930s, the Republicans were stronger in the industrial north of the USA while the Democrats had more support in the south. On the whole, Republicans in the 1920s and 1930s preferred government to stay out of people's lives as much as possible. The Democrats were more prepared to intervene in everyday life.

Causes and consequences of the economic boom

What was making all the fun and frolics of the Roaring Twenties possible? The short answer is a booming economy. US industries were producing more goods than the rest of the world put together (see Source 6). As well as higher production, these industries generally had higher productivity – they were operating more efficiently. While they were successful in selling goods around the world, most US companies could make a lot of money from the large internal market of the USA, with its population of 123 million (over half of them in towns or cities). Economic growth averaged just over 4 per cent per year – a healthy rate. Prices stayed relatively stable, even though wages for most workers rose. This resulted in an average increase in spending power of 11 per cent. So it was boom time!

Policies of the Republican governments of the 1920s

President Warren Harding had promised a return to 'normalcy' after the disruption of the war. For him and his Republican Party, this meant getting back to making money. Harding appointed men with strong backgrounds in business to key jobs in the government. Andrew Mellon, in charge of the Treasury, had become the second richest man in the USA from his aluminium and oil businesses. Herbert Hoover, the secretary of commerce, had made a fortune in mining and had also carried out important humanitarian work in Europe after the First World War. Hoover was a popular figure at the time, and the Democratic Party had also tried to recruit him. The rising young Democrat (and future president) Franklin D. Roosevelt said: 'Hoover is certainly a wonder. I wish we could make him president of the United States. There couldn't be a better one.' But Hoover joined the Republicans. Harding's Cabinet contained many other millionaires – the *New York World* newspaper estimated that their combined wealth was over $600 million.

Key policies

Republican policies were shaped by the views of Harding and his Cabinet:

1 Laissez-faire

Republicans believed that government should interfere as little as possible in the everyday lives of the people. This attitude is called laissez-faire. *Republicans felt that the government should leave businessmen alone to do their jobs. That was where prosperity came from. This was closely related to their belief in 'rugged individualism', which reflected an admiration of the way Americans were strong and got on with solving their own problems.*

2 Protective tariffs

The Republicans believed in import tariffs, which made it expensive to sell foreign goods in the country. For example, in 1922 Harding introduced the Fordney–McCumber tariff, which made imported food expensive in the USA. These tariffs protected businesses against foreign competition and allowed US companies to grow even more rapidly.

Republican policies

3 Low taxation

The Republicans kept taxes as low as possible. This brought some benefits to ordinary working people, but even greater benefits to the very wealthy. The Republicans felt that if people kept their own money, they would spend it on US goods and rich people would reinvest their money in industries.

4 Powerful trusts

Trusts were huge corporations that dominated industry. Woodrow Wilson and the Democrats had fought against trusts because they believed it was unhealthy for millionaires such as Andrew Carnegie (steel) and John D. Rockefeller (oil) to have almost complete control of one vital sector of industry. The Republicans allowed the trusts to do what they wanted, believing that these 'captains of industry' knew better than politicians did what was good for US business.

Source 7 President Calvin Coolidge, speaking to a gathering of US newspaper editors, 1925.

I am pleased that American newspapers take the trouble to understand and report on what happens in the business world. After all, the chief business of the American people is business. They are profoundly concerned with buying, selling, investing and prospering in the world.

Source 8 Herbert Hoover, speaking after being elected president in 1928.

We in America today are nearer to the final triumph over poverty than ever before in the history of any land. We shall soon, with the help of God, be in sight of the day when poverty will be banished from this nation.

Coolidge and Hoover

President Harding died suddenly in 1923 and was succeeded by his vice-president, Calvin Coolidge. Coolidge shared Harding's views. He earned the nickname 'Silent Cal' because he believed government should keep out of business and many other issues. Coolidge kept most of Harding's officials in his Cabinet. The American public seemed to like Republican policies and Coolidge was elected in his own right in 1925. However, he died three years later and Herbert Hoover became president.

ACTIVITY

Look at this exam-style question:

How are Sources 7 and 8 useful to historians studying the Roaring Twenties?

Now look at some example answers:
A   *Sources 7 and 8 are not useful. They are from politicians so they are biased.*
B   *Sources 7 and 8 are very useful. They are biased of course, because they are from Republican politicians. But that makes them useful because they reveal what Republican politicians thought and believed.*

1   Discuss why A is a very poor answer.
2   Discuss why B is a very good answer.
3   Improve answer B by adding two or three sentences that provide examples of how the sources are biased and what this reveals about the beliefs of Hoover and Coolidge.

The First World War

Another key factor in the economic boom was the First World War. The USA did not join the war until 1917, but from the start of the European war in 1914, US industries made money supplying weapons and equipment to Britain, France and their allies. US banks also made a fortune by loaning money to these countries. The USA benefited further because the war damaged the trade, industry and exports of the main fighting nations. For example, Germany had a leading chemical industry before the war, but by 1918 the USA had far overtaken it in the production of chemicals.

Source 9 A leaflet supporting Herbert Hoover's election campaign, 1928. ▼

The war stimulated the aviation industry as well. The aircraft industry flourished and increasing numbers of pilots were trained. These aircraft and pilots became the basis for an explosion in air travel and air mail (this was how Lindbergh got started). By 1930, around 162,000 commercial flights were operating a year.

ACTIVITY

We do not know what was on the other side of Source 9, but it is likely that there would have been some key campaigning points to convince people to support Hoover. Use pages 198–202 to produce a plausible reconstruction of what these notes might have said.

Resources and transport networks

One major factor in the success of the 1920s was the USA's vast natural resources (see Factfile). It is no coincidence that some of the USA's richest businessmen – Rockefeller, Carnegie and Mellon – were all involved in exploiting these resources.

Rockefeller was the boss of Standard Oil. The oil industry was booming because oil was taking over from coal as the most popular fuel for both industrial and domestic use. Demand was also rising as car ownership increased. At first there were many oil companies, making different grades of oil and petrol, but Rockefeller gradually bought most of them up to create one giant corporation that produced a single standard fuel.

Carnegie made his money from steel. Steel was required for the motor industry and the new consumer goods and, of course, the skyscrapers that now characterised the city skylines. The third businessman, Mellon, was a banker but he had an eye for successful businesses. His financial backing helped the growth of new industries such as electricity and aluminium. Aluminium was light but strong and especially useful for making cars, electrical appliances and aircraft. The USA also had a relatively young population, which provided a strong labour force for all these industries.

The Republican government initiated a major road-building programme in the 1920s. The road network doubled and the work employed more people than any other sector. In addition, the extended roads helped to boost the motor industry. Alongside the well-established rail network, the new road network helped businesses to transport goods efficiently (see Source 10).

Source 10 An advertisement for International Trucks, 1927. ▲

1 What key selling points is the manufacturer emphasising in Source 10?

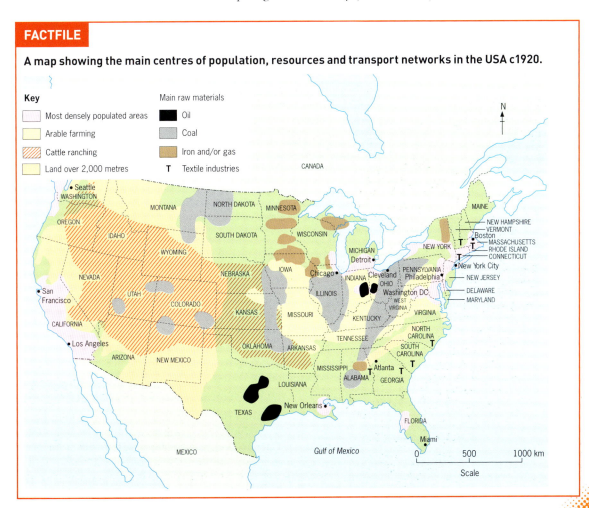

FACTFILE

A map showing the main centres of population, resources and transport networks in the USA c1920.

Source 12 An advertisement for stockings in the 1920s. Although the caption says silk, they were actually rayon. ▲

1 Who is the target audience of Source 12?
2 In what ways is Source 12 similar to Source 11? Explain your answer.

New industries, new methods

Through the 1920s, new industries and new methods of production were developed in the USA. Many companies adopted the principles of the Efficiency Movement. This emerged from the ideas of an engineer called Frederick Winslow Taylor. It was based on the theory that most companies (and the government) would be more effective if they eliminated activities that wasted time or resources. However, experts were needed to identify these areas of waste and so companies began to invest in research universities and schools of business and engineering. They recruited graduates from those institutions into their ranks. Federal and state governments invested in research on improving local administration and reform of hospitals and medical schools.

Businesses put these new ideas to work. The country was able to exploit its vast resources of raw materials to produce steel, chemicals, glass and machinery. Electricity was changing the USA too. Before the First World War, industry had still been largely powered by coal. By the 1920s electricity had taken over. In 1918, only a few homes were supplied; by 1929 almost all urban homes had electricity.

In turn, these new industries launched a boom in consumer goods. Telephones, radios, vacuum cleaners and washing machines were mass-produced on a vast scale. These new techniques, together with mass-production methods, meant that a high volume of goods could be produced much more cheaply, so more people could afford them. Items that were once luxuries were now more common. For example, silk stockings had once been a luxury that only rich women enjoyed. In 1900, only 12,000 pairs had been sold. In the 1920s, however, the invention of rayon – a cheaper substitute for silk – changed this. In 1930, 300 million pairs of stockings were sold to a female population of around 60 million.

The car

The most important of these new booming industries was the automobile industry. The motor car had first been developed in the 1890s and the first cars were built by blacksmiths and other skilled craftsmen. They took a long time to make and were very expensive. In 1900, only 4,000 cars were made.

Car production was revolutionised by Henry Ford. In 1913, he set up the world's first moving production line, in Detroit, Michigan. A skeleton car started at the beginning of the line. Each worker had one or two small jobs to do as the vehicle moved past him on the line. By the end of the line, a complete car had been built. The most famous of Ford's production-line cars was the Model T. More than 15 million were produced between 1908 and 1925. In 1927, they came off the production line at a rate of one every ten seconds. In 1929, 4.8 million Ford cars were made.

Ford was one of three huge corporations making cars – the others were Chrysler and General Motors. By 1929, they racked up sales of 29 million cars between them. There were also many smaller manufacturers making specialised vehicles such as trucks. In 1919, there were 1 million trucks in the USA. By 1929, there were 3.5 million. By the end of the 1920s, cars were the USA's biggest industry. As well as employing hundreds of thousands of workers directly, it also had a positive effect on other industries. Glass, leather, steel and rubber were all required to build the new vehicles. Cars accounted for 75 per cent of US glass production in the 1920s! In addition, of course, cars needed petrol to run and roads to drive on – road construction was the biggest single employer in the 1920s.

Owning a car was not just a rich person's privilege, as it was in Europe. There was one car to five people in the USA, compared with one to 43 in Britain, and one to 7,000 in Russia. Cars made it possible for people to buy a house in the suburbs, which further boosted house-building. For example, the New York suburb of Queens doubled in size in the 1920s. Grosse Point Park outside Detroit grew by 700 per cent!

Source 13 A still image of the Ford production line in 1920. This was taken from a promotional film made and released by the Ford company. ▶

ACTIVITY

1 Write a slightly more detailed caption for Source 13 (up to 50 words more).

3 Sources 11–13 are all promotional or advertising materials. Does that mean a historian should dismiss them because they are biased?

4 Why were mass production techniques so crucial to the new industries?

Mass consumption

It is no good producing lots of goods if people do not buy them – mass production requires mass consumption. So, the big industries used sophisticated sales and marketing techniques to get people to buy their goods. New electrical companies such as Hoover became household names.

- **Mass nationwide advertising:** This had been used for the first time in the USA during the war, to encourage people to support the war effort. Many advertisers who had learned the trade in wartime propaganda now set up agencies to sell cars, cigarettes, clothing and other consumer items. Posters, radio advertisements and travelling salesmen encouraged Americans to spend.
  - **Mail order:** There was a huge growth in the number of mail-order companies in the 1920s. People across the USA, especially in remote areas, could buy the new consumer goods from catalogues. In 1928, nearly one-third of Americans bought goods from the Sears, Roebuck and Company catalogue. This greatly expanded the market for products.
  - **Credit:** Even if they did not have the money, people could borrow it easily. Or they could take advantage of the new 'buy now, pay later' hire-purchase schemes. Eight out of ten radios and six out of ten cars were bought on credit. Ford and General Motors actually set up their own credit companies. Before the war, people expected to save up until they could afford something. Now they could buy on credit.
  - **Chain stores:** A brand-new kind of shop emerged in this period: the chain store. These were the same shops selling the same products all across the USA.

Source 14 Sales of consumer goods 1915–30. Overall, the output of US industry doubled in the 1920s. ▼

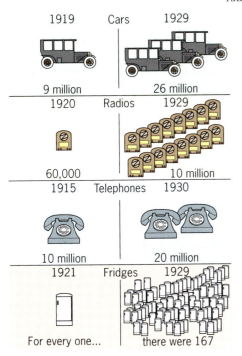

1919 Cars 1929
9 million 26 million
1920 Radios 1929
60,000 10 million
1915 Telephones 1930
10 million 20 million
1921 Fridges 1929
For every one... there were 167

5 'Source 14 is more *reliable* than Source 12 because it contains statistics.' Do you agree with this view?
6 'Source 14 is more *useful* than Source 12 because it contains statistics.' Do you agree with this view?

A state of mind: confidence and consumerism

One thing that runs through all the factors you have looked at so far is an attitude or a state of mind. Part of this was the Republican philosophy that 'business knows best'. People in the USA tended to trust and admire business leaders above politicians. Henry Ford was generally very popular. In one election he stood for Congress and despite running no election campaign, holding no meetings and publishing no promotional materials, he was only narrowly defeated!

At the same time, most Americans believed that they had a right to prosperity. They began to feel it was important to have a nice house filled with the latest consumer products, a good job and plenty to eat. In earlier decades, thrift (being careful with money and saving 'for a rainy day') had been seen as a good quality. In the 1920s, this was replaced by a belief that it was better to spend money. There was confidence in the USA during this period. Business people had the confidence to invest in the new industries, to experiment with new ideas and to set up new companies and employ people. Ordinary Americans had the confidence to buy goods, sometimes on credit, because they were sure they could pay for them, or to invest in industry itself by buying shares. Confidence is vital to any economic boom.

Wall Street and the stock market

It is impossible to set up a business without money. New companies raised money from investors (see Factfile). This was a critical part of the economic boom after the First World War. Before then, usually only the very wealthy had been investors and they sometimes bought whole companies. But in the 1920s, many Americans began to invest in the US stock market (known as Wall Street) with their own small savings. Some even borrowed money to invest and then paid back the loan when they made a profit (a practice called 'buying on the margin').

In 1920, there had been only 4 million share owners in the USA. By 1929, there were 20 million out of a population of 120 million (although only about 1.5 million were big investors). People could make a lot more money buying and selling shares on the stock market than they could in an ordinary job (see Figure 15). While the economy boomed and confidence was high, the stock market supported business and business supported the stock market. It seemed like a win–win situation.

Figure 15 A graph showing ways of making money in the 1920s. ▼

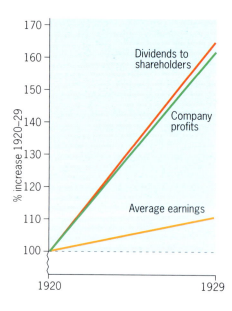

FACTFILE

Investment and the stock market

● To set up a company you need money to pay staff, rent premises, buy equipment, etc.
● Most companies raise this money from investors. In return, these investors own a share in the company. They become 'shareholders'. These shareholders can get a return on their money in two ways:
    – by receiving a dividend – a share of the profits made by the company
    – by selling their shares.
● If the company is successful, the value of the shares is usually higher than the price originally paid for them. Investors buy and sell their shares on the stock market.
● The price of shares varies from day to day. If more people are buying than selling, then the price goes up. If more are selling than buying, the price goes down.
● For much of the 1920s, the price of shares on the US stock market went steadily upwards.

FOCUS TASK

A What factors caused the economic boom?

1 In this section, you have read about eight different factors behind the boom of the 1920s. Create a 'factor card' for each one, summarising how it contributed to the boom.

2 Use your factor cards to design your own skyscraper summary of the factors behind the economic boom. We have shown one interpretation on this page, but you might want to do it differently. For example, you could have different factors as sections in the skyscraper or have the same sections but in a different order. Think about:
   a factors that could be combined on one floor because they are connected
   b which factor should go at the bottom, as the foundation
   c which factor should go at the top as the crowning glory
   d which factors should be left out altogether because they were not very important.

3 One historian has said: 'Without the new automobile industry, the prosperity of the 1920s would scarcely have been possible.' Do you agree? If so, where would this go in your diagram?

4 Once you are happy with your skyscraper, write a paragraph to explain it.

B How did the boom affect people's lives and standard of living?

5 Look back over pages 199–206 and find evidence of the way the boom affected people's lives. Copy and complete the table below to record your observations.

Aspect of life	Impact of boom	Examples/evidence
the jobs people did		
their income		
where they lived		
the homes they lived in		
what they owned		
their attitudes		
their leisure time		
anything else you can find		

6 Look back at your work on the Focus Task on page 200. Add extra details to your advice about the Roaring Twenties attraction, but try not to take it over 250 words.

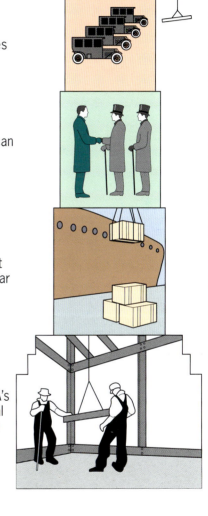

A state of mind

New industries

Republican policies

The First World War

The USA's industrial strength

Who did not share in the boom?

While many Americans were enjoying the economic boom, some were not so lucky.

Farmers

Total US farm income dropped from $22 billion in 1919 to just $13 billion in 1928. There were a number of reasons why farming had such problems:

- **Declining exports:** After the war, Europe imported far less food from the USA. This was partly because Europe was poor, and partly a response to US tariffs, which stopped Europe from exporting to the USA.
- **New competitors:** Farmers were also struggling against competition from the highly efficient Canadian wheat producers. All this came at a time when the population of the USA was actually falling so less food was needed.
- **Overproduction:** Underlying all these problems was the issue of overproduction. From 1900 to 1920, while farming was doing well, more and more land was being farmed. Improved machinery, especially the combine harvester, and improved fertilisers made US agriculture extremely efficient. The result was that by 1920 it was producing a SURPLUS.
- **Falling prices:** Prices plummeted as desperate farmers tried to sell their produce. In 1921 alone, most farm prices fell by 50 per cent. Hundreds of rural banks collapsed in the 1920s and there were five times as many farm bankruptcies as there had been in the 1900s and 1910s.

Not all farmers were affected by these problems. Rich Americans wanted fresh vegetables and fruit throughout the year. Shipments of lettuce to the cities, for example, rose from 14,000 crates in 1920 to 52,000 in 1928. However, for most farmers the 1920s were a time of hardship. This was a serious issue. Nearly half of all Americans lived in rural areas, mostly working on farms or in businesses that sold goods to farmers. Problems in farming therefore directly affected more than 60 million people. Six million rural Americans, mainly farm labourers,

Source 16 A cartoon from *The Chicago Daily Tribune*, April 1927. It was called 'The Farmer's Predicament'. ▶

1 Sometimes cartoonists are supportive or critical of something or someone. Sometimes they simply observe what is happening. Which applies to Source 16: is the cartoonist supportive or critical or simply observing?

were forced off the land in the 1920s. Many of these were unskilled workers who migrated to the cities, where there was little demand for their labour. African Americans were particularly badly hit. They had always done the least skilled jobs in the rural areas. As they lost their jobs on the farms, three-quarters of a million of them became unemployed.

Republican politicians were largely unsympathetic to famers. When Congress finally considered bringing in tariffs to protect farmers in 1929, the Republicans demanded similar protection for other industries and the plan became bogged down in political argument. It is no surprise that farming communities were the fiercest critics of the LAISSEZ-FAIRE policies of the Republican party.

Workers in traditional industries

In the traditional industries growth was slow and profits gradually declined. The coal industry employed lots of people, but as coal was replaced as a source of power by electricity and oil, the industry suffered. Other industries such as leather and shoe-making also struggled. The cotton industry in the south virtually collapsed and the workforce of the textile industries of the north-eastern USA fell from 190,000 to less than 100,000. The Republicans protected these industries to some extent by putting tariffs on foreign imports, but these were not growth markets like, for example, the markets for electrical goods.

Naturally this affected the people who worked in these industries. Skilled workers could not compete with machinery or cheap labour in the southern states. Labour unions tried to protect jobs and improve working conditions and wages and there were many strikes in this period. Some turned violent and troops were called in to control the situation. A few succeeded in improving the situation for workers, but overall things were difficult for the unions in the 1920s. Businessmen and politicians like Ford, Rockefeller, Mellon and Hoover were all extremely hostile to unions. So were many newspaper owners, who regarded them with suspicion and hostility.

Even if workers did get a pay rise, their wages did not increase on the same scale as company profits or the DIVIDENDS paid to SHAREHOLDERS. In 1928, there was a strike in the coal industry in North Carolina, where the male workers were paid only $18 and women $9 for a 70-hour week, at a time when $48 per week was considered to be the minimum amount required for a decent life. In fact, for the majority of Americans wages remained well below that figure through the 1920s. It has been estimated that 42 per cent of people in the USA lived below the POVERTY LINE, which meant they did not have enough money to pay for essentials such as food, clothing, housing and heating.

The unemployed and the poor

Unemployment also remained a problem throughout the 1920s. The growth in industry did not create many new jobs because companies were expanding by electrifying or mechanising production. The same number of people (around 5 per cent) were unemployed at the peak of the boom in 1929 as had been in 1920, yet the amount of goods produced had doubled. These millions of unemployed Americans were not sharing in the boom. They included many poor whites, but an even greater proportion of African American and Hispanic people and other members of the USA's large immigrant communities.

The plight of the poor was desperate for the individuals concerned, but it was also damaging to US industry. The boom of the 1920s was consumer-led, which means that it happened because ordinary people were buying things for their homes. With so many families too poor to buy consumer products, the demand was likely to dwindle eventually. However, Republicans stuck by their policy of not interfering, and took no steps to deal with unemployment or poverty.

Case study: Chicago in the 1920s

If you wanted to study poverty in the 1920s, Chicago was a good place to go. This was one of the USA's biggest cities. It was the centre of the steel, meat and clothing industries – traditional businesses that employed many unskilled workers. Such industries had busy and slack periods. In slack periods the workers would be 'seasonally unemployed'. Many of these workers were Polish or Italian immigrants, or African American migrants from the southern United States. In 1906, the harsh life of people who lived and worked in the Chicago meatpacking industry was exposed in the novel *The Jungle*, by the campaigning author and journalist Upton Sinclair. Sinclair's own publisher called the novel deeply depressing! When President Theodore Roosevelt first heard about it he called Sinclair 'a crackpot', but after reading the book he changed his views and ordered an investigation into the meatpacking district. But that was 1906. Had things changed by the 1920s? How far did the people Sinclair wrote about share in the prosperity of the 1920s?

- Only 3 per cent of semi-skilled workers owned a car. In richer areas, 29 per cent owned a car.
- Workers in Chicago did not like to buy large items on credit. They preferred to save their money for when they might not have a job. Many bought smaller items on credit, such as radios.
- Poor White people did not use the new chain stores that had revolutionised shopping in the 1920s. Nearly all of these were in middle-class districts. Poorer White industrial workers preferred to shop at the local grocer's, where the owner was more flexible and gave them credit.

FOCUS TASK

Who did not share in the boom?

1 Do either Task A or Task B below.

A Dear Mr Hoover …
Look back at Source 8 on page 202. Use pages 208–10 to go back in time and travel through poorer parts of the USA in the 1920s. Gather evidence to contest Hoover's claim and write a paper setting out in detail:
  – how badly off some farmers have become since the war
  – why farmers are poor
  – why workers in older industries are suffering
  – why immigrant workers and African Americans are not well off
  – how Republican policies have contributed to the problems (or failed to help).
Try to use specific examples such as Chicago in the 1920s.

B John, Joe and Jeff
John, Joe and Jeff are cousins. During the 1920s their families have moved. John is still in the rural Midwest trying to keep the family farm going. Joe moved to Chicago and now works in the meatpacking industry. Jeff is a travelling salesman working in New York. Write the script for a conversation between these three at a family reunion in 1928. They might talk about:
  – their families
  – their work
  – their homes
  – their hopes
  – their political views.
You could act the conversation out or even record it!

2 Look back at your work on the Focus Task on page 200. Add extra details to your proposal for the Roaring Twenties attraction but again limit yourself to 150 words.

PRACTICE QUESTIONS

1 Describe one example of Republican economic policies in the 1920s. (2)
2 Describe one example of social change in the 1920s. (2)
3 Explain why the Roaring Twenties got their name. (10)
4 Explain why some industries prospered in the 1920s. (10)
5 'Without the new automobile industry, the prosperity of the 1920s would scarcely have been possible.' How far do you agree with this view? (18)

How did women's lives change in the 1920s?

Women's lives in the 1900s

Before the First World War, middle-class women in the USA – like those in Britain – led restricted lives. They were expected to dress and behave in particular ways. They did not wear make-up, participate in sport or smoke in public. Their relationships with men were strictly controlled and they had to have a chaperone with them when they went out with a boyfriend. In most states they could not vote. Women were expected to be housewives. Very few paid jobs were open to women and those who did work had lower-paid jobs such as cleaning, dressmaking and secretarial work. In rural parts of the USA, where the attitude of the Church had a particularly strong influence, women were expected to follow traditional roles.

In the 1920s, however, many of these things began to change, especially for urban and middle-class women. Source 19 gives us a glimpse of this change. But what caused it?

Source 17 A photograph of a schoolteacher, 1905. ▲

1 How are Sources 17 and 18 useful to historians investigating the lives of American women in the 1920s?
2 Is it possible to say one source is more useful than the other?
3 Try to picture Carol (Source 18) in your mind. Do you think she looks like the woman in the photograph in Source 17?

Source 18 An extract from *Main Street*, a novel by Sinclair Lewis published in 1920. By 1922, it had sold around 2 million copies. In this extract one of the main characters, Carol, is talking to her husband Will.

Will: *That's the whole trouble with you! You haven't got enough work to do. If you had five kids and no hired girl, and had to help with the chores and separate the cream, like these farmers' wives, then you wouldn't be so discontented.*

Carol: *I know. That's what most men—and women—like you would say. These business men, from their crushing labours of sitting in an office seven hours a day, would calmly recommend that I have a dozen children. As it happens, I've done that sort of thing. I'm a good cook and a good sweeper, and you don't dare say I'm not!*

Will: *No-no, you're—*

Carol: *But was I more happy when I was drudging? I was not. I was just bedraggled and unhappy. It's work—but not my work. I could run an office or a library, or nurse and teach children. But solitary dishwashing isn't enough to satisfy me—or many other women. We're going to chuck it. We're going to wash 'em by machinery, and come out and play with you men in the offices and clubs and politics you've cleverly kept for yourselves! Oh, we're hopeless, we dissatisfied women! Then why do you want to have us about the place?*

Changes in the 1920s

You have already seen how the First World War had a huge impact on the US economy, an effect which continued into the 1920s. The war also had a big impact on the lives and role of women in society.

Source 19 A cartoon from the US magazine *New York Time Current History*, published in October 1920. The title was 'The sky is now her limit'. ▲

1 Is Source 19 supporting or attacking the 19th Amendment, which gave women the vote? How can you tell?
2 How is this source useful to historians looking at the position of women in society?

Women's movements and the vote

There had been an active SUFFRAGIST movement in the USA throughout the 1900s, campaigning for women's rights and particularly the right to vote. When the USA joined the war in 1917, Suffragists threw themselves into the war effort. The National American Woman Suffrage Association (NAWSA) took part in both civilian and military organisations, but it also seized the political opportunity that the war offered. The National Women's Party (NWP) organised demonstrations outside the White House (the home and offices of the president) to highlight the hypocrisy of fighting a war to preserve democracy while denying American women their democratic right to vote. By 1918, President Woodrow Wilson accepted that women should be given the vote. In August 1920, Congress finally approved the 19th Amendment to the Constitution, which gave women the vote.

The campaigning did not end there, however. NAWSA became the League of Women Voters, which offered women training on how to use their vote wisely. It would advise women on their legal rights and explain how to put pressure on their representatives in Congress to improve women's lives. The NWP continued to act as a pressure group. It put forward over 600 pieces of LEGISLATION promoting equality for women in health, working conditions, legal rights and many other areas. Around 300 of these were accepted. One of the key achievements was the Sheppard–Towner Act of 1921 (see Factfile).

FACTFILE

Sheppard–Towner Act 1921
- Morris Sheppard and Horace Towner were congressmen who supported women's SUFFRAGE and were interested in social reform.
- Both were appalled at the poor health care and high infant death rates in the USA (higher than any other industrialised country), particularly in rural areas.
- The Sheppard–Towner Act provided up to $2.6 million to help states improve maternity and child health care.
- Around 3,000 child and maternal health centres were created. Child mortality fell significantly during the 1920s (although the act was not the only reason for this).
- Getting the act through Congress proved to be a battle and even after it was approved there was still a lot of opposition to it from medical professionals and some women's groups. It was underfunded and not all states introduced the measures.
- However, the act brought real benefits and it was an important step forward for women. The federal government had agreed on the need for government involvement in a social issue. In an era of *laissez-faire* this was a significant achievement.

Political empowerment

Many women, especially those in the middle classes, gained a political education in these campaigns. One of the most high-profile examples was Eleanor Roosevelt, the wife of the future president Franklin D. Roosevelt. It is no coincidence that women went on to play a key role in campaigns on social issues during the 1920s. They supported moves for improved education and health care, and women were prominent in the TEMPERANCE movement and Prohibition (see pages 216–20).

Employment opportunities

During the First World War, women entered the workforce doing traditional 'men's' roles, just as they did in Britain. They also served in the Women's Land Army, the Red Cross and many local organisations. Although women were not allowed to serve in combat roles, many learnt new skills through their wartime work, including nursing, telegraphy and STENOGRAPHY, camouflage painting and MUNITIONS testing.

This trend continued after the war. In urban areas more women took on jobs – particularly middle-class women. They had more time to work because their jobs around the home had been made easier by new electrical goods such as vacuum cleaners and washing machines. Women typically took on jobs created by the new industries. There were 10 million women in paid employment in 1929 – 24 per cent more than in 1920.

Source 20 Women welding in a munitions factory in 1917. ▲

3 Why do you think Source 20 was published in 1917?
4 How did the photographer try to achieve this aim?

More money, greater freedom

With money of their own, working women became a new group targeted by advertisers. Even women who did not earn their own money were increasingly seen as the decision-makers about what new products their family should own. There is evidence that women's role in choosing cars triggered Ford, in 1925, to make them available in colours other than black.

Many of the traditional behavioural rules were eased as well. Women wore more daring clothes. They smoked in public and went out drinking and driving with men, without chaperones. They kissed in public. These 'flappers' were identified by their short skirts, bobbed hair, bright clothes and lots of make-up. They were the extreme example of liberated urban women.

Source 21 A publicity photograph for the Parody Club in New York, 1925. ▶

Source 22 The cover of *Life* magazine, 1926. The title is 'Teaching an old dog new tricks'. ▼

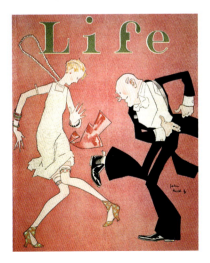

Films and novels also exposed women to a much wider range of role-models. Millions of women watched films with sexy or daring heroines, as well as those that showed women in more traditional roles. The newspaper, magazine and film industries found that sex sold much better than anything else! Women were also less likely to stay in unhappy marriages. In 1914, there had been 100,000 divorces; in 1929 there were twice as many.

5 Why did the Parody Club publish the photograph in Source 21?
6 What is the artist saying about women in Source 22?
7 Explain how Sources 21 and 22 are useful to historians as evidence about women in the 1920s.

Source 23 The US feminist campaigner Doris E. Fleischman, writing in 1932.

It is wholly confusing to read the advertisements in the magazines that feature the enticing qualities of vacuum cleaners, mechanical refrigerators and ... other devices which should lighten the chores of women in the home. On the whole these large middle classes do their own housework. ... Women who live on farms ... do a great deal of work besides the labour of caring for their children, washing the clothes, caring for the home and cooking ... labour in the fields ... help milk the cows. ... The other largest group of American women comprises the families of the labourers ... the vast army of unskilled, semi-skilled and skilled workers. The wages of these men are on the whole so small [that] wives must do double duty – that is, caring for the children and the home and toil on the outside as wage earners.

Continuing limitations ...

It might seem that everything was changing in the 1920s, and for young, middle-class women living in cities this was certainly true. However, this is only part of the story.

... at work

Women were still paid less than men, even when they did the same job. The employment of women increased while that of men did not, but this was partly because women were cheaper employees. However, a bigger issue was the lack of opportunities available to most women.

... in politics

In politics as well, women were still not equal with men. They may have been given the vote but this did not give them access to political power. Political parties wanted women's votes, but they did not want women as candidates – they considered them 'unelectable'. Although many women, such as Eleanor Roosevelt (see Profile), had a high public standing, only a handful of women had been elected to Congress by 1929.

PROFILE

Eleanor Roosevelt (1884–1962)

- Born into a wealthy family in 1884.
- Married Franklin D. Roosevelt (future president) in 1905.
- Heavily involved in:
    - League of Women Voters
    - Women's Trade Union League
    - Women's City Club (New York)
    - New York State Democratic Party (Women's Division).
- Work concentrated on:
    - uniting New York Democrats
    - public housing for low-income workers
    - birth-control information
    - better conditions for women workers.

... in the family

Films of the 1920s give the impression that women lived lives filled with passion and romance. However, novels and films of the period can be misleading. Women certainly did watch such films (in great numbers) but there is no evidence that many of them lived the sort of lives found in fiction like this. In fact, many women reacted with outrage. There remained a strong conservative element in US society. Traditional religion and old-fashioned values kept most women in a much more restricted role than young urban women enjoyed. For most, raising a family and keeping a good home for their husband were their main priorities. Conservative sections of society expressed strong disapproval of women who did seize the new opportunities that the 1920s offered.

1 Read Source 25 opposite. Which of these terms do you think best describes the overall tone of the source: optimistic, pessimistic, negative, cheerful, bitter, sad?

2 Does the author blame women or see them as victims? Explain your answer.

3 Would you say that Sources 24 and 25 take the same attitude towards women? Explain your answer fully.

Source 24 An article by the journalist Dorothy Ducas in the *New York Evening Post*, January 1929. Ducas graduated from university in 1926 and became an award-winning journalist in a long career.

Women's Economic Freedom Blamed in Marriage Decline

Marriage is declining in popularity in New York City, while divorce is gaining in favour, and the women are to blame.

In spite of the solemn pronouncement from pulpits and platform that the younger generation is, at heart, exactly like the elder, sociologists today have to admit a change has come over metropolitan young folk, especially women, in the face of figures now available for the year just ended. In 1928, the City Bureau of Vital Statistics reports today, there were 6,007 fewer marriages than in 1927. ...

AN AGE OF ADJUSTMENT

As for divorces ... it was estimated there would be some 1,300 decrees granted, an increase of more than 100 over those handed down in 1927. 'Women with their new opportunities won't stand for what they used to stand for,' is the way Professor Clarence G. Dittmer, head of the department of sociology at New York University, explained it. 'Increase in divorce accompanies growth, and expanding democracy comes along with new social and economic opportunities for women.'

Source 25 An extract from an article called 'Evils of Woman's Revolt against the Old Standards' by the Roman Catholic priest Hugh L. McMenamin. It was published in the magazine *Current History*, October 1927.

Look about you. The theatre, the magazine, the latest novel, the night clubs —all give evidence of an ever-increasing disregard for basic decency. You do not have to be a prude or a puritan to feel that something is passing in the hearts and in the minds of women of today that is leaving them cold and unwomanly. ... We may try to deceive ourselves and close our eyes to the conduct of the flappers. We may call it greater self-reliance or self-assertion, and try to pardon immodesty in dress by calling it style and fashion, but the fact remains that deep down in our hearts we feel a sense of shame and pity. Modern economic conditions have dragged woman into the commercial world and made her economically independent. It is quite impossible for a woman to engage successfully in business and politics and at the same time create a happy home. A woman cannot be a mother and a typist at the same time.

Source 26 A cartoon entitled 'Them Days Is Gone Forever', published in the *Chicago Tribune*, January 1925. ▼

THEM DAYS IS GONE FOREVER—Flout This on Your Flute—BY AL POSEN

PRACTICE QUESTIONS

1 Describe one example of how life changed for women in the 1920s. (2)
2 Describe one example of reactions to changes in the lives of women in the 1920s. (2)
3 Explain why life changed for some women in the Roaring Twenties. (10)
4 'The 1920s saw a revolution in the lives of American women.' How far do you agree with this view? (18)

FOCUS TASK

'Them Days Is Gone Forever!'

1 A popular cartoon strip called 'Them Days Is Gone Forever' ran in many US newspapers from 1921 to 1927. Most Americans would have come across it. Source 26 shows a typical example.
   a Study the source. What can you infer about women, and society generally, in the 1920s? Think about values, ideas, concerns, attitudes, changes.
   b Now put on your hindsight glasses and write a paragraph explaining whether you think this source really represents the experience of women in the USA in the 1920s.
   c Finally, take one step even further back and discuss the following question in pairs or small groups: Do you think people at the time really thought that cartoons like Source 26 were an accurate reflection or did they just see it as a joke?
2 Look back at your work on the Focus Task on page 200. Add extra details to your proposal for the Roaring Twenties attraction, but try not to add more than 150 words.

Prohibition: the 'noble experiment'?

Why was prohibition introduced?

In nineteenth-century rural America there was a very strong temperance movement. There were two main temperance organisations at the time: the Anti-Saloon League and the Women's Christian Temperance Union. Members of temperance movements did not drink alcohol and campaigned to persuade others to give up alcohol. Most members of these movements were devout Christians who wanted to prevent the damage that alcohol did to family life. They also argued that alcohol caused a wide range of health problems, particularly mental-health issues. The temperance movements were so strong in some areas that they managed to persuade their state governments to prohibit (ban) the sale of alcohol.

Through the early twentieth century such campaigns gathered pace, and eventually there was a national campaign to ban alcohol nationwide. Some powerful people supported the movement. Leading industrialists did so, believing that workers would be more reliable if they did not drink. Politicians backed it because it won them votes in rural areas. By 1916, 21 states had banned saloons.

Supporters of prohibition became known as 'dries'. The dries had some convincing arguments to support their case. For example, they claimed that '3,000 infants are smothered yearly in bed, by drunken parents'. The USA's entry into the First World War in 1917 boosted the dries' campaign. Drinkers were accused of being unpatriotic cowards. Most of the big breweries were run by German immigrants who were portrayed as the enemy. Drink was linked to other evils as well. After the Russian Revolution, the dries claimed that Bolshevism (communism) thrived on drink and that alcohol led to lawlessness in the cities, particularly in immigrant communities. Saloons were seen as dens of vice that destroyed family life. The campaign became one of country values against city values.

By 1917, the movement had won the support of enough state governments to propose the 18th Amendment to the Constitution, which 'prohibited the manufacture, sale or transportation of intoxicating liquors'. It became law in January 1920 and is known as the Volstead Act. Supporters saw it as a 'noble experiment' – 'noble' because of its good intentions and 'experiment' because the US government had never tried to force people to behave in a certain way before. Prohibition lasted from 1920 until 1933. Although it is generally seen as a failure, levels of alcohol consumption did drop by about 30 per cent in the early 1920s.

How was Prohibition enforced?

The government ran information campaigns and Prohibition agents arrested offenders. Two of the most famous agents were Isadore Einstein and his deputy Moe Smith, who made 4,392 arrests. Their raids were always low-key: they would enter SPEAKEASIES (illegal bars) and simply order a drink. Einstein had a special flask hidden inside his waistcoat with a funnel attached. He preserved the evidence by pouring his drink down the funnel and the criminals were caught!

◀ **Source 29** The front cover of a leaflet issued by the Scientific Temperance Federation, 1919.

Source 27 A temperance campaigner, speaking in 1917.

Our nation can only be saved by turning the pure stream of country sentiment and township morals to flush out the cesspools of cities and so save civilisation from pollution.

Source 28 The front cover of the magazine of a temperance organisation, published in 1919, shortly before the introduction of Prohibition. ▲

WHY AMERICA WENT DRY

Beer Doubled
The Child Death-Rate

IN THE FIRST FIVE YEARS OF LIFE

All in the same village. Beer practically the only drink used by the parents and not always immoderately.

Children of Sober Parents
23% DIED
(18.6% in first year)

Children of Beer Drinkers
45% DIED
(36% in first year.)

Alcohol whether in Beer or in Whisky is an Enemy to Child Life.

120 Sober Families with 650 Children.
18 Beer-Drinking Families with 125 Children.
All strictly comparable and free from hereditary disease.

Adolph Kiekh : Alcohol and Child Mortality in Durrenberg, Austria
Scientific Temperance Journal, Dec. 1914

COPYRIGHTED 1920
BY SCIENTIFIC TEMPERANCE FEDERATION
BOSTON, MASS.
PRINTED IN U. S. A.

THE AMERICAN ISSUE PUBLISHING CO.
WESTERVILLE, OHIO

---

1   How similar are Sources 28 and 29? Think about: their content (i.e. what they show), their aims and the methods they use to achieve those aims.

Source 30 A table showing the activities of federal Prohibition agents.

	1921	1925	1929
illegal distilleries seized	9,746	12,023	15,794
gallons (US) of spirit seized	414,000	11,030,000	11,860,000
arrests	34,175	62,747	66,878

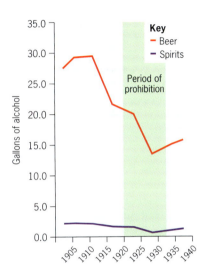

Figure 31 A graph showing alcohol consumption of Americans (in US gallons) per year, 1905–40. ▲

However, Prohibition proved impossible to enforce in the cities. There was not the money to finance all the raids that would be needed to close down all the illegal drinking establishments. There were also not enough agents – each agent was poorly paid and was responsible for a huge area. The biggest problem was that many ordinary people simply did not obey the law.

How did Americans respond to Prohibition?

Prohibition gained widespread approval in some states, particularly rural areas in the Midwest. It was much less popular in urban states and the state of Maryland never even introduced Prohibition.

Rich and powerful people thought Prohibition was a bad idea. It was not difficult for them to either avoid the law (see Source 36) or simply ignore it. Some even believed that this was a law that did not apply to them – they believed it was a way to improve 'ordinary people'. One of the most striking examples of this was George Cassidy, the official BOOTLEGGER for members of Congress. He made an average of 25 deliveries of alcohol to Congress every week while the police turned a blind eye. Cassidy was eventually caught by federal agents but he was given a light sentence of only 18 months.

Source 32 A medical note written by Winston Churchill's doctor in 1932. Churchill was on a speaking tour of the USA at the time, during which he had an accident.

This is to certify that the post-accident convalescence of the Hon. Winston S. Churchill necessitates the use of alcoholic spirits, especially at meal times. The quantity is naturally indefinite but the minimum requirements would be 250 cubic centimetres.

2 Study Sources 30–32. Do they provide evidence that Prohibition was a success or a failure or both? Explain your answer.

3 How is Source 32 useful as evidence about the difficulty of enforcing Prohibition?

4 Why do you think the authorities took and published Source 33?

Source 33 A photograph taken by the authorities and published in many newspapers. It shows federal agents tipping illegal (bootleg) liquor away. ▼

Source 34 Members of the American Liberties League parading on a horse-drawn cart to protest against Prohibition in 1925. The banner is a quote from the Bible. ▼

Supply and demand

It was not just the rich and powerful who ignored Prohibition. Millions of Americans, particularly in urban areas, were simply not prepared to obey the law. Bootleggers made vast fortunes. Al Capone made around $60 million a year from his speakeasies. He famously claimed: 'Prohibition is a business. All I do is supply a public demand.'

That demand was huge. By 1925, there were more speakeasies in US cities than there had been saloons in 1919. Izzy Einstein filed a report on how quickly someone could find alcohol after arriving in a new city. The results were:

- Chicago: 21 minutes
- Atlanta: 17 minutes
- Pittsburg: 11 minutes
- New Orleans: 35 seconds (he was offered a bottle of whisky by his taxi driver when he asked where he could get a drink!)

Illegal stills (short for distilleries) sprang up all over the USA as people made their own whisky, which became known as 'moonshine'. The stills were a major fire hazard and the alcohol they produced was frequently poisonous. Agents seized over 280,000 of these stills, but there were probably many thousands more that were never found. Most Americans had no need for their own still – they simply went to their favourite speakeasies, which were well supplied by bootleggers.

About two-thirds of the illegal alcohol came from Canada, because it was impossible for the authorities to monitor the whole of the long border between the two countries. Other bootleggers brought in alcohol by sea. They would wait in the waters outside US control until an opportunity to land their cargo presented itself. One of the most famous bootleggers was Captain McCoy, who specialised in the finest Scotch whisky. This is where the phrase 'the real McCoy' comes from.

Source 36 A cartoon from 1925 titled 'The National Gesture'. It was published in *Judge* magazine, a satirical journal similar to the British *Private Eye* or *Punch* magazines. ▼

What was the impact of Prohibition?

Corruption

Prohibition led to massive corruption. Many law-enforcement officers were themselves involved with the liquor trade. Big breweries stayed in business throughout the Prohibition era by bribing local government officials, Prohibition agents and the police to leave them alone. In some cities, police officers were prepared to tell people where they could find speakeasies if they wanted a drink! In Seattle one police officer, Roy Olmstead, was fired for importing alcohol and so became a full-time bootlegger. By the time he was caught in 1928 he had built up a large network of paid city officials and police officers. Even when arrests were made, it was difficult to get bootleggers convicted because senior officers or even judges were in the pay of the criminals.

The bootlegger George Remus certainly did well from the trade. He had a huge network of paid officials that allowed him to escape charge after charge against him. At one party he gave a car to each of the women guests, while all the men received diamond cufflinks worth $25,000. The head of the New York FBI, Don Chaplin, once ordered his 200 agents: 'Put your hands on the table, both of them. Every son of a bitch wearing a diamond is fired.' One in 12 Prohibition agents was dismissed for corruption.

1 What is the cartoonist trying to say in Source 36? Explain what you think his message is, whether he is supporting or criticising someone or something, and how he achieves his aim.

Gangsters

One of the most enduring images of the Prohibition era is that of the gangster. Estimates suggest that organised gangs made about $2 billion out of the sale of illegal alcohol during this period. The rise of the gangsters tells us a lot about US society at this time. They generally came from poor immigrant backgrounds: in the early 1920s the main gangs were Jewish, Polish, Irish and Italian. Gangsters were often poorly educated, but they were clever and ruthless. Dan O'Banion (an Irish gang leader murdered by Al Capone), Pete and Vince Guizenberg (hired killers who worked for Bugsy Moran and died in the St Valentine's Day Massacre) and Lucky Luciano (an Italian killer who spent ten years in prison) were some of the best-known gangsters. Gangs fought viciously with each other to control the liquor trade as well as the prostitution, gambling and protection rackets that were centred on the speakeasies. In Chicago alone, there were 130 gangland murders in 1926–27 – but not a single arrest. By the late 1920s, fear and bribery had made law enforcement ineffective.

Case study: Chicago and Al Capone

The gangsters operated all over the USA, but perhaps the best example of the power of the gangsters is Chicago gangster Al Capone.

Capone arrived in Chicago in 1919, on the run from a murder investigation in New York. He ran a drinking club for his boss, Johnny Torio. In 1925, Torio retired after an assassination attempt by one of his rivals, Bugsy Moran. Capone took over and proved to be a formidable gangland boss. He built up a huge network of corrupt officials among Chicago's police, local government workers, judges, lawyers and Prohibition agents. He even controlled Chicago's mayor, William Hale Thompson. By 1929, Capone had destroyed the influence of the other Chicago gangs, committing at least 300 murders in the process. The peak of his violent reign came with the St Valentine's Day Massacre in 1929, when Capone's men murdered seven of Moran's gang, using a fake police car and two gangsters in police uniform to put Moran's men off their guard.

Surprisingly, Capone was a high-profile and even popular figure in the city. He regularly attended baseball and American football games and was cheered by the crowd when he took his seat in the stadia! He was well known for giving generous tips (over $100) to waiters and shop girls and spent $30,000 on a soup kitchen for the unemployed (see Source 37).

Source 37 A photograph of a soup kitchen funded by Al Capone, 1931. ▶

219

Source 38 A crowd of applicants at the Board of Health, waiting for permits to sell beer in New York, 6 April 1933. The next day, the Cullen–Harrison Act became law, which legalised the sale of beer. ▲

1 If you look for images of Prohibition you will find many photographs of Americans celebrating the end of it. We chose Source 38 instead because we felt that it was more useful to historians studying the era. Do you agree?

Why was Prohibition ended?

The St Valentine's Day Massacre was a turning point. The papers screamed that the gangsters had graduated from murder to massacre. The 'noble experiment' had clearly failed. It had made the USA lawless, the police corrupt and the gangsters rich and powerful. With the Wall Street Crash in October 1929, and the ensuing Depression of the early 1930s, there were sound economic arguments for ending Prohibition. Legalising alcohol would create jobs, raise tax revenue and free up resources currently being used to enforce Prohibition. The Democratic president Franklin D. Roosevelt was elected in 1932 and Prohibition was repealed in December 1933.

PRACTICE QUESTIONS

1 Describe one example of the arguments made by supporters of Prohibition. (2)
2 Describe one example of how Prohibition affected US society. (2)
3 Explain why Prohibition ended in 1933. (10)
4 'Prohibition was a success.' How far do you agree with this view? (18)

FOCUS TASK

A Why did Prohibition fail?

Below are four groups who could be blamed for the failure of Prohibition.

A The American people, who carried on going to illegal speakeasies, making Prohibition difficult to enforce.

B The law enforcers, who were corrupt and ignored the law-breakers.

C The bootleggers, who continued supplying and selling alcohol.

D The gangsters, who controlled the trade through violence and made huge profits.

1 For each of group, find evidence on pages 216–20 to show that it contributed to the failure of Prohibition.
2 Which group do you think played the most important role in the failure? Explain your choice.
3 Draw a diagram to show any links between the groups.

B Why was Prohibition introduced in 1920 and then abolished in 1933?

4 Many people who were in favour of Prohibition before 1920 were equally convinced that it should be abolished in 1933. To make sure you understand this change in attitude, research and write reconstructions of two letters:
a The first should be from a supporter of Prohibition to his or her congressman in 1919, explaining why the congressman should vote for Prohibition. In your letter, explain how Prohibition could help to solve problems in the USA.

b The second should be from the same person to the congressman in 1933, explaining why the congressman should vote against Prohibition. In your letter, explain why Prohibition has failed.
5 Look back at your work on the Focus Task on page 200. Add extra details to your proposal for the Roaring Twenties attraction. Try not to add more than 150 words.

Prejudice and intolerance: the dark side of the Roaring Twenties

The experience of immigrants

The vast majority of Americans were either immigrants or descendants of recent immigrants. Immigration to the USA was at an all-time high in 1901–10, particularly Jews from eastern Europe and Russia who were fleeing persecution, and people from Italy who were escaping poverty. Many Italian immigrants did not intend to settle in the USA, but hoped to make money to take back to their families in Italy.

The USA had always prided itself on being a 'melting pot'. In theory, individual groups lost their ethnic identity and blended with other groups to become just 'Americans'. In practice, however, this was not always the case. In the big cities, the more established immigrant groups – Irish Americans, French Canadians and German Americans – competed for the best jobs and the best housing. These groups tended to look down on the more recent immigrants from eastern Europe and Italy, who in turn had nothing but contempt for African Americans and Mexicans, who were regarded as being at the bottom of the social scale.

Source 39 A cartoon entitled 'Come On!' showing attitudes to communism in the USA, 1919. The character in the black suit looks like the communist leader Leon Trotsky and has 'revolution maker' written on his chest. The piece of paper says 'Propaganda for US'. ▼

The Red Scare

In the 1920s, these racist attitudes were made worse by an increased fear of communism. The USA had watched with alarm as communists in Russia (Bolsheviks) took over the government in a revolution in 1917. People were afraid that the recent immigrants from eastern Europe and Russia would bring similar radical ideas to the USA. This reaction was called the 'Red Scare'. In 1919, this fear gave rise to a wave of disturbances. Around 400,000 workers went on strike. In Boston, even the police went on strike, and looters and thieves roamed the city. There were race riots in 25 towns.

The Palmer Raids

Today, most historians believe that the strikes were caused by economic hardship. However, many prominent Americans in the 1920s saw the strikes as the dangerous signs of communist interference. The fears were not totally unjustified. Many immigrants in the USA did hold radical political beliefs. ANARCHISTS published pamphlets calling for the overthrow of the government, and distributed them widely in US cities. In April 1919, a bomb planted in a church in Milwaukee killed ten people. In May that year, bombs were posted to 36 prominent Americans. In June, more bombs went off in seven US cities, and one of them almost succeeded in killing Mitchell Palmer, the US attorney-general.

In response to this wave of violence, all those believed to have radical political beliefs were rounded up. They were usually immigrants and the evidence against them was often flimsy. J. Edgar Hoover, a clerk appointed by Palmer, built up files on 60,000 suspects and in 1919–20 around 10,000 individuals were informed that they were to be deported from the USA.

2 According to the cartoonist in Source 39, is the USA afraid of communism?

3 As a historian, does Source 39 make you believe the USA is not afraid or actually that it is? Explain your answer.

4 How similar are Sources 39 and 40?

Source 40 Mitchell Palmer, US attorney-general, speaking in 1920.

The blaze of revolution is eating its way into the homes of the American workman, licking at the altars of the churches, leaping into the belfry of the school house, crawling into the sacred corners of American homes, seeking to replace the marriage vows with libertine laws, burning up the foundations of society.

1 How similar are Sources 40 and 41?
2 Explain how sources 39–41 are all extremely useful in revealing attitudes towards immigrants.

Source 41 Republican senator James Heflin, speaking in 1921 in a debate over whether to limit immigration.

The steamship companies haul them over to America and as soon as they step off the ships the problem of the steamship companies is settled, but our problem has only begun – Bolshevism, red anarchy, blackhanders [members of dangerous political groups] and kidnappers, challenging the authority and integrity of our flag. ... Thousands come here who will never take the oath to support our constitution and become citizens of the USA. They pay allegiance to some other country while they live upon the substance of our own. They fill places that belong to the wage earning citizens of America. ... They are of no service whatever to our people. ... They constitute a menace and a danger to us every day.

Source 42 A poster published by the Sacco and Vanzetti Commemoration Society, 2008. ▲

ACTIVITY

You have just received a photograph – Source 42 – on your phone from a relative who is on holiday in Boston. They have asked you what this is all about. Send a short message back, keeping it under 100 words if you can.

Sacco and Vanzetti

Two high-profile victims of the Red Scare were Italian Americans Nicola Sacco and Bartolomeo Vanzetti. They were arrested in 1920 on suspicion of armed robbery and murder, and they confirmed that they were anarchists. Anarchists hated the US system of government and wanted to destroy it by stirring up social disorder. The trial of Sacco and Vanzetti became more about their radical ideas than about the murder they were accused of. The prosecution relied heavily on racist slurs about their Italian origins and on stirring up fears about their radical beliefs.

The judge at the trial said that although Vanzetti 'may not actually have committed the crime attributed to him he is nevertheless morally culpable [to blame] because he is the enemy of our existing institutions'. Sacco and Vanzetti were convicted on flimsy evidence. A leading lawyer of the time said: 'Judge Thayer is … full of prejudice. He has been carried away by fear of Reds which has captured about 90 per cent of the American people.'

After six years of legal appeals, Sacco and Vanzetti were executed in 1927. There was a storm of protest around the world from both radicals and moderates, who believed they had not received a fair trial. To deflect the criticism, the governor of Massachusetts set up an enquiry (the Lowell Commission) headed by the president of Harvard University and former law professor Abbott Lawrence Lowell. Lowell found that the verdicts and the executions were completely justified. However, Lowell was known for his controversial views: he would not let Black students live in dormitories with White students; he believed immigrants could not become Americans unless they abandoned their ties to their homeland; he also introduced a quota for the number of Jews allowed to study at Harvard and expelled all homosexual students. As such, Lowell's findings on the Sacco and Vanzetti verdict did not appease the critics. Sacco and Vanzetti were eventually pardoned 50 years later.

Immigrant quotas

Partly as a result of the Red Scare, the government began to change its policy on immigration. In 1924, it introduced a quota system that ensured that the largest proportion of immigrants came from north-west Europe (mainly British, Irish and German). No Asians were allowed in at all. From a high point of more than 1 million immigrants a year between 1901 and 1910, by 1929 the number arriving in the USA had fallen to 150,000 per year.

The experience of African Americans

Look at Source 43. Do you notice anything about the crowd? If the camera had panned around the rest of the baseball ground you would have seen that in the other stand the spectators were all White. Such racial segregation was a common part of life in the USA in the 1920s.

African Americans had long been part of the country's history. The first Africans had been brought to the USA as slaves. By the time slavery was ended in the nineteenth century, there were more African Americans than White people in the southern United States. White governments, fearing the power of this large group of citizens, introduced many laws to control their freedom. These became known as the Jim Crow Laws. African Americans were segregated in many areas of life. They could not vote. They were denied access to good jobs and good education, and they suffered great poverty well into the twentieth century.

3 'Source 43 is just a photograph of a crowd. It is no use to historians.' Write a short paragraph explaining why this view is wrong.

Source 43 Part of the crowd at a baseball match in Tennessee, April 1922. ▼

The Ku Klux Klan

- The Klan was formed in the 1850s by former soldiers after the American Civil War, with the aim of keeping White people in control of the country.
- It used parades, beatings, lynchings and other violent methods to intimidate African Americans. It also attacked Jews, Catholics and foreign immigrants.
- It was strongest in the Midwest and rural south, where working-class Whites competed with African Americans for unskilled jobs.
- It declined in the late nineteenth century but started up again in 1915. It spread rapidly in the early 1920s, and Klansmen were elected to positions of political power.
- By 1924, the KKK had 4.5 million members.
- The governors of the states of Oregon and Oklahoma were Klan members and the organisation was especially dominant in Indiana.
- The Klan declined after 1925. One of its leaders, David Stephenson, was convicted of a vicious, sexually motivated murder. He turned informer and the corruption of the Klan became common knowledge.

Racial violence and the Ku Klux Klan

Poverty and segregation were not the worst hardship for African Americans. They also faced extreme racist violence, most notably from the Ku Klux Klan (see Factfile). In the 1900s the Klan had been in decline, but it was revived after the release of the film *The Birth of a Nation* in 1915. The film was set in the 1860s, just after the Civil War. It glorified the Klan as defenders of decent American values against traitorous African Americans and corrupt White businessmen. President Wilson said of the film: 'It is like writing history with lightning. And my only regret is that it is all so terribly true.'

With support from such prominent figures, the Klan became a powerful political force in the early 1920s. The Klan targeted Jews and many other minorities, but the worst violence was directed at African Americans.

African Americans throughout the southern states had to deal with severe racism. There were many cases of LYNCHING (hanging without trial), particularly when crimes had been committed against Whites which people thought had been committed by African Americans. In 1930, 16-year-old James Cameron was arrested, along with two other African American men, on suspicion of the murder of a White man and the rape of a White woman. They were in prison in Marion, Indiana when a mob arrived intending to lynch them. The mob broke down the doors of the jail and killed the other two accused men. Miraculously Cameron survived.

Source 44 The journalist R. A. Patton, writing about Klan violence in Alabama, 1929.

A lad whipped with branches until his back was ribboned flesh … a white girl, divorcée, beaten into unconsciousness in her home; a naturalised foreigner flogged until his back was pulp because he married an American woman; a negro lashed until he sold his land to a white man for a fraction of its value.

1   Source 44 is highly emotive and critical of the Klan. Does this make it an unreliable source about the Klan or the author?

Source 45 Panel 23 from the series *The Great Migration* by the African American artist Jacob Lawrence. The paintings tell the story of the migration of African Americans from the south to the north in the 1920s in 59 panels. The title of this panel is 'And the Migration Spread'.
▶

Cameron's experience was not unusual. Thousands of African Americans were lynched in this period. Many reports describe atrocities at which whole families of White people, including young children, clapped and cheered. Faced by such intimidation, discrimination and poverty, many African Americans left the rural south and moved to cities in the northern USA. The African American population of both Chicago and New York more than doubled in the 1920s: New York's from 150,000 to 330,000 and Chicago's from 110,000 to 230,000.

Opportunities and achievements

In the north, African Americans had a better chance of getting good jobs and a decent education. For example, Howard University had been set up exclusively for African Americans. In both Chicago and New York there was a small but growing African American middle class and a successful 'Black capitalist' movement encouraged African Americans to set up businesses. In Chicago this movement boycotted chain stores, protesting that they would not shop there unless African American staff were employed. By 1930, almost all the shops in the area where African Americans lived had Black employees.

There were internationally famous African Americans, such as the singer and actor Paul Robeson (see Profile). However, Robeson was a qualified lawyer and only became a singer because of the racial barriers he had faced when trying practise law. The popularity of jazz made many African American musicians into high profile media figures. The African American neighbourhood of Harlem in New York became the centre of the 'Harlem Renaissance' – a hub of creativity and a magnet for White customers who frequented the bars and clubs. African American artists and writers flourished in this atmosphere. The poet Langston Hughes wrote about the lives of working-class African Americans and the poverty and problems they suffered. Countee Cullen was another prominent poet who tried to tackle racism and poverty. In his poem 'For A Lady I Know', he tried to sum up attitudes of wealthy white employers to their African American servants:

She even thinks that up in heaven
Her class lies late and snores
While poor black cherubs rise at seven
To do celestial chores.

PROFILE

Paul Robeson (1898–1976)

- Born 1898, the son of a church minister who had once been a slave.
- Went to Columbia University and passed his law exams with honours in 1923.
- As a Black lawyer, it was almost impossible for him to find work, so he became an actor – his big break was in the hit musical *Showboat*.
- Visited Moscow in 1934 on a world tour and declared his approval of communism saying: 'Here, for the first time in my life, I walk in dignity.'
- As a communist sympathiser, Robeson suffered in the USA. He was banned from performing, suffered death threats and had his passport confiscated.
- He left the USA in 1958 to live in Europe, but returned in 1963.

Source 46 A poster published by the NAACP to support a bill being put to the US Senate in 1922 to make lynching a federal crime. This would have taken the role of investigation and prosecution out of the hands of local authorities and given it to government agents. The bill was not passed. ▼

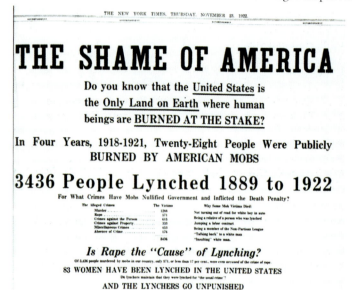

African Americans in politics

African Americans also entered politics. W.E.B. DuBois founded the National Association for the Advancement of Colored People (NAACP), which had 300 branches and around 90,000 members by 1919. The NAACP campaigned to end racial SEGREGATION laws and to get laws passed against lynching (see Source 46). The group did not make much headway at the time, but the number of lynchings did fall.

Another important figure at this time was Marcus Garvey, who founded the Universal Negro Improvement Association (UNIA). Garvey urged African Americans to be proud of their race and colour. He instituted an honours system for African Americans (like the British Empire's system of knighthoods). The UNIA helped African Americans set up their own businesses. By the mid-1920s there were UNIA grocery stores, laundries, restaurants and even a printing workshop. Garvey set up a shipping line to support both the UNIA businesses and also his scheme of helping African Americans to escape the racism of the USA by emigrating to Africa. Eventually Garvey's businesses collapsed, however. One reason for this was that he was prosecuted for exaggerating the value of the shares of his company. He was one of very few businessmen to be charged for this offence, and some historians believe that J. Edgar Hoover was behind the prosecution.

Garvey's movement attracted over 1 million members at its height in 1921. One of these was the Reverend Earl Little. Little was beaten to death by members of the KKK in the late 1920s, but his son went on to be the civil rights leader known as Malcolm X.

1 Why did the NAACP publish Source 46?
2 How did the poster try to achieve its aims?
3 Does this source prove that the NAACP was effective?

Limitations

These movements were important, but none managed to change attitudes towards African Americans in the USA significantly. In addition, while life expectancy for African Americans increased from 45 to 48 in 1900–30, they were still a long way behind the Whites, whose life expectancy increased from 54 to 59 over the same period. Many African Americans in the northern cities lived in great poverty. In Harlem they lived in worse housing than Whites, yet paid higher rents. They had poorer education and health services. Many Black women worked as low-paid domestic servants. Factories making cars employed few African Americans or operated a Whites-only policy. In Chicago, African Americans suffered great prejudice from longer-established White residents. If they attempted to move out of the African American areas to adjacent neighbourhoods, they were greeted with hostility (see Source 47).

They got a similar reception from poor Whites. In Chicago, when African Americans attempted to use parks, playgrounds and beaches in the Irish and Polish districts, they were set upon by gangs calling themselves 'athletic clubs'. African American communities in northern areas often became isolated ghettos.

Prejudice was also evident within these communities. Middle-class African Americans who were restless in the ghettos tended to blame newly arrived migrants from the south for intensifying White racism. In Harlem, the presence of some 50,000 West Indians was a source of inter-racial tension. Many of them were better educated, more militant and prouder of their colour than the newly arrived African Americans from the south.

Source 47 From the *Chicago Property Owners' Journal*, 1920.

There is nothing in the make-up of a negro, physically or mentally, that should induce anyone to welcome him as a neighbour. The best of them are unsanitary ... ruin follows in their path. They are as proud as peacocks, but have nothing of the peacock's beauty. ... [Negroes] are undesirable neighbours and entirely irresponsible and vicious.

FOCUS TASK

How should we tell the story of African Americans in the 1920s?

1   African American history is still a very difficult and controversial subject in the USA. Historians, journalists, writers and filmmakers all try to tackle it, and most attempt to be honest about the prejudice and suffering African Americans experienced. However, some African American historians have objected to this because it portrays them as passive victims who did nothing to improve their own position. Your task is to prepare a presentation with the title 'African Americans in the 1920s: a balanced view'.

You will need to include slides on:
   a   the difficulties suffered by African Americans
   b   the reasons for these problems
   c   the motives of those attacking them
   d   how they responded.

It is up to you how much coverage you give to the different aspects.

2   Look back at your work on the Focus Task on page 200. Add extra details to your proposal for the 'Roaring Twenties' attraction, but try not to add more than 200 words.

PRACTICE QUESTIONS

1   Describe one example of prejudice towards immigrants in the 1920s. (2)
2   Describe one example of discrimination against African Americans in the 1920s. (2)
3   Explain why the execution of Sacco and Vanzetti in 1927 was controversial. (10)
4   Explain why many African Americans migrated to towns in the northern USA in the 1920s. (10)
5   'For African Americans the 1920s were a time of great improvement.' How far do you agree with this view? (18)

TOPIC SUMMARY

The 'Roaring Twenties': the age of irresponsibility?

1   The Roaring Twenties saw significant changes in the lives of Americans. The majority now lived in towns and cities. They were enjoying economic prosperity and this spending power gave rise to entertainment and leisure industries, especially music and movies.
2   Attitudes changed as well. Young people, and especially young women, gained more independence than they had ever had before.
3   On the other hand many Americans did not share in the prosperity, especially in the farming industry. Also, the majority of women did not gain much extra freedom, they still worked for low pay or looked after the home and family, or both.
4   Some sections of society worried that the USA was going off the rails, morally and economically. This led to Prohibition, an attempt to ban the drinking of alcohol. It turned out to be a disastrous failure as the American people mostly refused to obey the law. It also gave rise to crime and corruption.
5   African Americans and other minorities gained little from the Roaring Twenties. They tried to advance their cause with organisations like the NAACP but they faced prejudice, discrimination and even violence from organisations like the Ku Klux Klan.

5.2

The 1930s: Depression and New Deal

FOCUS

The US economy boomed in the 1920s, but in 1929 everything went disastrously wrong. The economy crashed and a catastrophic depression followed. Millions of people went from comfort to poverty. In this topic, you will examine:

● the effects of the Wall Street Crash and the Great Depression on Americans

● the attempts to tackle the problems, particularly President Roosevelt's New Deal

● the extent to which the New Deal and the events of the 1930s actually changed the USA.

Why did the US economy crash in 1929?

On Margin.

Source 1 A cartoon entitled 'On Margin', November 1929. ▶

How would you describe the scene in Source 1? It is neither happy nor 'roaring'! It shows the sense of despair many Americans felt in the weeks and months that followed 29 October 1929.

As the economy boomed through the 1920s, the value of shares rose and this led to SPECULATION on the stock market. Speculators are not interested in long-term investment, just short-term profit. This fuelled a dangerous development – buying 'on margin'. People borrowed money to buy shares in companies, with the intention of selling those shares when they rose in value to pay back the loan and keep the profit. US banks lent $9 billion to speculators in 1929 alone. Ordinary people as well as institutions were buying on margin. Businesses, wealthy investors and even banks speculated because in the 1920s the value of shares just seemed to keep going up.

This system depends on confidence – shares continue rising in value as long as people believe they are valuable and keep buying them. In autumn 1929, investors began to lose confidence in the US economy. They believed they could see weaknesses and thought the value of shares had gone too high, so they began to

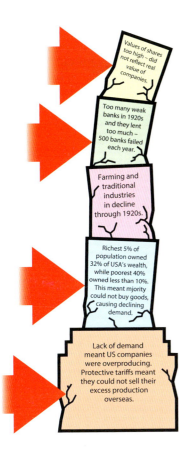

Values of shares too high – did not reflect real value of companies.

Too many weak banks in 1920s and they lent too much – 500 banks failed each year.

Farming and traditional industries in decline through 1920s.

Richest 5% of population owned 32% of USA's wealth, while poorest 40% owned less than 10%. This meant majority could not buy goods, causing declining demand.

Lack of demand meant US companies were overproducing. Protective tariffs meant they could not sell their excess production overseas.

sell them. This panicked other investors into selling their shares – particularly those who had bought 'on margin' who had to pay back their loans. All this had a dramatic effect. The value of US companies rapidly collapsed as investors desperately tried to sell their shares for any price they could get. Some shares (even shares in strong companies) became virtually worthless. Investors were ruined. In just four trading days, the market lost nearly half its value. This became known as the Wall Street Crash. The worst day was Tuesday 29 October 1929, often referred to as Black Tuesday, when more shares were sold than in any day in Wall Street history.

Speculation and speculators were blamed for the Crash. And the Crash in turn is often seen as the cause of the Great Depression that followed. But in reality both the Crash and the Depression were the result of much deeper problems.

How did the Crash affect Americans?

A change of circumstances

Source 1 gives a good sense of how the Crash affected people in the short term. Many high-profile figures were ruined:

- The Vanderbilt family lost $40 million.
- Businessman John D. Rockefeller lost 80 per cent of his wealth (although he still had $40 million).
- The British politician Winston Churchill lost $500,000.
- The singer Fanny Brice lost $500,000.
- Groucho and Harpo Marx (two of the Marx Brothers comedy team) lost $240,000 each.

Of course, millions of ordinary Americans were affected as well.

A new state of mind: the death of confidence

For a while it was not clear whether this would be a short- or a long-term crisis. President Hoover reassured the nation that prosperity was 'just around the corner'. He cut taxes to encourage people to buy more goods and by mid-1931 production was rising again. There was hope that the situation was more settled. But the Crash had destroyed the one thing that was crucial to the prosperity of the 1920s: confidence.

This was most evident in the banking industry. In 1929, 659 banks failed. This caused people to stop trusting them and many withdrew their savings. Consequently, in 1930 another 1,352 went bankrupt. These included the Bank of the United States in New York, which had 400,000 account holders – almost one-third of New Yorkers saved with this bank. Panic set in. Around the country a billion dollars was withdrawn from banks and put in safety deposit boxes or stored at home. People felt that only cash was safe from the effects of the Crash. Another 2,294 banks went under in 1931.

ACTIVITY

We think metaphors can be very useful in explaining history. Here we have used a crumbling skyscraper as a metaphor. In pairs or small groups either explain why this works or come up with a better metaphor.

◀ **Source 2** A photograph from 30 October 1929.

1   Source 2 is clearly posed for the camera. Does this mean it is not a useful source?

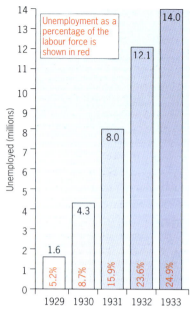

Source 3 A graph showing unemployment in the USA, 1929–33. ▲

1 Compare Sources 2 and 3. Is it possible to say whether one is more useful then the other as evidence about the Crash?

Source 4 US economist and politician J. K. Galbraith, speaking in 1979.

Every country has its great social memory. For the Japanese it is Hiroshima. For the Irish it is the Great Famine of the 1840s. For the British it is the trenches of World War I. For Americans it is the Depression. Even to this day, when something goes wrong with the economy you will hear Americans ask 'Does it mean another Depression?'

A downward spiral

While Hoover talked optimistically about the return of prosperity, Americans were showing their true feelings. They kept hold of their money instead of buying new goods or shares. This meant that banks had less money to offer in loans to businesses or to people as mortgages on homes. To make matters worse, banks began asking businesses to repay loans, although those businesses could not afford to do so. As loans were called in by the banks, many businesses collapsed or cut back.

The downward spiral was firmly established. Between 1928 and 1933 both industrial and farm production fell by 40 per cent, and average wages by 60 per cent. By 1932, the USA was in the grip of the most serious economic depression the world had ever seen. By 1933, there were 14 million unemployed and 5,000 banks had gone bankrupt. The collapse in urban areas soon had an impact on the countryside. Total farm income slipped to just $5 billion.

How did the Depression affect Americans 1929–33?

The human cost – in the countryside

People in agricultural areas had not enjoyed much of the prosperity that had characterised the 1920s, so they were the hardest hit by the Depression. As farm income fell, thousands of farmers were unable to pay their mortgages and went bankrupt. Some farmers organised themselves to resist banks taking back their homes. When sheriffs came to seize their property, bands of farmers holding pitchforks and hangman's nooses persuaded the sheriffs to retreat. Others barricaded highways to stop the authorities reaching them.

Despite these attempts at resistance, most farmers had no choice but to pack their belongings into their trucks and leave their homes. They became migrants, picking up work where they could. African American farmers and labourers were often worse off than their White neighbours as they lost their land and their farms first.

Bankruptcy was not the only problem. In the 1930s, the southern and Midwest states experienced a prolonged drought. Over-farming combined with the drought to cause the topsoil to turn to dust. This was then whipped up by the wind to create dust-storms that turned large areas into what was referred to as a 'dustbowl'.

Faced by this range of problems, many people in the rural USA faced hunger and MALNUTRITION. Images of these desperate migrants have formed the most enduring impression of the Great Depression.

Source 5 A photograph by Dorothea Lange, showing an abandoned farm swallowed up by dust in 1935. From 1933 onwards Lange was employed by two government agencies, the Resettlement Administration (RA) and the Farm Security Administration (FSA). She became famous as a photographer and journalist, recording the impact of the Depression. ▶

Source 6 A photograph by Dorothea Lange, showing a Mexican migrant worker in California. ▲

The human cost – in the towns

The situation was not much better in the towns. Unemployment rose rapidly. For example, in 1932, in the steel city of Cleveland, 50 per cent of workers were unemployed and in Toledo this figure was 80 per cent. Forced to sell their homes or evicted because they could not pay the rent, city workers joined the army of unemployed searching for work of any kind. Thousands were taken in by relatives but many ended up on the streets. At night the parks were full of the homeless and unemployed. A large number of men (estimated at 2 million in 1932) travelled from place to place on railway freight wagons seeking work. Thousands of children could be found living in these wagons or in tents next to the tracks. Every town had a 'Hooverville' – a shanty town of ramshackle huts where the migrants lived while they searched for work. The rubbish tips were crowded with families hoping to scrape a meal from the leftovers of more fortunate people. In 1931, 238 people were admitted to hospital in New York suffering from malnutrition or starvation. Forty-five of them died.

Attitudes to poverty

As Americans found their world turned upside down, their attitudes began to change. During the 1920s articles about migrant workers or the unemployed would have been dismissed as sob stories and the victims would be labelled idle layabouts who should show some 'rugged individualism'. During the 1930s, the work of photographers such as Dorothea Lange and the songs of musicians like Woody Guthrie showed the poor in a different light. Most Americans became more sympathetic towards them. They also became angry at a system in which workers who had contributed to the prosperity of the 1920s were now forced to queue for bread and soup dished out by charity workers. They became angry about a system which allowed banks to take people's money without guaranteeing it would be secure. They became angry that the Depression seemed to leave many of the rich untouched. By 1932, many Americans were beginning to question the Republican belief in *laissez-faire* and rugged individualism, and to wonder whether a different approach was needed.

Source 7 A Hooverville shanty town in Central Park, New York. The large building on the left is the Dakota Building, one of the most exclusive and expensive apartment buildings in New York. It was fully occupied during the Depression. ▶

◄ **Source 8** A cartoon by the US artist John McCutcheon, 1932. McCutcheon won a Pulitzer Prize for this cartoon.

Source 9 Some of the lyrics of 'Brother Can You Spare A Dime?', a song from a 1932 musical that became a huge hit.

They used to tell me I was building a dream
And so I followed the mob
When there was earth to plough or guns to bear
I was always there right on the job

They used to tell me I was building a dream
With peace and glory ahead
Why should I be standing in line
Just waiting for bread?

Once I built a railroad, I made it run
Made it race against time
Once I built a railroad, now it's done
Brother, can you spare a dime?

Source 10 An extract from *New Republic*, a liberal magazine, February 1933.

Last summer, in the hot weather, when the smell was sickening and the flies were thick, there were a hundred people a day coming to the dumps … a widow who used to do housework and laundry, but now had no work at all, fed herself and her fourteen-year-old son on garbage. Before she picked up the meat she would always take off her glasses so that she couldn't see the maggots.

Source 11 Evidence given by the US socialist and labour campaigner Oscar Ameringer to a government committee, 1932.

During the last three months I have visited some 20 states of this wonderfully rich and beautiful country. A number of Montana citizens told me of thousands of bushels of wheat left in the fields uncut on account of its low price that hardly paid for the harvesting. In Oregon I saw thousands of bushels of apples rotting in the orchards. At the same time there are millions of children who, on account of the poverty of their parents, will not eat one apple this winter. … I saw men picking for meat scraps in the garbage cans of the cities of New York and Chicago. One man said that he had killed 3,000 sheep this fall and thrown them down the canyon because it cost $1.10 to ship a sheep and then he would get less than a dollar for it. The farmers are being pauperised [made poor] by the poverty of industrial populations and the industrial populations are being pauperised by the poverty of the farmers. Neither has the money to buy the product of the other; hence we have overproduction and under-consumption at the same time.

Source 12 US writer Will Rogers, 1931. Rogers had a regular humorous column in a popular magazine.

There is not an unemployed man in the country that hasn't contributed to the wealth of every millionaire in America. The working classes didn't bring this on, it was the big boys. … We've got more wheat, more corn, more food, more cotton, more money in the banks, more everything in the world than any nation that ever lived ever had, yet we are starving to death. We are the first nation in the history of the world to go to the poorhouse in an automobile.

Source 13 A Dorothea Lange photograph showing unemployed workers in California waiting for benefit payments. ▲

Source 14 The president of the Farmers' Union of Wisconsin, A. N. Young, speaking to a Senate committee, 1932.

Farmers are just ready to do anything to get even with the situation. I almost hate to express it, but I honestly believe that if some of them could buy airplanes they would come down here to Washington to blow you fellows up. ... The farmer is a naturally conservative individual, but you cannot find a conservative farmer today. Any economic system that has in its power to set me and my wife in the streets, at my age what can I see but red?

Source 15 A cartoon published in the USA in 1932. This is thought to be the first time the term 'New Deal' was used. The cartoonist was John Miller Baer. He was also an independent member of Congress (neither Republican nor Democrat). ▶

The 1932 presidential election

These issues naturally became the focus of the presidential election of 1932 – the first opportunity for people to pass judgement on the Republicans who had been in charge during the boom years and then the crash. The sitting president, Republican Herbert Hoover, was up against the Democrat Franklin D. Roosevelt.

Herbert Hoover

In the 1932 election, Hoover paid the price for failing to solve the problems of the Depression. In fact, he was partly to blame for the severity of the situation. Until 1932 he refused to accept that there was a major problem, insisting that 'prosperity is just around the corner'. A famous banner carried in a demonstration of Iowa farmers read: 'In Hoover we trusted and now we are busted.'

With hindsight, it is easy to believe that Hoover did very little to resolve the crisis, but that is not entirely true. Hoover tried to restart the economy in 1930 and 1931 by implementing tax cuts. He tried to persuade business leaders not to cut wages because that would lead to lower spending and reduce demand. He set up the Reconstruction Finance Company, which propped up banks to stop them going bankrupt. He put money into public works programmes such as the Hoover Dam on the Colorado River. When these measures failed to make a significant impact, Hoover raised taxes. The Revenue Act of 1932 was the largest peacetime tax increase in US history and it doubled the rate of tax paid by the richest 1 per cent of the population.

Source 16 A photograph taken by an official military photographer in July 1932, showing police attacking the 'bonus marchers'. It was not published at the time. ▲

1 Does it surprise you that Source 16 was not published at the time?
2 If you were working for Hoover's opponents, how might you have made use of Source 16?
3 Why is Source 17 useful to historians studying this period?

Hoover was more of a practical manager than a politician. He took all these actions as short-term emergency measures and he planned to return to *laissez-faire* once the crisis was over. Hoover still felt that government intervention was not a long-term answer. The Republicans argued that business went in cycles of boom and bust, and therefore prosperity would soon return. In 1932, Hoover blocked the Garner–Wagner Relief Bill, which would have allowed Congress to provide $2.1 billion to create jobs. Historians are still debating whether or not Hoover was right to do this, but they do tend to agree that Hoover was out of step with public opinion. Most Americans believed the government should take some kind of action and maintain a watch over the economy and business to prevent a similar crisis in the future. In particular, they wanted leadership and reassurance. These were political skills that Hoover lacked. His opponent Roosevelt, however, had them in abundance.

Hoover's reputation was dramatically damaged by an event that took place in June 1932. Thousands of servicemen who had fought in the First World War marched on Washington asking for their war bonuses (a kind of pension) to be paid early. These 'bonus marchers' camped peacefully outside the White House and sang patriotic songs. Hoover refused to meet them. On 28 July, police and troops set on the marchers with guns and tear gas, killing two of them.

Source 17 Catholic priest Father J. Ryan. The Catholic Church had traditionally been bitterly opposed to communism.

When I think of what has been happening in this country since unemployment began, and when I see the futility of the leaders, I wish we might double the number of communists in this country, to put the fear, if not of God, then the fear of something else, into the hearts of our leaders.

Franklin D. Roosevelt

There could be no greater contrast to Hoover than his opponent in the 1932 election, Franklin D. Roosevelt:

- He was not a radical, but he believed in 'active government' to improve the lives of ordinary people, but only as a last resort if self-help and charity had failed.
- He had plans to spend public money on getting people back to work. As governor of New York, he had already started doing this in his own state.
- He was not afraid to ask for advice on important issues from a wide range of experts, such as factory owners, union leaders and economists.

PROFILE

Franklin D. Roosevelt (1882–1945)
- Born into a rich New York family in 1882.
- He went to university and became a successful lawyer.
- In 1910, he entered politics as a Democratic senator for New York.
- In 1921, he was paralysed by polio (he spent the rest of his life in a wheelchair).
- Elected president in 1933, in the middle of the economic crisis.
- Roosevelt was an excellent public speaker, an optimist and a believer in the 'American dream' – that anyone who worked hard enough could become rich.
- His 'New Deal' policies (see page 236), made him extremely popular.
- He was elected president four times.
- He led the USA through the Second World War until his death in April 1945.

Smile away the Depression!

Smile us into Prosperity!
wear a
SMILETTE!

This wonderful little gadget will
solve the problems of the Nation!

APPLY NOW AT YOUR CHAMBER OF COMMERCE
OR THE REPUBLICAN NATIONAL COMMITTEE

WARNING—Do not risk Federal arrest by looking glum!

The campaign

With such ill-feeling towards Hoover throughout the country, Roosevelt was confident of victory, but he took no chances. He went on a grand train tour of the USA in the weeks before the election and mercilessly attacked the Republicans.

Roosevelt's own plans were rather vague and general (see Source 19), but he realised that people wanted action – of any kind. Throughout a 20,800-km campaign trip, he made 16 major speeches and another 60 from the back of his train to gathered crowds. He promised the American people a 'New Deal'. It was not only his policies that attracted support; it was also his personality. Roosevelt radiated warmth and inspired confidence. He made personal contact with ordinary people and seemed to offer a way out of the terrible situation they were in. The election was a landslide victory for Roosevelt. He won by 7 million votes and the Democrats won a majority of seats in Congress. It was the worst defeat the Republicans had ever suffered.

◀ **Source 18** A Democrat campaign poster, 1932.

4 What is Source 18 trying to say about Hoover and the Republicans in 1932?

5 Politicians today are often criticised for negative campaigning (attacking their opponents rather than saying what they will do themselves). Is there any evidence that Roosevelt used negative campaigning?

6 Study Source 20 carefully. What is the main point it is trying to make about Hoover? Do you believe what the source says? Explain your answer.

Source 19 Franklin D. Roosevelt, in a speech given before his election, 1932

Millions of our citizens cherish the hope that their old standards of living have not gone forever. Those millions shall not hope in vain. I pledge you, I pledge myself, to a New Deal for the American people. This is more than a political campaign; it is a call to arms. Give me your help, not to win votes alone, but to win this crusade to restore America ... I am waging a war against Destruction, Delay, Deceit and Despair.

Source 20 An extract from an article called *Hero to Scapegoat*, the official biography of Hoover on the website of the Hoover Presidential Library and Museum.

In 1929 the Democratic Party hired former newspaperman Charles Michaelson to attack Hoover's image. Backed by a million dollar budget, Michaelson wrote speeches for Democrats on Capitol Hill and distributed a newspaper column. ... Comedian Will Rogers summed up the mood of a nation: 'If someone bit an apple and found a worm in it,' he joked, 'Hoover would get the blame.' Desperate encampments of tin and cardboard shacks were dubbed 'Hoovervilles'. There were 'Hoover hogs' (armadillos fit for eating), 'Hoover flags' (empty pockets turned inside out), 'Hoover blankets' (newspapers barely covering the destitute forced to sleep outdoors) and 'Hoover Pullmans' (empty boxcars used by an army of vagabonds escaping from their roots).

PRACTICE QUESTIONS

1 Describe one example of the impact of the Depression on Americans. (2)

2 Describe one example of Democrat campaign methods in 1932. (2)

3 Explain why the US economy crashed in the years 1929–33. (10)

4 Explain why Hoover lost the 1932 election. (10)

5 'The Depression was caused by speculators.' How far do you agree with this view? (18)

FOCUS TASK

Why did Roosevelt win the 1932 election?

In many ways, Roosevelt's victory needs no explanation. Indeed, it would have been surprising if any president could have been re-elected after the sufferings of 1929–32. But it is important to recognise the range of factors that helped Roosevelt and damaged Hoover. Write your own account of Roosevelt's success under the following headings:

- The experiences of ordinary people 1929–32
- The policies of the Republicans
- Actions taken by the Republicans
- Roosevelt's election campaign and personality.

The New Deal

During his election campaign, Roosevelt promised the American people a New Deal which would:

- get Americans back to work
- protect their savings and property
- provide relief for the sick, old and unemployed
- get US industry and agriculture back on their feet.

Hoover would have mostly agreed with these aims; the difference was that Roosevelt planned to use the full power of the government to achieve them. It would mean far more involvement in the lives of ordinary Americans and in the affairs of US businesses. Roosevelt's landslide election victory gave him the confidence to try this new approach.

The Hundred Days (the First New Deal)

In the first one hundred days of his presidency, Roosevelt worked with his advisers (known as the 'Brains Trust') to produce a huge range of sweeping measures.

The banks

One of the many problems was loss of confidence in the banks. The day after his INAUGURATION, Roosevelt ordered all banks to close and to remain closed until they had been assessed by government officials. A few days later 5,000 'trustworthy' banks were allowed to reopen, supported by government funds if they needed them. At the same time, Roosevelt's advisers had come up with a set of rules and regulations that would prevent the reckless speculation that contributed to the Wall Street Crash.

These actions were enabled by the Emergency Banking Act and the Securities Exchange Commission. These two measures gave a taste of what the New Deal would be. In this period, which became known as the 'Hundred Days', Roosevelt sent 15 proposals to Congress and all were adopted. Just as importantly, he took time to explain to the people what he was doing and why he was doing it. Every Sunday he would broadcast on radio to the nation. An estimated 60 million Americans tuned in to these 'fireside chats'. Nowadays, we are used to politicians addressing the nation but at the time it was a new idea.

Unemployment

The Federal Emergency Relief Administration tackled the urgent needs of the poor. $500 million was spent on soup kitchens, blankets, employment schemes and nursery schools. The Civilian Conservation Corps (CCC) was aimed at unemployed young men. They could sign on for a period of six months, which could be renewed if they could still not find work. Most of the work done by the CCC was on environmental projects in national parks. Most young men sent the money back to their families, and around 2.5 million people were helped by this scheme.

Source 22 A cartoon from 1933. The caption was 'Finis', which is Latin for 'End'. ▲

"Looks as If the New Leadership Was Really Going to Lead."

Source 23 A cartoon from 1933. The caption was: 'Looks as if the new leadership was really going to lead.' ▲

1 Study Source 22. How can you tell it was drawn by a supporter of the New Deal?
2 How far is Source 23 similar to Source 22?

Main events of the Hundred Days

4 March Roosevelt inaugurated.

5 March Closed banks.

9 March Selected banks reopened.

12 March Roosevelt's first radio 'fireside chat'. Encouraged Americans to put their money back into the banks. Many did so.

31 March The Civilian Conservation Corps set up.

12 May The Agricultural Adjustment Act passed.

18 May The Tennessee Valley Authority created.

18 June The National Industrial Recovery Act passed.

Main achievements of the Hundred Days

- It restored confidence and stopped investors pulling money out of the banks.
- Banking measures saved 20 per cent of home owners and farmers from repossession.
- Farmers were 50 per cent better off under AAA by 1936.
- TVA brought electrical power to underdeveloped areas.
- Public Works Administration created 600,000 jobs and built landmarks including San Francisco's Golden Gate Bridge.

A map showing the Tennessee Valley and the work of the TVA.

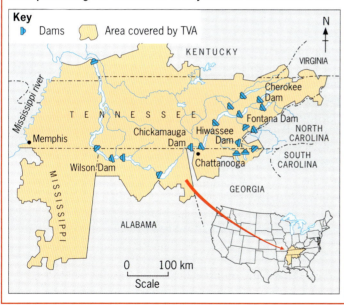

Farming

The Agricultural Adjustment Administration (AAA) tried to take a long-term view of the problems facing farmers. It set quotas to reduce farm production in order to force prices gradually upwards. At the same time, the AAA helped farmers to modernise and use farming methods that would conserve and protect the soil. In cases of extreme hardship, farmers were also given help with their mortgages. The AAA undeniably helped farmers, although modernisation also put more farm labourers out of work.

Industry

The final measure of the Hundred Days was the National Industrial Recovery Act (NIRA). This set up two important organisations.

- **The Public Works Administration (PWA)** used government money to build schools, roads, dams, bridges and airports. These would be vital once the USA had recovered, and in the short term they created millions of jobs.
- **The National Recovery Administration (NRA)** improved conditions in industry and outlawed child labour. It also set out fair wages and sensible levels of production. The idea was to stimulate the economy by giving workers money to spend, without overproducing and causing a slump. It was voluntary, and firms that joined used the blue eagle as a symbol of presidential approval. Over 2 million employers joined the scheme.

The Tennessee Valley Authority

The Tennessee Valley was a huge area that cut across seven states (see Factfile). In the wet season, the Tennessee River would flood; in the dry season it would reduce to a trickle. The farmland around the river was a dust bowl. The soil was eroding and turning the land into desert. The area also had great social problems. Within the valley people lived in poverty. The majority of households had no electricity. The problems of the Tennessee Valley were far too large for one state to deal with and it was very difficult for states to co-operate.

Roosevelt set up an independent organisation called the Tennessee Valley Authority (TVA), which cut across the powers of the local state governments. The main focus of the TVA's work was to build a series of dams on the Tennessee River (see Source 24). These transformed the region, bringing water to the dried-out land. They also provided electricity for this underdeveloped area. In the short-term, building the dams created thousands of jobs in an area badly hit by the Depression.

◀ **Source 24** The Fontana Dam, one of the TVA's later projects. Dams such as these revitalised farmland, provided jobs and brought electric power to the area.

Source 25 Raymond Moley, one of Roosevelt's advisers during the 'Hundred Days' Congress session.

The bank rescue of 1933 was probably the turning point of the Depression. When people were able to survive the shock of having all the banks closed, and then see the banks open up again, with their money protected, there began to be confidence. Good times were coming. It marked the revival of hope.

Source 27 Rudd Rennie, a US sports journalist, writing in 1934.

Wandering around the country with one of New York's baseball teams, I find that [what was] the national road to ruin is now a thriving thoroughfare. It has been redecorated. People have come out of the shell holes. They are working and playing and seem content to let a tribe of professional worriers do their worrying for them.

1 Do Sources 25–27 convince you that the New Deal was a success? Explain your answer based on:
   – what each source says about the impact of the New Deal
   – whether you think the source is reliable or unreliable about the impact of the New Deal.

The impact of the First New Deal

The measures introduced during the Hundred Days had an immediate effect. They restored confidence in government. Reporters who travelled the country brought back news of a boost in morale around the USA. Historians agree that Roosevelt's bold and decisive action had a marked effect on the American people.

Source 26 Frances Perkins, labour secretary under Roosevelt, writing in 1947.

As Roosevelt described it, the 'New Deal' meant that the forgotten man, the little man, the man nobody knew much about, was going to be dealt better cards to play with. ... He understood that the suffering of the Depression had fallen with terrific impact upon the people least able to bear it. He knew that the rich had been hit hard too, but at least they had something left. But the little merchant, the small householder and home owner, the farmer, the man who worked for himself – these people were desperate. And Roosevelt saw them as principal citizens of the United States, numerically and in their importance to the maintenance of the ideals of American democracy.

FOCUS TASK

What form did the New Deal take in 1933?

Look back over pages 236–38 and complete your own copy of this table.

New Deal measure/agency	Issue/problem it aimed to tackle	Action taken/powers of agency	Evidence it was/was not effective

The Second New Deal

Despite his achievements, by May 1935 Roosevelt was facing a barrage of criticism. Some people (like Senator Huey Long, see page 240) complained that he was doing too little, others (mainly the wealthy business sector) complained that he was doing too much. The USA was recovering from Depression less quickly than Europe. Business was losing enthusiasm for the NRA (for example, Henry Ford had cut wages). Roosevelt was unsure what to do. He had hoped to transform the USA, but it did not seem to be working.

On 14 May 1935, Roosevelt met with a group of senators and close advisers who shared his views and aims. They persuaded him to take radical steps to achieve his vision and make the USA a fairer place for all. One month later, the president presented the leaders of Congress with a huge range of laws that he wanted passed. This became known as the Second New Deal and was aimed at areas that affected ordinary people, such as strengthening unions to fight for the members' rights and for financial security in old age, as well as continuing to tackle unemployment. The most significant new features are outlined below.

Increased taxes on wealthy Americans

The **Revenue Act** of 1935 (also known as the Wealth Tax Act) introduced a 79 per cent tax on incomes over $5 million. It was more of a political measure than a tax-raising one, since only one person in the country had that kind of wealth! It was meant as a warning to the many wealthy Americans who were using a range of legal and illegal methods to avoid paying tax. By pursuing tax avoiders and introducing other taxes on the wealthy, Roosevelt raised the amount of tax paid by the wealthiest 1 per cent of Americans from 7 per cent in 1932 to 16 per cent in the Revenue Act of 1937. He also brought in taxes on business, such as the **Undistributed Profits Act** in 1936.

Strengthened trade unions

The **Wagner Act** forced employers to allow trade unions in their companies and to let them negotiate pay and conditions. It made it illegal to sack workers for being in a union.

Extra support and security for poor Americans

The **Social Security Act** provided state pensions for the elderly and for widows. It also allowed state governments to work with the federal government to provide help for the sick and the disabled. Most importantly, the act set up a scheme for unemployment insurance. Employers and workers made a small contribution to a special fund each week. If workers became unemployed, they would receive a small amount to help them out until they could find work.

Jobs for unemployed Americans

The **Works Progress Administration (WPA)**, later renamed the Works Project Administration, brought together all the organisations whose aim was to create jobs. It also extended this work beyond building projects to create jobs for office workers and even unemployed actors, artists and photographers. Source 5 on page 230 was taken by a photographer working for the Farm Security Administration. This project took 80,000 photos of farming areas during the New Deal. Source 28 was produced by an artist working for the Federal Arts Project. The government paid artists to paint pictures to be displayed in the city or town they featured.

Source 28 Costume design sketches for the first performance of the play *Pinocchio*. It was written and produced as part of the Work's Progress Administration's (WPA) Federal Theatre Project (FTP). ▲

Source 29 *Steel Industry* by Howard Cook, painted for the steel-making town of Pittsburgh, Pennsylvania. ▲

2 What impression of the New Deal does Source 29 attempt to convey?

3 Why do you think Roosevelt wanted artists and photographers to be employed under the New Deal?

Extra help for farmers

The **Resettlement Administration (RA)** helped smallholders and tenant farmers who had not been helped by the AAA. This organisation moved over 500,000 families to better-quality land and housing. The **Farm Security Administration (FSA)** replaced the RA in 1937. It gave special loans to small farmers to help them buy their land. It also built camps to provide decent living conditions and jobs for migrant workers.

FOCUS TASK

How far did the character of the New Deal change after 1933?

Draw two spider diagrams to compare the objectives and measures of the First New Deal and the Second New Deal. Then explain how the measures of the Second New Deal were different from those set out in 1933.

Reactions to the New Deal

Although the media and the US public were generally positive towards Roosevelt and the measures he took in the Hundred Days, not all Americans were enthusiastic supporters. Even some Democrats, including Huey Long and the American Liberty League, were anxious about the scale of government activity (see Source 31). Roosevelt and his New Deal faced significant opposition from some quarters.

1 Source 30 is critical of Roosevelt in the Hundred Days. Explain how you know this.
2 Do you think the cartoonist in Source 30 is opposed to any government action at all?
3 How similar are Sources 30 and 31?

◀ **Source 30** A cartoon from 1933. The caption was: 'How Much More Do We Need?' The figure in the water is Uncle Sam, who represents the USA.

Source 31 A cartoon published by the American Liberty League in 1935. The ALL was Democrats who were unhappy with Roosevelt's policies. ▼

It was criticised for not doing enough!

A number of high-profile figures complained that the New Deal was not doing enough to help the poor. Despite the measures, many Americans remained desperately poor. The hardest hit were African Americans and the poor in farming areas.

A key figure arguing on behalf of these people was Huey Long. Long became governor of Louisiana in 1928 and a senator in 1932. His methods of gaining power were unusual and sometimes illegal (they included intimidation and bribery). However, once he had power he used it to help the poor. He taxed big corporations and businesses in Louisiana and used the money to build roads, schools and hospitals. He employed African Americans on the same terms as Whites and clashed with the Ku Klux Klan.

Long supported the New Deal at first, but by 1934 he was criticising it for being too complicated and not doing enough. Instead he put forward a scheme called 'Share Our Wealth'. All personal fortunes would be reduced to $3 million maximum, and maximum income would be $1 million a year. Government taxes would be shared between all Americans. He also proposed pensions for everyone over 60, and free washing machines and radios.

Long was an aggressive and forceful character with many friends and many enemies. Roosevelt regarded him as one of the two most dangerous men in the USA. Long was assassinated in 1935.

Two other key critics were:
- **Dr Francis Townsend**, *who founded several 'Townsend Clubs' to campaign for a pension of $200 per month for people over 60, providing that they spent it that month. This would stimulate the economy in the process.*
- *A Catholic priest,* **Father Coughlin**, *used his own radio programme to attack Roosevelt. He set up the National Union for Social Justice, which gained a large membership.*

It was criticised for doing too much!

The New Deal came under fire from sections of the business community and from Republicans for doing too much. They argued that:
- *the New Deal was complicated and there were too many regulations that hampered business*
- *government should not support trade unions and it should not support calls for higher wages – the market should deal with these issues.*
- *schemes such as the Tennessee Valley Authority created unfair competition for private companies.*
- *The New Deal schemes were too like the economic plans being carried out in the communist USSR and were unsuitable for the democratic, free-market USA*
- *Roosevelt was behaving like a dictator*
- *high taxes discouraged people from working hard and gave money to people for doing nothing or doing unnecessary jobs.*

The New Deal is nothing more or less than an effort to take away from the thrifty what the thrifty and their ancestors have accumulated, or may accumulate, and give it to others who have not earned it and never will earn it, and thus to destroy the incentive for future accumulation. Such a purpose is in defiance of all the ideas upon which our civilisation has been founded.

Roosevelt was upset by the criticisms, but also by the tactics used against him by big business and the Republicans, who used a smear campaign to reduce support for the New Deal. They said that Roosevelt was disabled because of a sexually transmitted disease rather than from polio. Employers put messages into their workers' pay packets saying that New Deal schemes would never happen.

Roosevelt turned on these enemies bitterly (see Source 34), and it seemed the American people were with him. In the 1936 election he won 27 million votes, with the highest margin of victory ever achieved by a US president. He was then able to joke triumphantly: 'Everyone is against the New Deal except the voters.'

Source 33 An extract from a book by the prominent businessman Howard E. Kerschner, called *The Menace of Roosevelt and His Policies*, published in 1936.

Roosevelt took charge of our government when it was comparatively simple, and for the most part confined to the essential functions of government. He has transformed it into a highly complex, bungling agency for throttling business and bedeviling the private lives of free people. It is no exaggeration to say that he took the government when it was a small racket and made a large racket out of it.

4 Study Sources 32, 33 and 35. List the points they make against the New Deal.

5 In what ways are Sources 34 and 36 similar? How are they different?

6 How might the authors of Sources 32, 33 and 35 have reacted to Sources 34 and 36? Explain your answer.

Source 34 A speech by Roosevelt in the 1936 presidential election campaign.

For twelve years this nation was afflicted with hear-nothing, see-nothing, do-nothing government. The nation looked to government but government looked away. Nine crazy years at the stock market and three long years in the bread-lines! Nine mad years of mirage and three long years of despair! Powerful influences strive today to restore that kind of government with its doctrine that government is best which is most indifferent. ... We know now that government by organised money is just as dangerous as government by organised mob. Never before in all our history have these forces been so united against one candidate – me – as they stand today. They are unanimous in their hate of me – and I welcome their hatred.

Source 35 A cartoon from the 1930s. ▼

Source 36 A cartoon from the mid-1930s. ▼

Source 37 A cartoon from the British magazine *Punch*, published in 1935. The caption read: 'The Illegal Act. Preisdent Roosevelt: I'm sorry but the Supreme Court says I must chuck you back again.' ▲

Source 38 A cartoon published in the US newspaper the *Brooklyn Daily Eagle*, 1937. ▲

Opposition from the Supreme Court

Roosevelt's problems were not over with the 1936 election. In fact, he now faced the most powerful opponent of the New Deal – the American Supreme Court. This court was dominated by Republicans who opposed the New Deal. It could overturn laws if they were believed to contradict the Constitution. In May 1935, a strange case had come before the US Supreme Court. The Schechter Poultry Corporation had been found guilty of breaking NRA regulations because it had sold chicken that was unfit for humans to eat. It had also exploited workers and threatened government inspectors.

The corporation appealed to the Supreme Court. The court ruled that the government had no right to prosecute the company, because the NRA was unconstitutional. It undermined too much of the power of the local states.

Roosevelt was angry that this group of Republicans should deny democracy by throwing out laws that he had been elected to pass. He asked Congress to give him the power to appoint six more Supreme Court judges who were more sympathetic to the New Deal. However, Roosevelt misjudged the mood of the American public. The people felt that the president was attacking the system of government and were alarmed at the steps he was taking. Roosevelt had to back down and his plan was rejected. However, the Supreme Court had been shaken by Roosevelt's actions and was less obstructive in the future. It approved most of Roosevelt's Second New Deal measures from 1937 onwards.

The New Deal 1936 onwards

After the events of 1936, Roosevelt became more cautious. Early in 1937 prosperity seemed to be returning and Roosevelt did what all conservatives had wanted: he cut the New Deal budget. However, the cut in spending caused a new recession. Unemployment increased once more. The 1937 recession damaged Roosevelt's reputation. Middle-class voters lost confidence in him. In 1938, the Republicans did well in the congressional elections. However, Roosevelt was still enormously popular with many ordinary people and he was re-elected with a large majority in 1940. The USA was no longer as united behind his New Deal as it had been in 1933. But by 1940 Roosevelt and most Americans had other things on their minds – the outbreak of war in Europe and Japan's exploits in the Far East.

FOCUS TASK

Why did the New Deal encounter opposition?

The bullet points below show some of the reasons why people opposed the New Deal. Use the text and sources on these pages to find examples of individuals who held each belief. Try to find two more reasons why people opposed the New Deal.
- It won't work.
- It'll harm me.
- It'll harm the USA.

---

1 Look at Sources 37 and 38. One supports Roosevelt's actions and the other one does not. Which is which? How do you know?

Did the New Deal work?

Roosevelt won two peacetime elections and led the USA through the traumas of the Second World War. Many Americans still view him as a hero, and this attitude colours how people look at the New Deal. There is also another 'evidence' problem in assessing the New Deal.

- The programme was kind to photographers, film makers, writers and artists – who were the very people who created many of the sources about the New Deal. For example, Dorothea Lange's photographs (see pages 230–32) revealed the horror of the Depression to those who were not experiencing it first-hand and this in turn influenced people to support the New Deal. There was also a Federal Writers' Project and a Federal Arts Project. As a result, Roosevelt and the New Deal had a lot of supporters in the film and media industries.
- The New Deal agencies themselves produced a lot of 'information films' which emphasised the scale of the problems that Roosevelt inherited and the achievements of the New Deal.

So was the New Deal a success? In trying to answer this question we have to consider what Roosevelt was trying to achieve. We know that by 1940 unemployment was still high and the economy was certainly not booming. On the other hand, economic recovery was not Roosevelt's only aim. In fact it may not have been his main aim. Roosevelt and many of his advisers also wanted to reform society. When assessing whether or not the New Deal was a success, therefore, you will have to decide what its aims were and then whether or not they were achieved.

FOCUS TASK

How successful was the New Deal (Part 1)?

Pages 243–45 summarise the impact of the New Deal on various groups.

1 For each aspect of the New Deal, decide where you would place it on the scale below, indicating success or failure. Explain your score and support it with evidence from these pages.
2 Compare your six 'marks' on the scale with those of someone else in your class. Working together, try to come up with an agreed mark for the whole of the New Deal. You will have to think about the relative importance of different issues. For example, you might give more weight to a low mark in an important area than to a high mark in a less important area.

−5   0   +5

Source 39 A cartoon from the *Portland Press Herald*, showing Harold Ickes in conflict with big business, 1937. ▼

GIVING BUSINESS A NICE REST BETWEEN ROUNDS

Aspect 1: A new society?

- The New Deal restored the faith of the American people in their government.
- The New Deal was a huge social and economic programme. Government help on this scale would never have been possible before Roosevelt's time. It set the tone for future policies for government to help people.
- The New Deal handled billions of dollars of public money, but there were no corruption scandals. For example, the head of the Civil Works Administration, Harold Hopkins, distributed $10 billion in schemes and programmes, but never earned more than his salary of $15,000.
- The secretary of the interior, Harold Ickes, actually tapped the phones of his own employees to ensure there was no corruption. He also employed African Americans, campaigned against anti-Semitism and supported the cause of Native Americans.
- The New Deal divided the USA. Roosevelt and his officials were often accused of being communists and of undermining American values. Ickes and Hopkins were both accused of being anti-business because they supported trade unions.
- The New Deal undermined local government.

Aspect 2: Industrial workers

- The NRA and Second New Deal strengthened the position of labour unions.
- Roosevelt's government generally tried to support unions and make large corporations negotiate with them.
- Some unions combined as the Committee for Industrial Organization (CIO) in 1935 – large enough to bargain with big corporations.
- The Union of Automobile Workers (UAW) was recognised by the two most anti-union corporations: General Motors (after a major sit-in strike in 1936) and Ford (after a ballot in 1941).
- Big business remained immensely powerful in the USA despite being challenged by the government.
- Unions were still treated with suspicion by employers.
- Many strikes were broken up with brutal violence in the 1930s.
- Companies such as Ford, Republic Steel and Chrysler employed their own thugs or controlled local police forces.

Figure 40 A graph showing unemployment and the performance of the US economy during the 1930s.

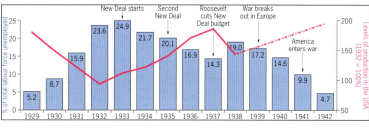

- By the end of the 1930s there were over 7 million union members and unions became powerful after the war.

Aspect 3: Unemployment and the economy

- The New Deal created millions of jobs.
- It stabilised the US banking system.
- It cut the number of business failures.
- Projects such as the TVA brought work and an improved standard of living to deprived parts of the USA.
- New Deal projects provided the USA with valuable resources such as schools, roads and power stations.
- The New Deal never solved the underlying economic problems.
- Confidence remained low – throughout the 1930s, Americans only spent and invested about 75 per cent of what they had before 1929.
- When Roosevelt cut the New Deal budget in 1937, the country went back into recession.
- There were still 6 million unemployed in 1941.
- Only the USA's entry into the Second World War brought an end to unemployment.

Aspect 4: African Americans

- Around 200,000 African Americans gained benefits from the Civilian Conservation Corps, other New Deal agencies and relief programmes.
- Many African Americans benefited from New Deal slum clearance and housing projects.
- Some New Deal agencies discriminated against African Americans.
- There was racial segregation in the CCC. Mortgages were not given to Black families in White neighbourhoods.
- More Black workers were unemployed (35 per cent living on relief in 1935) but they were much less likely to be given jobs, and the ones they did get were often menial.
- Domestic workers (the area in which many Black women were employed) were not included in the Social Security Act.
- Roosevelt failed to put through any civil rights legislation, particularly laws against the lynching of African Americans. He feared that Democrat senators in the southern states would not support him.

Source 41 Poor African American children in Alabama, c1936. ▼

Aspect 5: Women

- The New Deal resulted in some women achieving prominent positions. Eleanor Roosevelt became an important campaigner on social issues.
- Mary Macleod Bethune, an African American woman, headed the National Youth Administration.
- Frances Perkins was the secretary of labour. She removed 59 corrupt officials from the Labor Department and was a key figure in making the Second New Deal work in practice.
- Most of the New Deal programmes were aimed to help male manual workers rather than women (only about 8,000 women were involved in the CCC).
- Local governments tried to avoid paying out social security payments to women by introducing special qualifications and conditions.
- Frances Perkins was viciously attacked in the press as a Jew and a Soviet spy. Even her Cabinet colleagues tended to ignore her at social gatherings.

Aspect 6: Native Americans
- The Indian Reorganization Act 1934 provided money to help Native Americans buy and improve land and control their own tribal areas.
- The Indian Reservation Act 1934 helped Native Americans to preserve and practise their traditions, laws and culture, and develop their land as they chose.
- Native Americans remained a poor and excluded section of society.

FOCUS TASK

How successful was the New Deal (Part 2)?

1 In the previous Focus Task you evaluated the impact of the New Deal in certain areas. Now use that research to think through the issues more comprehensively. Here are some discussion questions to guide you.

Roosevelt's aims	Unemployment and the economy
• What were Roosevelt's aims for the First New Deal? • What new aims did he have in the Second New Deal? • Which of these aims did Roosevelt most succeed in? Which did he most fail in?	• Why did unemployment remain high throughout the 1930s? • Does this mean that Roosevelt's New Deal was not a success?
Opposition	**Criticisms and achievements**
• How did opposition to the New Deal make it hard for the programme to work? • How successfully did Roosevelt deal with such opposition?	• Which criticism of the New Deal do you think is most important? Why? • Which achievement do you think is the most important? Why? • Would Roosevelt have agreed with your choice? Why?

2 Now write your own balanced account of the successes and failures of the New Deal. Reach your own conclusion as to whether it was a success or not. Include:
   a the nature and scale of the problem facing Roosevelt
   b the action he took through the 1930s
   c the impact of the New Deal on Americans
   d the reasons for opposition to the New Deal.
   Make sure you include evidence to back up your judgements.

TOPIC SUMMARY

The 1930s and the New Deal

1 The US economy crashed in October 1929. It was tipped over the edge by the Wall Street Crash, but there had been many weaknesses building up.
2 The Crash led to a long economic depression, with high unemployment, poverty and hardship. American confidence largely disappeared and was replaced by anger at a system that had caused such misery and the politicians who were held responsible.
3 This anger led to a change of president. Roosevelt was elected in 1933, offering the American people a 'New Deal'. Massive state spending followed on welfare, job creation and banking reform.
4 Many Americans supported the New Deal but some criticised it for wasting money, holding back business and eroding freedoms. Despite the critics, Roosevelt was re-elected by a landslide in 1936.
5 The New Deal was never able to solve the economic problems completely. By the end of the 1930s, unemployment was still high.

PRACTICE QUESTIONS

1 Describe one example of the impact of the New Deal on Americans. (2)
2 Describe one example of the policies of the Second New Deal. (2)
3 How popular was the New Deal in the 1930s? (10)
4 'Roosevelt was not just trying to fix the US economy, he was trying to change the USA.' How far do you agree with this view? (18)

5.3

The USA 1941–48:
A land united?

FOCUS

The Second World War began in Europe in 1939, but fighting had started earlier in Asia when Japan invaded China in 1937. At first the USA tried to stay out of the conflict, but in 1941 Japanese forces attacked the US naval base at Pearl Harbor, drawing the USA into the war. In this topic, you will examine:
- how the USA mobilised for war
- the extent of support for the war in the USA
- the impact of war on the American people.

The war economy

When examining the USA's war effort, it is useful to start with some statistics about the country during this period:

- More Americans died in industrial accidents (300,000) on the home front than were killed in fighting the Japanese and the Germans (200,000).
- The war effort cost the USA approximately $400 billion.
- Six months after the attack on Pearl Harbor, US factories were producing more than those of Japan, Germany and Italy combined.
- By the end of the war, the United States alone was producing twice as much as its enemies.

Source 1 New York's Grand Central Station in 1942. The entire east wall was covered by a huge mural promoting war bonds. Ordinary people bought war bonds, which helped to pay for the war effort. ▼

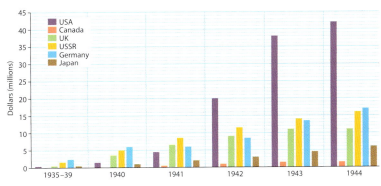

Source 2 A graph showing production of war resources in millions of dollars 1935–44. ▲

The achievements of the US war economy were staggering. In a summit meeting, Soviet leader Stalin proposed a toast: 'To American production, without which this war would have been lost.' The USA shifted from peacetime to wartime production amazingly quickly. Between 1941 and 1945, US factories produced 250,000 aircraft, 90,000 tanks, 350 naval destroyers, 200 submarines and 5,600 merchant ships. By 1944, the USA was almost half of global weapons production. US industry was also providing food, clothing, vehicles, rubber tyres, engines and engine parts, tools and countless other items not only for its own huge forces but also for those of the Allies.

Wartime prosperity

Of all the countries involved in the Second World War, the USA was the only one that emerged from the conflict economically stronger. There is little doubt that war brought a tremendous sense of energy and activity to the USA. Although Americans did not want war, they benefited from it in economic terms:

- More than half a million new businesses started up during the war. Many companies became extremely wealthy as a result of war contracts. For example, Coca-Cola set up production plants around the world to provide the troops with the drink, which became the most popular in the world. Wrigley took on the role of packaging rations for US forces, adding Wrigley's chewing gum to the packs of course.
- The war effort ended unemployment – something that Roosevelt's New Deal had failed to do.
- Even farmers, after almost 20 years of enduring low prices and economic crisis, began to enjoy better times as the USA exported food to its allies.

Mobilising the USA

How were these staggering results achieved? A whole range of factors combined to mobilise Americans so effectively.

Individual action

People recognised the urgency of the situation and responded positively. Morale was high at the start of the war and generally remained good throughout. Americans accepted rationing on items like gasoline and some types of food. Hunting and fishing were banned. Production of baseballs and tennis balls was ended so that factories could produce materials needed for the war effort. Clothing became simpler so it used up less material. Professional baseball was stopped and the players were conscripted into the armed forced. Golf courses were used as military parade grounds. Miss America for 1942, Jo Carroll Dennis of Texas, vowed to remain single for the duration of the war as her contribution to the war effort!

In some respects, the biggest problem was finding things for people to do. They went out on air-raid patrols, although the USA was never bombed. Millions of Americans grew vegetables in 'victory gardens'. When the War Production Board called for people to contribute 4 million tons of scrap metal in two months they responded with 5 million tons in three weeks.

Ordinary Americans invested their income in bonds (see Source 1). They effectively lent money to the government, with a promise that the bonds would be paid back with interest at the end of the war. In all, Americans contributed $129 billion to the war effort by buying bonds. This was a vote of confidence in their government – in marked contrast to the distrust of the post-Crash era just a decade earlier.

ACTIVITY

Study Source 1 carefully. The aim of the mural is to get people to buy war bonds, but as historians can we learn more from this source? In pairs or small groups decide what the mural is trying to say about:
- the strength of the USA
- why the USA is fighting
- US society
- the relationship between the people and the government.

247

Propaganda

In a democracy, it is vitally important for a government to have the support of the population when fighting a war. Dictators like Stalin and Hitler would execute opponents or put them in camps. Roosevelt did not have this option. One important element in Roosevelt's success was persuading people that they were in the right – they were fighting for a just cause, against tyranny and oppression. Propaganda reinforced this message.

Japan handed the government a powerful propaganda weapon when it attacked Pearl Harbor on 7 December 1941. Throughout the war, the US propaganda machine used the treachery of this attack as the basis for a great deal of material convincing the American public to support the war effort. The USA was also at war with Japan's ally, Germany. The racial policies of Nazi Germany gave the USA plenty of propaganda material to work with (see Sources 4 and 5).

The USA also had one propaganda weapon more powerful than any other nation – the entertainment industry, focused on Hollywood. Throughout the war, Hollywood turned out movies that glorified the USA and its troops while presenting the enemy as fiendish and cruel. Even Sherlock Holmes was relocated to Hollywood, with a series of popular films about the great detective being set in the 1940s and about foiling Nazi plots. Americans could also escape the reality of the war for a couple of hours with romantic comedies or musicals. Comic books about heroes such as GI Joe followed the same pattern.

ACTIVITY

Sources 4 and 5 are both examples of propaganda but in many ways they are very different. Make a list of the differences between the aims of the sources and the techniques each one uses.

Source 4 A US propaganda poster from 1942. ▼

Source 5 A US propaganda poster from 1943. ▼

A hands-on government

The extraordinary levels of wartime production in the USA are not only explained by individual spirit and a belief in the cause. The wartime economy was more closely controlled by the government than ever before. Between 1940 and 1945 the federal government spent nearly twice as much as it had spent in the preceding 150 years. Taxes like the Victory Tax (1942) were raised on people's income and their savings. They had to pay taxes on luxury goods such as nylon and alcohol. Nobody liked government control and taxes, but most people understood that such measures were necessary in times of war. There were no complaints that the government was 'doing too much', as there had been in the 1930s (see Source 6).

Willing industrialists

In January 1942, Roosevelt set up the War Production Board under the leadership of the industrialist William Knusden. Knusden believed the country would not be able to produce all the goods it needed without the co-operation of factory bosses. He asked other leading industrialists how they thought they could best meet war production needs rather than setting them targets. He even let them decide which companies would produce particular goods. For example:

- General Motors produced heavy machine guns and thousands of other war products
- the Chrysler Corporation produced anti-aircraft guns
- General Electric increased its production of turbines by 300 times in 1942.

Source 6 US historian Glenn Jeansonne, writing in 1995.

The increase in federal agencies in the New Deal was like a gentle breeze compared to the cyclone of federal expansion during the war. The politicians in Congress who had complained during the New Deal that the President had too much power now gave him more power than ever before. Businessmen who had complained about government interference now went to work for that government. Roosevelt, having complained at the attitudes of these men in the 1930s, now praised their patriotism.

The government clamped a ceiling on price increases, moved workers from marginal to essential industries, rationed scarce resources, and raised taxes to the highest levels in history. It created a synthetic rubber industry, established a national speed limit, eliminated the production of new cars and home appliances, and operated transportation as an integrated system. The federal government, which had grown 60 per cent under the New Deal, grew 300 per cent during the war.

FACTFILE

US government measures in the Second World War

Once war began, the government took over most aspects of life and work. In the course of 1942, a wide range of measures was introduced and government organisations were set up that remained in place for the rest of the war.

- Roosevelt got Congress to agree to higher taxes. Taxation remained a contentious issue throughout the war. However, by 1944 almost all working Americans were paying federal taxes compared with just 10 per cent in 1940.
- The War Production Board was created to manage war industries.
- The Office of Price Administration controlled prices and tried to stamp out illegal trading on the black market.
- Rationing was introduced on food and fuel. Clothing, cars and some other items were not rationed, but these were usually very expensive because they were not subject to price controls.
- The Office of Censorship published a code of guidelines for newspapers, magazines, broadcasters and film studios. There were no officials to enforce these guidelines; the organisation relied on co-operation from the media.

Source 7 An official US government photograph showing B-26 bombers being assembled in the Martin aircraft factory in Baltimore, 1941. It was used in a newsreel programme about aircraft production in wartime. ▲

Around 80 per cent of American contracts went to only 100 firms, although the work ended up with thousands of smaller companies, subcontracted to supply tools, materials and equipment. The large firms wanted to help the war effort, but they also saw that they could make a lot of money out of it.

One of the most significant industrialists at the time was Henry J. Kaiser. He had played an important part in the Tennessee Valley Authority during the New Deal programme (see page 237). During the war, Kaiser developed the USA's metal and shipbuilding industries. He designed and built the 'Liberty' ships, turning out one of these large cargo ships every 42 days by 1943.

1 Study Source 7. Why did the US government make a film about aircraft production in wartime?
2 Can you see any connections between Source 7 and Source 1?
3 The Studebaker company was not selling the vehicles shown in Source 8 to the public, so why do you think they published this poster?
4 Sources 7 and 8 are placed between the sections 'Willing industrialists' and 'Willing workers'. Do you think they belong more in one or other section, or are they in the right place? Explain your answer.

Willing workers

Around 16 million American men and women served in the US armed forces. This meant that many more workers were needed to fill their jobs at home. Fourteen million people worked in the factories. General Motors alone took on an extra 750,000 workers during the war. Most manufacturing jobs were in the industrial north or on the Pacific coast. Around 4 million workers migrated from the rural south to these areas, including significant numbers of African Americans. Nearly 750,000 African Americans found work in the war industries. Many more served in the armed forces (see page 254). California saw an influx of 1.5 million new workers.

US labour unions agreed not to strike and to accept increased federal control for the duration of the war. They agreed to the controls on wages that Roosevelt imposed – for the most part. Union membership rose from 9 million in 1941 to 15 million in 1945. In return the unions demanded improved conditions and managed to get allowances for women workers to help with child care. There were some strikes, such as the mine workers in 1943, but this was settled quickly when the government agreed to the miners' demands.

Nearly a million women were hired by the federal government. Many African American women moved out of domestic and agricultural work to take higher-paying jobs in war industries

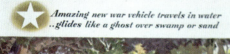

Source 8 A poster produced by the Studebaker company, 1944. Before the war Studebaker manufactured cars and trucks. ▲

All available women

Before the war, there were already 12 million working women. During the war, 300,000 women joined the armed forces and another 7 million joined the workforce. Women's air service pilots (WASPs) flew every type of US warplane in tests and delivery runs from the factories to the airfields where they were stationed. One in three aircraft workers was a woman. Women were often given difficult welding jobs in awkward parts of aircraft bodies because they were smaller and more agile than men.

Source 9 A wartime poster featuring Rosie the Riveter. ▲

5   What was the purpose of Source 9 and how does it try to achieve its aims?

6   How similar are Sources 9 and 10?

7   Is it possible to say whether one of Sources 9 and 10 is more useful to historians? Explain your answer.

Source 10 An official US government photograph of women riveting in an aircraft factory. ▼

In the munitions and electronics industries, one in two workers was a woman. Most fuses were made by women, because they generally had nimbler fingers. In a government survey, 60 per cent of US plant managers said that the women were their best workers. The media created a poster campaign featuring Rosie the Riveter (see Source 9). Hollywood even made a movie about Rosie.

However, it was not all positive for women. The vast majority of women in the military only served in the USA and were confined to clerical tasks, nursing or other traditionally female roles. Records show that many senior commanders were concerned that women would be a distraction to the troops.

Women workers were not always welcomed by their male colleagues or by trade unionists, who felt that they were a threat to jobs and to pay levels – women earned up to 60 per cent less than men for the same work. Congress resisted Roosevelt's plans to ensure equal pay for men and women in the armed forces. Factories made little or no effort to provide child-care facilities. Even when they did, the services were unreliable and most women had to ask friends and family to help out.

Women who did not work or serve in the military also played their part. They planted 'victory gardens', entertained soldiers at USO canteens, volunteered as nurses' aides, collected scrap, sewed and gave blood. Importantly, they also kept up morale on the home front.

After the war, many women simply left their wartime jobs so the men returning from combat could take them up again. However, many women did not give up paid work completely. They may not have been riveters any more, but they found work as secretaries, clerks and shop assistants. One result of wartime employment was a big shift in work patterns over the next 20 years.

All these changes put a strain on traditional family life. Working women had to juggle the demands of work and family. Many found that the money and confidence that they gained while working gave them a new outlook on life. The separation from husbands fighting overseas also took its toll. One-sixth of war wives and one-third of married male soldiers had affairs and there was a record number of divorces. There was also a rise in teenage crime and minor offences such as vandalism. Police reports show concerns about the emergence of youth gangs and teenage sex.

FOCUS TASK

Why was the USA able to produce so much in the Second World War?

Why was the USA able to achieve such great levels of war production in the Second World War? Draw a sports podium with an extra level for 'runners up who also helped'. Decide which position on the podium should go to:

● the government
● industrialists
● workers
● ordinary civilians (individual action)
● women
● the producers of propaganda.

Think carefully about your decision and write notes about the contribution of each. You may decide that you want to redraw the podium with fewer steps or more steps.

The US war effort: a different side to the story?

So far this story has been mostly about Americans rallying round to help with the war effort. That is how the government wanted it to be and how most of the media reported it. This positive version has entered into popular memory in the same way that the Depression entered popular memory in a powerfully negative way. But is this positive story *too* positive? Since the war, some historians have taken a different view.

The war according to Howard Zinn

Howard Zinn served in the US air force during the war and became very critical of the way in which the media, in his view, failed to tell the truth about what was taking place. After the war he became a university professor and an anti-war campaigner. In 1980, he wrote *A People's History of the United States*. This was a very different history from the traditional, pro-US popular textbooks of the time and it became a bestseller, in part because it was extremely controversial and many commentators disagreed strongly with Zinn's opinions. In the chapter on the Second World War, Zinn questioned whether it really was the popular war that people seemed to remember it as (see Source 11).

1. Many historians believe that Zinn's alternative view of the Second World War was extremely important. Study the extracts in Source 11 and select four examples mentioned by Zinn that do not fit the traditional story of the war.

2. According to Zinn, why did some Americans not fully support the war effort?

3. One common criticism of Zinn was that although his research was accurate he tended to assume that people thought like he did. Is there any evidence to support this in the source?

4. Zinn has also been accused of exaggerating the scale of opposition to the war. What evidence is there to support this view?

Source 11 Extracts from *A People's History of the United States* by Howard Zinn, published in 1980.

A Zinn on American labour

Despite the overwhelming atmosphere of patriotism and total dedication to winning the war, despite the no-strike pledges of the AFL and CIO, many of the nation's workers, frustrated by the freezing of wages while business profits rocketed skyward, went on strike. During the war, there were fourteen thousand strikes, involving 6,770,000 workers, more than in any comparable period in American history. In 1944 alone, a million workers were on strike, in the mines, in the steel mills, in the auto and transportation equipment industries. When the war ended, the strikes continued in record numbers—3 million on strike in the first half of 1946.

B Zinn on Americans joining the military

Beneath the noise of enthusiastic patriotism, there were many people who thought war was wrong, even in the circumstances of fascist aggression. Out of 10 million drafted for the armed forces during World War II, only 43,000 refused to fight. But this was three times the proportion of C.O.s (conscientious objectors) in World War I. Of these 43,000, about 6,000 went to prison, which was, proportionately, four times the number of C.O.s who went to prison during World War I. Of every six men in federal prison, one was there as a C.O. Many more than 43,000 refusers did not show up for the draft at all. The government lists about 350,000 cases of draft evasion, including technical violations as well as actual desertion, so it is hard to tell the true number, but it may be that the number of men who either did not show up or claimed C.O. status was in the hundreds of thousands—not a small number. And this was in the face of an American community almost unanimously for the war.

C Zinn on opposition to US involvement in the war

Only one organized socialist group opposed the war unequivocally. This was the Socialist Workers Party. The Espionage Act of 1917, still on the books, applied to wartime statements. But in 1940, with the United States not yet at war, Congress passed the Smith Act. This took Espionage Act prohibitions against talk or writing that would lead to refusal of duty in the armed forces and applied them to peacetime. The Smith Act also made it a crime to advocate the overthrow of the government by force and violence, or to join any group that advocated this, or to publish anything with such ideas. In Minneapolis in 1943, eighteen members of the Socialist Workers Party were convicted for belonging to a party whose ideas, expressed in its Declaration of Principles, and in the Communist Manifesto, were said to violate the Smith Act. They were sentenced to prison terms, and the Supreme Court refused to review their case.

Source 12 A Massachusetts local newspaper from 1943. The story was printed in the newspaper but this copy of the article was found in the newspaper clippings collection of the Office of Price Administration (OPA), which enforced price controls. ▶

CHRONICLE

ST 13, 1943 *August*   Price 7 Cents

Price Control Panel Wants Two Women to Investigate Local Retail Ceiling Prices

Board Member Says Work is not Snooping if Properly Done -- Many Say it is, and Refuse the Job

price investigation have refused. Most of them felt that it was "snooping" and some would apparently have taken on the work if they could have been paid for it. It is required, however, that the service be voluntary, the only paid em-

Source 13 The opening section of a radio broadcast from December 1943.

And now we are going to bring you a broadcast arranged in collaboration with the OPA. There has been a lot of trade lately against the OPA's fight against black markets. This fight is the most dramatic in the whole programme to enforce price control in order to keep your cost of living from getting out of hand. ... This morning we are going to tell you how that enforcement works, why it is important that it does work and what you as individuals can do to make it work.

ACTIVITY

1. Sources 12 and 13 are very useful to historians. Explain what they reveal about:
   a how prices were controlled
   b how people felt about price controls
   c how the government tried to enforce price controls.
2. Howard Zinn's work was based on searching the archives for material that supported his views. He did not use these two documents. If he had, what do you think he might have said?

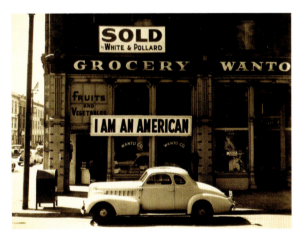

Source 14 A photograph taken by Dorothea Lange of a store belonging to a Nisei who was forced to close it down after being interned. ▲

5. You came across Dorothea Lange on pages 230–32. From what you know about her, why do you think she took the photograph in Source 14?
6. Write a more detailed caption for Source 14 to be used in a museum of the history of the home front in the USA.

Internment of Japanese Americans

The USA had a large Japanese immigrant population, particularly on the Pacific coast. The attack on Pearl Harbor created a wave of anti-Japanese feeling across much of the country, and official propaganda encouraged this attitude. Around 120,000 Japanese Americans from California, Washington State, Arizona and Oregon were interned in 1942. It was a brutal programme:

- They were transported to bleak internment camps in remote areas of the USA. Many of them lost their property, or were forced to sell it at very low prices.
- No account was taken of whether the people were Issei (born in Japan) or Nisei (children of immigrants, born in the USA).
- In other US states, Japanese people were subjected to vandalism, abuse and even murder.

Hindsight suggests that this policy owed more to racism than to security. The USA was also at war with Germany and Italy, but no German or Italian Americans suffered the same treatment. Chinese Americans were sometimes mistaken for Japanese and attacked.

The interned Japanese Americans amazed the guards in the camps with their dignity and patriotism, including raising the American flag each morning. In January 1943, Congress allowed Japanese Americans to serve in the armed forces and 33,000 immediately volunteered, including thousands from the internment camps. The all-Nisei infantry units in the US army were among the most highly decorated for bravery in the war.

Not all Americans supported the internment policy. Many lawyers argued that it went against the Constitution. As early as 1944, a Supreme Court judge called the policy 'government racism'.

African Americans

For African Americans the war effort was full of contradictions. While the war brought some advantages, many of these came at a price.

In the workplace

Over 400,000 African Americans migrated from the south to the USA's industrial centres in the north. On average, they doubled their wages to about $1,000 per year. However, they faced prejudice and discrimination, and African workers generally earned half what White workers earned.

Campaigners for the rights of African Americans, led by Philip Randolph, threatened to organise a march of 50,000 people to Washington to demand an end to discrimination at work. In June 1941, Roosevelt signed Executive Order 8802 (see Source 15), which ordered employers who were supplying goods for the war effort to end discrimination. But it would take more than executive orders to change attitudes. In 1942, at the Packard electronics company, 3,000 White workers walked out when three African American workers had their jobs upgraded as a result of the order. Members of management walked out too.

During the war, poor workers (both Africans and Whites) created racial tension. There were race riots in 47 cities during the war, the worst of which was in Detroit during June and July 1943 (see Factfile).

The war highlighted racial tensions, but it also sowed the seeds for the successes of the civil rights movement in the 1950s and 1960s (see Topic 6.2), changing attitudes among African Americans in several ways. First of all, the war was a war against the racist ideas of Nazi Germany. It made little sense to then make no challenge to racism at home. And this made more White Americans open to the arguments of civil rights campaigners. Activists also built up new membership and campaigning experience during the war, calling for better treatment of troops.

> **Source 15** An extract from Executive Order 8802.
>
> *It is the policy of the United States to encourage full participation in the national defence programme by all citizens of the United States, regardless of race, creed, colour or national origin, in the firm belief that the democratic way of life within the Nation can be defended successfully only with the help and support of all groups within its borders.*
>
> *Therefore, by virtue of the authority vested in me by the Constitution and the statutes, and as a prerequisite to the successful conduct of our national defence production effort, I do hereby reaffirm the policy of the United States that there shall be no discrimination in the employment of workers in defence industries or government because of race, creed, colour or national origin, and I do hereby declare that it is the duty of employers and of labour organisations, in furtherance of said policy and of this Order, to provide for the full and equitable participation of all workers in defence industries, without discrimination because of race, creed, colour or national origin.*

In the armed forces

US forces were fighting against Nazi Germany, a state that was openly racist. African Americans rallied to the cause. Over 1 million of them joined the armed forces. However, their wartime experience highlighted the extent of racism and discrimination in the USA itself. Black soldiers usually served in African American-only units with White officers. It was not until 1944 that the US marines allowed African American soldiers into combat. Up to that point, they had only been used for transporting supplies, or as cooks and labourers (they were often referred to as 'mules'). Many African women served in the armed forces as nurses, but they were only allowed to tend African soldiers. In one incident in the American south, a rail company restaurant refused to serve African American soldiers who were guarding German prisoners of war on a train, yet they were prepared to serve the White German prisoners.

FACTFILE

The Detroit Race Riots 1943
- Throughout the war, urban populations increased as migrant workers settled there to work in war industries.
- Hundreds of thousands of migrants, White and African American, arrived in the Detroit area to work in these industries.
- There was competition for the best jobs, housing and services such as schools and health care. This led to increased tensions between the existing populations and the migrants, as well as between different migrant groups.
- The exact trigger is not known but on 20 June 1943 riots broke out, with African American youths throwing stones and debris at the police. The riots continued for two days. By that point 6,000 troops had been moved into the area.
- Later investigations suggested that the causes of the riots were discrimination in housing and jobs and also police brutality. It was also discovered that large numbers of White youths travelled to Detroit once the riots began and effectively engaged in battles with African Americans or just attacked the Black neighbourhoods.
- Police and troops killed 34 people, 25 of them African Americans. Property worth around $2 million was destroyed. The worst damage was in Paradise Valley, the poorest area of Detroit.

Source 16 A US propaganda poster from 1943. ▼

By 1944, African American soldiers were fighting in combat units and there were hundreds of Black officers in the army and marines. These units distinguished themselves in Europe at the Battle of the Bulge (1944) and in the Pacific in the Battle of Iwo Jima (1945). There were also fighter squadrons of African American pilots, such as the 332nd Fighter Group commanded by Captain Benjamin Davis. By 1945, there were many integrated units in the army. US Supreme Commander General Eisenhower strongly supported integrated combat units.

Discrimination was worst in the navy. By the end of the war, only 58 African American sailors had risen to officer rank. It was exclusively African American sailors who were assigned to the dangerous job of loading ammunition on to ships bound for the war zones. In July 1944, an accident killed 323 people, most of them Black sailors (see Source 21 on page 256).

The government ordered the navy to end all racial discrimination by February 1946 but this was more hopeful than realistic. In 1948, President Harry Truman (Roosevelt had died in 1945) passed Executive Order 9981 (see Source 17). This was another step forward, but still only a small one. In 1949, Truman had to sack the secretary of the army because he refused to follow the terms of the executive order. In 1963, the secretary of defence, Robert McNamara, passed Order 5120.36, which banned segregation in living accommodation in the military.

ACTIVITY

Not all Americans were positive about their wartime experience. If people are angry, they sometimes comment on posters such as Source 16 by adding graffiti. Think carefully about the information above, then suggest what graffiti a disgruntled Black or White American worker might add.

Source 17 An extract from Executive Order 9981.

It is hereby declared to be the policy of the President that there shall be equality of treatment and opportunity for all persons in the armed services without regard to race, colour, religion or national origin. This policy shall be put into effect as rapidly as possible, having due regard to the time required to effectuate any necessary changes without impairing efficiency or morale.

Source 18 World heavyweight boxing champion Joe Louis, an African American who served during the war.

There may be a lot wrong in America, but there is nothing Hitler can fix.

Source 20 The 'Draftee's Prayer', published in an African American newspaper in 1943.

Dear Lord, today I go to war:
To fight, to die, Tell me what for?
Dear Lord, I'll fight, I do not fear,
Germans or Japs;
My fears are here.

Source 23 A letter from Crew Chief Patterson Field to the US army weekly magazine *Yank*, 1943. Zoot suits were fashionable suits of the 1940s, first worn by Mexican Americans.

Dear Yank

My plane was in Los Angeles at the height of the so called zoot suit riots. I saw several of them and was ashamed of the servicemen I saw. It must be understood, and no amount of baloney can hide it, that the zoot suit riots were really race riots, directed mainly against the Mexican, and to some extent the Negro citizens of Los Angeles. It's about time a certain element in the armed forces be told that a man can be a good American citizen regardless of the color of his skin, and has all the rights of a good citizen. To those servicemen who took part in the riots I'd like to ask a question: What the hell uniform do you think you're wearing, American or Nazi?

Source 19 An extract from a speech by the NAACP leader Walter White, 1943.

A professor at a US college which was only attended by African Americans told me about when he asked students why they did not want to join the army in 1943. One student told him: 'The army jim-crows us. The navy lets us serve only as messmen. The Red Cross refuses our blood. Employers and labour unions shut us out. Lynchings continue. We are disenfranchised, jim-crowed, spat upon. What more could Hitler do than that?'

Source 21 The wreckage that resulted along the Port Chicago waterfront after two ammunition ships blew up in the harbour. Almost 300 Black men died in the blast as they loaded ammunition on to the ships; no Whites had been ordered to help with the loading.

Source 22 A sign erected to prevent Black people moving into a government housing project, Detroit, 1942.

Source investigation

Study Sources 18–23 then answer the following questions.

1 What does Source 18 suggest about African American attitudes to the war?
2 What evidence is there that this attitude is either typical or exceptional?
3 Why do you think that the incident in Source 21 was so effective in stirring up public opinion?
4 Look at Sources 19–21. Which of these three sources do you think most accurately sums up the experience of Black people in wartime USA? Explain your answer.
5 Sources 18–23 show positive and negative aspects of the experience of Black Americans during the war. Write a paragraph explaining whether you think the balance of positive and negative aspects is too far one way or the other, or is about right. You will need to mention some of these points:
   a how far the positive sources are reliable (backed up by other sources or information) and typical (representative of people's experiences)
   b how far the negative sources are reliable and typical
   c whether there should be more on either aspect.

FOCUS TASK

Was the wartime USA united or divided?

Look back at Source 1 on page 246. This mural is promoting war bonds, but it also presents an interpretation of the USA at war. Is that a complete picture?

1 Look carefully at the mural. Make a list of all the ways in which it shows the USA united behind the war effort.
2 Now use the rest of your work from this topic to write a second paragraph or list of bullet points, adding features of the wartime USA that do not appear on the mural.
3 All governments control information and put their own 'spin' on events, especially during wartime. Do you think the government could have made this mural more representative, yet still achieved its objective of uniting people behind the war effort? Discuss your view with others in your class.

PRACTICE QUESTIONS

1 Describe one example of the extended government control in the Second World War. (2)
2 Describe one example of new opportunities for women in the war. (2)
3 Explain why several Executive Orders were passed relating to race in the period 1946–48. (10)
4 'Overall the people of the USA supported the government in the war effort.' How far do you agree with this view? (18)

TOPIC SUMMARY

The 1940s: a land united?

1 The USA joined the Second World War in December 1941. War finally ended the economic depression as US industries mobilised for war production.
2 The great majority of Americans supported the war effort and made individual efforts to support the war, particularly by buying war bonds, which were effectively loans to the government.
3 The US government began to take control of the economy in a way that went far beyond even the New Deal. Taxes rose and rationing and censorship were brought in. The achievements of US war production were staggering and the USA out-produced its enemies many times over.
4 Not all Americans benefited. Americans of Japanese origin were interned. Discrimination and prejudice against African Americans and other minorities did not disappear. Even presidential orders banning discrimination were unable to stop it.
5 Despite this, African Americans made a massive contribution to the war effort and partly as a result of this they gained support from others in US society to try to right many of their wrongs after the war.

KEY TERMS

Make sure you understand these key terms and can use them confidently in your writing.
- bootlegger
- *laissez-faire*
- lynching
- poverty line
- segregation
- speakeasies
- suffrage

ASSESSMENT FOCUS

How the non-British depth study on the USA 1919–41 will be assessed

This section is worth 40 marks – 20 per cent of your total GCSE. The questions could be on any part of the content, so you need to know it all.

Three questions will assess:
- AO1: knowledge and understanding (total 15 marks across all questions)
- AO2: explanation and analysis (15 marks across all questions).

One question will assess:
- AO3: analyse, evaluate and use sources (10 marks in one question).

Above all, the paper is trying to assess your ability to think and work like a historian. Before you read this guidance you might want to look back at the introduction on how historians think on page 4. There, we set out some steps that historians take:
1 focus
2 ask questions
3 select
4 organise
5 fine tune

The exam questions have already chosen a focus (stage 1) and they have asked questions (stage 2). What the examiner wants from you is stages 3, 4 and 5.

Question 1

Question 1 will usually ask for a short description of an event or feature from one section of the course. It is a simple knowledge question, usually requiring some accurate description. For example:

> *Describe one example of extra government powers during the Second World War. (2 marks)*

Advice

Select: Choose one action and either describe it in a couple of sentences or describe why the government took the action. You do not need every detail.

Organise: The main thing to remember here is not to write too much.

Fine tune: Make sure that your spellings and dates are correct. Make sure that your answer is clear – in the pressure of an exam it is easy to accidentally say something you do not mean to say.

Example answer

One example of extra government powers was wage control.

Question 2

Question 2 will demand more analysis and explanation than Question 1. It might ask you to judge the importance or impact of a factor, or how successful an organisation was. For example:

> *Explain why some industries in the USA prospered in the 1920s. (10 marks)*

To develop your answer, you could argue that one factor was more important than another or argue they were equally important – or perhaps that they were connected.

A useful way to improve your answers is to assess them yourself. Examiners use mark schemes but you do not really need anything that complicated. Think of it like an Olympic medal ceremony. Read some of your practice answers to this question and ask yourself which of these medals your answer deserves.

Aim of the question
This is designed to start the exam with a relatively simple, knowledge-based question. The examiner wants to see that you can select and describe important events accurately, without simply writing down everything you know.

This answer is correct and would get one mark. However …

Examiners are not looking for a lot, but they do want more than this. This answer is naming an action rather than describing it.

To improve this answer, the candidate could add:

When war broke out, the US government did not want strikes or other disputes to get in the way of war production so it took control of wages, making them fair but also making unions agree not to strike.

Aim of the question
'Explain why' means you are looking for reasons why something happened. There will usually be at least two reasons or factors you might write about for a question like this, and examiners want to see you explain them rather than just describe successful industries.

The Question 2 medal ceremony

 Bronze (up to 25% of marks): You list some successful industries in the 1920s (e.g. rayon, electricity) but do not go any further.

 Silver (up to 60% of marks): You describe the success of some of these industries in greater detail, e.g. '300 million pairs of rayon stockings sold in 1930 compared with 12,000 silk stockings in 1900' (which is good), but you do not explain why they prospered (which is a shame).

 Gold (up to 100% of marks): You go beyond description to explain *why* they prospered – what factors helped them (e.g. Republican policies, growing urban population) and *why* those factors helped them. Just naming a factor is not enough; you have to explain the link between the factor and the outcome.

Even a Gold answer can be improved by ensuring you have:
- a clear conclusion that rounds off your argument and makes it really clear what you think the answer to the question is
- a balanced answer that shows you understand that there might be more than one view about the question, or explains how the different elements are connected
- supporting evidence – using relevant knowledge and a good range of examples to support each point you make.

Advice
Select: Focus on factors rather than industries.

Organise: The important thing is to use your knowledge in a relevant way. In this question, a good way to organise your answer might be: 'Industry prospered in the USA for a number of reasons. To begin with ... This helped some industries because ...'

Fine tune: Make sure that your spellings and dates are correct. Make sure that your answer is clear – in the pressure of an exam it is easy to accidentally say something you do not mean to say. Above all make sure you have really explained how the various factors helped industries prosper and not just described what happened.

Example answer

In the 1920s, industry prospered in the USA for a number of reasons. One major success was the motor industry. It prospered because of the introduction of the production line for motor cars, particularly in the Ford motor company. This made them quicker and cheaper to build so more people could buy them. Ford also made good use of the new techniques of advertising and hire purchase to sell cars.

There were other reasons as well. New industries like electricity were emerging and there was a demand for consumer goods.

This is a good answer – a Gold! It would probably get 7 marks.

It has a clear opening and it then really does explain why the motor industry prospered.

It then goes on to list other factors – raw materials and demand. This is good in the sense that the candidate is focusing on reasons. Unfortunately these factors are simply named and not explained.

To improve this answer the candidate could:

- *simply focus on consumer demand – explain how the US population was becoming better off and more urbanised and wanted appliances like fridges, washing machines, etc.*
- *explain how demand for consumer goods was linked to electricity – many of the goods were powered by electricity.*

There is nothing wrong with the factors chosen, and the examiner does not want you to cover all of them. But it would have been just as acceptable to have explained government policies or the impact of the First World War or the economic confidence of the time.

Question 3

Question 3 requires an evaluation of sources. The question will always be worth 10 marks and it will always contain two sources. However, it can appear in two formats:

Format A: separate questions

This format asks a separate question on each source (worth 5 marks each). For example:
- Why was the source published?
- How is this source useful to historians?
- What is the viewpoint of the artist/author?
- How reliable is this source?

Format B: comparison question

This format asks you to compare two sources (10 marks). For example:
- How similar are Sources A and B?
- How far do the sources agree?
- Why do they disagree?
- Is one source more reliable than the other?
- Is one source more useful than the other?

Aim of the question
These questions ask you to show your understanding of two sources from the period you are studying by producing a clear answer and supporting that answer from the sources. Some examples of questions are shown below, but we cannot cover all types. You will find it helpful to look at the Assessment Focus for the other depth studies as well (pages 190 and 330), which give examples of the different types of questions and advice how to tackle them.

The Question 3 source evaluation guide

Here are some rules to help you evaluate sources.

Sources are not textbooks. Do not treat them like they are.

Textbook authors use many sources and then generalise to give the overall picture. Textbooks tell you what happened. Sources tell you how individuals or groups *felt* about what happened. If a source says something different from your textbook, this does not mean it is wrong. It might be attypical and something the textbook author did not have space to cover.

Do not criticise a source because of what it does not say.

You could make this point about almost any source – a source on the USA in this period does not tell you about Germany in the 1800s. Neither does this morning's newspaper. It is not a helpful approach.

Back up your points with examples from the source.

It is amazing how often candidates fail to do this. They may write something like 'Source B is hostile to immigrants', but then fail to say what they found in Source B that led them to this conclusion.

In comparison questions, compare content first ...

... Then go on to compare purpose, attitude, context, etc.

Use comprehension to work out *what the source says* and then use inference to see *what it can tell you.*

Comprehension means understanding what the source actually says – such as an advertisement trying to sell vacuum cleaners or a newspaper article criticising immigrants. An inference builds on your comprehension – it is something not stated in the source but which can be worked out from it. For example, you might be able to look at an advertisement from the 1920s and decide that it is aimed at women. This is an inference, because the poster does not state this openly. Similarly, you might be able to infer that the writer of an article wants controls in immigration, even though they might not actually say that. Using inferences can also stop you making mistakes about bias (see right).

Use your evaluation to answer the question – not for its own sake.

Candidates often use useful tools like the five Ws (Who? Why? When? Where? What?). However, it is also common for candidates to forget to use those findings to answer the question! If you are going to use the five Ws or a similar technique, make sure the information it gives you helps support your answer, otherwise it is irrelevant.

Never dismiss a source because it is biased or unreliable. All sources are useful about something and reliable about something.

The *story in the source* might be biased or unreliable (e.g. an election poster). However, that means *the story of the source* is very useful – somebody went to the trouble of exaggerating, lying or distorting the facts in order to achieve a particular aim. We can use the source to learn about the people who created it, their aims and their attitude towards the people they are lying about. Sources will almost always reveal something about values, attitudes, fears, concerns, beliefs and reactions.

Only use contextual knowledge when it helps you answer the question.

If you have some relevant contextual knowledge that supports your answer, use it. If you just want to show the examiner you know stuff, don't!

Commenting on tone or language is not evaluation.

A comment on the tone or language of a source can be used to support a point you make about purpose, attitude or some other aspect of evaluation, but in itself is not evaluation.

Example 3A: separate question format

One common question type is a 'message' question. For example:

Study Source A. What is the cartoonist's message? (5 marks)

Source A A cartoon from 1935. The figure in the boat is Roosevelt and the figure in the water in Uncle Sam (representing the USA).

The Question 3 medal ceremony (message question)

- **Bronze (up to 25% of marks):** You comment on details in the source (e.g. the sea represents the economic depression).

- **Silver (up to 60% of marks):** You explain one or more of the sub-messages (e.g. the Supreme Court is making Roosevelt throw Uncle Sam back in the water) rather than the main message.

- **Gold (up to 100% of marks):** You make an inference to explain the message of the cartoon (e.g. Roosevelt is unhappy because he is being forced to abandon some of his New Deal policies, shown by putting Uncle Sam back in the water) and support your answer with extracts or details from the source(s).

A Gold medal answer can be improved by ensuring you have:
- explained the attitude of the cartoonist, not just the message of the cartoon
- offered more than one type of evaluation: e.g. evaluation of the purpose or attitude of source, or what the context or provenance reveals about it.

Advice

Select: Source questions are slightly different from other types of questions. However, most examiners will tell you that many candidates need to be more selective when tackling this type of question. If you have some relevant contextual knowledge that supports your answer, use it. If you just want to show the examiner you know stuff, don't!

Organise: By far the most important thing is to work out what you want to say before you start writing. A good way to organise answers to message questions is:

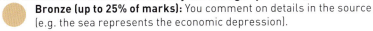

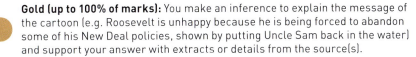

The cartoonist is praising / criticising ... because ...

We can tell this from the cartoon because ...

The cartoonist was making this point at this time because ...

Fine tune: Do all the usual checking, but here it is worth making sure you have answered the question using content and then evaluation.

Example answer

The message of the cartoonist is that **Roosevelt is unhappy** about being forced to throw Uncle Sam back into the water. In 1935, the Supreme Court ruled that many of President Roosevelt's actions in the New Deal were unconstitutional and he was not allowed to do them. Roosevelt was trying to help the US economy recover, and the cartoonist is clearly frustrated that he has been stopped. We can see this because Roosevelt obviously does not want to throw Uncle Sam back into the water. He says the Supreme Court is making him do it.

Example 3B: separate question format

Another common question type concerns the reliability of a source. For example:

> **Source B** An extract from a radio broadcast by Father Charles Coughlin, 1936.
>
> *The great betrayer and liar, Franklin D. Roosevelt, who promised to drive the corrupt out of America, has succeeded only in driving the farmers from their homesteads and the citizens from their homes in the cities. I ask you to remove the man who claims to be a Democrat, from the Democratic Party, and by this I mean Franklin Double–Crossing Roosevelt.*

● **Study Source B. How reliable is this source as evidence about the New Deal? (5 marks)**

Aim of the question

This question is asking you to show your understanding of two sources from the period you are studying by producing a clear answer and supporting that answer from the sources.

The Question 3 medal ceremony (reliability question)

Bronze (up to 25% of marks): You comment on the provenance (the author is a Republican, it was written at the time) or context (at this time X was happening) but do not tackle the question.

Silver (up to 60% of marks): You answer the question (e.g. why you think it is reliable or unreliable) and support your answer by evaluating extracts or details from the source(s).

Gold (up to 100% of marks): You answer the question in a balanced way and use context, provenance, purpose, attitude and other inferences (things that are not stated in the source but which can be worked out) to support the answer.

A Gold medal answer can be improved by ensuring you have:
● a valid conclusion
● offered more than one type of evaluation.

Advice

Select: Source questions are slightly different from other types of questions. However, most examiners will tell you that many candidates need to be more selective when tackling this type of question. If you have some relevant contextual knowledge that supports your answer, use it. If you just want to show the examiner you know stuff, don't!

Organise: By far the most important thing is to work out what you want to say before you start writing.

Fine tune: Do all the usual checking, but here it is worth making sure you have answered the question using content and then evaluation.

Example answer

This is a good answer – probably worth 4 marks.

There is a strong inference about the purpose of the source (shown in bold) and the candidate uses this intention to argue the source is not reliable about the New Deal.

This argument is then well supported with analysis of the language used in the source and the candidate's own knowledge of Father Coughlin.

The answer could be improved by pointing out that in some ways this is a reliable source – it is reliable as evidence about the opposition to the New Deal and how the opponents opposed it.

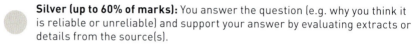
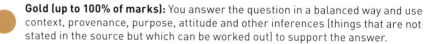

This source is not really reliable as evidence about the New Deal. It is obviously **trying to discredit Roosevelt.** Father Coughlin was a popular broadcaster with a very large audience estimated at 30 million. He basically felt that Roosevelt was not doing enough to help the poor or to control banks and big business. We can see how strongly Coughlin feels where he calls Roosevelt a liar and betrayer. This is clearly a very biased source.

Example 3C: comparison format
Another common question style compares the usefulness of sources.

> **Source A** An advertisement for stockings in the 1920s. Although the caption says silk they were actually rayon. ▶
>
> **Source B** The US feminist campaigner Doris E. Fleischman, writing in 1932.
>
> *It is wholly confusing to read the advertisements in the magazines that feature the enticing qualities of vacuum cleaners, mechanical refrigerators and … other devices which should lighten the chores of women in the home. On the whole these large middle classes do their own housework. … Women who live on farms … do a great deal of work besides the labour of caring for their children, washing the clothes, caring for the home and cooking … labour in the fields … help milk the cows. … The other largest group of American women comprises the families of the labourers … the vast army of unskilled, semi-skilled and skilled workers. The wages of these men are on the whole so small [that] wives must do double duty – that is, caring for the children and the home and toil on the outside as wage earners.*

The aim of the question
The focus of the question is on usefulness. Remember – every source is useful. You might find it helpful to keep thinking 'How is it useful?' rather than 'How useful is it?'

The best way to show that something is useful is to *use* it! So this question is testing whether you can make use of the sources – whether you understand the content and whether you can make inferences (things that are not stated in the source but which can be worked out) and support them.

● ***Study Sources A and B. Which is more useful about women in the 1920s? (10 marks)***

The Question 3 medal ceremony (usefulness)

Bronze (up to 25% of marks): You comment on the provenance or type of source (one is a poster, the other is an article) *or* argue they are not useful because of what they do not tell you. Neither of these approaches really answers the question.

Silver (up to 60% of marks): You answer the question and support your answer with extracts or details from the sources.

Gold (up to 100% of marks): You answer the question and use context, provenance, purpose, attitude or other *inferences* to support the answer.

A Gold medal answer can be improved by ensuring you have:
- a valid conclusion
- more than one type of evaluation.

Advice
Select: Candidates often criticise sources as not useful because they do not say what the candidate already knows. This is not a helpful approach so in some ways the best advice we can give is to *not* select knowledge from your wardrobe! Instead you are using your knowledge and understanding of the period to make use of the source. Similarly, stay away from comments about bias unless you can show how the bias makes it useful.

Organise: The most important thing is to work out what you want to say before you start writing. A good structure for this question is:

> Both of these sources are very useful to the historian even though they are about different things.
>
> For example, Source A is useful because from it we can see … We can tell this because …
>
> Source B is also useful because from it we can tell … We can tell this because …
>
> Overall …

Fine tune: Do all the usual checking, but here it is worth making sure you have answered the question using content and then evaluation.

This is a Gold medal answer – 9 out of 10!

It picks out information from each source and explains how the information is useful.

It then steps up a level and makes inferences from each source – two inferences from Source A. The inferences are shown in bold.

As if this is not enough the answer then supports the inference made with evidence for the sources to support the inference.

The only way you could improve it would be with a conclusion, perhaps like this:

On balance, I think Source B is more useful than Source A for two reasons. Firstly, it probably refers to the majority of American women and it also stops us from being misled by Source A into thinking that life in the Roaring Twenties was fun for all women.

Aim of the question
Examiners want to see a balanced answer. You can still state your view strongly and clearly but make sure you have fully considered the alternative view.

Example answer

Both these sources are very useful to the historian, even though they are about different things.

For example, Source A is useful because it tells us that companies were using advertisements to sell products like stockings. **Source A is also useful because we can infer from it that women are an important market for advertisers.** This poster is clearly aimed at women. For one thing it is an advertisement for stockings. But it is also trying to suggest that the stockings they sell are glamorous and luxurious like the woman in the poster, so women would want to be like her. **So the source is also useful because we when we look closely it reveals some of the techniques which advertisers were using at this time.** Advertising became a major industry in this period.

Source B is also useful because it tells us that not all women had vacuum cleaners and other modern gadgets and that women had to look after families and work as well. **This is useful because we can then infer that life was still very hard for American women and not all women had benefited from the Roaring Twenties.** We can tell this because she says the magazine adverts are misleading - not all women have vacuum cleaners and other modern gadgets, and women have to look after their families and work as well.

Question 4

Question 4 is a traditional essay-style question. For example:

'The people of the USA fully supported the government in the Second World War.' How far do you agree? (18 marks)

The Question 4 medal ceremony

 Bronze (up to 25% of marks): You describe events during the war (e.g. government actions) without addressing the question.

 Silver (up to 60% of marks): You argue yes or no and support your argument by describing example(s) of support or opposition.

 Gold (up to 100% of marks): You write a balanced answer which explains that there is evidence to support both a 'yes' and a 'no' argument. The answer may support one side or the other but must acknowledge that there is an alternative view even if you think it is wrong.

Even a Gold answer can be improved by ensuring you have:
- a clear conclusion that rounds off your argument and makes it really clear what you think the answer to the question is
- a balanced answer that shows you understand that there might be more than one view about the question or explains how the different elements are connected
- used relevant knowledge and a good range of examples to provide supporting evidence for each point you make.

Advice
Select: Focus on whether particular actions show support or opposition. A common error is to describe actions and forget to explain whether they are examples of support or opposition. It may seem obvious to you, but examiners cannot read your mind. They will not credit something unless you spell it out in your answer.

Organise: Take one factor and explain it in a paragraph of its own. Then move to the next paragraph.

Fine tune: Make sure that your spellings and dates are correct. Make sure that your answer is clear – in the pressure of an exam it is easy to accidentally say something you do not mean to say. In this question, examiners like you to say which side of the argument you support.

Example answer

I mostly agree with the statement although it might be going too far to say all the people of the USA fully supported the war.

The majority of Americans supported the war effort in the Second World War. To begin with, the majority of them supported going to war against Japan in particular after the attack on Pearl Harbor. This outraged Americans anyway and US propaganda made effective use of the attack. Germany declared war on the USA soon afterwards and US propaganda found it easy to convince Americans that Nazism was an evil which needed to be fought. Americans also gained a great deal from the war. More than half a million new businesses started up. The war ended unemployment which had been a massive problem in the 1930s. It brought opportunities for all workers, including women and African Americans as well.

On the other hand, not all Americans supported the war. There was very high taxation which was unpopular and some opposed America getting involved in the war in Europe. For many African Americans the war led to little or no improvement in racial discrimination. Units in the army and navy were segregated along racial lines. We also know that in war industries there were many strikes even though the unions made an agreement with the government not to go on strike.

Overall I agree with the statement. Far more Americans supported the war than opposed it. Perhaps the most striking example is the Japanese Americans. Despite their poor treatment by the government many Japanese Americans went on to serve with distinction in the armed forces, indicating how strong support was among the population as a whole.

This is an excellent answer – definitely a Gold – and would probably get 18 marks.

It has a clear opening and it then sticks to the line that the opening suggests it will follow.

There is a good analysis of two factors.

It is worth noting that this answer does not cover every aspect of the home front in the USA. It does not need to! The level of detail shown here is enough for a top mark.

Good conclusions are rare, and this one is particularly good.

KEYS TO SUCCESS

As long as you know the content and have learned how to think, this exam should not be too scary. The keys to success are:

1 Read the question carefully. This may sound obvious, but there is a skill to it. Sometimes students answer the question they *wish* had been asked rather than the one that has *actually* been asked. So identify the skill focus (what they are asking you to do). Do they want you to write a description, an explanation or a comparison? Identify the content focus (what it is about) and select from your knowledge accordingly.

2 Note the marks available. That helps you work out how much time to spend on answering each question. Time is precious – if you spend too long on low-mark questions you will run out of time for the high-mark ones.

3 Plan your answer before you start writing. For essays this is particularly important. The golden rule is: know what you are going to say; then say it clearly and logically.

4 Aim for quality not quantity: in the time limits of an exam you will not be able to write down everything you know and can think of – even if it is relevant. The marker would much rather read a short answer that really tackles the question than page after page of material that is not relevant.

5 Check your work. You will never have time in an exam to rewrite an answer but try to leave some time at the end to check for obvious spelling mistakes, missing words or other writing errors that might cost you marks.

The USA 1945–75 Introduction: 'It's the economy, stupid'

Have you ever heard this phrase? It was a key element of the election campaign for US president Bill Clinton in 1991. The point he was making was that of all the issues in politics, the most important is the economy. If the economy is strong, the politicians in power are popular and they can achieve things. If the economy is weak, the same politicians usually face disapproval and possibly even protest. So, before we investigate the USA in the years 1945–75 in more detail, this section gives an overview of the ups and downs of the US economy in that period and how this affected the priorities and decisions of its political leaders.

FACTFILE

The US economy after the Second World War

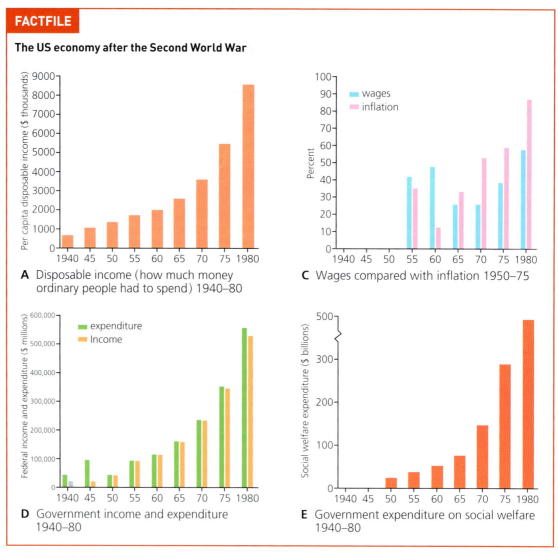

A Disposable income (how much money ordinary people had to spend) 1940–80

C Wages compared with inflation 1950–75

D Government income and expenditure 1940–80

E Government expenditure on social welfare 1940–80

1 Study the data in the Factfile carefully. What would you say are the three main patterns that can be seen in the economy and spending?

The USA was the world's richest country …

The USA emerged from the Swecond World War with a strong economy. Despite some unsteady years, it largely remained strong. The nation's wealth grew each year – sometimes very quickly. From 1945 to 1980 the USA was the richest country in the world.

Source 1 A photograph of the Czekalinski family from Cleveland, Ohio. The photo was taken in 1951 for an article in the DuPont company's employee magazine, *Better Living*. DuPont was a huge US chemicals company. The article was about the advantages of the US economy. The family of four is pictured alongside groceries a typical American family would consume over the entire year. ▲

2   Look at Source 1. Why was this photograph published by the company in its magazine?

... but how should it spend all that money?

The president was judged by whether he (they have all been men) kept the economy growing. He had to keep US business happy. On the other hand, such wealth gave the president enough money to do almost anything he wanted – whether that was a prestige project such as putting a man on the moon before the USSR did, a massive military project such as fighting a war in faraway Vietnam or a social project such as improving health care for children from poor families in the USA's inner cities.

... and who should decide?

In election campaigns, each president made bold promises about how he would use the government's income. After his election, the new president often faced a long tussle with Congress over whether or not these promises could be implemented – and frequently Congress won.

... and what if you didn't quite fit in?

Source 1 is a celebration of US prosperity, comfort and success. Americans like the Czekalinskis worked hard, obeyed the law and paid their taxes. They were typical of the vast majority of Americans in this period. They conformed to the main values of US society and they respected their church leaders, politicians and bosses at work. And of course they were middle class and White.

Now consider what life would be like if you were not like the Czekalinskis. What if you did not share all their beliefs? What if you were not prepared to do what the boss said? What if you thought that CAPITALISM was not a perfect system? What if you felt that wrongs should be righted? What if you were not middle class? What if you were not White? In the rest of this chapter, you will investigate the stories of some of these people.

6.1 The Red Scare: Post-war challenges in the USA 1945–54

FOCUS

The USA emerged from the Second World War as the most powerful nation on Earth. Despite this, in the years after the war Americans were gripped by fear and suspicion of communism, a period that became known as the 'Red Scare'. In this topic, you will examine:
- why there was a Red Scare
- how the Red Scare affected US society.

Why was there a Red Scare in the USA in the 1950s?

American fear of communism went back a long way: the USA was democratic, capitalist and largely Christian. In contrast, communists believed in a single-party state, centralised control of all industry, and atheism. With such different beliefs anti-communism was a fact of life in the USA. What is surprising is how strong the anti-communist feeling proved to be in the late 1940s and early 1950s. The reason for this was a complex interaction between the international situation and the internal political situation in the USA.

The international situation

You studied the tension and conflicts between the USA and USSR in the Cold War in Chapter 2. In summary, the USA emerged from victory in the Second World War only to face a new and formidable rival – the communist Soviet Union (USSR). President Truman took a tough stance against the USSR but many Americans still saw communism as a threat. This feeling increased in the later 1940s and early 1950s as a result of several developments.

- **The Soviet bomb:** In 1949, the USSR developed the atomic bomb. This was a massive shock to US politicians and the American public.
- **Communist China:** In the same year, China was taken over by communists led by Mao Zedong. A new communist nation of 500 million people had emerged. It was another shock, as the USA had backed Mao's opponents and given them massive aid in the form of weapons and equipment.
- **Southeast Asia:** Communism was also advancing in Malaya, Indonesia, Burma and the Philippines, encouraged by communist China.
- **The Korean War:** In 1950, communist North Korea invaded South Korea. The USA won United Nations support for a successful counter-attack, until China sent support to North Korea. Soon the USA was bogged down in the Korean War, which lasted until 1953.

The internal political situation in the USA

During the Second World War, the USA was united in a way that it had never been before. However, after the war some of the social and political divisions from the 1930s resurfaced. Racial tensions began to rise again. There were many strikes and disputes between unions and employers. Old and bitter political rivalries that had been put aside during the war re-emerged between the main political parties, and sometimes between members of the same party. In this tense atmosphere some rival politicians or groups genuinely wondered whether their opponents might be communists. Others saw communism as an effective (and easy) way to discredit an opponent.

1 Study Sources 1–5. Do you think the 11 communists got a fair trial? Explain your answer.

Source 1 A photograph of the 11 leaders of the US Communist Party imprisoned in 1949. ▲

Source 2 An extract from a US newsreel reporting the trial of the 11 leaders of the Communist Party of the United States in 1949. Note that they were not actually accused of plotting to overthrow the government.

Eleven of America's top communists are found guilty of conspiracy to overthrow the government. … This ends an investigation that has extended over ten years. The leading prosecution lawyer is now widely tipped to become a federal judge and possibly rise higher still. On the other hand the defence lawyers have been arrested and given jail sentences and fines for contempt of court for their behaviour in the trial. It cost the government almost $1million to achieve this result. It was a price paid gladly by a free people, to guarantee freedom of speech to all, and a fair trial provided by the government, even for those accused of plotting to destroy it.

The Red Scare

The rest of US society followed the example of the politicians. Government agencies, and even businesses and educational institutions, feared communist infiltrators at home – they saw 'Reds under the bed', as one saying of the time went. In one high-profile case, 11 leading members of the Communist Party of the United States were accused of violating the Smith Act in 1949. This act had been passed in 1940 and made it illegal not only to plan or attempt to overthrow the US government, but also to simply call for it. All 11 were found guilty. Ten of them were sentenced to five years in prison and a $10,000 fine, the other was given three years because he had served in the army in the Second World War. Source 2 shows how the case was reported.

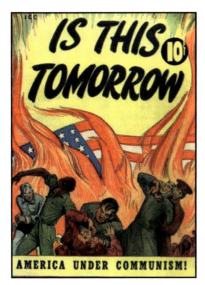

◄ **Source 3** The front cover of a comic book published in 1947 by the Catechetical Guild Educational Society. This organisation was formed in 1942 by a Catholic priest, Father Louis Gales. Comic books were immensely popular at the time and this publication used the same style as superhero comics to tell a story of what life in the USA would be like under atheist communism.

Source 4 Still images from a US film called *Make Mine Freedom*, broadcast in 1948. The film was one of a series funded (around $6 million) by the Sloan Foundation, a foundation set up by the chairman of the General Motors Corporation. The foundation commissioned the religious Harding College in Arkansas to make a series of nine short cartoon films that would 'portray simple economic truths about the US system of production and distribution in an interesting and entertaining manner'. ▶

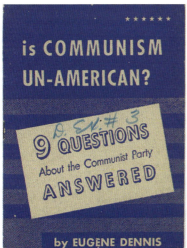

Source 5 The front cover of a book published in the USA in 1949. Eugene Dennis was one of the 11 communist leaders tried and jailed in 1949 (see Source 1). ▲

ACTIVITY

1   Choose one of these starter sentences and then write a paragraph explaining your choice.
    a   These sources are useful because they provide evidence that Americans were under threat from communism at this time. I think this because …
    b   These sources are useful because they provide evidence that many Americans felt they were under threat from communism at this time. I think this because …
    c   These sources are useful because they show that Americans who did not conform to capitalist ideals were treated harshly. I think this because …
    d   These sources are all biased so they are not useful. I think this because …

The effects of the Red Scare on the US government

The Red Scare was not confined to newspapers and newsreels. The government was fully involved in the process of hunting down communists in the USA.

The Federal Bureau of Investigation

The director of the Federal Bureau of Investigation (FBI), J. Edgar Hoover, was strongly anti-communist. He had been a driving force behind the first Red Scare, after the Russian Revolution. In 1947, Hoover set up the Federal Employee Loyalty Program. This allowed Hoover's FBI loyalty boards to investigate government employees to see if they were current or former members of the Communist Party. From 1947 to 1950, around 3 million people were investigated. Nobody was charged with spying, but 212 staff were identified as 'security risks' (that is, communist sympathisers) and were forced out of their jobs.

Source 6 FBI Director J. Edgar Hoover. ▲

The House Un-American Activities Committee

The US Congress is divided into two houses – the House of Representatives (usually referred to as 'the House') and the Senate. In the 1930s, Congress established the House Un-American Activities Committee (HUAC), a committee made up of members of the House of Representatives. HUAC had the right to investigate anyone who was suspected of doing anything un-American, which really meant anything communist. This was particularly true when Martin Dies was chairman. Dies and several other members of the HUAC were violently anti-communist and had even been members of the Ku Klux Klan.

At first, the committee did not get a lot of public attention. However, in 1947 it became big news when a new chairman, J. Parnell Thomas, was appointed. Parnell was even more radically anti-communist than Dies. The FBI had files on many Americans, which were passed to the HUAC. In particular the FBI suspected that that a number of prominent Hollywood writers, producers and directors were members of the Communist Party. The HUAC called these people in for questioning. It is important to remember that it was not illegal to be a communist in a free, democratic country such as the USA. So when the Hollywood Ten, as they became known, appeared before the committee they refused to answer any questions. Every time they were asked: 'Are you now or have you ever been a member of the Communist Party?', they referred to the First Amendment of the US Constitution, which guarantees all Americans freedom to believe what they want. They said that the HUAC did not even have the right to ask the question. They were each jailed for a year for contempt of court because they refused to answer questions. Hollywood studios 'blacklisted' the ten, and most of them never worked in the US film industry again. The case of the Hollywood Ten made the HUAC a household name.

Source 7 Hollywood star Robert Taylor with J. Parnell Thomas, chairman of the HUAC. ▲

Source 8 Robert Taylor giving testimony in front of HUAC, October 1947. 'Fellow travellers' was a common term for communists.

Chairman of the Committee: You would refuse to act in a picture in which a person whom you considered to be a communist was also cast; is that correct?

Robert Taylor: I most assuredly would and I would not even have to know that he was a communist. This may sound biased; however, if I were even suspicious of a person being a communist with whom I was scheduled to work, I am afraid it would have to be him or me, because life is a little too short to be around people who annoy me as much as these fellow travellers and communists do.

The Rosenbergs

The USSR developed an atomic bomb in 1949. Although the USA was aware that the Soviets were working on a nuclear weapon, this was much sooner than anyone expected. The US government strongly suspected that spies had passed information to the USSR. In 1950, a German-born British physicist, Klaus Fuchs, was convicted of passing US and British atomic secrets to the USSR. The investigation into Fuchs also led to suspicions against Julius Rosenberg and his wife Ethel. At their trial in March 1951 they denied all the charges against them. Despite this, they were found guilty and executed in June 1953. The evidence that convicted the Rosenbergs appeared to be flimsy. However, historians today believe that the Rosenbergs were guilty. They now know of coded telegrams between the Rosenbergs and Soviet agents that began in 1944. The telegrams were eventually published in 1995.

The Hiss case

In 1948, Whittaker Chambers faced the HUAC. He admitted to being a communist in the 1930s and said that Alger Hiss, a high-ranking member of the US State Department, had been a member of his group. Hiss accused Chambers of lying and Truman dismissed the

Source 9 Alger Hiss, speaking before the HUAC, 1948. ▲

case. However, a young politician called Richard Nixon (a member of the HUAC) decided to pursue the case. He found convincing evidence that Hiss did know Chambers, and debatable evidence that Hiss had passed information to the USSR during the war. Hiss was never tried for spying, but he was convicted of perjury in 1950 and spent nearly five years in prison. It is still not known whether or not Hiss was really guilty of passing secrets.

The McCarran Act

The Hiss and Rosenberg cases encouraged Congress to pass the Internal Security Act of 1950 (also known as the McCarran Act, after Senator Pat McCarran). President Truman opposed it because he claimed it would make a mockery of the USA's Bill of Rights. However, Congress voted 80 per cent in favour of the act. The main measures it encompassed were as follows:

- All communist organisations had to be registered with the US government and their members finger-printed.
- No communist could carry a US passport or work in the defence industries.
- The act even allowed for the setting up of detention camps in emergency situations.

ACTIVITY

Write a sentence for each of the following, explaining its role in the Red Scare:
- Federal Employee Loyalty Program
- McCarran Act
- The HUAC
- J. Edgar Hoover
- Hiss case
- Richard Nixon
- The Rosenbergs.

4 Study Source 9. Does this source reveal more about Hiss or about the HUAC? Explain your answer.

Source 10 The stage and Hollywood film star Lee J. Cobb, speaking in the late 1950s about his experiences. He was originally blacklisted but eventually agreed to do a deal with the HUAC.

When the facilities of the government of the United States are drawn on an individual it can be terrifying. The blacklist is just the opening gambit – being deprived of work. Your passport is confiscated. That's minor. But not being able to move without being tailed is something else. After a certain point it grows to implied as well as articulated threats, and people succumb. My wife did, and she was institutionalised. In 1953 the HUAC did a deal with me. I was pretty much worn down. I had no money. I couldn't borrow. I had the expenses of taking care of the children. Why am I subjecting my loved ones to this? If it's worth dying for, I am just as idealistic as the next fellow. But I decided it wasn't worth dying for, and if this gesture was the way of getting out of the penitentiary I'd do it. I had to be employable again.

1 What do Sources 7 and 8 tell you about Robert Taylor?
2 Are they useful evidence of anything else?
3 Describe the differences between Taylor and Lee J. Cobb (Source 10).

The reaction of the American people

How did the American people react to this Red Scare? Most evidence suggests that they lapped it up! Some were hysterically anti-communist themselves and welcomed every exposé as another victory for US values. Even those who were not strongly anti-communist got caught up in the drama of it all, especially when so many famous names from Hollywood were called before the committee.

Interrogations were filmed and photographed. Simply appearing before the HUAC could ruin a career. 'Suspects' were asked to 'name names' – tell the committee about other communists. If they refused, they were suspected of being a communist. If they did, then those they named were in turn investigated.

Some politicians, journalists and cartoonists were disgusted by the spectacle and were brave enough to say what they thought. However, politicians on all sides could also see how much publicity the hearings were generating and they realised that being seen as tough on communism would win them votes at election time. Into this troubled atmosphere stepped a ruthless and ambitious young Republican senator called Joseph McCarthy.

Source 12 A cartoon by Herbert Block (known as Herblock), 1947. It was published in the *Washington Post*. The title of the cartoon was: 'It's okay – We're hunting communists.' The men in the car represent HUAC members. ▶

ACTIVITY

Study Sources 11–15. They are all comments on the Red Scare. Which is the odd one out? You will need to examine each source and consider:

- what it is saying about the HUAC or communism
- its attitude towards HUAC or communism (e.g. support, criticism, ridicule)
- what you can tell about the author/artist of each source and how you reached this judgement.

Remember that many cartoons try to make a point by seeming to make the opposite point but in a mocking way. See how many of you got the answer right when your teacher tells you!

Source 13 Hollywood movie stars posing for a photograph before delivering a letter of protest to Congress about the activities of the HUAC, October 1947. The line-up includes Lauren Bacall, Humphrey Bogart and Danny Kaye. These would be regarded as A-list celebrities today. ▲

Source 14 A US cartoon from the early 1950s. ▲

Source 15 Another Herblock cartoon published in the *Washington Post* in 1949. The title of the cartoon was 'You read books, eh?' The investigators represent HUAC. (Note: Americans usually call the square root symbol a radical.) ▲

Source 16 A photograph of Senator Joseph McCarthy giving a press conference. ▲

The rise and fall of McCarthyism

In 1950, McCarthy was in search of a headline – and he found it! He claimed that he had a list of over 200 communists in the State Department. He had not found these communists himself; the names came from the official report from the FBI's loyalty board investigations. This claim that there were communists working for the government sent shockwaves around the country.

After his initial claims of 200 (made in a speech), McCarthy revised the number downwards to approximately 80. When he finally submitted a written report to the Senate, the number dropped to 57. In fact, 35 of these had been cleared and the other 22 were still being investigated. McCarthy confessed that he was amazed by the amount of publicity his announcement generated, but he was determined to use his new-found prominence in the upcoming elections. The Democrat senator Millard Tydings declared that there was little real evidence against the government workers. In response, McCarthy accused Tydings himself of being 'un-American'. McCarthy had a lot of support from fellow Republicans and in the 1952 Senate elections they reaped the benefits. Tydings lost his seat to a McCarthy supporter.

As a member of the Senate, McCarthy could not be on the HUAC, but after the election President Eisenhower appointed him as head of a separate White House committee to investigate communist activities in the government. The HUAC continued to operate as it had done, while McCarthy's committee did the same. Throughout 1952 and 1953, McCarthy extended his own investigations and turned his committee into a weapon to increase his own power and terrify others. His methods mainly involved false accusations and bullying. He targeted high-profile figures and accused anyone who criticised him of being a communist.

The 'witch hunts'

McCarthy claimed that General George Marshall (the much-admired US army general who had launched the Marshall Plan to give aid to Europe after the Second World War – see page 61) was at the centre of a conspiracy against the USA. President Eisenhower was close friends with Marshall, but surprisingly did very little to protect him when McCarthy made these accusations. Thousands of others also found their lives and careers ruined by this 'witch hunt'. False accusations led them to be blacklisted, which meant that they could not work. Over 100 university lecturers were fired, as universities came under pressure from McCarthy. The HUAC blacklisted 324 Hollywood personalities. Studio bosses such as Walt Disney, Jack Warner and Louis Mayer supported the HUAC and refused to employ anyone who was suspected of having communist sympathies. They also increased the anti-communist hysteria by producing science-fiction films such as *Invasion of the Body Snatchers* and *The War of the Worlds*, which showed the threat of alien invaders, clearly representing the communist threat to the USA.

The return of Captain America

Captain America was a comic-book superhero who had been created in 1941 as a character fighting the Nazis. At the end of the war, Marvel comics killed him off. However, in 1953, they brought him back to life to help vanquish this new enemy. He was given the title 'Captain America, Commie Smasher'. The story ran that he had not actually died, but had in fact been frozen in ice. What do you think this teaches us about the Red Scare? It may seem silly, but comics and cartoons are a good source of evidence about the public mood at a particular time – they were as popular at the time as computer games are today.

Source 17 A poster for *The War of the Worlds*, one of the most successful films in 1953. It painted a picture of a world where the USA and all it stood for was under attack from Martian invaders. ▼

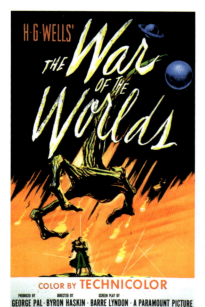

Source 18 Captain America in action, 1944. ▲

Did anyone oppose McCarthy?

Many senators spoke up against McCarthy, including the Republican Senator fmor Vermont, Ralph Flanders. Quality newspapers such as the *Washington Post, New York Times* and *Milwaukee Journal* produced sensible and balanced reporting that damaged McCarthy's credibility. Herbert Block continued to attack McCarthy (and those who failed to oppose him) with cartoons in the *Washington Post* (see Sources 19 and 20).

Some big names from Hollywood protested at the treatment of actors, writers and producers. Many movies made sly references to the paranoia within the movie industry and society as a whole, and the tendency people had to enjoy gossip and shocking stories. A good example was the 1951 movie *People Will Talk*.

In 1952, one of the USA's leading playwrights, Arthur Miller, wrote *The Crucible*. This was about real witch hunts in the early days of the United States, but his audiences knew that he was using his play as a way of condemning the methods used by McCarthy in the anti-communist witch hunts.

Source 19 A Herblock cartoon from 1951. President Roosevelt had talked of 'freedom from fear' as one of the Four American freedoms. Chiang and Franco were brutal dictators who ruled Taiwan and Spain. ▼

FOCUS TASK

Why did people support McCarthyism?

Support for McCarthy depended on four things:

Which of these do you think was the strongest leg of McCarthy's stool? Copy the diagram and add notes to it to show how this contributed to support for McCarthy. Include examples and evidence from these pages.

"Say, What Ever Happened To 'Freedom-From-Fear'?"

Source 20 Another Herblock cartoon, from 1974. McCarthy is on the left and Eisenhower is on the right. The president is pulling a feather instead of a sword from the scabbard. The title was 'Have a care', which was an old-fashioned threat used when gentlemen fought a duel. ▼

Source 21 Professor Owen Lattimore at the HUAC hearings, 1952.

The technique apparently used by Senator McCarthy against me is apparently typical. He first announced at a press conference that he had discovered the top Russian agent in the United States. At first he withheld my name, but later, after the drama of his announcement was intensified by delay, he then whispered my name to a group of newspaper reporters with full knowledge that my name would be bandied about by rumour and gossip and eventually published. I say to you that this was unworthy of a Senator or an American.

Source 22 An extract from Ed Murrow's *See It Now* broadcast attacking McCarthy, March 1954.

We must not confuse dissent with disloyalty. We must remember always that accusation is not proof and that conviction depends upon evidence and due process of law. We will not walk in fear, one of another. We will not be driven by fear into an age of unreason, if we dig deep in our history and our doctrine, and remember that we are not descended from fearful men.

Owen Lattimore

Another significant opponent of McCarthy's was also one of his victims – the university professor Owen Lattimore. Lattimore was an expert on China and East Asia, and had been the top adviser to President Truman when China fell to the communists in 1949. Lattimore was brought before the HUAC and questioned for 12 days. Although he fought back strongly, McCarthy's ally Senator Pat McCarran accused Lattimore of PERJURY (lying under oath). The FBI carried out five investigations on Lattimore until a federal judge finally threw out all the charges against him in June 1955.

Ed Murrow

McCarthy's most influential opponent was the TV journalist Ed Murrow. On 20 October 1953, Murrow broadcast a programme that criticised the methods used by the US air force to investigate one of its servicemen. On 9 March 1954, Murrow broadcast an entire episode of his show *See It Now* attacking McCarthy and showing damning footage of the senator and his methods. Murrow's broadcast is generally seen as one of the most influential and damaging attacks on McCarthy, and an important factor in his decline.

The decline of McCarthyism

Despite these opponents, it was four years before McCarthy's power and influence finally waned. The turning point was when he began to attack the army, claiming there were communist sympathisers in the high command. His accusations seemed increasingly ridiculous. In televised hearings, McCarthy was steadily humiliated by the lawyer representing the army, Joseph Welch. At one point, McCarthy reminded Welch that he had an employee in his law firm who had belonged to an organisation accused of communist sympathies. The court burst into applause for Welch when he replied 'Have you no sense of decency, sir? At long last, have you left no sense of decency?'

Eventually McCarthy lost all credibility, and he was even CENSURED by Congress for his actions. Anti-communist feeling in the USA remained, but the methods used by McCarthy were discredited. Some people said McCarthyism was doing as much damage to the USA as the supposed communist spies could ever do. Eisenhower, who had supported and promoted McCarthy, now made the joke that McCarthy*ism* has become McCarthy*was*m! McCarthy himself had become an alcoholic and he died of liver disease three years later.

The end of the Red Scare

With McCarthy's decline the intensity of the Red Scare began to wane. Anti-communist feeling remained strong but Americans were no longer convinced there were Reds under every bed. The HUAC continued to operate but it gradually lost status and importance as only the most extreme anti-communists were investigated by it. By the later 1950s and early 1960s, it was no longer taken seriously by presidents or other leading figures. In fact several of them openly challenged it. In 1959, the former president Harry Truman called the HUAC the most un-American thing in America. In the 1960s, academics and students at universities such as Berkeley criticised the past record of the HUAC in print – something that would never have happened ten years earlier.

ACTIVITY

Imagine the publishers of this book have received a letter complaining about Source 23 because it is one-sided. The letter-writer wants the source removed from the book. Discuss what you would do if you were the publisher and then write an email or letter explaining your decision.

The legacy of McCarthyism

McCarthyism had a huge impact on the USA and its history. In 1994, the US government published National Standards for history for high-school students. The document mentioned McCarthy 20 times and stressed the need to study McCarthyism as an example of how fundamental American values were violated. Few US politicians or historians have been prepared to defend McCarthy in any way. Most agreed with the views of Bill Myers (Source 23). However, in 2004 the US historian Ted Morgan published a book called *Reds*. He argued that the USA had faced a real threat from Soviet spies in the late 1940s and early 1950s, but that McCarthy's actions made it more difficult to catch these spies because he was so incompetent. Even this view was controversial, because writing anything that appears to support McCarthy opens up deep wounds even today.

Source 23 An extract from the commentary of a 1984 US TV documentary called *A Walk Through the Twentieth Century* with Bill Myers. Myers was a respected broadcaster and journalist.

Looking for an issue that would get him re-elected, he seized on the fears of millions, and launched the squalid campaign that became known as McCarthyism. Its tactic: reckless and undocumented accusation against government employees. Intimidation bred audacity and audacity fed upon itself. McCarthy soon had the celebrity he sought. The stage was his alone to command.

1 Read Source 23. It is fairly clear that Bill Myers was not an admirer of McCarthy. How do the tone and language of the source demonstrate this?

FOCUS TASK

Why did McCarthyism decline?

1 Go back to the stool diagram that you drew in the Focus Task on page 275.
In small groups, discuss the following questions:
  a Which of the legs do you think were the first to give way?
  b Why did these legs give way?
  c Which legs did not give way?
  d Why did those legs stay strong?
2 Now use the discussion to write your own paragraph(s) explaining the reasons for the decline of McCarthyism.

PRACTICE QUESTIONS

1 Describe one example of the actions of the HUAC. (2)
2 Explain why Senator McCarthy rose to prominence in the 1950s. (10)
3 'In the years 1945–53 the USA was a deeply divided nation.' How far do you agree with this view? (18)

TOPIC SUMMARY

The Red Scare

1 In the 1940s and 1950s, many Americans felt deeply worried about the spread of communism around the world, and this fuelled suspicion of Americans with left-wing ideas. They were felt to be un-American.
2 The government was worried too, and under the influence of FBI head J. Edgar Hoover it set up a loyalty programme to root out government employees who had communist sympathies.
3 The House of Representatives already had a House Un-American Activities Committee (HUAC) with the power to question anyone it suspected of being a communist sympathiser. This committee became much more significant than ever before.
4 Although they did not have the power to put people on trial, the committee hearings became trial by media because they questioned high-profile people and generated lots of publicity. Just to be called up to the Committee could ruin someone's career.
5 Senator Joseph McCarthy seized on this anti-communist feeling to advance his own career by making public but unsubstantiated accusations that there were communists in powerful positions in government and even in the army.
6 The Red Scare declined from the mid-1950s, largely because McCarthy's extremism had discredited the whole process.

6.2 Righting wrongs: African Americans and the struggle for civil rights in the USA 1945–75

FOCUS

You have seen that the USA was a troubled society despite its wealth and power. Perhaps the greatest problem of all was the position held by African Americans in society. Although they fared worse in the southern United States, they faced discrimination everywhere. From the early 1950s, however, African Americans mounted increasingly effective campaigns both locally and nationally to challenge discrimination and to ensure their civil rights. In this topic you will examine:
- the status of African Americans in the years after the Second World War
- the emergence of the civil rights movement
- the methods used by the civil rights movement
- the impact of the movement
- reactions to the movement.

The origins of the post-war civil rights movement

African Americans had lived in the USA for hundreds of years. For much of that time they had been slaves to White Americans, although there were also many free African Americans. African Americans like Harriet Tubman and Frederick Douglass had campaigned against slavery, particularly in the late eighteenth and nineteenth centuries. But even when slavery was abolished at the end of the Civil War in 1865, they had nothing like true equality with Whites. In the twentieth century, organisations such as the National Association for the Advancement of Colored People (NAACP) had supported African Americans and called for changes to the law. However, after the Second World War the African American campaign for equality and civil rights moved up a level, becoming larger, better organised and more assertive.

African Americans in US society: the 'Jim Crow' laws

The government tried to enforce fairer treatment and equality in defence industries and in the armed forces during the Second World War, but the situation did not really improve elsewhere. In the 1940s, discrimination and prejudice were still rife, particularly in the South (see Factfile).

Source 1 A US propaganda poster from 1943. ▲

Some of the discrimination was in the form of actual laws, but much of it was in the unfair enforcement of laws:
- **Segregation:** Seventeen states fully enforced the 'Jim Crow' laws, which segregated everyday facilities such as parks, buses and schools. In theory these facilities were separate but equal. In reality, services for African Americans were usually poor on non-existent.
- **Voting rights:** African Americans had officially been given the right to vote early in the century, but various practices were used to prevent them from voting – most commonly the threat of violence. In Mississippi, for example, African American people who tried to register to vote faced intimidation or even lynching. Only 5 per cent of the African American population in Mississippi was registered to vote.

1 Explain the message of Source 1.
2 Search the internet for other US posters from the Second World War. Use the search terms 'USA posters World War II'. What proportion of these are like Source 1?
3 Write your own definition of Jim Crow for a historical dictionary.

- **Law enforcement:** Police not only failed to stop attacks on African American people, they also frequently took part in them. White juries almost always acquitted Whites accused of killing African Americans.
- **Employment and pay:** African Americans faced official and legal discrimination at work. For example, in the south White teachers earned 30 per cent more than African American teachers.
- **Education**: In the southern states, schools were racially segregated. The best universities were closed to African Americans. In 1958, an African American teacher called Clemson King was committed to a mental asylum for applying to the University of Mississippi.

There was also the ever-present threat of violence. The Ku Klux Klan, a vicious WHITE SUPREMACY movement, was powerful in many of the Southern states. Even some police and other officials were members. The Klan intimidated, beat, tortured and killed African Americans. Usually those targeted were accused of some crime, but the real point was to intimidate African Americans.

FACTFILE

A map showing the main Jim Crow states in the USA around 1950. These states saw the worst discrimination, but African Americans faced poor treatment across the whole USA.

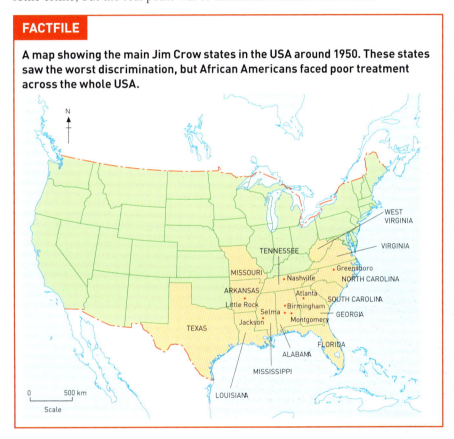

African Americans fighting for change

Amid the hysteria of the Red Scare, one small event caused some discomfort at the HUAC hearings in 1949. The baseball star Jackie Robinson was called to testify before the committee. He was an all-American hero: the first African American to play major league baseball. The HUAC was holding hearings about the danger of communist influence on minority groups such as African Americans. In April 1949, the radical African American singer and actor Paul Robeson (see Profile on page 280) claimed that African Americans would not fight for the USA against the USSR because of the discrimination they faced. Robinson was invited by the committee as a 'friendly' witness to deny Robeson's claims. (The photo in the Profile shows him waiting to be interviewed by the committee.) Robinson was a reluctant witness and did not want to be seen criticising Robeson, who was admired by many. But Robinson felt that he did have something to say (see Source 2 on page 280).

Jackie Robinson (1919–72)

- Born 1919 to a poor family in Georgia.
- Grew up to be an exceptionally talented sportsman, eventually specialising in baseball.
- Drafted into the military in 1942. While serving he applied to become an officer but his application was blocked. He was helped by the intervention of former heavyweight world champion boxer Joe Louis; his application was approved and became a lieutenant in 1943.
- Played in African American Leagues 1945–47 before joining the Brooklyn Dodgers in 1947 – the first African American to play major league baseball. By 1949, there were still only seven African American professional players.
- Enjoyed several seasons as a successful player and even had a film made of his life, *42*, in 1950.
- He continued to campaign for better opportunities and treatment for African American players and an end to segregation in all baseball leagues.
- Robinson was a strong supporter of the civil rights campaign and believed in non-violent protest.

Write a summary of Jackie Robinson's testimony to the HUAC. Source 2 is 488 words long. Try to summarise his points in 150.

Jackie Robinson's testimony

Source 2 An extract from Jackie Robinson's evidence to the HUAC, 1949.

It isn't exactly pleasant to get involved in a political dispute but I am testifying out of a sense of responsibility. I don't pretend to be any expert on communism or any other kind of a political 'ism'. But I am an expert at being a coloured American, with 30 years of experience at it.

I respect Mr Robeson as a famous ex-athlete, singer and actor, but his statement about Negroes not wanting to fight the Soviets sounds very silly to me. I do not believe he speaks for the majority of coloured Americans. I believe that most would do their best to help their country win the war, against Russia or any other enemy that threatened us. I am a religious man. Therefore I cherish America, where I am free to worship as I please, a privilege that other countries do not give. And I suspect that 999 out of almost any thousand coloured Americans you meet will tell you the same thing.

But my disagreement with Mr Robeson doesn't mean that we're going to stop fighting race discrimination in this country until we've got it all licked. It means that we're going to fight all the harder because our stake in the future is so big. We can win our fight without the communists and we don't want their help.

The White public should start toward real understanding by appreciating that every single Negro who is worth his salt is going to resent any kind of slurs and discrimination because of his race, and he is going to use every bit of intelligence such as he has to stop it. This has got absolutely nothing to do with what communists may or may not be trying to do. And white people must realise that the more a Negro hates communism because it opposes democracy, the more he is going to hate any other influence that kills off democracy in this country – and that goes for racial discrimination in the army, and segregation on trains and buses, and job discrimination because of religious beliefs or colour or place of birth.

And one other thing the American public ought to understand, if we are to make progress in this matter: The fact that it is a communist who denounces injustice in the courts, police brutality, and lynching when it happens doesn't change the truth of his charges. Just because communists kick up a big fuss over racial discrimination when it suits their purposes, a lot of people try to pretend that the whole issue is a creation of communist imagination.

But they are not fooling anyone with this kind of pretence, and talk about 'communists stirring up Negroes to protest' only makes present misunderstanding worse than ever. Negroes were stirred up long before there was a Communist Party, and they'll stay stirred up long after the party has disappeared – unless Jim Crow has disappeared by then as well.

Paul Robeson (1898–1976)

- Born 1898, the son of a church minister who had once been a slave.
- Went to Columbia University and passed his law exams with honours in 1923.
- As a Black lawyer, it was almost impossible for him to find work, so he became an actor – his big break was in the hit musical *Showboat*.
- Visited Moscow in 1934 on a world tour and declared his approval of communism saying: 'Here, for the first time in my life, I walk in dignity.'
- As a communist sympathiser, Robeson suffered in the USA. He was banned from performing, suffered death threats and had his passport confiscated.
- He left the USA in 1958 to live in Europe, but returned in 1963.

Robinson's testimony was not what the HUAC had been expecting. Some HUAC members approved – after all, he had disagreed with Robeson (who worried the HUAC) and argued that African Americans would fight against the USSR if it came to it. On the other hand, he had criticised the USA and its treatment of African Americans – a brave move in those times. The FBI opened a file on Robinson and continued to monitor him for many years. However, this did not stop him being an active campaigner for civil rights generally and for INTEGRATION in baseball particularly.

Robinson was not unique. Despite the pressures on them, African Americans began to organise protest campaigns and challenge the forces that held them back. They had plenty to build on in the campaigns of the 1920s and 1930s (see pages 224–26), but the advances towards equality during the war fuelled their efforts. Executive Orders such as Source 15 on page 254 showed that presidents were on their side. Most significantly, though, they were driven by the sense of injustice that the USA had fought racism abroad only to enforce it at home.

Brown vs Board of Education of Topeka, 1954

The first target of the post-war civil rights campaign was education. For decades, it had been legal in the USA for states to have separate schools for Black and White children. The states argued that separate education did not mean unequal education. They claimed that schools for Black children were equally well-equipped, although this was rarely true.

In September 1952, the National Association for the Advancement of Colored People (NAACP) brought a court case against the Board of Education in Topeka, Kansas. The case was about a girl called Linda Brown who had to travel several kilometres and cross a dangerous rail track to get to school, because she was not allowed to attend a Whites-only school closer to her home. Civil rights campaigners chose this as a test case to see whether the Supreme Court would allow states to continue segregating schools. They knew that if they won this case, the whole 'separate but equal' argument could no longer be used.

In May 1954, Chief Justice Earl Warren finally announced in favour of Brown and the NAACP, declaring that segregated education could not be considered equal. He said it created a feeling of inferiority for Black students and that meant that all segregated school systems were unequal ones. He ordered the southern states to set up integrated schools 'with all deliberate speed'.

PRACTICE QUESTIONS

1 Describe one example of discrimination against African Americans. (2)
2 Explain how far African Americans made progress in the years 1945–54. (10)

FOCUS TASK

What progress had civil rights campaigners made by 1954?

● 'African Americans made no progress in the years after the Second World War.'
● 'African Americans were powerless against discrimination in the years after the Second World War.'

Study each of these statements. Choose one of them and write two paragraphs about it. One paragraph should set out the evidence *for* the statement. The other paragraph should set out the evidence *against* it.

FACTFILE

The civil rights struggle – the long view

This topic focuses on the key years of the civil rights struggle (1945–75) but is only one part of a longer story that begins well before 1945. Here is an overview of the main events.

1619   First known sale of African American slaves (in Virginia).

1776   Declaration of Independence published, stating that 'We hold these truths to be self-evident, that all men are created equal, that they are endowed by their Creator with certain unalienable Rights, that among these are Life, Liberty and the pursuit of Happiness.' Many of the men who signed it were slave owners.

1840s–50s   Growing attention to anti-slavery thanks to campaigners such Tubman and Douglass.

1865   End of American Civil War and abolition of slavery.

1870   The 15th Amendment to the Constitution enacted, guaranteeing the right to vote. At the same time, however, the first 'Jim Crow' (segregation) law passed in Tennessee.

1896   Supreme Court upholds segregation.

1900   Lynching becomes a popular means of intimidating African Americans. By 1914, more than 1,100 people had been lynched.

1910   National Association for the Advancement of Colored People (NAACP) founded.

1941   President Roosevelt issues an Executive Order banning discrimination against minorities in defence industries.

1948   Supreme Court upholds practice of housing contracts that allow areas to remain segregated.

1952   Tuskegee Institute reports that, for the first time in the 71 years it has been keeping records, no African Americans had been lynched during the year.

1954   Supreme Court rules against segregation in schools.

1955   Emmet Till murdered. Montgomery bus boycott, led by Martin Luther King, Jr.

1957   President Eisenhower sends troops to force school in Arkansas to integrate.

1960   Lunch-counter sit-ins throughout the South. Student Non-Violent Coordinating Committee (SNCC) founded.

1961   Congress of Racial Equality (CORE) organises Freedom Rides.

1962   James Meredith becomes the the first African American student admitted to the University of Mississippi.

1963   Over a quarter of a million people participate in the March on Washington on 28 August 1963, and hear Martin Luther King, Jr. deliver his 'I have a dream' speech. King receives the Nobel Peace Prize.

1964   Civil Rights Act passed by President Johnson.

1965   Voting rights campaign in Selma, Alabama. The Voting Rights Act passes and is signed into law. Assassination of militant African American rights leader Malcolm X.

1966   Stokely Carmichael, head of the SNCC, introduces the phrase 'black power' during a voter registration drive in Mississippi. The phrase divides the civil rights movement.

1967   Race riots in Detroit and other US towns and cities. Thurgood Marshall becomes the first African American justice of the Supreme Court.

1968   Kerner Commission warns that the USA is becoming two separate societies: one Black and poor, the other affluent and White. King is murdered. This sparks unrest and civil disorders in 124 cities across the country. Shirley Chisholm is the first African American woman elected to Congress.

1971   The Supreme Court upholds actions of school boards in Boston in bussing students as a means to achieve desegregation.

A turning point? The murder of Emmet Till

The victory of Brown vs Topeka in 1954 was widely celebrated. However, the following year the USA was given a sobering reminder of how far African Americans still had to go in terms of winning equality and freedom from discrimination.

Emmet Till was a 15-year-old African American from Chicago. While visiting his cousins in the small town of Money, Mississippi in August 1955, he went into a general store. There are conflicting accounts of exactly what happened, but it seems that Till tried to flirt with the (White) woman running the shop and later, when she left the shop, he wolf whistled her. Till had broken an unspoken law and he would pay with his life. Three days later he was kidnapped, beaten so badly that his face was unrecognisable, had an eye gouged out and was then shot in the head. His body was dumped in the river. Two local men were arrested but they were found not guilty at trial. They later admitted they had carried out the murder but denied they had done anything wrong.

Till's case suggested that little had changed in the USA since the times of slavery. It was certainly not unusual: lynchings, beatings, intimidation and discrimination were everyday experiences for African Americans. The difference in this case was the public reaction to Till's murder. His mother, Mamie, insisted that his coffin should be left open so that the thousands of Chicago people who came to pay their respects could see what had been done to him. The African American magazine *Jet* published photographs of the horrific injuries. Public outrage galvanised the civil rights movement once again. There were protest rallies across the country, with Mamie speaking to crowds of 10,000 or more.

1   As Source 3, we could have shown the photographs of Till's injuries. Instead we chose this photograph. Do you think we made the right decision? Explain your answer.

Source 3 Mourners at Emmet Till's funeral September 1955. ▼

The Montgomery bus boycott: non-violent direct action

Although people were already campaigning for African American rights in the 1950s, many people date the start of the civil rights movement to December 1955, when events in the town of Montgomery, Alabama, gained widespread attention.

Montgomery had a local law that African Americans were only allowed to sit in the middle and back seats of a bus, and they had to give up those seats if White people wanted them. One version is that Rosa Parks was riding on one of these buses. She was feeling tired and her feet hurt, and she just did not want to get up and give her seat to a White man on the bus. This suggests that her action and the protest that followed it were spontaneous. In fact, this is an example of effective 'spin' after the event. It does not mean she was any less brave or determined, but Rosa Parks was a civil rights activist and she decided to make a stand against Montgomery's racially segregated bus service. She knew what would happen next: when she refused to give up her seat to a White man she was arrested and convicted of breaking the bus laws. If her action had been spontaneous, there would not have been a photographer on hand to take the carefully posed photograph in Source 4!

Source 4 Rosa Parks having her fingerprints taken in Montgomery police station after her arrest. ▲

The MIA

In response to this event, the civil rights movement helped the African American people of Montgomery to form the Montgomery Improvement Association (MIA). The MIA decided that the best way to protest and to generate publicity was to boycott the buses. On the first day of the boycott, the buses were empty and 10,000–15,000 people turned out to hear a speech from the newly elected MIA president, Martin Luther King (see Source 5). The boycott was a great success. The African American community organised a car pool that carried about two-thirds of the passengers that the buses would have taken and the rest walked. The bus company lost 65 per cent of its income.

This was the first major example of the power of non-violent direct action – that is, challenging discrimination by refusing to co-operate with it. It showed how powerful people could be when they worked together, although it took great courage to stand up to take such action. Throughout the boycott, MIA leaders suffered serious intimidation. King was arrested twice. Local judges passed an INJUNCTION declaring the car pool to be illegal. Churches and homes were set on fire and racially integrated buses were shot at by snipers (seven bombers and snipers were charged, but all were acquitted).

At the same time, civil rights lawyers fought Rosa Parks' case in court. In December 1956, the Supreme Court declared Montgomery's bus laws to be illegal. This meant that all similar bus services were illegal and, by implication, that all segregation of public services was illegal.

Source 5 An extract from Martin Luther King's speech in Montgomery, Alabama, announcing the bus boycott in December 1955.

The great glory of American democracy is the right to protest for right. There will be no crosses burned at any bus stops in Montgomery. There will be no white persons pulled out of their homes and taken out on some distant road and murdered. There will be nobody among us who will stand up and defy the constitution of the Nation.

Source 6 Rosa Parks' body lying in state in the Capitol building in Washington DC, after her death in 2005. She was the first American woman ever to be given this tribute. ▲

Source 7 A Herblock cartoon from March 1956. The caption was: 'Lif' dat boycott! Ride dat bus!' This was a reference to a song from the popular musical *Showboat*, which was set in the South. ▲

1 Source 7 is about the Montgomery bus boycott but it does not show Rosa Parks, Martin Luther King or even any buses. Do you think this makes it an ineffective cartoon? Explain your answer.
2 Is Source 7 a critical cartoon or one which praises? Explain your answer.

Source 8 The Rosa Parks bus, which is now an exhibit in a museum in the USA. There is a statue of Parks inside. ▲

FOCUS TASK

Why were the civil rights education campaign and the Montgomery bus boycott important?

1 Both the campaigners and the US government clearly thought these campaigns to desegregate schools and buses were important. Working in pairs, take one case study each – either schools or buses.
   a List all the evidence on these pages that shows the campaigners thought it was important.
   b Write a paragraph to explain why they thought it was so important.
   c Swap your information with your partner to see if they came up with different or similar conclusions.
2 Historians rely a lot on hindsight. Sometimes events that seem important at the time seem less important to historians. Sometimes it is the other way around. Do you think the Montgomery bus boycott has become more or less important with hindsight? Explain your answer.

The political response: President Eisenhower

The Montgomery bus boycott was an important victory for civil rights campaigners. Martin Luther King was already a well-known figure among activists, but the Montgomery boycott increased his fame and his standing within the movement and among White Americans. King and other activists were now pressing for greater equality. In particular, they wanted the government to pass a Civil Rights Act that would force states to end discrimination. The campaign for the Civil Rights Act was a key part of the civil rights story for the next decade. President Eisenhower addressed some of these issues in his State of the Union address in 1956 (see Source 9). In two significant ways Eisenhower stood by his word: he used his power to enforce integration of schools and he passed the first Civil Rights Act.

> **Source 9** President Eisenhower's State of the Union address, January 1956. The State of the Union is a speech given by the president each year, analysing the main issues facing the country.
>
> *We are proud of the progress our people have made in the field of civil rights. In Executive Branch operations throughout the nation, elimination of discrimination and segregation is all but completed. Progress is also being made among contractors engaged in furnishing Government services and requirements. Every citizen now has the opportunity to fit himself for and to hold a position of responsibility in the service of his country. In the District of Columbia, through the voluntary cooperation of the people, discrimination and segregation are disappearing from hotels, theatres, restaurants and other facilities.*
>
> *It is disturbing that in some localities allegations persist that Negro citizens are being deprived of their right to vote and are likewise being subjected to unwarranted economic pressures. I recommend that the substance of these charges be thoroughly examined by a Bipartisan Commission created by the Congress. It is hoped that such a commission will be established promptly so that it may arrive at findings which can receive early consideration.*
>
> *The stature of our leadership in the free world has increased through the past three years because we have made more progress than ever before in a similar period to assure our citizens equality in justice, in opportunity and in civil rights. We must expand this effort on every front. We must strive to have every person judged and measured by what he is, rather than by his colour, race or religion. There will soon be recommended to the Congress a programme further to advance the efforts of the Government, within the area of Federal responsibility, to accomplish these objectives.*

1 According to Source 9, what progress has been made?
2 Is there any evidence that the president is putting a slant on the situation?
3 Is this source more useful as evidence about government action or the effectiveness of the civil rights movement? Explain your answer.

Eisenhower and Little Rock, Arkansas 1957

In 1954, civil rights campaigners achieved an important victory in the battle for equal education with the Supreme Court judgement outlawing school segregation (see page 281). However, the verdict met with bitter resistance in some states, including Arkansas. Three years after the judgement, this state government had done very little to integrate its schools.

In 1957, the Supreme Court ordered the governor of Arkansas, Orval Faubus, to let nine African American students attend a White school in the town of Little Rock. In an act of defiance, Faubus ordered the Arkansas National Guard (reserve soldiers) to prevent these students from entering. He claimed it was because he could not guarantee their safety. Faubus only backed down when Eisenhower sent federal troops to protect the students and make sure that they could join the school. The troops stayed for six weeks.

Source 10 A White House press release containing a telegram from President Eisenhower to Governor Faubus, 5 September 1957. ▶

IMMEDIATE RELEASE   September 5th 1957

- -

THE WHITE HOUSE

THE PRESIDENT TODAY
SENT THE FOLLOWING TELEGRAM TO THE
HONOURABLE ORVAL E FAUBUS,
GOVERNOR OF ARKANSAS

The Honourable Governor Orval E Faubus
Governor of Arkansas
Little Rock, Arkansas

I have received your telegram requesting my cooperation in the course of action you have taken on school integration recommended by the Little Rock School Board and ordered by the United States Supreme Court.

When I became President I took an oath to support and defend the Constitution of the United States. The only assurance I can give you is that I will uphold the Constitution with all legal means at my command.

There is no basis in fact to your claims that the federal authorities are planning to arrest you or that your phone lines have been tapped.

At the request of Judge Davies, the Department of Justice is currently collecting facts as to your interference with or failure to comply with the Supreme Court's order. I expect you and other state officials   who are partially paid for and sustained by the government   to give full cooperation to the Court and the Justice Department.

Dwight D Eisenhower.

4 What does Source 10 reveal about the relationship between Eisenhower and Faubus? Explain your answer.
5 Why did the president publish the telegram from himself to Faubus?
6 Explain why the press release containing the telegram is more useful to historians than just the telegram on its own.

Eisenhower and the Civil Rights Act 1957

In 1957, Eisenhower fought fierce opposition in Congress to bring in a new Civil Rights Act. It was the first act of this type since the end of the Civil War and the abolition of slavery in 1865. The Civil Rights Act of 1957 outlawed many of the Jim Crow measures designed to stop African Americans voting. It also set up a process by which people could complain about voting irregularities.

This act proved difficult to enforce in practice and the numbers of African Americans voting increased by only 3 per cent. However, it proved that the president was willing to support African American rights and brought Eisenhower and his vice president Richard Nixon into contact with civil rights leaders, notably Martin Luther King.

1 Does Source 11 help to explain why King was not satisfied with the 1957 Civil Rights Act?
2 How far does Jackie Robinson in Source 12 agree with King in Source 11?
3 In what ways is Source 13 similar to other Herblock cartoons you have studied in this chapter, such as those on pages 275 and 285?

The campaigners' response: Martin Luther King and the SCLC

Eisenhower had hoped that the passing of the 1957 Civil Rights Act would reduce the actions of campaigners. In fact, the opposite happened. Under King's leadership, the civil rights movement was preparing to increase its actions. In 1957, King formed the Southern Christian Leadership Conference (SCLC). This group ran conferences and trained civil rights activists in techniques of non-violent protest, how to deal with the police, the law and the media.

Source 12 Civil rights activist Jackie Robinson (see page 280), writing to President Eisenhower in May 1958.

I was in the audience at the Summit Meeting of Negro Leaders yesterday when you said we must have patience. I felt like standing up and saying 'Oh no, not again!'. I respectfully remind you sir that we have been the most patient of all people. We cannot do as you suggest and wait for the hearts of men to change. We want to enjoy now the rights that we feel entitled to as Americans. We need an unequivocal statement from you – if necessary backed up by action such as you took against Governor Faubus last year – making it clear that America is determined to give negroes the freedoms we are entitled to under the constitution.

Source 14 President Eisenhower meeting with civil rights leaders in 1958. Martin Luther King is second from left. Eisenhower is fourth from the left. ▲

Source 13 A Herblock cartoon from 1960. The title was 'Pray Keep Moving Brother'. ▼

FOCUS TASK

What progress had been made in civil rights by 1960?

Source 9 on page 286 is an extract from Eisenhower's State of the Union address for 1956. Use pages 278–88 to write a 'State of Civil Rights for African Americans' address at the end of the 1950s. You could mention:
- barriers facing African Americans
- how African Americans have challenged these barriers
- which barriers have been overcome
- which barriers remain
- individuals or groups who deserve credit.

Source 15 The logo of the SNCC. ▼

The Civil Rights Act 1960

The 1960 Civil Rights Act was an attempt by Eisenhower to improve the act of 1957. It allowed the federal authorities to inspect the process of voter registration and introduced penalties for anyone who obstructed someone trying to register to vote. Eisenhower also authorised the continuation of the Civil Rights Commission he had set up in 1956.

Eyes on the prize: moving up a gear

In the 1980s, a US TV series called *Eyes on the Prize*, about the civil rights movement, was aired (the 'prize' being equal rights). It has become a widely used term when discussing the history of this period. So what did the civil rights movement do to try to gain the prize?

Direct action gathers pace 1960–61

The success of the Montgomery bus boycott showed the power of non-violent direct action. Martin Luther King was widely regarded as the leader of the civil rights movement, but a number of different groups began to organise similar direct action:

- **SNCC:** African American and White American students were deeply moved by the civil rights movement and played a major role in it. In April 1960, they set up the Student Non-violent Coordinating Committee (SNCC).
- **CORE:** Another key organisation was the Congress of Racial Equality, which had been founded by civil rights activist James Farmer in 1942.

These groups, often working together as well as with King's SCLC, staged many different protests.

Sit-ins

In 1960, in Greensboro, North Carolina, SNCC students began a campaign to end segregation in restaurants in the town. Their local branch of Woolworths had a lunch counter that had chairs/stools only for Whites, while African Americans had to stand and eat. Four African American students sat on the White-only seats and would not leave even when they were refused service. The next day, 23 more students did the same; the next day there were 66 students. Within a week, 400 African American and White students were taking part in sit-ins at lunch counters all over the town. With support from the SNCC, this non-violent tactic spread to other cities. By the end of 1960, lunch counters had been desegregated in 126 cities.

Similar protests took place in other towns – and not just in restaurants. In February 1960, in Nashville, Tennessee, 500 students organised sit-ins in restaurants, libraries and churches. Their college expelled them, but then backed down when 400 teachers threatened to resign if the students were not readmitted. By May 1960 the town had been desegregated.

4 Study sources 16 and 17. Make a list of the similarities and differences between the two scenes.

5 Which of these two sources would you choose as the image for the front cover of a book on the civil rights movement? Explain your answer.

6 Does it surprise you that Source 16 was published much more widely than Source 17? Explain your answer.

Source 16 A photograph of SNCC students in a sit-in protest in Jackson, Mississippi, 1963 ▼

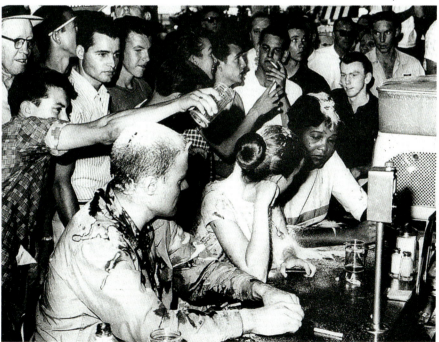

'Freedom rides'

In May 1961, CORE activists began a form of protest called 'freedom rides'. Many states were not obeying the order to desegregate bus services after the Montgomery ruling. 'Freedom riders' were people who deliberately rode on buses in the city of Birmingham, Alabama, to highlight this. They faced some of the worst violence of the civil rights campaigns. When the SNCC joined the freedom rides it met with the same violent reaction. Two hundred freedom riders were arrested and spent 40 days in jail. The governor of Alabama, John Patterson, did little to protect the riders until he came under pressure from the new president, John F. Kennedy, to do so. African Americans and their White supporters had shown that they were no longer prepared to be intimidated.

Source 17 Freedom riders sitting next to their burning bus near Anniston, Alabama. A mob of White people met the bus at the bus terminal, stoned it and slashed the tyres, then followed the bus out of town and set fire to it. They attacked the passengers as they fled the bus. ▶

ACTIVITY

Imagine you are a member of the SNCC in June 1961. Someone asks you why you are part of the movement, suggesting that all you and the other civil rights groups have achieved is a bus ride, getting beaten up and being arrested. Give an answer (either written or verbally) to this criticism. You could mention:

- the practical advances made since the late 1950s (for example, desegregation)
- the moral importance of these advances
- why you believe non-violence is the right tactic
- where you think your protests might go from here.

James Meredith and 'Ole Miss'

The freedom riders gained a great deal of publicity but they, and King and the SNCC, were all part of a much larger movement. Sometimes the protesters were groups, sometimes they were individuals. In 1962 an African American student, James Meredith, applied to study at the famous 'Ole Miss' – Mississippi State University. He was rejected but he won his appeal (with help from the NAACP) to overturn the decision to exclude him from the university. Mississippi state and university officials objected, so the US attorney-general sent in federal marshals to make sure Meredith could attend his classes. Violence erupted, two marshals were killed and 160 people were wounded, but Meredith entered 'Ole Miss'. The Bob Dylan song 'Oxford Town' celebrates this breakthrough.

Source 18 Martin Luther King, commenting on his tactics in Birmingham, Alabama, in 1963. Critics had accused him of deliberately stirring up violence.

Instead of submitting to surreptitious cruelty in thousands of dark jail cells and on countless shadowed streets, we are forcing our oppressor to commit his brutality openly – in the light of day – with the rest of the world looking on. To condemn peaceful protesters on the grounds that they provoke violence is like condemning a robbed man because his possession of money caused the robbery.

Taking stock, 1962

By 1962, the civil rights movement had achieved some notable successes:

- It had developed a style of protest – non-violent direct action – that earned the campaigners much support and respect, and gave them moral authority when their opponents were all too ready to use violence against them.
- Notable individuals had emerged as leaders, in particular Martin Luther King and Malcolm X (see page 301).
- Civil rights was becoming a major national issue, affecting and of interest to ethnic minorities and the White majority throughout the USA. The movement had built up great momentum.
- The new, young, popular president, John F. Kennedy, had committed himself to a wide-ranging civil rights programme of laws and regulations.

However, there was still a long way to go. Racism was still a fact of life in many parts of the USA. Black people faced much greater poverty and deprivation than White people and many Black people still felt helpless to change their lives. On the very night that Kennedy pledged his support for the movement, the leading Black activist in the state of Mississippi, Medger Evans, was murdered by a known racist. The court acquitted him.

The next three years saw the most dramatic progress of the whole civil rights story, as politicians and campaigners, White and Black, men and women in the north and south, used a range of strategies to keep up the pressure for change.

Source 19 Fire hoses being used against protesters in Birmingham, Alabama, 1963. The water pressure was so powerful that it could knock bricks out of walls. ▲

The Birmingham civil rights march 1963

The helplessness that Black people felt at this time was particularly strong in Birmingham, Alabama. Six years after the Montgomery decision, Birmingham was not desegregated. Its police force was notoriously racist and had links to the Ku Klux Klan.

In April 1963, Martin Luther King organised a civil rights march through the city. The aim of the march was to turn media attention on Birmingham to bring its policies to national attention. King knew that, with civil rights now a national issue, the US and international media would cover the march in detail. In the full glare of media publicity, police chief Bull Connor ordered police and fire officers to turn dogs and fire hoses on the peaceful protesters. The police arrested over 1,000 protesters and put many in jail, including King himself. Critics accused King of provoking the violence by staging this march. Source 20 is his reply.

Source 20 An extract from Martin Luther King's letter from Birmingham jail, Alabama, 1963.

But when you have seen vicious mobs lynch your mothers and fathers at will and drown your brothers and sisters at whim; when you have seen hate-filled policemen curse, kick and even kill your Black brothers and sisters; when you see the vast majority of your twenty million Negro brothers smothering in an airtight cage of poverty in the midst of an affluent society; when you are harried by day and haunted by night by the fact that you are a Negro … when you are forever fighting a degenerating sense of nobodiness; then you will understand why we find it difficult to wait.

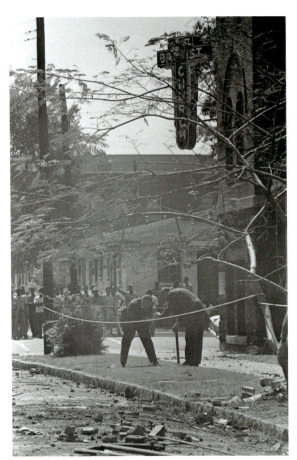

The president steps in

In May 1963, President Kennedy intervened. He put pressure on the governor, George Wallace, to force the Birmingham police to release all the protesters, to give more jobs to Black Americans and to allow them to be promoted. Birmingham officially outlawed segregation, but in practice it remained a bitterly divided place. In September 1963, a Ku Klux Klan bomb killed four Black children in the 16th Street Baptist Church in Birmingham.

Source 22 A protest march organised by CORE in response to the bombing, 22 September 1963. ▼

Source 21 A photograph of federal investigators searching through debris after the bombing of the church in Birmingham, Alabama, 15 September 1963. ▲

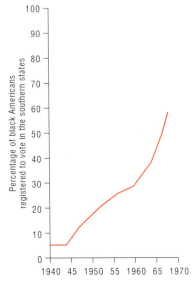

Figure 23 A graph showing the numbers of African Americans registered to vote in the southern states. ▲

ACTIVITY

Write an article for a US newspaper in 1963. You have a choice of two headlines:
a The weakness of African Americans today
b The strength of African Americans today

Use the information and sources on pages 289–92 to write the article. Your target word limit is 150 words.

Voting rights

The Birmingham march demonstrated the power of peaceful protest to challenge racism, but it also showed that states would only end segregation if they were forced to. Civil rights leaders wanted Kennedy to pass a stronger Civil Rights Act that would enshrine Black civil rights in law and prevent racism and discrimination such as that seen in Alabama. They thought this would ensure that, while racist attitudes might persist, the law would safeguard the rights of Black people.

President Kennedy and his brother Robert, the attorney-general, saw things differently. They wanted to concentrate on the issue of voting rights, believing that if enough Black people registered to vote, they would have power over the decisions that politicians made locally or at state level. Kennedy felt that this was where the big changes were needed. There were more Black people than White people in Birmingham, so if they could all vote they could oust the White racists.

The civil rights movement began to move its protest in the same direction. It organised courses for Black Americans in voting procedures and taught them how to register to vote (see Figure 23).

The march on Washington 1963: 'I have a dream'

At the same time, campaigners also kept up the pressure on the government. In August 1963, organised by Martin Luther King, over 200,000 Black people and 50,000 White people marched together to Washington DC, to call on the president to introduce a civil rights bill. At the rally, King gave his famous 'I have a dream' speech (see Source 24). The event had a huge impact on public opinion in the USA.

> 1 Which of Sources 24–26 is most useful to historians investigating the civil rights march of 1963?

Source 24 Part of an interview for a TV programme in 2003, marking the 40th anniversary of the March on Washington and Martin Luther King's 'I have a dream' speech. You can read the text and hear recordings of this speech online at the US National Archives website abd other sites.

In 1963 I was an eight-year-old boy living in Pasadena, California. It was a hot summer day and the television was on. The March on Washington was being broadcast and my mother told me never to forget this day. She said it was history in the making. This was so unusual – my mother never used language like this nor drew my attention to the television.

For a white boy in a racially segregated city, this was a powerful message and it has stayed with me. Hopefully, one day, we'll all rise up in the words of the hymn which Dr King quoted: 'Free at last, free at last. Thank God Almighty, I'm free at last.'

Source 25 A reconstruction drawing of a banner from the march on Washington, 1963. ▶

Source 26 A photograph of the march on Washington, 1963. ▼

The Civil Rights Act 1964

By 1963, almost everyone in the USA had a view on the issue of civil rights. In November 1963, Kennedy was assassinated. His successor Lyndon B. Johnson was just as committed to civil rights and used his skills as a politician to push through important laws. On 2 July 1964, he signed the Civil Rights Act. This made it illegal for local government to discriminate in areas such as housing and employment.

FOCUS TASK

What progress had civil rights campaigners made by 1965?

Look back at your work in the Focus Task on page 288 where you wrote a 'State of Civil Rights for African Americans' address at the end of the 1950s. Now write a new address for January 1965. You could mention:

- the barriers still facing African Americans
- how African Americans have challenged these barriers
- which barriers have been overcome
- which barriers remain
- individuals or groups who deserve credit
- how much progress has been made since 1945
- what will happen next.

Civil rights campaigns after 1964

Martin Luther King, the SCLC, CORE and the other civil rights groups did not pack up and go home after the Civil Rights Act was passed in 1964. The programme of non-violent protest continued, with a focus on voting rights.

The 'freedom summer'

The summer of 1964 has been called the 'freedom summer'. With the momentum gained from the Civil Rights Act, King and the SCLC continued to encourage Black Americans to register to vote. They were helped by young White people from the northern states who came south in great numbers to help. In the 20 months that followed the Civil Rights Act, 430,000 Black Americans registered to vote.

Selma

King deliberately targeted areas where discrimination was worst. In early 1965, he organised a 'voting rights' march through Selma, Alabama. The population of Selma was 29,000; 15,000 of these were Black adults old enough to vote, yet only 335 (just 2.4 per cent) were registered to do so. The town was also notorious for its racist sheriff, Jim Clark. The authorities banned the planned march. When, on 7 March, about 600 people went ahead with it anyway, they were brutally attacked. The media called it 'Bloody Sunday' and the TV pictures of the violence horrified the USA. King tried to keep the pressure on and rearranged the march. However, he compromised on 11 March by leading a token procession that turned back after a short distance. In 2014, an African American woman, Ava duVernay, who grew up near Selma, made a movie to mark the anniversary of this event (see page 304).

The Voting Rights Bill 1965–68

King's compromise at Selma avoided more violence, but it annoyed the more radical activists, who felt that the march should have gone ahead properly. However, King's restraint probably helped the president force through the Voting Rights Bill in 1965. It became law three years later, in 1968. The bill allowed government agents to inspect voting procedures to make sure that they were taking place properly. It also ended the literacy tests that voters had previously had to complete before they voted. These discriminated against poor African Americans in particular. After 1965, five major cities, including Detroit, Atlanta and Cleveland, all had African American mayors. In Selma, African Americans began to register to vote and in the next election Jim Clark lost his job.

Source 27 A cartoon published by Martin Luther King's SCLS in Selma, Alabama, 1965. ▼

HENRY BROWNLEE
1/28/65

1 Why was this carton (Source 27) published?
2 Do you think the cartoonist was thinking more about the past or the future?

Source 28 An extract from a lecture given by the US author and peace activist James Douglass, 2006.

Martin Luther King became a mortal enemy of Washington on April 4, 1967, one year to the day before his assassination, when he said in his great Riverside Church Address against the Vietnam War: 'I could never again raise my voice against the violence of the oppressed in the ghettos without having first spoken clearly to the greatest purveyor of violence in the world today – my own government.' Dr King saw the Vietnam War as the revelation of a profound systemic evil.

Source 29 A press release from the SCLC about King's speech in February 1967.

Civil rights leader Andrew Young today said the American economy has developed into a system of "socialism for the rich and free enterprise for the poor." … He said the idea that the Civil Rights Movement is "dead" is as much a myth as the idea that "God is dead." "As long as there is a little boy going hungry in Atlanta, and slums in our cities, and inferior education in crowded classrooms, and other injustices, there will be a Civil Rights Movement," he declared.

Rev. Young is Executive Director of the Southern Christian Leadership Conference and a close associate of Dr. Martin Luther King, Jr., SCLC President.

In a luncheon speech to the Hungry Club at the Atlanta YMCA, Rev. Young said the struggle for human rights and self-determination in America and throughout the world is becoming a contest between "haves" and "have-nots."

He told his integrated audience: "You must decide which side you are on."

Rev. Young said resistance to the Civil Rights Movement is stiffening because poor people now are demanding political and economic power, and "when you come to grips with established powers in society, you have no friends. People do not readily give up power. But we have faced challenges to freedom before, and we accept the new challenge."

Source 30 US historian Thomas Jackson, writing in 2007.

But Martin Luther King Jr. was no mere dreamer. As the civil rights revolution's most famous strategist and self-proclaimed 'symbol', King stood at the forefront of a mass political movement with many leaders and agendas. Like Lincoln and the Emancipation Proclamation, African Americans and their white allies organized, protested, and voted, forcing politicians to make hard choices and progressive commitments. … In the end King concluded that Lyndon Johnson had failed to mobilize and sustain a constituency of poor and working-class Americans that might defend a Great Society dedicated to real equal opportunity.

Source 31 A comment by US civil rights historian Ralph E. Luker on King's plagiarism.

Fifteen years ago I was responsible for directing research on Martin Luther King's early life for the Martin Luther King Papers Project. … What became increasingly clear as we worked through the papers from King's early career is that there were serious problems of plagiarism in his academic work. … When word of our findings leaked to the press, it appeared first in England and only later in the American press. It was, for several days, very big news indeed. Our five minutes of infamy waned and scholarly reflection took over. Boston University convened a panel to assess the situation. It concluded that there were serious problems with King's dissertation, made note of that, and concluded, nonetheless, that his doctorate should not be revoked.

3 Explain how Sources 28 and 29 are useful in showing King's new direction to historians.

4 Which source is more useful about the effects of King's new thinking?

A change of direction?

After 1964, King began to feel that while the civil rights campaign had achieved much, the work of improving the USA had still only just begun. He widened his criticisms to include the Vietnam War – the reasons the USA was involved, the way fighting was going and the effects it was having at home and abroad. Soon, King was voicing even more radical thoughts. The civil rights campaign had been based on the assumption that the USA was basically a fair place but that African Americans were not sharing in that equality. By 1968, however, King was beginning to question fundamental American values and ideals. He was worried that only middle-class African Americans had really benefited from the progress made by the civil rights movement, and that the odds were stacked unfairly against the poor, whether they were African American or not.

The significance of Martin Luther King

We will never know how this new direction would have turned out. In 1968, Martin Luther King was assassinated. This was probably the work of a hired killer, although it has never been proved which of King's enemies employed the assassin. King's death marked the end of an era for the civil rights movement. During his life, he had helped to transform the movement from a southern sideshow to a national movement. Major battles had been fought and won. Segregation was now illegal; the Civil Rights Act had enshrined African American rights in law; African American people in the south now held real political power.

We can see his importance today by the fact that around 125 schools are named after him and around 770 streets also bear his name. Martin Luther King Day is a public holiday in the USA – one of only four days dedicated to individuals. Most young Americans learn about Martin Luther King and the civil rights movement. King is usually presented as a saintly figure, and some historians have expressed concerns that this approach fails to represent his story fully and accurately. King himself got involved in the hard realities of politics in his own way, and was prepared to pressurise politicians to make changes (see Source 30). President Kennedy's wife Jackie later commented on how she disliked King as a person because he was a tough negotiator with her husband. Lyndon Johnson had King's phones bugged and kept him under surveillance by the security services, and in private he often referred to him in unfavourable and sometimes unpleasant terms.

Criticisms of King

Some members of the civil rights movement felt that King ignored important issues like poverty. Some 'White Nationalist' websites in the USA have been calling for the repeal of the King holiday. The calls are based on claims that King committed adultery and that he was guilty of plagiarism (copying the work of other scholars) when he got his doctorate in 1955 (see Source 30). The revelations shocked many people, but should these issues affect our judgement as historians?

FOCUS TASK

Which decade saw most progress?

Discuss these statements with a partner and then decide which one you agree with most:

- Civil Rights movements achieved more in the 1950s than in the 1960s.
- Civil Rights movements achieved more in the 1960s than in the 1950s.
- Civil Rights movements were only able to achieve what they did in the 1960s because of the foundations laid in the 1950s.

You could put this to a class vote.

Source 32 A mural commemorating King at the Washington DC public library. ▼

1 In what ways is Source 32 similar or different to the Rosa Parks' memorials and museum exhibits on page 285?

ACTIVITY

A visitor has walked into the Washington DC public library and seen the mural in Source 32. The visitor does not know anything about King. Write a commentary to go with the mural explaining what it shows.

Black power

Historians write history in books or make TV programmes and one thing they have in common with playwrights, novelists and film makers is that they cannot have all the action going on at the same time. Instead, they show you what is happening to some people in one scene, then they shift to a different scene. We are now going to change scene. Through the 1960s, at the same time that the campaigns you have studied so far were taking place, there were other developments within the Black communities of the USA. Black nationalism was one of these. Most Black nationalists rejected the non-violence of the civil rights movement. They felt that force was justified in order to achieve equality for Black Americans. Others fought not for equality but for complete separation.

One movement that attracted many disillusioned Black Americans was the NATION OF ISLAM, headed by Elijah Muhammad. The Nation of Islam attracted figures such as boxer Cassius Clay (who later changed his name to Muhammad Ali), who was an outspoken critic of racial discrimination. Another follower of the Nation of Islam was Malcolm Little, better known as Malcolm X. He was critical of Martin Luther King's methods and believed that the civil rights movement held back Black people. He wanted to see Black Americans rise up and create their own separate Black state in the USA, by force if necessary (see Source 33). Malcolm X was assassinated in 1965.

2 Write a sentence to describe each of the following:
  a Malcolm X
  b Black power
  c Black Panthers.

Source 33 Comments made by Malcolm X in the 1960s.

A The white man has taught the Black people in this country to hate themselves as inferior, to hate each other, to be divided against each other. The brainwashed Black man can never learn to stand on his own two feet until he is on his own. We must learn to become our own producers, manufacturers and traders; we must have industry of our own, to employ our own. The White man resists this because he wants to keep the Black man under his thumb and jurisdiction in White society. He wants to keep the Black man always dependent and begging – for jobs, food, clothes, shelter, education. The White man doesn't want to lose somebody to be supreme over.

B I am for violence if non-violence means we continue postponing a solution to the American Black man's problems. If we must use violence to get the Black man his human rights in this country then I am for violence.

The SNCC itself became more radical when the Black student Stokely Carmichael was elected chairman in 1966. He talked in terms of 'Black power'. He set out a radical view of it and in the process he was critical of Martin Luther King: 'This nation is racist from top to bottom, and does not function by morality, love and non-violence, but by power.'

Even more radical than Carmichael were the Black Panthers. This was a political party with a small private army, and it had around 2,000 members. They believed that Black Americans should arm themselves and force the Whites to give them equal rights. They clashed many times with police forces, killing nine police officers between 1967 and 1969.

Source 34 Members of the Black Panther Party protest against the arrest of one of their leaders, Huey Newton, 1967. ▶

Source 35 A Black Panther campaign poster. ▼

3 Which of Sources 34–36 is most useful as evidence about the Black Panthers?

Source 36 FBI director J. Edgar Hoover, quoted in the *New York Times*, 9 September 1968.

The Black Panthers are the greatest threat to the internal security of the country. Schooled in communist ideology and the teaching of Chinese Communist leader Mao Tse–tung, its members have perpetrated numerous assaults on police officers and have engaged in violent confrontations with police throughout the country. Leaders and representatives of the Black Panther Party travel extensively all over the United States preaching their gospel of hate and violence not only to ghetto residents, but to students in colleges, universities and high schools as well.

Source 37 A highway patrolman stands guard over protesters after the Watts riots, Los Angeles, 1965. There were an estimated 30,000 rioters in this incident and 34 deaths. ▲

Race riots and the Kerner Report

From 1965 to 1967, US cities suffered a wave of race riots. These were not the cities of the southern states, where Black people faced the most obvious discrimination. They were cities in the north and west, which had large Black populations. The cause of the riots in most cases was poor relations between the police and Black people. Most of the USA's cities were divided along race lines. Most police forces were White and many Black working-class people who lived in the inner cities felt that they did not get the same protection from crime as Whites. They distrusted the police. African American rioters were influenced by the radical Black nationalists. Others joined the riots as an expression of their frustration about the way they were treated in the USA. The most serious riots took place in the Watts area of Los Angeles in August 1965 and in Detroit in July 1967. President Johnson asked governor Otto Kerner of Illinois to investigate the riots and in his conclusion the governor cited racism as the cause and talked of two USAs: one Black and one White.

What was the impact of Black Power?

There is no doubt that Black Power groups brought to national attention the disillusionment of many African Americans. But did this have a positive or a negative impact on the struggle for civil rights? There is much evidence from the time that the more radical elements of Black Power groups alarmed moderate opinion and alienated many white Americans who might otherwise have been sympathetic towards the civil rights movement. The Black Power movement was seen as at least partly responsible for the race riots of 1965. The movement was also criticised by civil rights leaders such as Roy Wilkins because it gave law-enforcement authorities the opportunity and the excuse to crack down on all African American activists. The FBI established a special counterintelligence programme called COINTELPRO, which monitored thousands of activists and put many Black Power members in prison.

The debate continues to this day. As historians rethink and reinterpret the evidence they point out:

- that the Black Power movement has been misrepresented and was much more complex than was portrayed at the time
- that media coverage of Black Power at the time was misinformed and based more on ignorance and fear than on an attempt to understand the movement
- that whereas Black Power and the civil rights movements are often portrayed as two separate, divided movements, actually the two strands shared a lot of common ground. Stokely Carmichael and Martin Luther King were quite friendly and agreed on the need to fight poverty (Carmichael offered support for the 1968 Poor People's Campaign). Both were opposed to the Vietnam War. In 1967, King spoke at the SCLC Convention and told the audience to be proud of Black pride and Black culture.

Source 38 A report from officials in the British Embassy in Washington to the Foreign Office in Britain on the use of the 'Black Power' slogan, 5 August 1966.

CONFIDENTIAL

BRITISH EMBASSY, WASHINGTON, D.C.,
5 August 1966.

As you will know from the newspapers there has been a lot of activity recently in the civil rights field and much unrest among the Negroes. I thought, therefore, that it might be useful to give you a few details of developments. …

2. One of the most significant new features has undoubtedly been the emergence of the slogan Black Power which, so far as I can trace, first began to be used publicly during the Mississippi civil rights march in June. It has been traced by the Christian Science Monitor to Mr Stokely Carmichael, Chairman of the Student Non-violent Coordinating Committee.

3. The slogan has to most people rather an alarming ring about it, with implications of violence and extremism and a blatant appeal to racism. In fact no one seems to know exactly what it means, and perhaps this was deliberate, at least to start with. It is a striking slogan which could lend itself to all kinds of interpretations according to the needs of the moment. Nonetheless, as mentioned later in this letter, attempts have been made to define it because many people came to regard it as the battle-cry of black violence.

4. However, the main significance of Black Power is that it has threatened to split the civil rights movement. Earlier this month both the National Association for the Advancement of Colored People (N.A.A.C.P.) and the Congress of Racial Equality (C.O.R.E.) held their national conventions at roughly the same time. The slogan Black Power was used constantly at the C.O.R.E. convention, and, according to the Press, was endorsed there and 'adopted as the dominant philosophy of the movement' (Washington Post).

5. It was obvious that somebody of Dr Martin Luther King's mentality (he is the leader of the Southern Christian Leadership Council (S.C.L.C.) would disagree profoundly with it, and he made his opposition known at once. So did Roy Wilkins, Executive Director of the N.A.A.C.P. on 4 July at the convention in Los Angeles. He told his audience that the slogan meant 'anti-White power … we of the N.A.A.C.P. will have none of this'. …

9. Floyd McKissick, Executive Director of C.O.R.E., criticised the Administration for not doing enough for the Negroes, but the interesting thing about his Press conference was that he clearly sought to reassure the public that the term Black Power did not, as he put it, mean 'black supremacy' and 'does not mean the exclusion of white Americans from the negro revolutions, does not advocate violence and will not start riots'.

1 According to Source 38, why is it hard to define Black Power?
2 What effect does the source say Black Power was having in the civil rights movement?
3 Explain why Source 38 is useful as evidence about the effects of Black Power in US society.

Source 39 Historian Peniel E. Joseph, writing in 2006.

Historians tend to regard black power's speeches and boisterous nationalism as the opposite of the civil rights movement's dreams of community. Its reputation as having helped unleash urban violence – and a white backlash – remains a fixed part of civil rights scholarship and public memory. … Civil rights struggles are rightfully acknowledged as having earned black Americans a historic level of dignity. 'Black Power' accomplished a no less remarkable task, fuelling the casually assertive identity and cultural pride that is part of African-American life today. In this way, in spite of the hostilities between the two movements, there remains between them a shared history of struggle that briefly transcended political differences while ultimately transforming the landscape of race relations.

Source 40 Historian Yohuru Williams, writing in 2006.

Race riots in fact coincided with Black Power; they did not cause it. However, they did provide Black militants with a bargaining chip that many unfortunately misused, playing into the popular mindset that all Black militants supported violence.

Source 41 Historian Clayborne Carson, writing in 1994.

Both civil rights and black power leaders were able to gain national prominence most readily by emphasizing intangible goals – civil/human rights and increased group pride – rather than tangible, especially economic, goals. … Black power proponents and black nationalist leaders challenged civil rights leaders to transform the living conditions of the black masses, but all black leaders found it easier to transform the status and esteem of African Americans than to change racial realities. As a result, the black consciousness movements of the 1960s and 1970s achieved psychological and cultural transformation without having much impact on the living conditions of poor and working-class blacks. The black masses acquired an ideological vocabulary to express their anger and frustration but still lacked the political awareness necessary for effective action.

FOCUS TASK

Did the Black Power groups harm the struggle for civil rights?

1 Study the information and sources about the Black Power groups on these two pages and then discuss these questions in small groups:
   a What positive contributions of Black Power groups can you identify?
   b What examples of harm are mentioned?
   c What areas of agreement or disagreement can you find between the historians?
2 If you were able to ask each historian in Sources 39–41 the question 'Did the Black Power groups harm the struggle for civil rights?', which of these opinions do you think they each would take?
   a Black Power groups made a mainly positive contribution.
   b Black Power groups did more harm than good.
   c The issue is too complex for a simplistic question like this.

Source 42 An extract from a letter written by Malcolm X to Martin Luther King, July 1963.

A united front involving all Negro factions, elements and their leaders is absolutely necessary. A racial explosion is more destructive than a nuclear explosion. If capitalistic President Kennedy and communistic Chairman Khrushchev can find something in common on which to form a united front despite their tremendous ideological differences, it is a disgrace for Negro leaders not to be able to submerge our 'minor' differences in order to seek a common solution to a common problem posed by a common enemy.

Source 43 Historian Clayborne Carson, writing in 2006.

Had they lived, Malcolm and Martin might have advised their followers that the differences between the two were not as significant as was their shared sense of dedication to the struggle for racial advancement. Malcolm came to realize that non-violent tactics could be used militantly and were essential aspects of any mass struggle. Indeed, he was himself a peaceful man who never used violence to achieve his goals. Martin, for his part, remained philosophically committed to the ideals of non-violence, but he increasingly recognized that mass militancy driven by positive racial consciousness was essential for African American progress. 'I am not sad that black Americans are rebelling,' he remarked in his last published essay. 'Without this magnificent ferment among Negroes, the old evasions and procrastinations would have continued indefinitely.'

Comparing Martin Luther King and Malcolm X

You have come across these two figures many times. Now you are going to look at them in a little more detail and compare them. Both fought to represent the African American community, and many historians have compared every detail of their lives and thoughts. Until recently, most accounts focused on the differences between them, particularly their methods (violence or non-violence), their attitudes to segregation (integration or separation) and their religious beliefs (Christianity or Islam). From the Profiles opposite you can see some of the other differences that are often emphasised, such as their early lives. However, the two men actually shared much common ground.

PROFILE

Dr Martin Luther King (1929–68)

- Born as Michael but later changed his name to Martin.
- Father was a Baptist minister who spoke out against inequality.
- Grew up in relative comfort during the Depression. Graduated with a degree from the all-black Morehouse College in Atlanta in 1948.
- Studied in Pennsylvania and then gained his doctorate in Theology from Boston University in 1955.
- Married Coretta Scott in 1953 and they had two sons and two daughters.
- He was a Baptist minister like his father and grandfather, as well as a leader of the civil rights movement.
- He was a mesmerising speaker whose 'I have a dream' became
- He believed passionately in non-violent protest, but he was not afraid to face confrontation and was subject to considerable violence himself. He favoured actions such as the bus boycott and the sit-in.
- In December 1964 he was awarded the Nobel Peace Prize.
- Assassinated in 1968 by Earl Ray. There have been many theories that Ray was simply a hired killer, and that he was employed to murder King by one of King's opponents.

PROFILE

Malcolm X (1925–65)

- Born May 1925 as Malcolm Little.
- Father was a Baptist minister who spoke out against inequality.
- Family threatened by Ku Klux Klan and forced to move. Father killed in 1931; strongly suspected of being a racist murder but never proved.
- The death of his father plunged the family into poverty, especially in the Depression. His mother was taken into a mental hospital.
- Became involved in drugs and crime and imprisoned for burglary in 1946. Joined the Black Muslim faith while in prison.
- After release in 1952 he joined Elijah Muhammad's Nation of Islam in Chicago. Changed his name to X, symbolising the African name that had been taken from his ancestors by slavery.
- Quickly became a leading figure in the movement. Went on speaking tours advocating Black power and founding new mosques. Became minister of the New York mosque.
- Openly criticised Whites and the US system as a whole. He also disagreed with Elijah Muhammad's policy of non-involvement in politics and criticised Martin Luther King for holding back African American radicalism with non-violent methods. Elijah Muhammad suspended Malcolm X in 1963 and he left to establish the Organization of Afro-American Unity in March 1964.
- By this time he was beginning to adapt his views on Black separatism and began to urge African Americans to work with sympathetic Whites to achieve progress.
- Malcolm X was shot dead at a party meeting in Harlem on 21 February 1965. Three Black Muslims were later convicted of the murder.

ACTIVITY

Study the sources and Profiles of Martin Luther King and Malcolm X. Now make your own copy of the table below and use it to record the key points about each one. You can refer to previous sections of this chapter as well to help you complete it.

	Martin Luther King	Malcolm X
Origins/background		
Beliefs		
Methods		
Key achievements		
Reaction of others		
Significance (immediate)		
Significance (longer term)		

Source 44 The only meeting between Malcolm X and Martin Luther King, March 1964. ▶

The significance of Malcolm X

In many ways, Malcolm X's contribution is difficult to sum up. He never led a mass movement in the way that King did. However, he did manage to inspire and energise young African Americans who were disillusioned with their treatment by American society but who also felt that the civil rights movement was not achieving anything.

His main impact was intellectual. His ideas played a key role in the development of the Black Power movement, the Black Arts movement and the widespread development of the concept of being proud to be Black. He also brought the issue

> **Source 45** Historian Clayborne Carson, writing in 2005.
>
> *Rather than recognizing the common ground in the ideas of Martin and Malcolm, most black leaders of the era after King's death in 1968 saw them as irreconcilable alternatives. Black people were advised to choose between Martin and Malcolm, rather than affirming that each offers a partial answer to the problem of race. Unlike many of their followers, the two men understood at the end of their lives that their basic messages were compatible rather than contradictory. Both saw that the building of strong, black-controlled institutions in African American communities did not contradict the goal of achieving equal rights within the American political system; indeed, they came to understand that achieving one goal could contribute to the achievement of the other. Perhaps the most important consequence of their tragic deaths was that they were unavailable to serve as elder statesmen for the African American leader who followed them.*

> **Source 46** An extract from Malcolm X's autobiography.
>
> *When I am dead ... I will be labelled as, at best, an 'irresponsible' black man. I have always felt about this accusation that the black 'leader' whom white men consider to be 'responsible' is invariably the black 'leader' who never gets any results. You only get action as a black man if you are regarded by the white man as 'irresponsible'. In fact, this much I had learned when I was just a little boy. And since I have been some kind of a 'leader' of black people here in the racist society of America, I have been more reassured each time the white man resisted me, or attacked me harder – because each time made me more certain that I was on the right track in the American black man's best interests.*

of civil rights to prominence in the large northern cities of the USA, helping to make civil rights a national issue rather than one confined to the southern states. As historian Bruce Perry said: 'He made clear the price that white America would have to pay if it did not agree to Black America's legitimate demands.' Malcolm X also played a powerful role in raising the self-belief of many African Americans by getting them to see that they had a long and distinctive heritage that could be traced back to their African roots. He had a major impact in bringing many African Americans into contact with Islam.

Although he is not revered in the same way as King, Malcolm X does have his share of memorials. There are many schools and streets named after him and there is an educational centre at the University of Columbia named after him. He has featured more prominently than King in film portrayals, and this probably reflects the fact that he appealed more to the kind of younger, urban African Americans who make films, rather than the more respectable Martin Luther King.

Can they be compared?

You have already seen that it is difficult to compare the ideas of these two men. It is similarly difficult to compare their significance. This is partly because both Malcolm X and Martin Luther King were intelligent enough to realise how important they were. They knew that the African American protest movement was in fact a grassroots movement, based in local communities and often centred on church communities. Look back through this section and see how many organisations are mentioned that admired King and accepted him as a figurehead but which he did not actually lead (e.g. CORE). Malcolm X was in a similar position, and towards the end of his life he worked to bring greater unity and co-ordination between the different African American organisations. Perhaps the most important contribution of both men was to provide some degree of unity to organisations that were difficult to hold together. The fact that many of these organisations splintered after their deaths is an indication of this.

> **FOCUS TASK**
>
> ### Who did more for civil rights: Martin Luther King or Malcolm X?
>
> 1 Work in pairs or small groups. You are going to prepare for a debate in which you will have to support the claims of either Martin Luther King or Malcolm X as the greater contributor to the civil rights movement. The problem is that your teacher is not going to tell you which man you are supporting until the last moment. You will have to:
>   a prepare points to support the claim of each leader
>   b prepare points that could be used to criticise each leader
>   c prepare to make any other points that you think are relevant.
> 2 Discussion: It might not surprise you to learn that there are fewer memorials to Malcolm X than to Martin Luther King. Do you think Malcolm X deserves to be remembered as much as Martin Luther King?

Source 47 Comments by Professor Brian Balogh in a radio discussion about the movie *Selma*, 2015.

Duvernay [the director] has been very eloquent in interviews, saying she wanted to make a film about the people who make up the movement. The problem is she doesn't do that. She is so intent on displacing the great white saviour Johnson that she replaces him with the great black saviour – Martin Luther King. ... That was one of the fundamental African American criticisms of King. He was the great man who would sweep in for those photo opportunities to get on the front pages. And as you can see in the film, that is part of his strategy. All I'm saying is that for somebody who wants to make a film about the people, there were precious few scenes with the actual people in the film.

Who else deserves credit?

So far this section has focused on the civil rights movements and its leading figures. But the achievements of the movement actually involved many other people and organisations.

Ordinary people

To begin with, thousands of African Americans and small numbers of White Americans marched, demonstrated, protested and suffered verbal and physical abuse during these campaigns. In fact when the movie *Selma* was shown in 2014, one eminent American historian felt that the ordinary campaigners did not get enough credit (see Source 47). *Selma* also caused uproar over its portrayal of President Lyndon Johnson. In the movie Johnson was portrayed as a scheming and unscrupulous politician who had little sympathy for Civil Rights. Not surprisingly, this led to comments from some people.

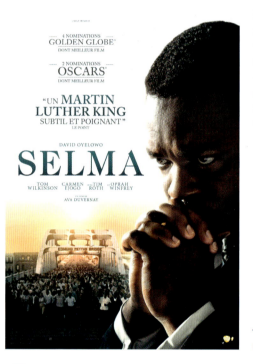

So was Johnson given a raw deal in the movie? Clearly the author of Source 49 thinks so. However, some historians think Johnson is overrated in this area and that the contribution of President Kennedy is underrated. You will compare their contributions on page 327.

◀ **Source 48** A poster for the 2014 movie *Selma*.

Source 49 An extract from 'What *Selma* gets wrong' by Mark K. Updegrove, historian and director of the L.B.J. Presidential Library and Museum.

Selma gets much right. The film humanizes Dr. Martin Luther King, Jr., and the colossal burden he faced in 1965 leading a fractious movement. But "Selma" misses mightily in faithfully capturing the pivotal relationship—contentious, the film would have you believe—between King and President Lyndon Baines Johnson.

In the film, President Johnson resists King's pressure to sign a voting rights bill, which—according to the movie's take—is getting in the way of dozens of other priorities. Indeed, "Selma's" obstructionist LBJ has no real conviction on voting rights. This characterization of the 36th president flies in the face of history. In truth, the partnership between LBJ and MLK on civil rights is one of the most productive and consequential in American history.

Yes, Johnson advocated stripping a potent voting rights component out of the historic Civil Rights Act he signed into law in the summer of 1964. A master of the legislative process—and a pragmatist—he knew that adding voting rights to the Civil Rights Act would make it top-heavy, jeopardizing its passage. Break the back of Jim Crow, Johnson believed, and then we'll tackle voting rights.

---

1 Why is the author of Source 49 defending Johnson?
2 Does this mean his comments cannot be accepted?

Source 50 A Herblock cartoon from 1961. The waitress is starting to tell the foreign visitors they cannot be served when the manager comes up and says 'It's all right to seat them. They're not Americans.' ▲

'Route 40'

One group who helped the campaign for the Civil Rights Act of 1964 were surprisingly not even from the USA. In the 1950s and early 1960s, many African colonies gained independence from their former rulers (mostly Britain and France). When this happened they usually set up diplomatic links with other countries, particularly the USA. Their diplomats would fly to New York to visit the United Nations, then they would drive down to Washington on 'Route 40' to meet US government officials and sometimes even the president. It was a long drive and many of them tried to take a break on the journey. The problem was that on Route 40 they were often stopped by police – it was unusual to see Black men in cars. They also found that they were refused service or accommodation in segregated restaurants and hotels. It was the same story when they tried to find offices and accommodation either in Washington itself or in neighbouring Virginia.

This behaviour was a propaganda gift for the USSR, embroiled in the Cold War against the USA. The USA took any opportunity it could to embarrass the USSR and the lack of freedom in communist countries was a favourite for US propaganda. In the civil rights campaign the Soviets had a perfect propaganda weapon to strike back. They highlighted the racial discrimination and intimidation of the USA generally in their anti-US propaganda, but they also highlighted particular events, such as the Birmingham bombing or the attacks on marchers in Selma. One of their favourite tactics was to describe the treatment of foreign diplomats, particularly those from Africa.

This is a small part of the story but it caused major embarrassment to presidents Eisenhower, Kennedy and Johnson and all added to the pressure for the Civil Rights Act. The act did not solve this problem entirely. Hotel owners in Virginia and Atlanta challenged the right of the government to make them serve Africans or African Americans. They took their case all the way to the Supreme Court, but the court backed the government. This was a victory for civil rights but it reveals how it takes more than a government act to change attitudes.

FOCUS TASK

Which method of campaigning was most effective?

You have been creating record cards for each of these methods used by civil rights campaigns:
- court case/legal challenge
- non-violent direct action
- empowering ordinary people
- marches and demonstrations
- violent protest.

Now use these cards to tackle one of the following tasks:
1 Explain which method got the most publicity and why.
2 Explain which method you think was the most effective and why.
3 Explain how two or more of these methods worked together.

Which president did the most for civil rights?

John F. Kennedy 1961–63

Civil rights was not one of Kennedy's priorities when he took office in 1961. However, thanks to the actions of civil rights activists he was forced to deal with the issue. Most historians agree that Kennedy was surprised by the developments of the early 1960s but that he was basically sympathetic to the aims of the civil rights activists. During his presidential campaign he promised to end discrimination in federally owned housing and he helped to get Martin Luther King out of jail.

Once in office he took other important measures:

Source 51 President Johnson introducing the Voting Rights Act 1965 to Congress.

The Constitution says that no person shall be kept from voting because of his race or his colour. We have all sworn an oath before God to support and defend that Constitution. We must now act in obedience to that oath. Their cause must be our cause too, because it is not just Negroes, really it's all of us who must overcome the crippling legacy of bigotry and injustice. And we shall overcome.

- He made high-level Black appointments: the NAACP lawyer Thurgood Marshall became the first African American US circuit judge and Robert Weaver became head of the Housing and Home Finance Agency – the first African American senior government official.
- He stood up to the governors of the southern states and tried to force them to defend the freedom riders (see page 290).
- The Justice Department, under JFK's brother Robert, successfully attacked segregation in southern airports and brought more lawsuits than any previous government against organisations breaking the 1957 Civil Rights Act.
- In October 1962, he sent 23,000 government troops to ensure that just one Black student, James Meredith, could study at the University of Mississippi.
- In September 1963, Kennedy made a major speech on nationwide TV committing himself to the cause of civil rights and calling for a new federal civil rights act.

Source 52 Roger Wilkins, assistant attorney-general 1964–67 and one of the few top African American officials of the time.

It was very rare in those days to have the experience of white people in positions of power react positively to their perceptions and to adopt their vision. Johnson did this, and he also adopted the call of the movement: 'We Shall Overcome'.

Kennedy's achievements were genuine and important. However, he moved too slowly for civil rights activists. Critics said he was not interested enough in the issue. It certainly was not his top priority and he probably did not understand how passionately civil rights campaigners felt about it. His first proposed Civil Rights Bill was very moderate and disappointed activists. In Kennedy's defence, he probably understood public opinion better than the activists and was trying not to alarm the public by being too radical. He also had to deal with the fact that many members of Congress would have delayed and fought against measures that they thought were too radical. In the end, Kennedy's assassination meant that we cannot know how much more he would have done. However, he undoubtedly laid the foundations of what became the Civil Rights Act passed by President Johnson.

Lyndon Johnson

Lyndon Johnson has a reputation of being a difficult, even unpleasant man. There is no doubt that he was prepared to be aggressive and forceful and to pressurise friends and opponents to achieve what he wanted. As soon as he came to power he introduced $800 million of measures to wage a 'war on poverty'. Although not a civil rights measure, this helped many African Americans who were among the poorer members of society.

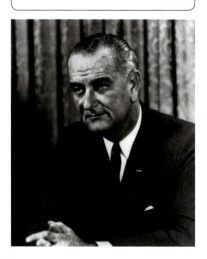

Johnson also brought in the Civil Rights Act 1964. His key contribution here was his ability to manage Congress. Unlike Kennedy, Johnson was an experienced politician with many allies in the House and the Senate, and this helped him to pass controversial measures. He made the 1964 act much more radical than Kennedy's original proposal and forced it through by pressuring members of the Senate who were planning to delay it. Johnson then pressured Congress into further civil rights legislation, the Voting Rights Act, in 1965. This put voter registration in the hands of federal rather than local authorities and banned literacy tests. The act gave the vote to thousands of African Americans who had effectively been denied it. It also led to the election of record numbers of African American officials to positions of authority in the South.

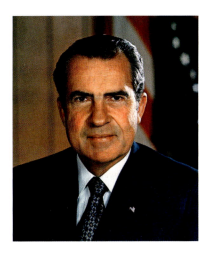

Richard Nixon, 1969–74

Nixon was president for just six years. However in this time he took steps that had a real impact on civil rights:

- Desegregation of schools and colleges went from being a legal requirement to a reality. Desegregation was supposed to have happened after the Brown vs Topeka case of 1959 but in 1968 almost 70 per cent of African American students still went to segregated schools. By 1974, the figure was 8 per cent. However, housing was still largely segregated and students going to integrated schools were often taken long distances by bus.
- Nixon extended key sections of Johnson's Voting Rights Act (the sections on literacy tests) which were due to expire in 1970. He banned these tests across the whole of the country, not just in the South.
- Nixon brought in quotas for the numbers of African American students who should be taken into universities, and also quotas for the employment of African Americans in areas such as public administration, the police, judiciary, etc. This policy became known as 'affirmative action'.
- Nixon also tried to build up African Americans' sense of having a stake in American society. He tried to tap into the Black Power consciousness, but to turn its energy into education and business. He wanted minorities to become managers and owners and not just workers. Nixon set up the Office of Minority Business Enterprise, which gave federal contracts to businesses owned by African Americans or Hispanics. He also ploughed funding into the largest African American colleges and universities. By 1971 there were 13 African American Congressmen, 81 mayors, 198 state legislators and 1,567 local office holders.

These were huge steps forward. So why have Nixon's achievements not always been recognised?

- First of all, other aspects of his presidency have overshadowed his record on civil rights. Nixon's presidency ended in failure. He was forced to resign (the only president ever to do so) over the Watergate scandal after he ordered the bugging of his political opponents and then tried to hide his involvement through an elaborate series of cover-ups.
- He got on badly with many of the leading civil rights campaigners (see Source 54). He was right-wing while civil rights activists tended to be left wing. As a young senator he helped in the McCarthy anti-communist witch hunts (see page 274). He was recorded making racist comments in the Oval Office, which did not help his case.
- His so-called 'southern strategy' also alienated many civil rights leaders. This strategy involved working with governors and state governments in the southern states rather than challenging and criticising them as Kennedy and Johnson had done. Nixon even tried to appoint Supreme Court judges who were sympathetic to southern segregationist policies. The southern strategy was partly driven by politics. Nixon needed to keep voters and southern congressmen on his side. However, it was also driven by realistic politics. By working with the southern states rather than antagonising them it could be argued that Nixon actually got laws put into action on the ground rather than simply passed in Congress.

Source 53 Joseph Smitherman, Mayor of Selma, Alabama.

When we heard Johnson on the radio and he said 'we shall overcome' it felt like somebody had just stuck a knife in your heart. All you fought for was over – our President had sold us out.

Source 54 Historian Dean Kotlowski, writing in 2001.

Why has it taken so long to credit Richard Nixon with advances in civil rights? For one thing, Nixon alienated civil rights leaders and African Americans. The president dragged his heels on integration of suburbs and northern schools. He made few addresses to the nation on civil rights and he inflamed racial tension through his 'southern strategy'. Incensed black leaders criticized Nixon harshly. Their critique has remained the standard interpretation of Nixon's policies. Nixon's relations with civil rights leaders became like the Cold War. Each side became suspicious of the other. Yet realising they had to do deals with each other, the two sides on rare occasions cooperated in areas of mutual benefit.

FOCUS TASK

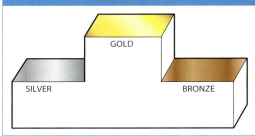

Who did more for civil rights: Kennedy, Johnson or Nixon?

Consider the work of Kennedy, Johnson and Nixon on civil rights. Where would you put them on the podium below? Write a brief paragraph explaining why each one has been given the position they have.

Source 55 President Barack Obama and his wife Michelle at the celebrations of his inauguration as President of the USA in January 2009. He was the first African American president in the country's history. ▲

Fast forward: 2009

The fact that an African American could stand for and become president of the USA in 2009 shows how far the cause of civil rights had come by the end of the twentieth century. Obama himself said during the 2008 campaign that the USA was 'light years away from the time of Martin Luther King'. In fact, Obama tried to make race a very small issue in the campaign because he wanted to be accepted as a politician rather than as an African American politician. But it is easy to trace the events of 2009 back to the historic impact of the civil rights movement of 1950–75. For example:

● From the later 1960s the voting campaign began to pay dividends – African American senators were elected, such as Edward Broke of Massachusetts. In 1967, the city of Cleveland elected an African American mayor. The Reverend Jesse Jackson, one of Martin Luther King's closest supporters, became a leading figure in the Democratic Party and still is today.

● In 1988, the government passed the Civil Rights Restoration Act, which forced private organisations that received government money (e.g. companies working on government contracts) to ensure they applied anti-discrimination rules fully. Other private organisations were not affected.

● At a local level many local authorities began to bring in anti-discrimination policies towards the workers they employed and also in areas such as housing. At the same time, statistics reveal that early in the twenty-first century, African Americans were still more likely to live in poverty than other groups, even other minority groups such as Asian or Arab Americans or Hispanic Americans. Unemployment rates for Black Americans in 2000 were around 8 per cent – twice the rate for White Americans. Around 8 million Black Americans were officially classed as living in poverty in 2000, which was nearly three times the rate for White Americans. They also suffered from greater levels of physical and mental health problems and higher rates of crime and family breakdown.

FOCUS TASK

The civil rights Hall of Fame

1 Create your own civil rights Hall of Fame for the activists of the period 1945–74. There will be paintings, photographs and statues of key figures in the civil rights movement. Each person or group will have a display with information about them including video clips, images, web pages and so on. You have six panels, which should go to the six most important people or groups of people. Decide what order they should come in so the most important comes first. The order is up to you but you need to be able to back it up with evidence and argument.

Turning points in the civil rights movement

2 You have now studied the history of the civil rights movement 1948–68. Historians often look for turning points when they describe a historical process. A turning point is usually:
 – an event that makes the events after it possible and/or
 – an event that has a huge impact on the way people think or behave.
Do you think there was a turning point in this story? If so, what was it? Here are some possible candidates:
 – 1954 Brown vs Topeka Board of Education
 – murder of Emmet Till
 – Civil Rights Act 1957
 – Civil Rights Act 1964
 – Selma 1965
 – assassination of King
You can select one from the list or choose one not on the list. Whatever you choose you should be able to explain why it qualifies as a turning point.

PRACTICE QUESTIONS

1 Describe one example of the actions of SNCC. (2)
2 Describe one example of the actions of the Black Panthers. (2)
3 Describe one example of discrimination against African Americans in the early 1960s. (2)
4 Explain why civil rights was such a major issue in the period 1954–64. (10)
5 Explain how far African Americans made progress in the years 1954–64. (10)
6 'Presidents did more than campaigners in achieving civil rights for African Americans between 1954 and 1974.' How far do you agree with this view? (18)

TOPIC SUMMARY

The struggle for civil rights in the USA 1945–74

1 In the 1940s, African Americans faced severe prejudice and discrimination, particularly in the 17 Jim Crow states, which operated a policy of segregation of Black and White people.
2 Civil rights campaigners challenged this situation in various ways, including legal challenges (such as Brown vs Topeka), non-violent direct action (such as lunch-counter sit-ins) and marches (such as Birmingham or Washington in 1963).
3 The civil rights movement was very diverse. Different organisations worked in their own way, but their leading spokesman was Martin Luther King, and groups such as SNCC, CORE and the NAACP acknowledged his leadership. It was, however, a grass-roots movement. Millions of people, including many White people, joined campaigns and protests.
4 Under King, the best-known strategy was non-violent direct action – refusing to co-operate with segregated facilities. The success of the Montgomery bus boycott showed how powerful this strategy could be. It led to the segregation of bus services being declared illegal by the Supreme Court.
5 Another key strategy was voting rights. Politicians such as President Kennedy particularly championed this because it dealt with the problem at a local level. If more Black people voted then racist politicians would not get elected. However, this would be a slow process that would take a generation to achieve results.
6 Other civil rights campaigners, such as Malcolm X and the Black Panthers, believed in violent protest. They called for African Americans to use their power (Black Power) to scare America into change. Historians argue whether this violence or the threat of it held back or sped up the granting of civil rights.
7 One key objective of the civil rights movement was to secure a Civil Rights Act that enshrined their rights in law and made illegal the many practices that states and individuals used to prevent African Americans being treated equally.
8 All the post-war presidents officially agreed the objectives of the civil rights movement and successive presidents introduced a series of Civil Rights Acts, each stronger than the one before. The greatest improvements were made under President Johnson, but historians argue over which president made the greatest contribution.
9 By 1975 African Americans had made major progress towards equality, with many elected to political office and all schools and colleges and public spaces officially desegregated. However the process of change was still not complete.

6.3 The times they are a-changing? Government and dissent c1964–75

FOCUS

With hindsight, some historians believe that the Civil Rights Act of 1964 was a turning point in US history. Things did not change overnight, of course, but the act did seem to indicate a shift in attitudes. It made the civil rights movement more determined to campaign for equality, and this in turn encouraged other groups to campaign for their rights as well. In this topic, you will examine:

- the emergence of other protest campaigns including other minorities
- the emergence of the women's movement.

Background: 'The Times They Are A-Changin''

This is the title of a 1964 song by the folk singer and US megastar Bob Dylan. You can listen to the song online. You might think that Dylan was writing about civil rights – and in some ways he was. However, he was really writing about even more fundamental and wide-reaching events. To many Americans at the time it did seem that times were changing. The conformity and barriers that held back certain groups were being broken down. The economy took a downturn, especially in the later 1960s, and this particularly affected the poorest in society. Above all there was the Vietnam War, which had an immense financial, political and psychological impact on the USA in this period. Bear this in mind as you read through this topic. You may want to look back at pages 80–89 to remind yourself about the war. As you read, think about the types of changes taking place. You will be asked to note them at the end of the topic.

How far did other groups achieve civil rights in the USA?

The campaign for Black civil rights was a major achievement in its own right. But it also gave many groups in the USA a sense that other inequalities in society could be removed if enough people worked to that end. In this way, the Black civil rights movement gave birth to other protest movements. You are going to investigate the experiences and achievements of four other groups or campaigners for their civil rights: Hispanic Americans, Native Americans, women and gay Americans.

Case study 1: Hispanic Americans

Hispanic Americans are either immigrants from Spanish-speaking territories that border the USA, or the descendants of Spanish-speaking Americans who lived in areas that had formerly been part of the Spanish Empire. By far the largest Hispanic group were the Mexican Americans.

Immigration from Mexico to the USA was a fact of life for both countries during the twentieth century. Mexico was poor compared with the USA and the USA offered the prospect of regular work for wages that were high by Mexican standards. These wages could be sent home to support families, educate younger brothers and sisters or help buy medicines. There were major waves of immigration in the early 1900s, at the time of the Depression in the 1930s and during and after the Second World War.

Most Mexicans worked as agricultural labourers. In 1942, the US and Mexican governments agreed the 'bracero' programme, which brought thousands of Mexicans to work as contract labourers on US farms. The Mexicans had the necessary skills from their own rural backgrounds, and they tended to concentrate in the states closest to their homeland: Arizona, California, Colorado, New Mexico and Texas. The programme continued until 1964, after which many Mexicans decided to settle in the USA rather than returning home as they were supposed to. As a result, the Mexican American population of the USA began to grow and they became a prominent community. Their numbers swelled in 1965 when the US Congress passed the Immigration and Nationality Act. This opened up the USA's strict quotas on immigration from Mexico and other countries. It also had a family reunification clause, which allowed immigrants living in the USA to bring their families into the country and become US nationals.

There was a long tradition of illegal as well as legal immigration from Mexico, so it is almost impossible to be sure of the exact levels of immigration. What is certain is that by 1978 there were over 7 million Mexican Americans in the USA, with 1 million in Los Angeles alone (one-third of the population).

Source 1 Supporters of Mexican civil rights leader Reies Tijerina protesting about land rights in Washington DC in 1968. Their protests were co-ordinated with Martin Luther King's Poor People's Campaign. ▼

Discrimination

Mexican immigrants suffered the same intolerance and discrimination as Black Americans and Native Americans. Mexican Americans endured high unemployment, ill treatment and low wages in the workplace, poor housing, educational segregation and discrimination by the police. They were generally discouraged from joining trade unions or political parties. They were under-represented in local politics because they were discouraged from registering to vote, and the number of elected Mexican American officials was tiny in relation to the size of their community. All of these factors led Mexican Americans to reject this term and begin to call themselves 'Chicanos'. This was the beginning of the Chicano civil rights movement.

Chicano nationalism

The first stage of the movement was an assertion of Chicano national pride and identity. In the mid-1960s, Reies Tijerina launched a legal campaign based on a treaty between the USA and Mexico in 1848 to return large areas of land in New Mexico to Chicanos. The campaign was defeated by a combination of legal action and intimidation, resulting in Tijerina launching a raid on a court house in New Mexico. Tijerina's action failed but he did succeed in highlighting the issue of the state of Chicanos in the USA. His actions also appealed to young Chicanos, giving them a sense of pride and identity.

Rodolfo 'Corky' Gonzales had a similar effect. He founded the Crusade for Justice in Denver in 1966, which campaigned for better treatment for Chicanos. He was part of the Poor People's Campaign, which Martin Luther King had established to protest about poverty and discrimination generally in the USA, not just on behalf of Black people. Gonzales led Chicano representatives from the south-western USA in the Poor People's March on Washington in 1968. He linked issues of race, poverty, discrimination and the Vietnam War, and was an inspiration to many young Chicanos to protest against the injustices they faced. He provided active help and support to Chicano high-school students in their protests in 1968.

Cesar Chavez

One of the most high-profile Chicano campaigns was led by Cesar Chavez. He was co-founder of the National Farm Workers Association, which later became the United Farm Workers (UFW). In 1966, he led a strike by California grape pickers for higher wages and safer working conditions. Chavez believed passionately in non-violent action and went on a hunger strike himself. The UFW called for a national boycott of grapes by the American public, and it was common to see car bumper stickers saying 'No Grapes'. The strike dragged on for five years, but it attracted national attention and led to an investigation by a Senate subcommittee.

Chavez gained the support of Senator Robert Kennedy, and in the early 1970s most of the farm owners signed bargaining agreements with the labourers for better wages. In 1966 and 1967, Chavez's activities inspired similar actions in Texas, Wisconsin and Ohio. These were important achievements, although Chicanos generally remained one of the poorest and most discriminated-against sections of US society.

Source 2 Police arrest a Chicano demonstrator, 1971. ▼

High-school walk-outs

The way to integrate and achieve in US society was through education and qualifications, and the Chicanos were very aware of this. However, very few Chicanos went on to college after high school. In fact, their schools were plagued by a high dropout rate. They were also segregated from white students, suffered crumbling buildings, lacked Mexican American teachers and studied a curriculum that left young Chicanos feeling like outsiders in their own country.

In March 1968, student activists organised a mass walk-out of Chicano students from high schools in eastern Los Angeles. The protest brought some 20,000 teenagers on to the streets of the city to protest. Newspaper and television coverage of the incident was high, and Robert Kennedy came to talk to the student leaders. This action was also a success in that many of the student leaders went on to become successful activists helping other Chicanos. However, the walk-outs failed to achieve their aim. There were violent clashes as the school boards called in the police to force the students back to school and it resulted in no substantial changes to educational conditions for Chicanos. There were further walk-outs in 1971, 1972 and 1974, but many of the complaints that inspired the protests of 1968 can still be heard today.

Source 3 Cesar Chavez, explaining his views on action in the 1960s.

It is not good enough to know why we are oppressed and by whom. We must join the struggle for what is right and just. Jesus does not promise that it will be an easy way to live life and His own life certainly points in a hard direction; but it does promise that we will be 'satisfied' (not stuffed; but satisfied). He promises that by giving life we will find life – full, meaningful life as God meant it. Until the chance for political participation is there, we who are poor will continue to attack the soft part of the American system – its economic structure. We will build power through boycotts, strikes, new unions – whatever techniques we can develop. These attacks on the status quo will come, not because we hate, but because we know America can construct a humane society for all its citizens – and that if it does not, there will be chaos. Those who are willing to sacrifice and be of service have very little difficulty with people. They know what they are all about. People can't help but want to be near them. They help them; they work with them. That's what love is all about. It starts with your heart and radiates out.

Source 4 Chicano students protesting in front of the Denver Schools Administration Building in 1973. The protesters were locked out. ▶

1 What does Source 4 reveal about the reasons for Chicano protests in this period?

FOCUS TASK

What did the Hispanic Americans achieve in their campaign?

The Chicano civil rights movement is much less well known than the Black civil rights movement. Write a report or create a presentation on the Chicanos, comparing their movement with the Black civil rights movement. You should consider:
- aims and motives
- methods
- impact
- long-term legacy.

Add a final section indicating whether you think that the Chicano movement deserves to be overshadowed by the Black civil rights movement to such a great extent.

Traditional tribal governing systems, particularly justice systems, came under strong attack. The Bureau of Indian Affairs established tribal police forces and courts under the administrative control of its agents, the reservation superintendents and other efforts designed to erode the power and influence of Indian leaders and traditions. Everything Indian came under attack. Indian feasts, languages, certain marriage practices, dances and any practices by medicine or religious persons were all banned by the Bureau of Indian Affairs.

Source 6 American Indian Movement protesters at a rally in 1970. ▼

Case study 2: Native Americans in the 1970s

One November day in 1972, a 26-year-old Native American woman walked into the office of Dr Connie Pinkerton-Uri in Los Angeles and asked for a womb transplant because she and her husband wished to start a family. Dr Pinkerton-Uri had to explain that there was no such operation. She also enquired as to why the woman had no womb. Some years earlier, a doctor from the Indian Health Service (IHS) had been treating her for alcoholism. In the process he had given her a hysterectomy. This was not related to her treatment and the IHS doctor had told her the process was reversible. The Native American woman was completely devastated and left the doctor's office in tears.

In many ways, this story sums up the grievances that Native Americans had in the early 1970s. Ever since their defeat by the emerging USA in the 1800s, most Native Americans had been forced to live on RESERVATIONS. Here their opportunities were limited. There were few decent jobs and education was poor. Throughout the twentieth century conditions for Native Americans got worse, and by the 1950s they had some of the highest rates of alcoholism, mental-health problems, economic deprivation, illiteracy and lack of opportunity of any racial group in the USA. This was partly the result and partly the cause of the US government's policy of trying to assimilate Native Americans into mainstream US society.

This policy began unofficially in the 1870s and it became official in the 1920s under the government's Bureau of Indian Affairs (BIA). By the 1950s it had had a devastating effect on Native American people. Their traditions and cultures were under attack. They were often denied the full value of resources such as timber or minerals that were taken from their lands by big corporations. Even their existence was under threat – the example of sterilisation above was not unusual. Native American organisations claimed that the IHS sterilised around 25 per cent of Native American women of child-bearing age during the 1970s.

One of the reasons for the sterilisation policy was that after the Second World War the Native American birth rate rose. By 1980, there were nearly 1 million Native Americans. Many began to migrate to US towns and cities in search of opportunities under a government programme designed to help. Here they met the same discrimination and problems as other ethnic minority groups in the USA and around one-third of all those who relocated eventually returned to their tribal homelands. Some of those who remained did flourish in the urban environment and gained an education. Many of these Native Americans began to organise themselves to protest about the hardships faced by their people. It was generally the younger ones who protested, partly because in the towns they were no longer constrained by the more conservative tribal elders.

Radical protest

In 1969 a young Sioux writer, Vine Deloria, published a book called *Custer Died for Your Sins*. The book attacked US policy towards Native Americans and called for an uprising of Red Power, along the same lines as the Black Power protests. In the same year, Native American demonstrators of the American Indian Movement (AIM) occupied Alcatraz Island and offered to buy it from the government for $24. The point they were making was that this was the sum that European settlers had originally paid for New York in the 1600s. More protests followed. In 1972, a Native American march on Washington ended with the protesters taking over

Source 7 An extract from the Wounded Knee information booklet, published by the AIM after the siege.

The equipment maintained by the military while in use during the siege included fifteen armored personal carriers, clothing, rifles, grenade launchers, flares, and 133,000 rounds of ammunition, for a total cost, including the use of maintenance personnel from the national guard of five states and pilot and planes for aerial photographs, of over half a million dollars.

the offices of the Bureau of Indian Affairs. Even more seriously, AIM activists occupied the trading post at Wounded Knee on 27 February 1973, claiming it on behalf of Native Americans to be run free of US government control. They chose Wounded Knee because it had been the site of an infamous massacre of Native Americans by US government forces in 1890, effectively marking the end of the struggle between Native Americans and the settlers for control of a vast area of central USA. They were protesting against discrimination generally, but they also had specific complaints:

- They accused the local BIA head agent, Dick Wilson, of mishandling federal funds which were supposed to be spent on the welfare of local Native American people.
- They accused Wilson of using the reservation police force as his own private army.
- They also wanted to draw attention to the disastrous environmental and health effects of the mining operations being carried out in the Dakota hills.

The result was a siege that lasted 71 days and resulted in two deaths. Eventually the protesters abandoned the siege, but the huge scale of the government operation attracted nationwide publicity (see Source 7). Native Americans used other tactics, too. They hired lawyers to press their claims for land ownership, claiming that in the 1800s the Native peoples had been forced or tricked into giving up their lands.

All this activity forced President Richard Nixon to act. In 1969, he appointed Louis R. Bruce (a Mohawk-Sioux) as Commissioner for Indian Affairs. Nixon returned 48,000 acres of sacred tribal lands to the Taos Pueblo Indians. Further measures followed in the 1970s, including the Indian Child Welfare Act 1974 (to prevent government agencies taking children away from Native American territories to be brought up elsewhere) and the Indian Self Determination Act 1975. This act effectively ended the US policy of trying to assimilate Native Americans and guaranteed that they would be free to govern themselves while still receiving aid from the US government.

Source 8 A US government armoured vehicle at Wounded Knee, 1973. ▲

FOCUS TASK

What were the issues faced by Native Americans in the 1970s?

The year is 2013. You have been asked to create a podcast to be broadcast on the 40th anniversary of the takeover of Wounded Knee in February 1973. Your podcast needs to explain why this event is significant. Your podcast is limited to two minutes. It should summarise:

- why Native Americans were protesting in the early 1970s
- how their situation compared with the situation of other ethnic minorities
- why the protest of the 1970s was significant. You could emphasise its symbolic significance (why Wounded Knee was such an important site) or its practical significance in the Native American campaign for civil rights.

---

1 Why do you think the AIM published the information in Source 7?
2 How reliable do you think Source 7 is as a source of information about events at Wounded Knee in 1973?
3 How does Source 8 help you decide how far you think Source 7 is reliable?

Case study 3: **The women's movement**

One of the most important protest movements of the 1960s and 1970s was the women's movement, which aimed to win equal rights for women. Since the Second World War, women's role had been changing. Such change was resisted by conservative Americans, who thought it was women's job to keep the home and bring up a happy family, and a man's role to work. But by the 1960s, that view was clearly out of date. It was being undermined by two trends.

Trend 1: More women workers

The Second World War had increased the number of working women. That trend continued after the war.
- In 1940 women made up 19 per cent of the workforce.
- In 1950 women made up 28.8 per cent of the workforce.
- In 1960 women made up almost half of the workforce.

In 1960, Eleanor Roosevelt, the widow of President Franklin Roosevelt, pressured President Kennedy to set up a commission on the status of women and particularly on their status at work. It reported in 1963. Women were almost half of the workforce, yet:
- 95 per cent of company managers were men.
- 88 per cent of technical workers were men.
- Only 4 per cent of lawyers and 7 per cent of doctors were women.
- Women earned around 50–60 per cent of the wages of men, even for the same work.
- Work for women was overwhelmingly low paid, part time and low level with no responsibility.
- Women could still be dismissed when they married.

> **Source 9** Congresswoman Martha Griffiths asked the directors of National Airlines about its policy on female flight attendants, who were fired when they married or reached the age of 32.
>
> *You are asking that a stewardess be young, attractive and single. What are you running, an airline or a whorehouse?*

Trend 2: Changed expectations

After the Second World War, many women had rushed to get married and have children. Fifteen years later, a lot of these women were extremely disillusioned. In 1963, Betty Friedan described the problem in her influential million-copy best-seller, *The Feminine Mystique*. The 'feminine mystique' was her term for the set of ideas that said that women's happiness came from total involvement in their role as wives and mothers. Friedan said that married women must be helped to continue in paid employment, if they were not to get bored, frustrated and de-skilled. Friedan asked hundreds of college-educated women what they wished they had done differently since graduating in the 1940s. She found a generation of educated and capable women who felt like domestic servants – there simply to meet the needs of their families, with little chance to develop their own careers or expand their horizons. They felt undervalued and depressed.

> **Source 10** From *The Feminine Mystique* by Betty Friedan, 1963. Friedan called women's deep sense of dissatisfaction with their traditional role 'the problem that had no name'.
>
> *As the American woman made beds, shopped for groceries, matched slipcover material, ate peanut butter sandwiches with her children, chauffered Cub Scouts and Brownies, lay beside her husband at night, she was afraid to ask even of herself the question: 'Is this all?'*

Source 12 Feminist campaigner Betty Friedan, president of the National Organization for Women, talks to reporters in the lobby of New York State Assembly. ▲

Source 11 US author and journalist Anna Quindlen's introduction to a new (2002) edition of Betty Friedan's *The Feminine Mystique*.

Betty Friedan's book 'The Feminine Mystique' changed my life and that of millions of other women who became engaged in the women's movement and jettisoned empty hours of endless housework and found work, and meaning, outside of raising their children and feeding their husbands. Friedan's argument was that women had been coaxed into selling out their intellect and their ambitions for the paltry price of a new washing machine.

The women's movement

These trends led to what was called the women's movement. This was not a single organisation; there were thousands of different groups, all with different angles but with similar aims – to raise the status of women and end discrimination against women in all areas of life. Following the Status Commission's report in 1963, the government passed the Equal Pay Act. Equally important was the Civil Rights Act of 1964, which outlawed discrimination against women. However, women's groups felt these acts were not being fully implemented, so Betty Friedan founded the National Organization for Women (NOW) in 1966.

NOW

By the early 1970s, NOW had 40,000 members. It co-operated with a wide range of other women's movements, such as the National Women's Caucus, the Women's Campaign Fund, the North American Indian Women's Association and the National Black Feminist Organization. NOW learned some tactics from the civil rights movement and organised demonstrations in the streets of American cities. It also challenged discrimination in the courts. In a series of cases between 1966 and 1971, NOW secured $30 million in back pay owed to women who had not been paid wages equal to those of men. In 1972 the Supreme Court ruled that the US Constitution did give men and women equal rights.

Source 13 Journalist and feminist campaigner Gloria Steinem, speaking in a TV interview in 2014.

The predominant reaction to the women's movement at first was ridicule. It took a long time for us to be taken seriously enough to be opposed.

Source 14 An extract from a talk on the early days of the women's movement, given in 1971 by Jo Freeman. Freeman was a civil rights activist, feminist campaigner and political writer.

While few were students, all were under 30 and had received their political education as participants in the student movements of the last decade. Many came direct from ... civil rights organisations where they had been shunted into traditional roles and faced with the self-evident contradiction of working in a 'freedom movement' but not being very free. In 1964, Stokely Carmichael, later chairman of SNCC, made his infamous remark that 'The only position for women in SNCC is lying down.'

ACTIVITY

Write sentences or draw a diagram to show how each of the following factors helped create the women's movement:
- the Second World War
- the struggle for Black civil rights
- actions of individuals
- availability of education
- opportunities to work.

Include the evidence on the next three pages in your sentences or chart.

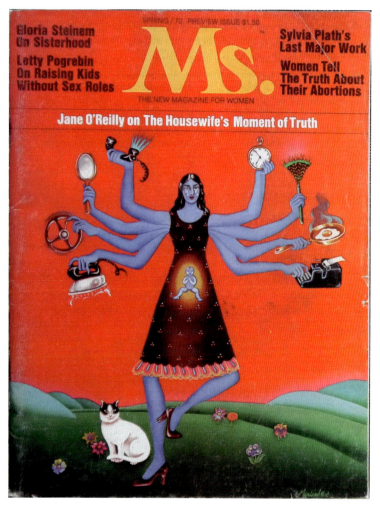

Source 15 A front cover of *Ms* magazine. This was set up by Gloria Steinem (see Source 16) and other feminists and was first published in January 1972. It was very popular and sold in large numbers, particularly in the early 1970s. ▲

Women's Lib

NOW was at one end of a broad spectrum of women's movements. Friedan, for example, was a feminist but she still believed in traditional family values and marriage. NOW used conventional methods, such as political pressure and court cases. At the other end of the spectrum were younger feminists with more radical objectives and different methods to achieve them. They became known as the Women's Liberation movement (or Women's Lib).

Feminists ran 'consciousness-raising' groups, where women could talk about their lives in depth and discuss how to challenge discrimination. They said that 'the personal was political' – everything you did in your personal life could affect the way people treated all women. For example, it was an act of protest against male supremacy to go out without make-up. It was like saying, 'Look at me – I don't care if you think I am pretty or not.' Some of the most radical members of Women's Lib were lesbians who regarded men as surplus to requirements. One saying went: 'A woman without a man is like a fish without a bicycle.'

Some groups hit the headlines. In 1968, radical women picketed the Miss World beauty contest in Atlantic City. They said that the contest treated women like objects not people. To make their point, they crowned a sheep as Miss World. Demonstrations such as this raised the profile of the feminist movement and the media loved it. However, some critics felt that it did not help its cause because the protests were not taken seriously.

Source 16 An address to the women of America in 1971 by Gloria Steinem, who became the leader of what was known as 'second-wave feminism'.

This is no simple reform. It really is a revolution. Sex and race, because they are easy, visible differences, have been the primary ways of organising human beings into superior and inferior groups, and into the cheap labour on which this system still depends. We are talking about a society in which there will be no roles other than those chosen, or those earned. We are really talking about humanism.

Source 17 Flo Kennedy, speaking in the 1970s. Kennedy was both a leader of the civil rights movement and a leading feminist.

As a Black woman when she applied to law school she was refused and was told this was not because she was Black but a woman. She threatened legal action and was enrolled and was the only Black woman on the course – alongside seven White women. It's interesting to speculate how it developed that in two of the most anti-feminist institutions, the church and the law court, the men are wearing the dresses!

ACTIVITY

Read Sources 16–18. These three speakers emerged as significant leaders of the women's movement. Work in threes. Choose one woman each: Gloria Steinem, Bella Abzug or Flo Kennedy, and use the internet to find out more about her and to write a Profile in the style of the Profiles on page 301.

Source 18 Statements by Bella Abzug, US congresswoman and feminist leader, in the 1970s.

a) We are coming down from our pedestal and up from the laundry room. We want an equal share in government and we mean to get it.

b) A woman's place is in the house! The House of Representatives!

Roe vs Wade – the right to abortion

One of the most important campaigns for radical feminists was the campaign to legalise abortion. This procedure was illegal in the USA but feminists believed that the law discriminated against women. They said they should not be forced to bear a child they did not want. They said that a woman had the right to choose what happened to her body and so should have the right to have an abortion if she wished.

The struggle over abortion began in the early 1960s. A young medical technician, Estelle Griswold, challenged the anti-abortion laws in her home state of Connecticut. It was not only abortion that was illegal in there. Contraceptive devices were also illegal and even giving information about contraception was against the law. Griswold's lawyers challenged Connecticut's laws. They handled their case cleverly. They did not argue directly against the abortion laws; instead they claimed that these laws were an illegal restriction on the privacy of ordinary Americans. The right to privacy was contained in the 14th Amendment to the US Constitution. The case went all the way to the Supreme Court. In 1965, the Supreme Court judges ruled 7–2 in favour of Griswold.

1   Study Sources 20 and 21. In your view, where have the largest changes taken place?

2   In what areas have the fewest changes taken place?

3   Do these sources support the view that there was little change in the role of women in the USA in this period?

Source 19 Gloria Steinem, speaking in 2014.

I used to hand my stories to my editor and then I would be told I could go to a hotel room with him for the afternoon or mail his letters. Needless to say I mailed his letters. That did not make me a feminist. I thought that kind of thing was normal and you had to put up with it. I don't think I understood the need for a women's movement until I went to cover an abortion hearing. I had had an abortion when I first graduated from college and had never told anyone. I listened to women testify about all they had to go through – the dangers, the injuries, the infection and the humiliation you had to endure to get an illegal abortion. I began to understand that my experience was not just me but an almost universal female experience and that meant that only if you got together with other women was it going to be changed in any way.

Source 20 A graph showing the reported numbers of abortions 1972–90. ▼

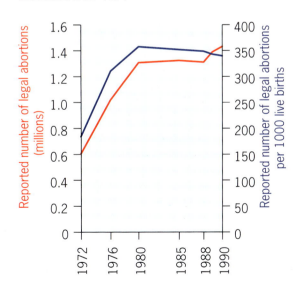

Source 21 A graph showing the proportion of women in the workforce in selected occupations in the USA. ▼

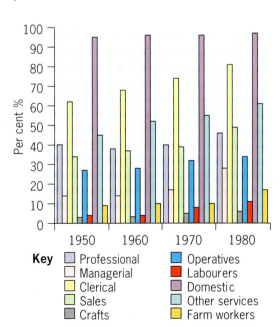

Opposition to the women's movement

At a time when attacking communists had gone out of fashion, many people on the political right enjoyed attacking the extremes of feminism. This may explain the success of some of the anti-feminist movements that also arose in this period. The most high-profile was STOP ERA, led by Phyllis Schlafly. ERA stood for the Equal Rights Amendment, which was a proposal to amend the US Constitution specifically to outlaw sex discrimination. In the reforming climate of the 1960s, Congress was in favour of ERA, and so was 63 per cent of the population. However, Phyllis Schlafly led a successful campaign to prevent it becoming law. She argued that feminists devalued the woman's role by making it equal with a man's, and that they denied the rights of the unborn child by their support for abortion. She compared the feminist woman's complaints with the 'positive' woman's approach (see Source 22).

The Equal Rights Amendment became bogged down in Congress as a result of Schlafly's campaign. The measure was finally defeated by three votes in 1982. Schlafly was helped by the fact that by 1980 people were turning away from radicalism once again. The anti-abortion movement was growing stronger. Economic problems for poor women were getting worse, not better – feminism did not seem to be relevant to their lives. Even mainstream feminists were prepared to accept that women had their own values and that equal rights might be a false objective.

FOCUS TASK

A What methods did American women use to achieve equality?

1 Below are the methods of campaigning used by Black civil rights activists:
 – court case/legal challenge
 – non-violent direct action
 – empowering ordinary people
 – marches and demonstrations
 – violent protest.
  a Which of these were also used by feminists? Give examples.
  b Which do you think was most important for the Women's Liberation movement?

B What did the women's movement achieve?

2 Imagine you work for *Ms* magazine. You are writing an article for the January 1975 edition. The theme is 'How far have we come?' Your aim is to explain the main achievements of the last ten years. You will need to plan it carefully as you have a limit of 300 words and two images.

Source 23 A fake film poster prepared by the feminist group Guerilla Girls in 2001. ▼

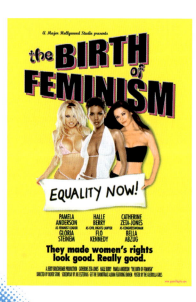

ACTIVITY

Study Source 23. This poster was made by a group of feminists in 2001 to satirise the attitudes of the film industry to women and to the women's movement in particular. You can find their reasons for doing this on the internet. This activity is in two stages:

1 Discussion:
  a What is this poster saying about the way that the women's movement is seen in the twenty-first century?
  b Choose one of these words to describe this poster and explain your choice (or choose another word of your own): rude; clever; demeaning.
  c What would be the reaction of Gloria Steinem, Flo Kennedy or Bella Abzug to this poster (see Sources 16–18)?
2 Your interpretation:
  Now get serious! Create or describe your own film poster that sums up the origins and methods of the women's movement.

Case study 4: Gay rights

The Stonewall riots 1969

In the early hours of 28 June 1969, a police raid took place on the Stonewall Inn in Greenwich Village, Manhattan. The bar was said to be owned by the Mafia and so the police watched it carefully. It was downmarket, unlicensed and had only the most basic facilities. However, Stonewall was one of the few places where gay people could gather, socialise, listen to music and generally be themselves. This was another reason why the bar was raided. Homosexual activity was illegal in all but one of the states of the USA, and could result in a prison sentence of up to 20 years. At this time, homosexuality was classified as a psychological illness and was treated with electroshock therapy.

New York had by far the largest gay community in the USA. Despite this – or perhaps because of it – the city authorities were aggressively anti-gay. The New York Police Department (NYPD) had its own vice squad and used surveillance, informers and even undercover police to trap gay men and women. By 1966, the police were arresting over 100 gay men a week. It must have felt very similar to the McCarthy witch hunts for many gay New Yorkers. There was fear, of course, but also great resentment that they could not simply live their lives.

There had been raids on the Stonewall before, but they usually ended peacefully. The bar would close for a short while and a few arrests would be made. But on this occasion it was different. Some of the Stonewall regulars resisted arrest and the police quickly lost control of the situation. A crowd gathered on the street and the atmosphere soon became ugly. Police riot officers wearing helmets and armed with nightsticks descended on the scene. The violent protests and demonstrations that erupted that night continued for almost a week.

Gay Liberation Front and the Gay Activists Alliance

The Stonewall riots are widely regarded as a turning point in the campaign for gay rights. They galvanised gay Americans into action. Within six months of the riots, three gay newspapers had been started. The newspapers – *Gay!*, *Gay Power* and *Come Out* – had a circulation of around 20,000–25,000. Soon after the riots, the Gay Liberation Front was also formed. Other campaigning groups started up, notably the Gay Activists Alliance (GAA). The GAA focused exclusively on gay issues and was a well-organised and well-run campaigning machine.

Despite these developments, the police continued to raid gay establishments. In March 1970, a gay bar called the Snake Pit was raided. Around 170 people were arrested and one young man was killed trying to escape by jumping from a window. The GAA used this incident to increase its campaigns against raids, gaining the backing of local congressman Ed Koch. After a huge amount of determined campaigning, GLF activists persuaded the American Psychiatric Association to stop classifying homosexuality as a psychological disorder.

Source 24 Historian William Eskridge, speaking in a TV documentary in 2011.

It was a nightmare for the lesbian or gay man who was arrested and caught up in the juggernaut but it was also a nightmare for the lesbians or gay men who lived in the closet. This produced an enormous amount of anger within the lesbian and gay community in New York City. Eventually something was bound to blow.

Source 25 Gay rights marchers, 1970. ▼

Source 26 Gay activist Frank Kameny, speaking in the late 1970s.

By the time of Stonewall, we had fifty to sixty gay groups in the country. A year later there was at least fifteen hundred. By two years later, to the extent that a count could be made, it was twenty-five hundred.

Gay Pride

A year after the riots, the first Gay Pride marches took place in New York and Los Angeles. These soon became a regular fixture and were replicated in many other cities.

> 1   What comparisons are being made in Sources 27 and 29?
> 2   What comparisons might be made with other campaign groups?

Source 28 Historian Lillian Faderman, writing in 2015.

The Stonewall Rebellion was crucial because it sounded the rally for that movement. It became an emblem of gay and lesbian power. By calling on the dramatic tactic of violent protest that was being used by other oppressed groups, the events at the Stonewall implied that homosexuals had as much reason to be disaffected as they.

Source 30 Joan Nestle, co-founder of the Lesbian Herstory Archives, 1974.

I certainly don't see gay and lesbian history starting with Stonewall ... and I don't see resistance starting with Stonewall. What I do see is a historical coming together of forces, and the sixties changed how human beings endured things in this society and what they refused to endure. ... Certainly something special happened on that night in 1969, and we've made it more special in our need to have what I call a point of origin ... it's more complex than saying that it all started with Stonewall.

Source 31 Mario Savio, a Berkeley student radical in the 1960s. Berkeley University, California, was one of the centres of student radicalism.

There is a time when the operation of the machine becomes so odious, makes you so sick at heart, that you can't take part; you can't even passively take part and you've got to put your bodies upon the gears and upon the wheels, upon the levers, upon all the apparatus and you've got to make it stop.

Source 27 Historian Nicholas Edsall, writing in 2003.

Stonewall has been compared to any number of acts of radical protest and defiance in American history from the Boston Tea Party on. But the best and certainly a more nearly contemporary analogy is with Rosa Parks' refusal to move to the back of the bus in Montgomery, Alabama, in December 1955, which sparked the modern civil rights movement. Within months after Stonewall radical gay liberation groups and newsletters sprang up in cities and on college campuses across America and then across all of northern Europe as well.

Source 29 Historians Dudley Clendinen and Adam Nagourney, writing in 2001.

Before the rebellion at the Stonewall Inn, homosexuals were, as a secret legion of people, known of but discounted, ignored, laughed at or despised. And like the holders of a secret, they had an advantage which was a disadvantage, too, and which was true of no other minority group in the United States. They were invisible. Unlike African Americans, women, Native Americans, Jews, the Irish, Italians, Asians, Hispanics, or any other cultural group which struggled for respect and equal rights, homosexuals had no physical or cultural markings, no language or dialect which could identify them to each other, or to anyone else. ... But that night, for the first time, the usual acquiescence turned into violent resistance. ... From that night the lives of millions of gay men and lesbians, and the attitude toward them of the larger culture in which they lived, began to change rapidly. People began to appear in public as homosexuals, demanding respect.

FOCUS TASK

Why did the Stonewall riots have such an impact?

Study the information and sources on these pages. You have seen examples in this chapter of how significant people and places have been remembered by memorials and monuments. Write a short report for the city of New York, explaining why you think the Stonewall Inn should be made into a monument.

Trying to change the USA

The student movement

Although the various groups you have examined in this chapter were all fighting their own causes, they also shared a vision – to make the USA a better, fairer place. This vision meant different things to different people. One of the biggest areas in which it differed was between the younger and the older generation of mostly white, middle-class Americans.

Getting involved: student radicalism

Many different groups were involved in student protests. One of the main organisations was Students for a Democratic Society. This was set up in 1959 with the aim of obtaining for students more say in how their courses and universities were run. Soon there were 150 colleges involved. This number rose to 400, with 100,000 members, by the end of the 1960s.

Student movements were not isolated from other protest movements. Students were heavily involved in the Black civil rights campaign and also the women's movement. The civil rights movement was particularly influential. Idealistic young students had been appalled at the injustices experienced by Black people.

In 1964, radical students in many different universities organised rallies and marches to support the civil rights campaign. They tried to expose racism in their own colleges. Some universities tried to ban these protests but students responded with a free-speech campaign to demand the right to protest. This was not a small minority of students: up to half of Berkeley's 27,500 students were engaged in the free speech movement.

Across the USA there were demonstrations on campuses as students rejected the values and the society that their parents had created. Society was often referred to as 'the system' or 'the machine' (see Source 31). Any individual or group whom students saw as victims of the machine could count on the support of student groups and could expect to see demonstrations on their behalf. Student groups backed campaigns for nuclear disarmament and criticised US involvement in South America. They supported the Black civil rights movement, taking part in marches and freedom rides (see page 290).

Source 32 Student protesters stage a sit-in at Columbia University, New York, April 1968. ▲

Source 33 From the song 'I Feel Like I'm Fixin' to Die' by Country Joe and the Fish.

And it's one, two, three, what are we fighting for?
Don't ask me I don't give a damn.
Next stop is Vietnam
And it's five, six, seven, open up the pearly gates
Well I ain't got time to wonder why.
We all gonna die.

The Vietnam War

Critics said that students simply adopted any radical cause, whether or not they really understood its motives and aims. However, one issue above all others united student protest – the Vietnam War. Half a million young Americans were fighting in the war, and the conflict was very unpopular with students. Anti-war protests reached their height in 1968–70 (see page 87). In the first half of 1968, there were over 100 demonstrations against the Vietnam War, involving 40,000 students. Frequently, the protests would involve burning the American flag – a criminal offence in the USA and a powerful symbol of the students' rejection of American values.

Anti-war demonstrations often ended in violent clashes with the police. At Berkeley, Yale and Stanford universities, bombs were set off. The worst incident by far came in 1970. At Kent State University in Ohio, students organised a demonstration against President Nixon's decision to invade Vietnam's neighbour, Cambodia. Panicked National Guard troopers opened fire on the demonstrators. Four students were killed and 11 others were injured. The press in the USA and abroad were horrified. Some 400 colleges were closed as 2 million students went on strike in protest at the action.

Source 34 The Kent State University demonstrations in Ohio, 4 May 1970. ▶

3 Explain why the violence at Kent State was such an important event.

Dropping out: the hippy movement

Some young people took up an entirely different kind of protest. They 'dropped out' and became hippies. They did not work or study. They grew their hair long and travelled around the country in buses and vans, which they decorated with flowers or psychedelic designs. They talked about peace and love. They experimented with sex and drugs and went to huge open-air concerts to listen to musicians like Bob Dylan.

For many Americans, this was a more deeply disturbing form of protest than student radicalism. The parents of these hippies were ordinary middle-class American families. They had been brought up to believe in the virtues of working hard in school and then working hard at a career to earn more money, buy a bigger house or car. They were also the generation that had fought to preserve American ideals of democracy in the Second World War and the Korean War. Now their children were rejecting their lifestyles. They were refusing to join the army and fight in Vietnam. In many ways, people thought that the USA was in crisis.

Links

It is easy to see history in isolated patches because it is easiest to study it that way. However, movements in history are often linked to one another. The protest movements of the 1960s are a good example. People were not members of just one group. A radical young student might at different times have taken part in:

- the civil rights freedom rides (see page 290)
- a feminist consciousness-raising group (see page 318)
- a free speech sit-in
- an anti-Vietnam march (see page 87)
- the Woodstock Festival.

Source 35 Hippies at the Woodstock Festival, 1968. Woodstock, in New York state, attracted half a million young Americans. It was a rock festival, but it was also a celebration of an 'alternative' drop-out lifestyle mixed with a strong element of anti-war protest. ▼

ACTIVITY

In 1966, one right-wing politician described the student protest movement as all about 'sex, drugs and treason'. Write your own phrase to sum up the student movement. It should be no more than five words long, but you should be able to explain fully why you think your phrase is effective.

PROFILE

John F. Kennedy (1917–63)

- Nickname JFK.
- Born 29 May 1917 into a wealthy and influential Massachusetts family of Irish descent.
- During the Second World War he commanded a torpedo boat.
- After the war, he became a Democratic congressman in 1947, then in 1952 he was elected to the US Senate.
- In 1953 he wrote an award-winning book called *Profiles in Courage*, about US politicians who risked their careers to stand up for things they believed in.
- In 1960 the Democrats chose him to run for president, with Lyndon Johnson as his vice-president.
- Kennedy narrowly defeated Republican Richard Nixon and was sworn in as president in January 1961.
- Kennedy's short time as president was dominated by Cold War tensions with the USSR (see Topic 2.2).
- He was assassinated in November 1963, while driving in an open car through Dallas, Texas.

Presidents and poverty

So far we have looked mostly at campaigners in this chapter. We should remember that politicians also wanted to improve the USA. Many wanted to help tackle the problem of poverty. We are now going to examine the track records of three presidents on this issue.

John F. Kennedy 1961–63

Kennedy narrowly beat Republican Richard Nixon in the election of November 1960 to become the youngest elected US president. He emphasised youth and idealism, and talked of the USA being at the edge of a 'New Frontier'. He wanted to make the country a better, fairer place for all Americans and to carry its ideals and messages around the world. He asked people to join him in being 'new frontiersmen'. In his inaugural speech, he urged them to 'ask not what your country can do for you, ask what you can do for your country'. He also asked the nations of the world to join together to fight what he called 'the common enemies of man: tyranny, poverty, disease, and war itself'. The great 'what if' in Kennedy's case is whether he would have achieved these aims if he had not been assassinated in November 1963.

What was the New Frontier?

Kennedy's New Frontier might sound like just a political slogan and to begin with that was true. Kennedy needed a powerful 'big idea' to unite the American people behind him after a desperately close election. He wanted them to sense they were on the edge of something new and exciting. However, the New Frontier developed into a series of reforms designed to improve the USA and the lives of its people.

The most controversial aspects of his New Frontier were social reforms to help poor Americans. Kennedy hoped to make the USA a fairer society by giving equal civil rights to all Blacks, and by helping people to better themselves. He knew many Americans were against these reforms, so the title was meant to make Americans feel involved and keen to a help other people, so that they would give his proposed social legislation a smoother ride! As part of his New Frontier he created the 'Peace Corps'. This was an organisation that sent young American volunteers to less economically developed countries to work as doctors, teachers, technical experts, etc. This greatly appealed to idealistic young Americans.

Despite his strong reputation there was another side to Kennedy's presidency. There were always claims about his possible links with leaders of organised crime and also about his many extramarital affairs.

Poverty
Aim: to tackle deprivation and ensure poor Americans had the opportunity to help themselves.

Achievements
- Kennedy increased the minimum wage.
- Under his Area Redevelopment Act, poor communities could get loans, grants or advice from the government to start new businesses or build infrastructure (roads, telephone lines, etc.).
- Under his Housing Act, people in run-down inner-city areas could get loans to improve their housing; or local authorities could get money to clear slums.
- Under his Social Security Act, more money was available for payments to the elderly and unemployed.
- His Manpower Development and Training Act retrained the unemployed.

But ...
- The minimum wage only helped those who already had a job.
- The housing loans did not help the poorest people since they could not afford to take out loans.
- Slum clearance led to housing shortages in the inner cities.
- Many poor Black families from the south moved to northern cities looking for work, where they experienced poverty and racial tension.

Lyndon B. Johnson 1963–69

Lyndon Johnson and the 'great society'

Johnson became president when Kennedy was assassinated in 1963. One year later, he had to seek election in his own right. He won a sweeping victory, partly because of the American public's sympathy after Kennedy's assassination. When he came to power, he wanted to take Kennedy's work much further. In his first speech as president, he talked in terms of a 'great society' – a place where the meaning of man's life matched the marvels of man's labour. He declared 'unconditional war on poverty' and called for 'an immediate end to racial injustice'. However, unlike Kennedy, Johnson does not have a reputation as a great president. Conservatives in Congress attacked him for spending too much on welfare reform. Liberals think badly of him because he escalated US involvement in the Vietnam War. His 'great society' is largely forgotten. See if you think this is fair.

Johnson's style might have been different from Kennedy's, but the policies were not. Johnson is often contrasted with Kennedy but he believed even more strongly in social justice and tackling poverty. His 'great society' tried to bring about radical social change. It was less moral and theoretical than the New Frontier – and more practical. Johnson tackled areas that Kennedy had not been able to touch, for example 'medicare', which provided free medical care for the poor.

PROFILE

Lyndon B. Johnson (1908–73)

- Nickname LBJ.
- Born 27 August 1908 in Texas.
- He saw poverty around him as he grew up and as a teacher he came into contact with many poor immigrant children, which gave him a commitment to social reform.
- He was elected to Congress as a Democrat in 1937 and was a strong supporter of President Roosevelt's New Deal (see page 236).
- He served in the navy in the Pacific during the Second World War.
- Johnson became a senator in 1948. He led the Democrats in the Senate from 1953.
- In the 1960 election campaign he was chosen to be JFK's vice-presidential candidate. As a mature, respected, skilful congressman he was seen as the ideal balance for Kennedy's youthful idealism. It was thought that he would know how to handle Congress.
- He became president when Kennedy was assassinated in 1963 and he successfully carried through Kennedy's planned measures, cutting taxes and introducing a new civil rights bill.
- Johnson was elected president again in his own right in 1964, with the widest margin of victory ever achieved in a presidential election.
- Johnson pushed through a huge range of radical measures on medical care, education, conservation, and help for economically depressed areas.
- His domestic achievements were overshadowed by the USA's involvement in the unpopular war in Vietnam.
- In 1968, Johnson announced he would not seek re-election for the presidency.
- He died of a heart attack in January 1973.

Source 36 Johnson with his long-time friend and adviser Abe Fortas in 1965. Johnson had a very direct approach when dealing with people – friends and rivals alike. ▲

1 What can you learn about Johnson from Source 36?

Poverty

Johnson's war on poverty involved a range of measures:

- The Medical Care Act (1965) put federal funding into health care along the lines of Britain's National Health Service, but it was not as comprehensive. It funded health care for elderly people and for families on low incomes.
- Johnson increased the minimum wage from $1.25 to $1.40 per hour.
- He increased the funding to the Aid of Families with Dependent Children (AFDC) scheme. This gave financial help to 745,000 families on low incomes.
- Poorer families also received food stamps to buy groceries.
- The VISTA programme tried to create work in poor inner city areas.
- The Head Start and Upward Bound programmes tried to persuade inner city populations of the importance of education.
- The Elementary and Secondary Education Act (1965) put federal funding into improving education in poorer areas. Until this time, the USA's education system had been locally funded. This meant that poorer areas found it harder than wealthier areas to raise enough money for good schooling. This was a major innovation in government policy, designed to back up the Head Start and similar programmes.
- There was a Job Corps to help school dropouts find work.
- The Neighbourhood Youth Corps did a similar job, encouraging local youngsters to do work such as clearing graffiti or keeping parks clean.
- The Model Cities Act (1966) linked to the other inner-city employment programmes. It improved inner-city environments by clearing slums or providing parks or sports facilities. It also gave top-up payments to people on low incomes to help pay their rents.

Johnson stands down

Johnson decided not to run for president again in 1968. It was an admission of defeat. With race riots, high inflation and high unemployment, government spending out of control and the anti-Vietnam War movement at its peak, it is doubtful whether Johnson would have won the election. In the event, the Democrats lost by a landslide and the nation gave its verdict on the eight years of Democratic presidency. How far this was a rejection of the radical social reforms and how far it was a reaction to the Vietnam War is a matter of debate, but a combination of the two meant the end for Johnson.

FOCUS TASK

Comparing Kennedy and Johnson

Here are some factors that have affected the reputations of Kennedy and Johnson:
- social policy
- the civil rights movement
- leadership style
- speeches
- the nature of their deaths
- the Vietnam War.

1 For each factor explain, with examples, whether it affected each president's reputation positively or negatively.
2 Which do you think was the biggest factor in making or breaking their reputation?
3 Out of a possible score of ten what would you give to each of the presidents? Write a paragraph to explain your scores and how far you think each president deserves his reputation.

Richard Nixon (1913–94)

- Born in California in 1913.
- Established a reputation as a brilliant scholar and lawyer.
- Served as a navy lieutenant commander in the Pacific during the Second World War.
- Elected to Congress from his California district after the war. In 1950, he won a seat in the Senate. He helped in the McCarthy anti-communist witch hunts.
- In 1952, he became Eisenhower's running mate for the presidential elections, and was vice-president 1953–61.
- He was the Republican candidate in the 1960 election and was narrowly defeated by John F. Kennedy.
- He stood again in 1968 and was elected president.
- He was re-elected in 1972. However, controversy over the Watergate affair plagued him. He was about to be IMPEACHED when he resigned in 1974.

Richard Nixon 1969–74

How many times have you heard of a scandal of any kind being called 'something-gate'? The name goes back to the Watergate scandal that rocked the USA in the early 1970s, which was seen as the single greatest threat to the US Constitution in its history. The scandal started with a small revelation but gradually snowballed into a constitutional crisis. Nixon had been running a campaign of dirty tricks against his opponents, including breaking into homes and offices to bug them, and trying to subvert legal cases.

Watergate also completely overshadowed some of the other aspects of Nixon's time in power. One of these areas was social policy. Although he criticised Johnson's 'great society' programme as too big and inefficient, and claimed he believed in small government, he actually expanded government spending on welfare and cut relatively few of Johnson's programmes. Nixon passed numerous welfare reforms of his own. These included:

- National Health Insurance Partnership Program 1974 – a reform of medical insurance which aimed to bring decent health care particularly to the poorest, who could usually not afford good medical insurance. This never went forward because of Nixon's resignation.
- Supplemental Security Income (SSI), which provided a guaranteed income for elderly and disabled citizens.
- Tax reform to help the ill and disabled, tax cuts for the low paid and to encourage the unemployed into work.
- Reform of the Food Stamp programme, taking it under federal control and making food aid more accessible to the poorest.
- A 20 per cent increase in spending on social security.
- Large amounts of funding injected into training and housing through the Comprehensive Employment and Training Act (CETA) and the Housing and Community Development Act.

FOCUS TASK

Which president did the most to tackle the problem of poverty?

On page 3-7 you rated the contributions of Kennedy, Johnson and Nixon on civil rights. Do the same task again in relation to their achievements in fighting poverty.

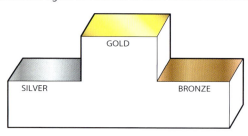

PRACTICE QUESTIONS

PRACTICE QUESTIONS

1 Describe one example of discrimination against women in the 1960s or 1970s. (2)
2 Explain why gay rights protesters became more active after 1969. (10)
3 Explain how far Native Americans and Chicanos made progress in the years 1954–64. (10)
4 'The main reason for protests in the USA in this period was economic hardship.' How far do you agree with this view? (18)

TOPIC SUMMARY

Government and dissent 1964–74

1 The success of the civil rights movement empowered many other groups to think that unfair aspects of American society could be challenged and changed.
2 In many ways Hispanic Americans faced as much discrimination and prejudice as African Americans. Rodolfo Gonzales and Cesar Chavez led non-violent protests and strikes to improve pay and working conditions for Hispanics, and succeeded in raising awareness of the discrimination they faced. They also focused on education but achieved little success in improving the quality of their schools.
3 Native Americans had also been mistreated by the US government for centuries. They focused on national identity, on preserving their traditions, languages and cultures, and on land rights. Using strategies such as occupying high-profile sites like Alcatraz and Wounded Knee they managed to force the government to end the policy of assimilation, leaving them free to govern themselves within their territories.
4 Women's rights campaigning focused around two key issues – equal treatment in the workplace and abortion. They used similar strategies to the African American Civil Rights campaigners to campaign for an Equal Rights Amendment to the constitution that would explicitly state that all aspects of the constitution (its freedoms and rights) applied equally to women as to men. This never became law. It was bogged down in political process but also faced many opponents, including many women who saw the women's movement as too extreme and anti-family.
5 Gay liberation became a national issue after the Stonewall riots, as gay people organised themselves into a national movement campaigning against discrimination for the first time.
6 Students and young people were involved in all the protests above, but they also had a particular focus on protesting against the Vietnam War. Anti-war feeling was at its height in the late 1960s because of the casualties but also because of the hypocrisy of spending billions of dollars a year fighting a war in Vietnam while doing little about poverty at home.
7 Some young people protested against American values by dropping out altogether and becoming hippies, using drugs and dressing differently.
8 The problem of poverty (economic inequality) in America united many of these protests.
9 Successive presidents tried to tackle these issues and change the USA for the better. Kennedy opened a 'New Frontier', calling on all Americans to do their bit for America; Johnson called for a 'great society', declaring war on poverty; Nixon disliked these phrases but spent an enormous amount of government money on welfare.

KEY TERMS

Make sure you understand these key terms and can use them confidently in your writing.
- boycott
- integration
- Nation of Islam
- white supremacy

ASSESSMENT FOCUS

How the non-British depth study on the USA 1945–75 will be assessed.

This section is worth 40 marks – 20 per cent of your total GCSE. The questions could be on any part of the content, so you need to know it all.

Three questions will assess:
● AO1: knowledge and understanding (total 15 marks across all questions)
● AO2: explanation and analysis (15 marks across all questions).

One question will assess:
● AO3: analyse, evaluate and use sources (10 marks in one question).

Above all, the paper is trying to assess your ability to think and work like a historian. Before you read this guidance you might want to look back at the introduction on how historians think on page 4. There, we set out some steps that historians take:
1 focus
2 ask questions
3 select
4 organise
5 fine tune

The exam questions have already chosen a focus (stage 1) and they have asked questions (stage 2). What the examiner wants from you is stages 3, 4 and 5.

Question 1

Question 1 will usually ask for a short description of an event or feature from one section of the course. It is a simple knowledge question, usually requiring some accurate description. For example:

> ● *Describe one example of protest in the period 1964–74. (2 marks)*

Advice
Select: Choose one example of protest and either describe it in more detail or describe why the government took the action. You do not need every detail.

Organise: The main thing to remember here is not to write too much.

Fine tune: Make sure that your spellings and dates are correct. Make sure that your answer is clear – in the pressure of an exam it is easy to accidentally say something you do not mean to say.

Example answer

> One example of protest in this period was the occupation of Wounded Knee by Native Americans. They occupied the trading post at Wounded Knee and declared it to be independent of the government. They were protesting about discrimination against them.

Aim of the question
This is designed to start the exam with a relatively simple, knowledge-based question. The examiner wants to see that you can select and describe important events accurately, without simply writing down everything you know.

This answer is good and would get 2 marks.

It is clear what the protest was and what the protest was about and how the Native Americans protested.

There is no need to improve this answer. The candidate could write a lot more of course but that would be a poor use of time.

Aim of the question

There will usually be at least two reasons in a question like this, and examiners want to see an explanation rather than just a description of McCarthy's actions. You can argue that one reason was more important than another or argue they were equally important – or perhaps that they were connected.

Question 2

Question 2 will usually demand more analysis and explanation than the outline in Question 1. It will ask you about the importance or impact of a factor, or how successful an organisation was. For example:

> ***Explain why McCarthy became important in the 1950s. (10 marks)***

A useful way to improve your answers is to assess them yourself. Examiners use mark schemes but you do not really need anything that complicated. Think of it like an Olympic medal ceremony. Read some of your practice answers to this question and ask yourself which of these medals your answer deserves.

The Question 2 medal ceremony

Bronze (up to 25% of marks): You list some of McCarthy's actions or events at the time but don't go any further (e.g. 'The Cold War was happening' *or* 'McCarthy held enquiries').

Silver (up to 60% of marks): You describe McCarthy's actions in greater detail (e.g. 'He claimed there were 200 communists in the state department.') but you do not explain why he became important (i.e. why anyone took any notice of him).

Gold (up to 100% of marks): You go beyond description to explain what McCarthy did and why these actions made him important (e.g. the context of the Cold War, following on from the Red Scare of the late 1940s) and why those factors helped him.

Even a Gold answer can be improved by ensuring you have:
- a clear conclusion that rounds off your argument and makes it really clear what you think the answer to the question is
- a balanced answer that shows you understand that there might be more than one view about the question, or explains how the different elements are connected
- supporting evidence – using relevant knowledge and a good range of examples to support each point you make.

Advice

Select: Focus on reasons why McCarthy became important rather than lots of detail of what he did.

Organise: The important thing is to use your knowledge in a relevant way. In this question a good way to organise your answer might be: 'McCarthy became important for a number of reasons. To begin with …. This helped him because …'

Fine tune: Make sure that your spellings and dates are correct. Make sure that your answer is clear – in the pressure of an exam it is easy to accidentally say something you do not mean to say. Above all check – have you really explained why McCarthy became important or have you just described events at the time? It is a very common error to just list events and assume you have answered the question. You need to spell out your points!

Example answer

This is a good answer – a Gold! It would probably get 8 marks.

It has a clear opening and it then really does explain why McCarthy became important, giving two reasons.

The first reason is explained very well. The second reason is sound but it is a bit lightweight. To improve this answer the candidate could explain the actions of McCarthy's committee in more detail, or his methods. This would explain why people were afraid to stand up to him.

There is nothing wrong with the factors chosen by the candidate and the examiner does not want you to cover all of them. But it would have been just as acceptable to have argued that McCarthy followed on from the work of the HUAC or that he was successful in gaining the support of many Americans.

McCarthy became important in the 1950s for a number of reasons.

Firstly, McCarthy became important because of the 'Red Scare'. There was an atmosphere of fear in the USA in the late 1940s because of the threat from the Communist USSR, which had made huge gains in territory after the Second World War. In 1949, it had developed its own atomic bomb. China was also taken over by Communists. The USA was determined to stop the spread of Communism, so McCarthy's claim that he had a list of over 200 Communists in the US government generated a lot of publicity.

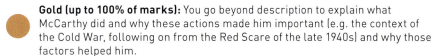

Another reason why McCarthy became important was that many people were afraid to stand up to him. McCarthy was made head of a White House committee to investigate Communist activities. Even President Eisenhower did not want to clash with McCarthy. When McCarthy accused his close friend and ally George Marshall Eisenhower did not defend Marshall.

Aim of the question

These questions ask you to show your understanding of two sources from the period you are studying by producing a clear answer and supporting that answer from the sources. Some examples of questions are shown on the following pages, but we cannot cover all types. You will find it helpful to look at the Assessment Focus for the other depth studies as well (pages 190 and 258), which give examples of the different types of questions and advice on how to tackle them.

Question 3

Question 3 requires an evaluation of sources. The question will always be worth 10 marks and it will always contain two sources. However, it can appear in two formats:

Format A: separate questions

This format asks a separate question on each source (worth 5 marks each). For example:

- Why was the source published?
- How is this source useful to historians?
- What is the viewpoint of the artist/author?
- How reliable is this source?

Format B: comparison question

This format asks you to compare two sources (10 marks). For example:

- How similar are Sources A and B?
- How far do the sources agree?
- Why do they disagree?
- Is one source more reliable than the other?
- Is one source more useful than the other?

The Question 3 source evaluation guide

Here are some rules to help you evaluate sources.

Sources are not textbooks. Do not treat them like they are.

Textbook authors use many sources and then generalise to give the overall picture. Textbooks tell you what happened. Sources tell you how individuals or groups *felt* about what happened. If a source says something different from your textbook, this does not mean it is wrong. It might be atypical and something the textbook author did not have space to cover.

Do not criticise a source because of what it does not say.

You could make this point about almost any source – a source on the USA in this period does not tell you about Germany in the 1800s. Neither does this morning's newspaper. It is not a helpful approach.

Back up your points with examples from the source.

It is amazing how often candidates fail to do this. They may write something like 'Source B is hostile to immigrants', but then fail to say what they found in Source B that led them to this conclusion.

In comparison questions, compare content first ...

... Then go on to compare purpose, attitude, context, etc.

Use comprehension to work out *what the source says* and then use inference to see *what it can tell you.*

Comprehension means understanding what the source actually says – such as an advertisement trying to sell vacuum cleaners or a newspaper article criticising immigrants. An inference builds on your comprehension – it is something not stated in the source but which can be worked out from it. For example, you might be able to look at an advertisement from the 1920s and decide that it is aimed at women. This is an inference, because the poster does not state this openly. Similarly, you might be able to infer that the writer of an article wants controls in immigration, even though they might not actually say that. Using inferences can also stop you making mistakes about bias (see right).

Use your evaluation to answer the question – not for its own sake.

Candidates often use useful tools like the five Ws (Who? Why? When? Where? What?). However, it is also common for candidates to forget to use those findings to answer the question! If you are going to use the five Ws or a similar technique, make sure the information it gives you helps support your answer, otherwise it is irrelevant.

Never dismiss a source because it is biased or unreliable. All sources are useful about something and reliable about something.

The *story in the source* might be biased or unreliable (e.g. an election poster). However, that means the *story of the source* is very useful – somebody went to the trouble of exaggerating, lying or distorting the facts in order to achieve a particular aim. We can use the source to learn about the people who created it, their aims and their attitude towards the people they are lying about. Sources will almost always reveal something about values, attitudes, fears, concerns, beliefs and reactions.

Only use contextual knowledge when it helps you answer the question.

If you have some relevant contextual knowledge that supports your answer, use it. If you just want to show the examiner you know stuff, don't!

Commenting on tone or language is not evaluation.

A comment on the tone or language of a source can be used to support a point you make about purpose, attitude or some other aspect of evaluation, but in itself is not evaluation.

Example 3A: separate question format

Source A A cartoon published in the USA in 1947. The title of the cartoon was 'It's okay – We're hunting communists'.

Study Source A. What is the message of the cartoonist? (5 marks)

The Question 3A medal ceremony (message question)

 Bronze (up to 25% of marks): You comment on details in the source (e.g. 'The car represents the HUAC.').

 Silver (up to 60% of marks): You explain one or more of the sub-messages (e.g. 'The HUAC is investigating communists.') rather than the main message.

 Gold (up to 100% of marks): You make an inference to explain the message of the cartoon (e.g. 'The HUAC is hurting innocent people.') and support your answer with extracts or details from the source.

Even a Gold medal answer can be improved by ensuring you have:
- explained the attitude of the cartoonist, not just the message of the cartoon
- included than one type of evaluation.

Advice
Select: Source questions are slightly different from other types of questions. However, most examiners will tell you that many candidates need to be more selective when tackling this type of question. If you have some relevant contextual knowledge that supports your answer, use it. If you just want to show the examiner you know stuff, don't!

Organise: By far the most important thing is to work out what you want to say before you start writing. A good way to organise answers to message questions is:

> The cartoonist is praising/criticising ... because ...
>
> We can tell this from the cartoon because ...
>
> The cartoonist was making this point at this time because ...

Fine tune: Do all the usual checking, but here it is worth making sure you have answered the question using content and then evaluation.

Example answer

The message of the cartoonist is that **the HUAC is damaging the lives of innocent people.** The HUAC investigated many cases of suspected Communists. They were in high profile areas, particularly the entertainment industry. Most of the people accused were innocent but many people had their careers ruined. The cartoon represents this by showing the HUAC car running over innocent civilians and claiming this is OK because they are hunting Communists.

Aim of the question

This question is primarily asking you to show your understanding of the content of the source but also the purpose of the source – the intended impact on the audience. This means showing you understand what changes the author was trying to bring about. These might be changes in laws, or in specific actions or in attitudes.

As always, it is a good idea to try to assess your own answer. Read your practice answers and ask yourself which of these medals your answer deserves.

Source B An extract from a newspaper article written by Martin Luther King, published while he was in prison in Birmingham, Alabama, 1963.

There can be no denying that racial injustice engulfs this community. Birmingham is probably the most segregated city in the United States. Its ugly record of police brutality is widely known, as is its treatment of Negroes in courts. There have been more unsolved bombings of Negro homes and churches in Birmingham than in any other US city. Our intention is to create a tense situation, full of crisis. We have not made a single gain in civil rights without determined legal and moral pressure.

Study Source B. Why was this source published in 1963? (5 marks)

The Question 3B medal ceremony (message question)

 **Bronze (up to 25% of marks):** You comment on the general context (e.g. 'At this time there was a lot of discrimination against African Americans.')

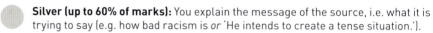 **Silver (up to 60% of marks):** You explain the message of the source, i.e. what it is trying to say (e.g. how bad racism is *or* 'He intends to create a tense situation.').

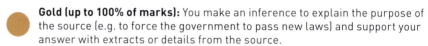 **Gold (up to 100% of marks):** You make an inference to explain the purpose of the source (e.g. to force the government to pass new laws) and support your answer with extracts or details from the source.

Even a Gold medal answer can be improved by ensuring you have:
- explained the attitude of the writer, not just the message of the article
- included more than one type of evaluation.

Advice

Select: Source questions are slightly different from other types of questions. However, most examiners will tell you that many candidates need to be more selective when tackling this type of question. If you have some relevant contextual knowledge which supports your answer, use it. If you just want to show the examiner you know stuff, don't.

Organise: By far the most important thing is to work out what you want to say before you start writing. With purpose questions a good way to organise your answer is:

> The purpose of this source was to ... [change laws/attitudes/X ...]
>
> The author tries to achieve this by ...

Fine tune: Do all the usual checking, but here it is worth making sure you have answered the question using content and then evaluation.

Example answer

> This source was published in 1963 **in order to put pressure on the government to pass a Civil Rights Act** to protect African Americans. King tries to achieve this first of all by deliberately writing from a prison cell, which he hopes will gain sympathy. He also tries to achieve his aim by pointing out the terrible discrimination faced by African Americans in Birmingham in particular. The article was part of a wider campaign for civil rights which started up with the Montgomery bus boycott in 1955.

This is a top-level answer, probably worth 5 marks.

The candidate makes a clear statement about the purpose of the source (in bold). This makes clear the intended audience (the government) and the change that King wants (a Civil Rights Act).

Notice this is more than just the message. The message is the racism in Birmingham but that is not King's purpose.

Details of the source are used well to support the answer. We have some supporting detail from the article used to support the answer. We also have contextual knowledge used in a relevant way to support the answer.

The answer does not really need improving. It is worth noting that it would have been an acceptable alternative to argue that his purpose was to stop the racism in Birmingham

Example B: Comparison format

Source C A report from Governor Otto Kerner of Illinois, who was appointed by the president to investigate the riots which took place in several American cities in 1968.

This is our basic conclusion: these were race riots, pure and simple. Our nation is moving towards two societies, one black, one white – separate and unequal. Segregation and poverty, discrimination at the hands of police and other authorities have created black ghettos and an environment unknown to any white Americans. White society is deeply implicated. White institutions created it, white institutions maintain it, and white society condones it. This deepening division is not inevitable. The movement apart can be reversed. Choice is still possible. Our principal task is to define that choice and press for a national resolution. The Civil Rights Act of 1964 was a start and no more. More measures like it are needed if all are to live equally under one flag.

Source D The reaction of President Lyndon Johnson to the riots of 1968.

It is not enough simply to decry disorder and blame those who rioted in the streets. We must also strike at the unjust conditions from which disorder largely flows. As I have said time and time again, aimless violence finds fertile ground among men living in the poverty of slums, facing their future without education or skills and with little hope of rewarding work. These ills, too, we are working to wipe out. It is these conditions we must wipe out. Civil Rights is a distraction. Our real enemy is poverty and ignorance and we must continue with our programmes to fight it.

Aim of the question
This question is designed to see what use you can make of sources – whether you understand the content and whether you can make inferences and support them.

Study Sources C and D. How similar are these two sources? (10 marks)

The Question 3B medal ceremony

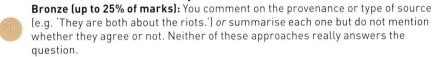 **Bronze (up to 25% of marks):** You comment on the provenance or type of source (e.g. 'They are both about the riots.') *or* summarise each one but do not mention whether they agree or not. Neither of these approaches really answers the question.

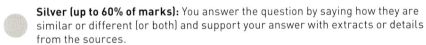 **Silver (up to 60% of marks):** You answer the question by saying how they are similar or different (or both) and support your answer with extracts or details from the sources.

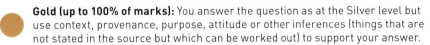 **Gold (up to 100% of marks):** You answer the question as at the Silver level but use context, provenance, purpose, attitude or other inferences (things that are not stated in the source but which can be worked out) to support your answer.

Even a Gold medal answer can be improved by ensuring you have:
- a valid conclusion
- offered more than one type of evaluation.

Advice

Focus: The focus of the question is on similarity and difference. Think through what each source is saying overall – you can even draw up a mini-plan of similarities and differences.

In some ways these sources are similar in that they say similar things …

On the other hand, they also say things which contradict each other …

We can also see that they are similar or different in terms of emphasis/attitude/purpose/audience

Select: In some ways the best advice we can give is to not select knowledge from your wardrobe! Just use your understanding of the period to make use of the sources. You might be able to use your knowledge to make comments about the purpose or context of the sources, but make sure your knowledge is supporting a point about similarity or difference. Stay away from comments about bias unless you can show how the bias is relevant.

Organise: By far the most important thing is to work out what you want to say before you start writing. A good structure for this questions is shown on the left.

Fine tune: Do all the usual checking, but here it is worth making sure you have answered the question using content and then evaluation.

Aim of the question
Examiners want to see a balanced answer. You can still state your view strongly and clearly.

Example answer

In some ways these sources are similar in that they say similar things. Both sources agree that one of the causes of the riots was poverty. Source C mentions poverty. So does Source D, along with lack of education.

On the other hand, they also say things which contradict each other. Source C says they were race riots. Source C lists many different ways in which race and discrimination was really the issue. It blames white institutions and white people generally. In contrast Source D really only focuses on poverty and ignorance and ignores discrimination.

The two sources are very different in terms of their **purpose**. Source C really wants to see one or more **new Civil Rights Acts**. It claims the 1964 Act was just a start. This is certainly true. We can tell this because in 1968 Black Power leaders like Malcolm X and the Black Panthers were protesting about discrimination. In contrast Johnson in Source D does not want to pursue Civil Rights. **He is more interested in his great society programme** which aimed to improve health care and fight poverty.

Question 4

Question 4 is effectively a traditional essay-style question. For example:

'The main reasons for protest in the period 1964–74 were economic.' How far do you agree? You should consider a range of possible reasons. (18 marks)

The Question 4 medal ceremony

Bronze (up to 25% of marks): You describe events during the period (e.g. government actions) without addressing the question.

Silver (up to 60% of marks): You argue yes or no and support your argument by describing example(s) of support or opposition.

Gold (up to 100% of marks): You write a balanced answer which explains that there is evidence to support both a 'yes' and a 'no' argument. The answer may support one side or the other but must acknowledge that there is an alternative view even if you think it is wrong.

Even a Gold answer can be improved by ensuring you have:
- a clear conclusion that rounds off your argument and makes it really clear what you think the answer to the question is.
- a balanced answer that shows you understand that there might be more than one view about the question or explains how the different elements are connected.
- supporting evidence and a good range of examples to support the points you make.

Advice
Select: First of all, you *do not* need to cover every protest movement in this period. You should probably cover two or three. Focus on the reasons for particular protests – they might be based on economic reasons or other reasons (or both). A common error is to describe protests and forget about the reasons for them. It may seem obvious to you but examiners cannot read your mind. They will not credit something unless you spell it out in your answer.

Organise: Take one factor and explain it in a paragraph of its own.

Fine tune: Make sure that your spellings and dates are correct. Make sure that your answer is clear – in the pressure of an exam it is is easy to accidentally say something you don't mean to say. In this question examiners like you to say which side of the argument you support.

Example answer

It is true that economic factors played a large role in protests in this period. They played a direct role in that economic problems in this period tended to hit the poor the hardest. So, for example, when the Vietnam War began to damage the American economy it was often African Americans and other minorities who were worst affected. This is why Martin Luther King was beginning to shift the focus of his campaigning on to economic affairs in the later 1960s before he was murdered. The Watts riots of 1965 in Los Angeles were also sparked by poverty.

However, other protests in this period had a more political focus. For example, in 1968–70 there were massive protests against the Vietnam War. Many students opposed being drafted in to fight a war they thought was wrong, especially after the media highlighted the actions of US troops at the My Lai massacre. Thousands refused to serve when they received the draft. 40,000 students protested against the war in the first part of 1968 alone. The largest protest was in 1969 when almost 700,000 people demonstrated in Washington. Students were injured and even killed in the 1970 protests at an Ohio university after the USA invaded Cambodia.

So the statement is partially correct. Economic factors did create protests. It is true that some protests were not primarily economic but economic problems often influenced them. The civil rights campaigns had great support partly because it was a just cause but also because African Americans suffered economically because of discrimination. This is also true of other groups like the Native Americans and Chicanos so it is very difficult to separate these factors out.

This is an excellent answer – definitely a Gold – and would probably get 18 marks.

It has a clear opening and it then sticks to the line which the opening suggests it will follow.

There is a good analysis of two factors.

It is worth noting that this answer does not cover every aspect of protest in the period. It does not need to! The level of detail shown here is enough for a top mark.

Good conclusions are rare, and this one is particularly good.

KEYS TO SUCCESS

As long as you know the content and have learned how to think, this exam should not be too scary. The keys to success are:

1   Read the question carefully. This may sound obvious, but there is a skill to it. Sometimes students answer the question they *wish* had been asked rather than the one that has *actually* been asked. So identify the skill focus (what it is asking you to do). Does it want you to write a description, an explanation or a comparison? Identify the content focus (what it is about) and select from your knowledge accordingly.
2   Note the marks available. These help you work out how much time to spend on answering each question. Time is precious – if you spend too long on low-mark questions you will run out of time for the high-mark ones.
3   Plan your answer before you start writing. For essays this is particularly important. The golden rule is: know what you are going to say; then say it clearly and logically.
4   Aim for quality not quantity: in the time limits of an exam you will not be able to write down everything you know and can think of – even if it is relevant. The marker would much rather read a short answer that really tackles the question than page after page of material that is not relevant.
5   Check your work. You will never have time in an exam to rewrite an answer but try to leave some time at the end to check for obvious spelling mistakes, missing words or other writing errors that might cost you marks.

Glossary

Agent Orange a poisonous chemical used by US forces in Vietnam to defoliate (remove leaves) from forest areas to deprive the enemy of cover

ambush a surprise attack

anarchist someone with particular political beliefs, which challenge the authority of the state

armistice a temporary end to fighting while opposing sides decide whether to make peace or continue fighting

artillery heavy missile weapons; the term usually refers to cannon but can also include catapults

Big Three (1) the three main leaders at the Paris Peace Conference after the First World war – Lloyd George (Britain), Wilson (USA) and Clemenceau (France); (2) the leaders at the Yalta Conferences in 1945 – Roosevelt/Truman (USA), Churchill/Atlee (Britain), Stalin (USSR)

bootlegger someone who supplies illegal alcohol

boycott refusing to trade or have other types of dealings with a country

capitalism a political, social and economic system centred on democracy and individual freedoms such as free speech, political beliefs and freedom to do business

censured criticised for particular actions

coalition a group of countries or political parties that have agreed to work together

collective security a key principle of the League of Nations, which stated that all members could expect to be secure because the other members would defend them from attack

Cominform an organisation set up to spread communist ideas and to ensure that communist states followed the methods and ideas of communism that were practised in the USSR

Comintern an organisation set up by the USSR to help spread communist ideas and influence

communism a political, economic and social system involving state control of the economy and less emphasis on individual rights than under apitalism

concentration camps special camps used by the Nazis to hold political opponents before and during the Second World War

conscription compulsory service in the armed forces

containment the policy adopted by the USA under President Harry Truman of trying to stop the spread of communism

coup a revolution, often intended to overthrow a leader

covenant an agreement or set of rules

defect to change sides

defoliate to remove leaves from trees and other plants, usually with chemicals, to stop an enemy hiding there

delegates representatives of a country at meetings or organisations (e.g. the League of Nations or the United Nations Organization)

democracy a political system in which the population votes for its government in regular elections

détente reducing tension or improving relations

disarmament the process of scrapping land, sea or air weapons

dividends a proportion of the profits of a company paid to its shareholders

doctrine a set of beliefs

drug trafficking transporting and selling illegal substances

economic sanctions refusing to supply goods (e.g. oil) to a country as a punishment for particular actions

economy the trade and value of the work of a country

euthanasia killing people, usually the sick or disabled

exile being forced to live outside your own country against your will

fascism a set of beliefs based on the importance of loyalty to a leader and using force to solve disputes

Fourteen Points the key points set out by US president Woodrow Wilson for negotiating peace at the end of the First World War

Führer literally 'the leader', usually referring to Adolf Hitler in Nazi Germany

genocide the murder or attempted murder of an entire people or race

ghetto a segregated area, usually referring to places were Jews were forced to live, but also used to describe areas where minority groups such as African Americans lived or simply poor parts of a city

glasnost openness and transparency – a policy of Soviet leader Mikhail Gorbachev in the 1980s, designed to allow people to have their views heard and to criticise the government

guerrilla warfare a type of warfare that avoids large-scale battles and relies instead on hit-and-run raids

Ho Chi Minh Trail a route in Cambodia used by North Vietnamese and Viet Cong forces to supply those fighting South Vietnamese and US forces

Holocaust the name given to the mass murder of the Jews and other racial groups by the Nazis in the Second World War

hyperinflation a process in which money becomes worthless; the most notable example of hyperinflation occurred in Germany in 1923

ideology a set of beliefs, usually political beliefs or religious beliefs that have a political element

impeached accused of wrongdoing and investigated

inauguration a ceremony to begin the time in office of a politician such as a president

injunction a legal ruling, usually preventing something

insurgency an uprising, usually against a government

integration mixing together, usually referring to different groups of people such as immigrants or minority groups mixing with the majority of the population

internationalism an approach to solving problems between countries based on co-operation (e.g. treaties or other agreements) rather than conflict

jihad an Arab term for the Muslim concept of a holy war

laissez-faire to leave alone – a political idea that involved removing government interference or involvement in business or other aspects of people's lives

League of Nations an organisation set up to manage international disputes and prevent wars after the First World War; it was the brainchild of US president Woodrow Wilson

Lebensraum 'living space' – this idea became part of Hitler's plans to conquer an empire for Germany in the 1930s

legislation laws

Locarno Treaties agreements made in the 1920s by which Germany accepted the western borders outlined in the Treaty of Versailles in 1919

lynching illegal killing, usually of African Americans in the southern USA

malnutrition lack of adequate food

military dictatorship a country where the government is run by the armed forces

military-industrial complex the relationship identified by US president Eisenhower in the 1950s between big businesses and the armed forces, which suggested the two helped each other too much

missile gap a term used to describe the alleged advantage of the USSR over the USA in nuclear missiles; historians doubt whether the missile gap was as large as people thought

munitions material for fighting wars, such as bullets and shells

napalm a highly explosive chemical weapon that spread a fireball over a large area; used extensively in the Vietnam War

Nation of Islam an African American movement in the USA in the 1960s

nationalism a strong sense of pride in your own country, sometimes addressed aggressively towards other countries or minority groups

Northern Alliance a group of states that worked together to overthrow the Taliban in Afghanistan in the early 2000s

paramilitary a group that uses armed force but is not a normal army

Paris Peace Conference a conference that ran from 1919 to 1923, to decide how to officially end the First World War; it resulted in the Treaty of Versailles with Germany and treaties with three other defeated nations

peaceful co-existence a policy of Soviet leader Khrushchev in the 1950s and 1960s, involving the USA and USSR accepting their differences and not fighting each other

perestroika 'restructuring' – the idea of Soviet leader Gorbachev in the later 1980s that the USSR needed to reform

perjury lying in a courtroom

plebiscite a vote, usually to determine a system of government or the future of a country

Politburo the main decision-making group of the Communist Party in the USSR (similar to the British Cabinet)

poverty line the minimum amount of earnings needed by a family to live

propaganda a particular set of ideas or information that is spread for a political purpose; propaganda can take many different forms

purge a policy pursued by Stalin in the USSR in the 1930s to remove potential opponents; the purges involved arrests, torture, show trials, executions and deportations to labour camps

rearmament building up arms and the armed forces; rearmament was used as a way of dealing with unemployment by many states in the 1930s, including Nazi Germany

Reichstag the German parliament

reparations money that Germany had to pay in compensation to Belgium, France, Britain and other states as a result of the First World War

reservations areas of land set aside by the US government for Native Americans to live on

revisionism the process of rethinking and changing interpretations of historical events

rhetoric speech or writing that sets out a point of view

Ruhr the main industrial region in Germany

segregation the separation of a person or group from mainstream society, such as African Americans in the USA

self-determination the right of nations to rule themselves rather than being part of larger empires

shareholders people who have bought shares in a company and receive a share of the profits

socialism a political system in which the government takes strong control of economic and social life; in theory, socialist societies would eventually become communist

speakeasies illegal drinking establishments, which sprang up during the era of Prohibition in the USA

speculation buying shares in the hope that their value will rise so they can then be sold at a profit

stenography writing something in shorthand and then turning it into longhand on a typewriter

sterilisation making a person unable to have children

stockpile to gather a large supply of something

suffrage the right to vote

suffragists campaigners for female suffrage in the early twentieth century, who believed in peaceful and legal protest

superpowers countries in a dominant international position, making them able to influence global events; after the Second World War, the USA and the USSR were the world's two superpowers

surplus an amount of something that is more than is needed

tariffs taxes on imported goods, which made them more expensive; tariffs were often designed to protect makers of home-produced goods

temperance a movement that opposed alcohol

think tank an organisation that researches issues and suggests policies to tackle them

totalitarian a system of government in which the state has total control

treason to speak or act against the monarch of a country

Treaty of Versailles the treaty that officially ended the First World War between the Allies and Germany; the treaty was controversial because some believed that its terms were excessively harsh

tribunal a type of court that investigates and makes judgement

war guilt a clause in the Treaty of Versailles that forced Germany to accept blame for the First World War

White supremacy the belief that White people should rule over other races

Young Plan a US economic plan revealed in 1929, designed to reorganise reparations payments to make it easier for Germany to pay them

Index

abortion rights 319, 320
Abyssinian crisis 302
Adenauer, Konrad 183, 184, 185
Afghanistan 8
    and alQaeda 11920, 121, 124
    Soviet war in 67, 906, 105, 106, 107, 119
    the Taliban 118, 121, 124
Africa
    African diplomats in the USA 305
    alQaeda bombings in 1223
    and the Paris Peace Conference 15
African Americans 209, 2237
    lynchings 2245, 283
    migration to the north 254
    and the New Deal 244
    politicians 308
    poverty and unemployment 308
    race riots 254, 255, 2989
    and the Second World War 2546
    segregation ('Jim Crow') laws 223, 2789, 287
    and the Vietnam War 87
    voting rights 278, 292, 307
    see also civil rights movement
AIM (American Indian Movement) 31415
Albania 59, 60
alQaeda 8, 119, 11924
Andropov, Yuri 91, 94, 107
Angola 65
AntiComintern Pact 35
Appeasement 3841, 4454, 56
    Churchill's view of 44, 45, 489
    counterrevisionist view of 44, 523
    Guilty Men view of 44, 467, 48, 52
    popular majority view of 44, 45
    revisionist view of 44, 501, 52
armed forces
    African Americans in the US 2545
    Britain 50, 51
    Germany 13, 34, 136
atomic bomb 58, 64, 65, 268
Australia 40
Austria
    Anschluss 389
    and the League of Nations 18, 19
    and the Versailles Treaty 11, 12
Axis alliance 35
Azzam, Abdullah 120
Baltic republics 113
banks
    and the Depression 229, 231, 236
Batista, Fulgencio 74
Belgium 11
Berlin
    in 1925 1324
    Blockade 623, 64, 65
Berlin Wall
    crisis 67, 6973
    fall of the 103, 111, 113, 114
bin Laden, Osama 1201, 122, 123, 124
Black Panthers 297

Black Power movement 296303, 307
Blair, Tony 49, 124
Brezhnev, Leonid 90, 92, 93, 94, 107
Britain
    and the Cold War 56
    'hinge years' 24
    and Hitler 36, 37, 38, 42
        Appeasement policy 38, 3940, 41, 51, 52
    and the League of Nations 20, 30, 31
    and the Spanish Civil War 35
    and the Versailles Treaty 14
British Empire 51
Bulgaria 19, 20, 59, 60, 113
Bush, George W. 124
businesses in Nazi Germany 163
Cambodia 85, 88
Canada 40
Capone, Al 219
Carmichael, Stokely 297, 298, 317
cars 200, 2045
Carter, Jimmy 91, 92
Castro, Fidel 74, 75, 78, 100
Chamberlain, Neville 35, 37
    and Appeasement 38, 39, 40, 41, 42, 4454
Chavez, Cesar 31213
chemical weapons 84, 88
Chiang Kaishek 64
Chicago 210, 21920
Chicano nationalism 31113
China
    and Afghanistan 91
    communist 64
    and the Korean War 67
    and Manchuria 267
    and the postCold War world 117
    and the USA 8, 88, 268
    and the Vietnam War 80, 81
Churchill, Winston 217
    and Appeasement 44, 45, 47
        The Gathering Storm 489
    'Iron Curtain' speech 59, 60
    Yalta Conference 56, 57
Civil Rights Acts 287, 289, 293, 294, 306, 308
civil rights movement 254, 278309
    Birmingham march (1963) 291
    and Black Power 296303, 307
    Freedom rides 290, 306
    'freedom summer' 294
    and Hispanic Americans 31013
    march on Washington (1963) 293
    Montgomery bus boycott 2845, 286, 289, 290
    organisations
        CORE 289, 290, 292, 303
        SCLC 288, 298
        SNCC 289, 297, 317
    origins 27881
    race riots 2989
    and 'Route 40' 305

    and school segregation 281, 2867, 307
    Selma march 294, 305
    and Selma (movie) 304
    sitins 289
    and student radicalism 3223
    see also African Americans; King, Martin Luther
Clemenceau, Georges 11, 12, 15, 17
Cold War 55115
    and Afghanistan 8
    causes of the 5566
    Churchill's 'Iron Curtain' speech 59, 60
    Churchill's view of Appeasement 48
    confrontations
        Soviet war in Afghanistan 67, 906, 105, 106, 107, 119
        see also Vietnam War
    crises 65, 6779
        Berlin Wall 67, 6973
        Cuban Missile 49, 67, 70, 749
    détente 88, 102, 105
    end of the 103, 10515
    and Gorbachev 94
    historians 97104
        new Cold War 97, 103
        postrevisionist view 97, 102
        US orthodox view 97, 989, 104
        US revisionist view 97, 1001
    key conflicts 65
    Korean War 65, 67
    and Operation Unthinkable 57
    origins of the, changing interpretations 97104
    and peaceful coexistence 68
    'proxy wars' 65
    and Russia 8
    see also nuclear weapons
collective security
    and the League of Nations 17
COMINFORM (Communist Information Bureau) 60
communism 25
    and Afghanistan 90, 93, 119
    AntiComintern Pact 35
    in China 64, 268
    and the Cold War 56, 64, 73
    in Germany 135, 137, 140, 142, 144, 145, 183
        East Germany 187
    and Hitler 33, 37
    Red Scare in the USA 98, 2212, 26877, 297
    and the Soviet Union 25, 108
    and the Vietnam War 80, 81, 88
Conference of Ambassadors 17, 20
consumer goods
    United States 204
Coolidge, Calvin 202
Corfu crisis (1923) 19, 20
Cuba
    Bay of Pigs invasion 70, 75

Missile crisis 49, 67, 70, 749
revolution 74, 100
culture
Nazi Germany 153
United States in the 1920s 199
Weimar Germany 134, 135, 138
Czechoslovakia 39, 40, 41, 45, 61
and the fall of communism 113
Daladier, Edouard 38, 40, 41, 42
'the dark valley' 2943
Dawes Plan (1924) 21, 133
Depression (192934) 238, 51, 22836, 310
and the Nazis 139, 140, 141
Detroit Race Riots (1943) 254, 255
Diem, Ngo Dinh 80
Dietrich, Marlene 134, 159
disarmament
and the League of Nations 21, 278
and the Versailles Treaty 11, 13, 14
Disarmament Conference (1932) 278
divorce
in the United States 213, 215
drug trafficking 18
eastern Europe
and the Cold War 57, 58, 601, 62, 105
fall of communism 11113, 114
and the Versailles Treaty 11
Edelweiss Pirates 158, 174
education in the USA
Chicano students 312
civil rights and school segregation 281,
2867, 307
and Johnson's war on poverty 327
Eisenhower, Dwight D. 74, 80, 255
and civil rights 2867, 288, 305
and McCarthyism 274, 275
farmers
and Nazi Germany 163
in the United States 2089
and the Depression 229, 230, 232,
233
and the New Deal 237
fascist Italy 25
First World War 8
and Germany 132
and the United States 202, 212, 213
France
'hinge years' 24
and Hitler 36, 37, 38, 40, 41, 42
and the League of Nations 20, 30, 31, 32
Mutual Assistance Pact with the USSR
36, 41
and the Rhineland 34
and the Spanish Civil War 35
and the Versailles Treaty 11, 14
Franco, General Francisco 35
Friedan, Betty 316, 317, 318
Fukuyama, Francis
'The End of History?' 11618
gangsters 21920
Garvey, Marcus 226
gay rights 3212
Germany
in 1925 1325
armed forces 13, 34
assessment of depth study on 1907
and the Cold War

Berlin Blockade 623, 64, 65
Berlin Wall 67, 6973
zones of occupation 57, 63
democratisation and rebuilding
Eastern Zone 1858
Western Zone 1835
and the Depression 23, 24, 25
East Germany 68, 69, 111, 113, 114, 1868
economy 133, 135, 161, 171, 1845
and the League of Nations 13, 14, 19, 21,
134, 135
rearmament 24, 25, 28, 30
reunification 114
Saar region 34
and the Spanish Civil War 35
Weimar Republic 1325, 186
Constitution 133, 134
and the Nazi Party 133, 1368
West Germany 63, 69, 114, 1835
see also Berlin; Hitler, Adolf; Nazi
Germany; Versailles Treaty
Goebbels, Joseph 138, 140, 145, 1524, 172,
178
Gonzales, Rodolfo `Corky' 311
Gorbachev, Mikhail 94, 10811, 113, 114
Greece 19, 20
Harding, Warren 201, 202
Hindenburg, Paul von 134, 143, 144, 145,
146
hinge years 238
hippy movement 324
Hispanic Americans 31013
Hiss, Alger 271
historians 45, 9
Hitler, Adolf 25, 30, 132
Anschluss with Austria 389
and Appeasement 3841, 50, 52
and Britain 36, 37
the Hitler myth 167
and Japan 35
Mein Kampf 136, 153
Munich Putsch (1923) 132, 136
Nazi ideology 33
and the Olympics (1936) 154
rearmament 28, 34, 36, 46, 161
Rhineland remilitarisation 32, 34, 36
rise to power 1367, 138, 140, 141, 1436
Rome-Berlin axis 32
and the Spanish Civil War 35
suicide 178
and the Versailles Treaty 25, 33, 34, 36,
37
vision for Germany 1489
and war 33, 42, 148, 178
see also Nazi Germany
Hitler Youth 137, 157, 158
Hoare-Laval Pact 31, 32
Ho Chi Minh 80, 82, 83
Hollywood
movies and the Cold War 99
personalities and the Red Scare 270,
273, 274
Honecker, Erich 111, 112, 113
Hoover, Herbert 27, 201, 202, 229, 230
and the presidential election (1932)
2334, 235
Hoover, J. Edgar 221, 226, 270, 297

HUAC (House UnAmerican Activities
Committee) 2701, 272, 274, 276
and civil rights 279, 281
Hungary 18, 19, 60, 68, 113
IMF (International Monetary Fund) 18
immigration
immigrant communities in the US 209,
210, 2212, 226, 31011
and nationalism in Europe 8
industrial workers
Germany 133, 162, 172, 185
United States 209, 210
and the New Deal 237, 244
Second World War 2501, 252
industries
United States 201, 202, 203, 2045
wartime 24950
Weimar Germany 133
internationalism
and the hinge years 23
and the League of Nations 1622, 32
and the Versailles Treaty 11
International Labour Organisation 18
Iranian revolution 90
Iraq 8, 121
Islam
and Afghanistan 90, 93, 119
and alQaeda 8, 119, 11924
Nation of Islam 296, 301
Islamic State 8, 124
Israel 118
Italy
Axis alliance 35
and Corfu 20
fascist 25
and the Spanish Civil War 35
and the Versailles Treaty 11
see also Mussolini, Benito
Jackson, Jesse 308
Japan
invasion of Manchuria 267
Pearl Harbor 246, 248
Japanese Americans 253
Jews
and Nazi Germany 135, 140, 148, 151,
154, 155, 156
persecution of 1645, 166, 1756
Johnson, Lyndon
and civil rights 293, 295, 298, 304, 305,
306, 307
and the Vietnam War 81, 82, 87, 88
war on poverty 3267
KelloggBriand Pact (1928) 21
Kennedy, John F.
assassination 293, 326
Berlin Wall crisis 70, 72, 73
and civil rights 290, 291, 292, 304, 305,
306, 307
Cuban Missile crisis 49, 70, 74, 756, 77,
78
and Johnson 326, 327
New Frontier 325
Vietnam War 80
Kennedy, Joseph 45
Kennedy, Robert 292, 306, 312
Khomeini, Ayatollah 90
Khrushchev, Nikita 68

Berlin Wall crisis 70, 71, 72
Cuban Missile crisis 74, 756, 78
King, Martin Luther 284, 286, 287, 288, 290, 2945
    assassination 295
    and the Birmingham march (1963) 291
    and Black Power 298
    'I have a dream' speech 293
    and Kennedy 306
    and Malcolm X 291, 3003
    and the Poor People's Campaign 298, 311
    in *Selma* (movie) 304
    significance of 295
Kissinger, Henry 88
Klemperer, Victor 155, 168, 186, 187
Kohl, Helmut 107
Korea 117
Korean War 65, 67, 268
Ku Klux Klan 224, 226, 270, 279, 291, 292
Laos 85, 88
Lattimore, Owen 276
League of Nations 1622
    and the Abyssinian crisis 302
    commissions 18
    Covenant 16
    and disarmament 21, 278
    failure in Manchuria 267, 30
    and Germany 13, 14, 19, 21, 134, 135
    and Hitler 34
    international security 1920
    and the Paris Peace Conference 11, 13, 14
lesbians 318, 321, 322
Lindberg, Charles 198, 199, 202
Lloyd George, David 11, 12
    and the League of Nations 17
Locarno Treaties (1925) 20, 21, 34, 134, 135
Long, Huey 238, 240
McCarran Act 271
McCarthy, Joseph 98, 272, 2747, 307
McNamara, Robert 77, 81, 89, 255
Malcolm X 2003, 226, 291, 2967
Manchurian crisis 267, 30
Mao Zedong 64
Marshall Aid 61, 62
Metelmann, Henrik 157, 158
Mexicans in the USA 31013
Middle East 8, 15
Miller, Arthur 275
Munich Agreement 3940, 45
Murrow, Ed 276
Mussolini, Benito 20, 25, 47
    Abyssinian crisis 302
    and Japan 35
    and the Munich Agreement 40
    Rome-Berlin axis 32
    and the Spanish Civil War 35
Myers, Bill 277
nationalism 8, 29
    Black Power 296303, 307
    Chicano 31113
    Nazi Germany 25
Nation of Islam 296, 301
Native Americans 245, 311, 31415
NATO (North Atlantic Treaty Organization) 64, 68, 114, 185

Nazi Germany 15, 25, 13297
    concentration camps 145, 151, 164, 171
    creating a National Community 15563, 169
    death camps 175
    Hitler's vision for 1489
    media and culture 1534
    middle classes 163
    Nuremberg rallies 152
    Olympics (1936) 154
    opposition to
        churches 167, 177
        lack of 1668
        wartime 177
    persecution of minorities 1646
    police state 1501
    racism 136, 149, 154, 1645
    rise and consolidation of 13247
    the SS 137, 141, 145, 150, 154, 165, 172
    TwentyFive Point Programme 136, 140
    and the Wandervogel movement 135
    women in 155, 15960
    and young people 1568
    see also Hitler, Adolf; Second World War
NaziSoviet Pact 412
New Deal (United States) 23645
Nicaragua 106
Nixon, Richard 88, 102, 271, 325
    and the civil rights movement 287, 307
    Native American policy 315
    Watergate scandal 328
    welfare reforms 328
Northern Ireland 117
NOW (National Organization for Women) 317, 318
nuclear weapons
    arms race 68, 105, 106
    atomic bombs 58, 64, 65, 268
    Cuban Missile crisis 49, 67, 70, 749
    disarmament 110
    and Gorbachev 94
    Nuclear Test Ban Treaty 78
    Strategic Arms Limitation Treaty (SALT) 88, 92, 102
    Strategic Defense Initiative (SDI) 106, 107
Nuremberg rallies 152
Obama, Barack 308
Olympics (1936) 154
Pakistan 91, 92, 93, 119
Paris Peace Conference 1015
Parks, Rosa 2845
Pearl Harbor 246, 248
Philippines 117
Poland
    and the Cold War 58, 59, 60, 68, 105
    fall of communism 111, 113
    Hitler's invasion of 41, 42, 46
    Jewish ghettos 175
    and the League of Nations 19
    Solidarity 105, 113
Potsdam Conference (1945) 589, 60
poverty in the USA 20910, 2312, 308
    Poor People's Campaign 298, 311
    and US presidents 3258
propaganda
    and the civil rights movement 305

    and the Cold War 55, 62, 65
    Nazi 136, 138, 140, 145, 149, 1524, 172
    US wartime 248
protectionism 24
public opinion
    and Appeasement 51
Rapallo Treaty (1922) 21
Reagan, Ronald 103, 105, 1067, 108
    and Afghanistan 93, 119
    and Gorbachev 108, 10910, 111
Rhineland 13
Robeson, Paul 225, 27980
Robinson, Jackie 27981, 288
Romania 59, 60, 111, 113
Roosevelt, Eleanor 212, 214
Roosevelt, Franklin D. 201, 212, 220, 248, 255
    and international relations 56, 57, 58
    and the New Deal 23645
    and the presidential election (1932) 233, 2345
Rosenberg, Julius and Ethel 271
Russia 8, 11, 117
    see also Soviet Union
Rwanda 117
Saarland 13
Saudi Arabia 90, 93, 119
    and Osama bin Laden 120, 121
Schlafly, Phyllis 320
Second World War
    and Appeasement 46, 47, 48
    Germany 15, 36, 42, 17182
        defeat, division and denazification 17982
        German people and the war effort 1714
    United States 242, 24657, 268
        African Americans 2546
        women 2501, 316
    and Vietnam 80
Selma (movie) 304
Serbia 11
South America 65
Soviet Union
    Afghan war 67, 906, 105, 106, 107, 119
    and Appeasement 51, 52
    and the civil rights movement 305
    collapse 103, 114
    and communism 25
    Gorbachev and reform 108, 109, 110
    and Hitler 34, 36
        NaziSoviet Pact 412
    and nuclear weapons 64, 65, 68
    and the origins of the Cold War 97, 989
    and the Second World War 172, 175, 180
    and the Spanish Civil War 35
    and the USA 268
    see also Cold War; Khrushchev, Nikita; Stalin, Josef
Spanish Civil War 35
Stalin, Josef 25
    and the Cold War 48, 68
        Berlin Blockade 62, 63
        Churchill's `Iron Curtain' speech 59
        eastern Europe 57, 58, 601, 62
        postwar conferences 56, 57, 58
    and East Germany 187

and Hitler 41 2
Steinem, Gloria 318, 319
Stonewall riots 321, 322
STOP ERA 320
Stresa Pact (1935) 30
Stresemann, Gustav 133, 134, 135, 138
student protests 322 3
suicide bombers 122
superpowers
    and the causes of the Cold War 55 66
        breakdown of relations 62
        conflicting ideologies 58
    telephone hotline 78, 92
    see also Soviet Union; United States
Swing movement 158
Syria 8
Taraki, Nur Mohammad 90, 91
terrorism 119, 122 4
Thatcher, Margaret 107
Tijerina, Reies 311
Till, Emmet 283
Truman, Harry 47, 59, 65, 104, 255, 276
    and the atomic bomb 58, 64
    and the Berlin Blockade 62, 63
    and the Korean War 67
    Truman Doctrine 49, 61, 62
Turkey 11
Ukraine 8
Ulbricht, Walter 187 8
unemployment
    Germany 25, 139, 141, 161, 184
    United States 209, 231
    and the New Deal 236, 239, 242, 243, 244
United Nations 17, 22
    WHO (World Health Organization) 18
United States
    and Afghanistan 8, 90, 118, 119
    and Appeasement 40, 47
    and China 8, 88
    CIA (Central Intelligence Agency) 74, 75
    and the Cold War
        causes of the 59, 61 3

Marshall Aid 61, 62
the Depression 23, 24, 25, 228 36, 310
    Wall Street Crash 23, 228 9, 236
economy 210 10, 266
    wartime 246 7, 249
gay rights 321 2
Hispanic Americans 310 13
and Hitler 37
immigrant communities 209, 210, 221 2, 226, 310 11
and Iraq 8
and the League of Nations 17, 27, 32
military industrial complex 81
Native Americans 245, 311, 314 15
New Deal 236 45
post Cold War world 117
    9/11 and the War on Terror 119, 121, 123 4, 124
presentday problems 8
presidential election (1932) 233 5
Prohibition 212
protest movements 322 4
Red Scare 98, 221 2, 268 77, 297
'Roaring Twenties' 198 227
    economic boom 201 8
    leisure and entertainment 199
    Prohibition 216 20
    Sheppard Tower Act (1921) 212
    and the Second World War 242, 246 57, 268
social security reforms 239
stock market 206
system of government 201
towns and cities 199, 231
War Powers Act (1973) 88
women 200, 211 15, 226, 244
    war work 250 1, 316
women's movement 316 20
    see also African Americans; civil rights movement; Cold War; Vietnam War
USSR see Soviet Union
Venezuela 117
Versailles Treaty 10 15, 28, 33, 36, 37, 41

and Germany 10, 11, 15, 140, 149
    reparations 12, 13, 14, 25, 133, 134
Vietnam War 8, 51, 65, 67, 80 9, 310
    and Afghanistan 90, 94
    antiwar protests 323, 324
    and the civil rights movement 294, 298
    as a Cold War confrontation 80 1
    and Cold War historians 100
    ending of and 'Vietnamisation' 88
    guerrilla warfare 80, 82
    Ho Chi Minh trail 81, 83, 84
    impact of 88 9
    local background 80
    and the media 86, 87
    My Lai massacre 86
    Operation Rolling Thunder 81
    Tet Offensive 86, 87, 88
    and the US peace movement 87
    US tactics 84 5
    Viet Cong 81, 82, 83, 85
Wallace, George 292
Warsaw Pact 64
Washington Conference (1921) 21
Wilson, Woodrow 10 11, 12, 14, 15
    Fourteen Points 10, 11
    and the League of Nations 16, 17
    and women's suffrage 21 2
women
    in Nazi Germany 155, 159 60, 174
    in the United States 200, 211 15
        African Americans 226
        employment of 211, 213, 214
        and the New Deal 244
        suffragist movement 212
        war work 250 1, 316
Women's Liberation Movement 318
women's movement 316 20
Yalta Conference (1945) 56 7, 58
young people
    in Nazi Germany 156 8, 174
Young Plan (1929) 21, 134
Yugoslavia 117
Zinn, Howard 252

Acknowledgements

The Publishers would like to thank the following for permission to reproduce copyright material.

Photo credits

p.4 Illustration by David Parkins for *The Economist*; **p.7** © United Nations Archives at Geneva; **p.10** Hulton Archive/Stringer/Getty Images; **p.11** © David Low/Associated Newspapers Ltd/Solo Syndication; **p.14** © The British Library Board; **p.17** *l* Hulton Archive/Stringer/Getty Images, *r* Ria Novosti/TopFoto; **p.18** *t, b* © United Nations Archives at Geneva; **p.21** © David Low/Associated Newspapers Ltd / Solo Syndication; **p.24** © David Low/Associated Newspapers Ltd/Solo Syndication; **p.26** © David Low/Associated Newspapers Ltd/Solo Syndication; **p.27** *t* © David Low/Associated Newspapers Ltd/Solo Syndication, *b* By permission of the Estate of Rollin Kirby Post/Library of Congress; **p.31** © David Low/Associated Newspapers Ltd/Solo Syndication; **p.32** © DACS 2016/bpk; **p.35** © Topham Picturepoint/Topfoto; **p.36** © David Low/Associated Newspapers Ltd/Solo Syndication; **p.39** *t* © World History Archive/TopFoto, *b* © Topfoto; **p.40** © McCord Museum/Drawing, cartoon | The Umbrella Man. | M965.199.4099; **p.41** *t, b* © Topfoto; **p.45** © Popperfoto/Getty Images; **p.46** *b* © Ullstein Bild/Getty Images; **p.47** By permission of the People's History Museum; **p.48** Reproduced with permission of the Master and Fellows of Churchill College, Cambridge; **p.49** © PA Photos/Topfoto; **p.50** © LSE Library; **p.52** R.A.C Parker, *Chamberlain and Appeasement: British Policy and the Coming of the Second World War (The Making of the Twentieth Century)*, 1993, Palgrave Macmillan, reproduced with permission of Palgrave Macmillan; **p.55** © Bettmann/Getty Images; **p.57** © Bettmann/Getty Images; **p.59** © Sputnik/TopFoto; **p.70** *l* © dpa picture alliance/Alamy Stock Photo, *r* © Popperfoto/Getty Images; **p.72** © Keystone/Getty Images; **p.73** © Ernst Maria Lang; **p.76** © Vicky/Associated Newspapers Ltd./Solo Syndication;